COMPUTER SOLUTION OF DIFFERENTIAL EQUATIONS

COMPUTER SOLUTION OF DIFFERENTIAL EQUATION

Arun Ghosh MSc

New Central Book Agency (P) Ltd
LONDON
HYDERABAD ERNAKULAM BHUBANESWAR
NEW DELHI KOLKATA PUNE GUWAHATI

REGD. OFFICE
8/1 Chintamoni Das Lane, Kolkata 700 009, India
email: ncbapvtltd@eth.net

OVERSEAS
NCBA (UK) Ltd, 149 Park Avenue North, Northampton, NN3 2HY, UK
email: ncbauk@yahoo.com

EXPORT
NCBA Exports Pvt. Ltd, 212 Shahpur Jat, New Delhi 110 049
email: ncbaexp@ncbapvtltd.com

BRANCHES

212 Shahpur Jat
New Delhi 110 049
email: ncbadel@ncbapvtltd.com

House No. 3-1-315, 1st Floor
Nimboliadda, Kachiguda, Hyderabad 500 027
email: ncbahydb@ncbapvtltd.com

Shop Nos. 3 & 4, Vinayak Towers
681/B Budhwar Peth, Appa Balwant Chowk
Pune 411 002
email: ncbapune@ncbapvtltd.com

GSS Shopping Complex, 1st Floor
Opposite College Post Office, Convent Road
Ernakulam 682 035
email: ncbaernk@ncbapvtltd.com

Shop No. 15, Bharati Towers, Ground Floor
Forest Park, Bhubaneswar 751 001
email: ncbabub@ncbapvtltd.com

Radhamayee Complex (Second Floor)
Opp. SBI, Panbazar, Jaswanta Road
Guwahati 781 001
email: ncbaguwahati@ncbapvtltd.com

COMPUTER SOLUTION OF DIFFERENTIAL EQUATION • Arun Ghosh

First Published: 1999
Reprinted: 2008, 2013

PUBLISHER
New Cental Book Agency (P) Ltd
8/1 Chintamoni Das Lane, Kolkata 700 009

TYPESETTER
A. G. Enterprise
1A 107 Salt Lake, Sector III, Kolkata 700 091

PRINTER
New Central Book Agency (P) Ltd
Web-Offset Division, Dhulagarh, Sankrail, Howrah

COVER DESIGNER
Angik

COVER PRINTER
Biswanath Studio
3 Garanhatta Street, Kolkata 700 006

ISBN: 978 81 7381 338 2

Price ₹ 495.00

Dedicated to

my Parents and my twins
Steven (Surojit) and
Benjamin (Biswajit)

Preface

The objective of this book is to present a substantial introduction to the ideas, phenomena and methods of ordinary differential equations that are frequently found in engineering, physics, chemistry and mathematics. The book can be appreciated at a considerable number of levels and is designed for everyone from amateurs to research workmen.

It can also be considered as an important reference for engineers and mathematicians belonging to this field. Included throughout are applications with appropriate suggestions and discussions, whenever needed, that form a significant and integral part of the textbook.

In a word, the text directs at an all-embracing and practical treatment of differential equations with some specific methods controlled by computer programs. I intend to treat the differential equations using initial or boundary conditions and the operation has been performed by the programming language C++ based on any MS-DOS computer system (Version 6.0) applying the classical methods, such as Euler, Simpson, Runge-Kutta, Richardson, Finite-Difference, etc.

The effects of this treatment, the computerised solutions in compact form for each problem have been provided for further study.

Prerequisites to make use of this text include good theoretical knowledge of Calculus and differential equations and acquaintance with high-level computer language C++. Some experience with computer programming using C++ will be a great assistance understanding the subject matter of the text.

The materials contained in this volume cover the following :

A short description of the high-level language C++, Integration of functions, Initial-value and boundary-value problems, the appropriate Numerical methods for the approximations of the differential equations, the Computer programs required for the purpose written in C++, some important relations from Mathematics. The volume concludes with a very short discussion on FORTRAN V programming language for future use.

Emphasis has been placed on section 4.1 in chapter 4 that deals with the problems concerning areas of bounded surfaces enclosed by plane curves, because the subject matter of numerical evaluation for areas of plane curves is a predominant topic within the extent of integration.

Special attention is focussed on chapters 5 and 9 in view of the fact that the differential equations with initial or boundary conditions are the kernels of the physical and technical problems.

I prepare this manuscript on personal computer from COMPAQ (Type : Presario CD/TV/528) and on Laptop from TOSHIBA (Type : T1910) operated on MS-DOS 6.0 and WINDOWS 95.

A software supplement consisting of a set of programs and subprograms designed in C++ (Turbo) and in FORTRAN V will be provided for the reader to work out the related mathematical models referred to the text in chapter 11.

A Diskette (3.5 inch/1.44 MB) in Standard PC-compatible form containing this supplement is available for the reader on request.

I think, my anticipation to believe is not indifferent, that the students, instructors and other readers who use this text can enjoy the development just as well the author has taken joy in the preparation.

I wish to express my very great thanks to my beloved Professor Pranabesh Sinharay of Calcutta University who has motivated me with an interest. I am grateful to the friends of the Computer centre in Hannover for their very helpful suggestions for improving the edition of the manuscript. In this connection I should not forget to mention the names of my twins : Steven and Benjamin and our affectionate Munmun who have contributed much to this volume.

Finally, I express my gratitude to Mr. Amitabha Sen of New Central Book Agency (P) Ltd., publisher in Calcutta.

October, 1997 **Arun Ghosh**
Hannover, Germany

Contents

Chapter 1

About C++ Fundamentals

C++ is an object-oriented programming language. Initially named "C with classes", the language was developed by Bjarne Stroustrup in 1980, while engaged at AT & T Bell Laboratories in Murray Hill, New Jersey, USA. In 1983 it had been changed to a standard name C++.

Specifically, C++ is built on the foundation of C language. All C++ compilers can be used to compile C programs. In fact, C++ is a superset of C. That is to say, it is an enhanced version of C. The language C was first implemented by Dennis Ritchie in the 1970s on the computer type PDP-11 from Digital Equipment Corporation.

Turbo C++ is a powerful compiler. It is very fast and efficient compiler for creating practically any application program. Turbo C++ provides an incorporate atmosphere for further developement of the program. It includes C++ and ANSI C. ANSI is the abbreviation for American National Standards Institute, founded in 1918.

Basically, the object is the main attraction of object-oriented programming. An object is a data type that has structure and state. Every object defines operations which can have access on that state. The object-oriented programming language allows us to take advantage of the advanced design methodology and labour-saving specialities.

Basic structure of a C++ program

A typical program written in C++ language contains basically five sections as represented by the constructional figure.

Preprocessor Directives : INCLUDE files
Common definition block with # define
CLASS declaration
Class : definition of member functions and data type items
Main function with Main () : entry of the program

Every function and every file must be signified by a name followed by a parenthesized parameter list. The list consisting of the names and types of variables will show what type of information it contains. If the parenthesis is empty (void), the function works without any parameter. The body of the function is enclosed by "{ }". The function terminates and returns to the next calling function after the closing brace is reached. A return statement has the same function as the closing brace.

The Keywords from C++

Keywords in C++ are the reserved words that are used for some special purposes and must not be employed as identifier names in C++ program. Identifier names are the user-defined names. In the discussion about identifiers afterwards you can find the distinction between the keywords and identifiers. I make use of the following very common keywords in the programs designed for the approximation of the Differential Equations. Some of them are apparently simple to understand and the others have been explained in this chapter in course of time.

auto	break	case
char	class	const
continue	default	do
double	else	endl
enum	float	for
goto	if	inline
int	interrupt	long
public	private	return
short	switch	void
while		

The case of the keywords is very significant. All the keywords must be typed in lowercase, that is one of the requirements of C++ program. The word RETURN typed in uppercase cannot be accepted as the keyword return.

Identifiers in C++

In C++ program an identifier is defined as a name that is used for a function, a variable or any other defined item. An Identifier is allowed to begin only with any letter of the alphabets or the underscore character. The rest may be letters (a through z) or digits (0 through 9). Here I mention some names as acceptable identifiers.

Temp_file; myProgram; first_name; _file01; macro_type; Name10; address3; etc.

The reserved words from C++ such as **char** cannot be used as identifier. ANSI C recommends only the first 32 characters as an identifier name. The limit of using characters as a name in C++ is very significant. The first 1024 (= 2^{10}) characters are accepted as identifier in C++ language.

The Features of C++

// Program for Differential Equations with Variables Separable.

The line represented here is a comment. A **comment** is identified by the symbol // (double slash). Basically, a comment followed by double slash is a single line comment. A multiline comment would be surrounded by the symbols, starting with /* (a slash followed by an asterisk) and ending with */ (asterisk followed by a slash). The compiler disregards the text that is enclosed by these symbols.

Cout <<"*\n\tThe Computer Solution of the IVP of order 1 : "<< Dtyp;*

The Cout statement with the operator << causes the information in quotation marks and the contents of the variable *Dtyp* to be displayed on the screen. The information and the contents are displayed in one line. The code \n, the most commonly used escape sequence, is the new-line character and the escape sequence \t (horizontal tab) moves the cursor to the next tab position before display.

Cout <<"Type (e) to exit :"; *cin* >> tch;

Cin and **cout** are predefined identifiers. Cin stands for console input. The input statement here holds the program until the value of the variable tch is set by the user.

It is noticeable that each statement terminates with a semicolon (;) meaning the end of the statement.

 # include < iostrean.h >

#include is a preprocessor directive. It is an instruction to the compiler for inclusion into another source file. The expression < iostream.h > is termed as header file contains information to support C++ I/O system. C++ language has been provided with several header files that are very useful for the developement of the program. I shall discuss on this subject matter later in this chapter.

#define Dtyp "Sev"

#define w 0.01

#define is one of the preprocessor directives. This directive is employed to define an identifier for a character sequence or a definite value in the source file. This is called a **macro** identifier.

#define Dtyp "Sev" is a command that yields the instruction to the preprocessor to substitute the string "Sev" when the macro name Dtyp is encountered. The substitution process is known as macro substitution. Each preprocessor directive begins with a symbol #. The C++ preprocessor contains the following directives :

# if	# ifdef	# else
# elif	# endif	# include
# define	# line	# error

For instance, # error directive instructs the compiler to print an error message and stop the compilation when the condition is encountered.

Basically, one can experience three types of errors when running a C++ program. Such errors could be detected by the compiler or by the linker or by the librarian. Inspite of successful compiling and linking the execution of the program sometimes comes to an end before completion due to run-time errors. These errors include logical errors, stack overflow, non-permissible division, abnormal program termination, null pointer assignment, etc.

```
Class SolDeq
{ int k,l;
  double ACT[11], Err[11];
```

```
public :
void setDE ()
{   SEVdx = 1+y*y;
    SEVdy = x;
    ............
    ............
}
void setACT ()
{   ...........
    ...........
}
void sevdata ()
{   ...........
    ...........
    gotoxy (10,10); cout << Xval;
    gotoxy (10,11); cout << Appval;
    gotoxy (10,13); cout << Aerr << endl ;
}
};
```

This is a declaration of a class named SolDeq. A class is used to create an object. The body of the class is embedded in two curly brackets { } followed by a semicolon. The variables and functions defined inside the declared class are the members of that class. The keyword **public** signifies that the member functions and variables are common to all. That is to say, all the member functions after the specifier public can be accessed by other members of the class and by any other part of the program.

Returning to the class declaration I see that the variables k, l, ACT, Err are defined in the Private sector of the class and are to some extent protected. They have been accessible only by the functions of the class.

double ACT [11];

It is a one-dimensional array with data type double. With this instruction C++ stores eleven elements under the name ACT in a contiguous memory location. The arrays have been placed in order, such as, ACT[0] ACT[1] ………. ACT[10].

void setDE ()

Functions are the building blocks of C++ programs and they are the central figures in C++ programming. This is a definition of a function declaration named setDE followed by the body of the function, delimited by braces. The fundamental difference between a definition and a declaration is that the definition has a function body.

The specifier **void** signifies that the function setDE has no return value and the empty parentheses indicate that it takes no arguments. As a whole, it is simply a declarator. Void is used to explicitly tell the compiler that something has no value. All functions, except those declared to be of type void, return a value. This value is explicitly specified by the return statement.

The class SolDeq, mentioned before, has another member function named setACT (). The definition is the same as that of setDE ().

The member function Sevdata () has a function body surrounded by the braces. Please don't forget to notice the manipulator **endl** placed at the end that causes a linefeed in the output. It has the same effect as the newline character code \n.

main ()

```
{  SolDeq.deqn;
   int i, j;
   ...........
   ...........
   for (i=1; i<=m; i++)
{  deqn.setDE ();
   ...........
   ...........
```

```
    deqn.setACT ();
    ...........
}
    ...........
    return 0;
}
```

Each C++ program must have a single external function named main, which is fundamentally a group of related program instructions, If a program consists of many functions including classes and other program elements, the execution of the program begins with the main function called **main** (). This is the real entrance of the program and without this function the linker does not work at all.

SolDeq. deqn;

With this specification we define only an object **deqn** of class SolDeq. The object is a discrete quantity and with that we can send messages to other parts of the program. Now I call two other member functions

deqn. setDE ();

deqn. setACT ();

by means of the object as the program shows along with other functions and set them in loop to perform the for-statement until the specified condition is satisfied.

A function returns to its calling station in two ways. When the closing brace '}' of the active function is encountered or when a return statement is executed, the function is caused to return immediately to its calling routine. The return statement can be used with a value associated with it. It's not always a condition, it depends on the declaration of the function. Non-void return type functions must return a value.

clrscr ();

gotoxy(60,1); cout << "Program :" << Pgname;

Allset :

gotoxy (5,8);

cout << "\aHave you set up the IC/PS/DE (y/n) ?";

```
ans = getche();
switch (ans)
{    case 'y'; break;
     case 'n'; cout << '\a'; sleep(1); return 0;
     default : gotoxy(8,10); cout << "\aINVALID CHOICE ........... Try again";
               sleep(2);
               goto Allset;
}
```

This a collection of related program instructions with a multipurpose switch statement. The **switch** statement in C++ is a control statement, better say, selection statement, that is advantageous over if statement which selects between two alternatives. In this connection a list of variables or character constants have been tested in succession and when the match is encountered, that means, when the case-statement meets the demand, the statement sequence related that match is executed. The execution of switch terminates with break or return. If the case-statements do not find the suitables, the default specifier takes in charge and leads the procedure to repeat.

ans = getche ();

This version indicates that the character you type for the variable ans is visible. If getch () is used instead, the entered character is not displayed in the screen.

\a

is an escape character used to make the user alert with a beeping sound.

sleep (1)

is an instruction for holding the program for one second. It is just like the wait-function as applied in other programming languages.

clrscr ()

means to clear the screen for further writing.

gotoxy (5,8)

This function positions the cursor within a text window that has a measure of 80 x 25 display. Basically, a window has 80 columns and 25 rows and the text written by some functions will appear within it. The gotoxy () function takes two integer parameters, the x and y coordinates. The command gotoxy (5,8) positions the cursor in the 5th column and in the 8th row.

Library functions and Header files

Now we want to conclude the brief outline on C++ with a description of header files in short. Many C++ tasks have been performed by library functions. Among others the commonly needed tasks are to mention, such as, string handling, data conversion, mathematical computations, I/O operations and graphics.

A library function has been conducted by the corresponding header file. The header files provide, among other matters, the prototypes for the library functions. Hence, whenever we use a library function in the program, the corresponding header file must be included.

A retrospective survey of the necessary header files for particular purposes has been made next.

< assert .h >	:	Supports debugging; tests a condition and possibly aborts; includes the files < stdio .h > and < stdlib .h >
< conio .h >	:	Declares various functions used in calling DOS I/O operations
< ctype .h >	:	Supports character handling ; contains information for character classification and character conversion
< dir .h >	:	Contains macros, structures and functions for working with directories and path names
< dos .h >	:	Defines various constants and declares specific calls necessary for DOS and 8086-processor
< errno .h >	:	Reports error messages
< float .h >	:	Defines related floating-point values
< fstream .h >	:	Declares the C++ streams that support file I / O; includes < iostream .h >
< graphics .h >	:	Declares prototypes for the graphics functions, such as, getcolor, setcolor, getx, gety, etc.

< io .h >	:	Contains information about the structures and declarations for low-level I / O routines like access, eof, open, write, etc; includes the file < stdarg .h >
< iomanip .h >	:	Declares the C++ streams I / O manipulators and contains macros
< iostream .h >	:	The basic C++ (earlier version) streams I / O routines are defined
< math .h >	:	Provides all possible mathematical functions
< memory .h >	:	Memory manipulation functions have been declared
< stdio .h >	:	Defines types and macros required for standard I / O (gets, puts, etc.)
< stdlib .h >	:	Supports commonly used routines : conversion routines, search / sort routines and others
< string .h >	:	Deals with string handling (strcpy, strlen, movedata, etc.)
< time .h >	:	Provides time and date functions

Some Points To Note

In connection with the mathematical problems worked out in this text one has to set up the mathematical functions in terms of programming language C++. Here are some instances.

Mathematical functions		**Conversion in C++**
$\text{Cos}^3 x$	→	pow(cos(x),3)
e^{xy}	→	exp(x*y)
$xy^{1/3}$	→	x* pow(y,0.33333333)
$(1-y^2)^{1/2}$	→	sqrt(1-y*y)
$\tan^{-1}(x^2+1)$	→	atan (x*x+1)
$\text{Ln}(x^2+y^2)$	→	log (x*x+y*y)
Sec x	→	1/ cos (x)
$(x^2+y^2)^{3/2}$	→	pow(sqrt (x*x+y*y),3)

Chapter 2

Preliminary Viewpoints

2.1. Numerical Development of Differential Equations

Almost all the physical problems and many practical applications of technology are dependent on mathematical formulations, specially in terms of **differential equations**, one of the important disciplines of mathematics.

If I approach the problem of differential equation with analytical philosophy, I should be really almost certain as to my ability to determine the solution of the problem, but the question arises at this stage, how many particulars and how many difficult steps may be required. The operations of arithmetic and the algebraic moves in the intermediate steps, required for the solution of the problem, can be sometimes complicated and cumbersome.

A large number of differential equations that have been met casually in the practical field, would be sometimes difficult to solve analytically. Numerical analysis would, thus, be a necessary and an inevitable fitting for the purpose of obtaining the numerical solutions of differential equations that cannot be solved or rather difficult to be solved by the standard methods that I want to discuss later in chapters 5 and 6. In view of that some methods or techniques are needed for the solutions of the equations that are numerically developed and these methods are known as **numerical methods**.

The numerical methods provide the most impressive and favourable results when they have been applied to difficult problems. There are many numerical methods, some of them are widely known because of precision and accuracy. With precision and accuracy I mean that they produce precise and accurate results by degrees.

The numerical methods are, at present age, very different and prevalent because of widespread acclamation in practice. In particular, the advent of digital computer has brought a revolution to the system of numerical analysis that involves the methods for the numerical development of the solutions. In other words, numerical methods have been successfully employed for numerically developed solutions of differential equations. I consider the numerical procedures throughout this textbook analytically and use them in solving the problems of differential equations and the related problems with the aid of Personal Computer.

The approximation of the solution of differential equations has been performed by the program instructions designed by the programming language C++ from BORLAND International using the appropriate numerical methods that are well fitted.

2.2. Error Propagation and Analysis

In attempting to determine the numerical solutions of mathematical problems I confront with the number system that in general involves errors.

Error propagation is defined as the means of developing at a certain phase of a calculation further error that arises out of the error at a previous point of calculation. Unfavourable propagation of error might be sometimes serious and could influence the computed results. The approach by which indefinite assumptions of initial and boundary conditions propagate in the final results can be manipulated properly applying a good numerical method.

Basically, the errors are inherent in the formulation of mathematical or physical problem. Mathematical constants like π(Pi), e(exponential function), Ln 2 (logarithmic function) and physical parameters, such as, force of attraction, velocity of light (c), etc. cause the formulation of the problem inaccurate when I apply the parameters rounding to some decimal places.

Most of the arithmetical or algebraic calculations produce numbers that contain unlimited decimal representations. Such long representation cannot be accepted in the approximation process because of limited word-length capacity of the computer. For the sake of convenience, I restrict myself to a limiting decimal representation rounding the number up or down. The error caused by rounding a number is known as **roundoff** error. The roundoff error plays an important role in the approximation system. In order to determine the accurate representation of a number the value of the error, that is rounded, must be added to approximate value.

There is another type of error called **truncation** error that arises generally in the definition of an elementary mathematical function. Applying the series expansion theorem it is obtained for

$$\text{Sin } x = \sum_{\infty}^{k=0} (-1)^k \frac{x^{2k+1}}{(2k+1)!} = x - x^3 / 3! + x^5 / 5! - x^7 / 7! + \ldots$$

To approximate the function sin x by a numerical procedure considered in this textbook, the series must be bounded by limiting the value of k. The truncation error is the result of truncating an infinite series in order to obtain a finite series.

In view of the above considerations let us now formulate the definition of **error**.

$$\text{Error} = \text{True value - Approximate value}$$

Definition of an error yields assuming the values Tv = 0.96543425 and Av = 0.96542310

$$\text{Error} = 0.96543425 - 0.96542310 = 0.00001115 = 1.115 \times 10^{-5}$$

Dividing the error by the true value I obtain the relative error that is defined by

$$\text{Relative error} = \frac{\text{error}}{\text{true value}}$$

The use of relative error is significant when the true value of a quantity is very small or too large. Sometimes I express the error with the symbols | error | denoting the **absolute error**. The floating-point representation of a number that is rounded or chopped in a computational procedure causes often the development of an error. The error that committed once, can affect the intermediate results of the operations leading to erratic final results.

Let us consider a simple equation. It is nothing but a problem of finding the two roots of a quadratic equation

$ax^2 + bx + c = 0$, where a, b, c are constants

Example $x^2 + 185.21x + 12.451 = 0.$

Applying the quadratic formula from algebra for determining the roots that state

$$x_{1;2} = \frac{-b \pm \sqrt{(b^2 - 4ac)}}{2a}$$

Here $b^2 = 34302.744$ (rounding to 3 decimal places)

$b^2 - 4ac = 34252.940$ (rounding to 3 decimal places)

$\sqrt{(b^2 - 4ac)} = 185.075$ (rounding to 3 decimal places)

True roots $x_{1,2} = -0.0672508$ & -185.1427492

and approximate roots $x_{1,2} = -0.06750$ & -185.14250

It is evident that there are discrepancies in the value between true and approximate roots. The discrepancies are due to roundoff errors that arise in the decimal representation for the quantity b^2 considered at start. The error developes step by step in further rounding a quantity and produce the unwanted results in subsequent operations. In this manner an error propagate through succeeding estimations that yield finally inaccurate results. At this stage I like to make another approach to roundoff error propagation considering an **Initial Value Problem**.

Example $Dy/dx = 2y\ (x\ Ln\ x) + 1/x$

with the initial condition $y(e) = 1.0$ $(e = 2.71828182)$

The exact solution of the IVP is $y(x) = Ln\ x\ (2Ln\ x - 1)$.

The initial condition $y(e) = 1.0$ satisfies the exact solution by setting $x_0 = e$. The approximation of $y(x)$ developes with a rounding error when I set the representation of e with 5 decimal places, that means, accepting the value for $x_0 = e = 2.71828$. All the succeeding approximations starting with y_0 provide inaccurate results because of rounding errors once determined for x_0.

In the exact solution I could substitute the accurate incremental values of x in order to get the exact values for $y(x_0)$, $y(x_1)$, etc. But the acceptance of the rounded initial condition for $x_0 = 2.71828$ and its imposition on the formula for the determination of the approximations produce error in the computed solutions. The errors develope gradually in unallowed magnitudes.

Error Analysis

I have so far discussed about the possible types and sources of error occured in the approximate solutions. I want to point out now some techniques in order to reduce the errors. The escape from error *in toto* is almost out of the question, even if a realistic estimation is achieved. A **numerical method** is a complete and unambiguous process for the constructive solution of mathematical problems that require particular numerically developed solutions together with a suitable error analysis. A numerical method is an integral part of numerical analysis, an important subject matter of mathematics, that deals with the various aspects of error development in numerical methods.

The most important fundamental requirement for computable error estimate is the convergence of an algorithm, a set of well-defined steps for the solution of a problem. An algorithm is said to be convergent, if the approximations are more closely to the sequence of true solutions of the problem. The efficiency of the convergence of algorithm is as well important. The size of the error after a finite number of operations must be estimated when the condition of convergence is not satisfied in some cases. The **error estimates** are extensively accepted by the numerical methods that are developed step-by-step for the approximation of differential equations. In order to make the estimate accurate, the value of width (w) must be considered very small.

Forward error analysis and backward error analysis are the two methods that are very known and useful in numerical analysis. The procedures have been preferred to successful analysis of errors. The backward error analysis reveals that the numerical solution satisfies exactly a disturbed form of the original problem. The bounds for the perturbations have been determined and will be imposed on the results considered standard as to find a bound for the error in the numerical solution.

The most simple case of error estimate is to make use of double precision. The representation of a number that is double that usual number of bits, is known as double precision representation. The double precision arithmetic can be used to achieve a required level of accuracy.

Chapter 3

Numerical Integration

3.1. Evaluation of the Definite Integral

We consider a function $f(x)$ that is supposed to be finite and continuous on an interval $[\alpha, \beta]$, assuming $\beta > \alpha$.

$$\text{The function} \qquad y = f(x) \tag{3.1}$$

is integrable on $[\alpha, \beta]$ based on the aforesaid considerations and represents a curve that is moving continuously in a path curving outwards or inwards.

Let us now make some mathematical observations on the function $f(x)$ with some presumed values of x within the range of the interval $[\alpha, \beta]$.

The base of the field of observation amounting to $\beta - \alpha$, is divided into m parts each of width w providing the values for x finite in quantity: α, $\alpha + w$, $\alpha + 2w$, …, $\alpha + (m - 1)w$, $\beta = \alpha + mw$. Without loss of generality we can erect perpendiculars on these points in the x-axis which aid us to form rectangular figures connecting the curve represented by the equation (3.1). The aggregate of the rectangles in the limits yields the area of the space enclosed by the curve $y = f(x)$, the x-axis and the two fixed ordinates corresponding to $x = \alpha$ and $x = \beta$. The spatial area can now be represented by the numerical measure

$$I = \int_{\alpha}^{\beta} f(x)\, dx = F(x) \Big|_{\alpha}^{\beta} = F(\beta) - F(\alpha) \tag{3.2}$$

The geometrical interpretation of definite integral exposes a clear view when it is described graphically as shown.

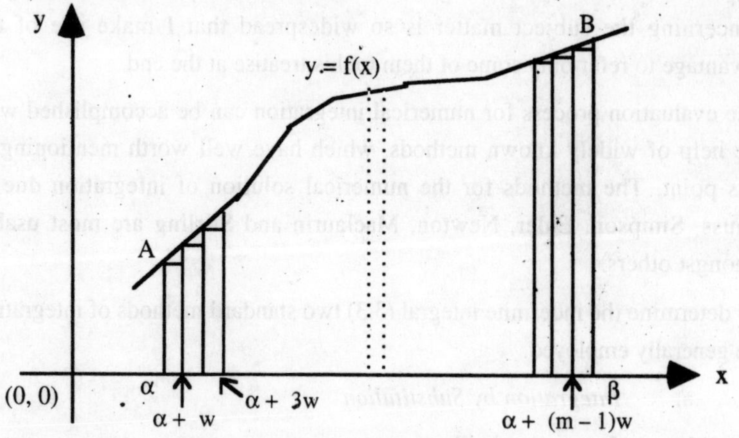

Graphical representation of the integral $\int_{\alpha}^{\beta} f(x)\,dx$

The expression in equation (3.2) is interpreted as the integral of $f(x)\,dx$ from α to β ; α is the lower bound, β is the upper bound, the function $f(x)$ to be integrated is called the **integrand** and the differential dx indicates that x is the **index of integration**. Another name for integrand is the subject of integration as suggested by Prof. G. H. Hardy of Cambridge University. The measure $F(\beta) - F(\alpha)$ that depends only on α and β and the shape of the function $f(x)$, is termed as the integral sum or the **difinite integral** or simply, the integral. It is also called the **Riemann** integral. The operational technique by which we get at the integral is known as the numerical integration.

This is a brief study for the evaluation of difinite integral from the point of view of the limit of a sum, provided that the function $f(x)$ satisfies certain fundamental necessary and sufficient conditions, such as, existence, continuity, integrability in certain domain. Because of the fact that the indefinite integral

$$\int f(x)\,dx \tag{3.3}$$

supplies consistently a definite value provided that the integral (3.3) is defined by finite limits, it is called the definite integral.

I need not be concerned here in detailed discussion about the general properties of definite integrals and also about the proofs of the theorems related to the throry of integration. The availability of standard books concerning the subject matter is so widespread that I make use of the advantage to refer only some of them to this treatise at the end.

The evaluation process for numerical integration can be accomplished with the help of widely known methods, which have well worth mentioning at this point. The methods for the numerical solution of integration due to Gauss, Simpson, Euler, Newton, Maclaurin and Stirling are most usable amongst others.

To determine the indefinite integral (3.3) two standard methods of integration are generally employed.

a) *Integration by Substitution*

b) *Integration by Parts.*

The case a)

Integration by substitution means only a change of the independent variable in an indefinite integral and the substitution reduces the integral to another form that is readily integrable as shown in the example.

Example Integrate $\int x^2 e^{x^3}\, dx$

The substitution $x^3 = t$ makes a change in the indefinite integral and by means of differentiation we obtain $3x^2 dx = dt$.

Hence $I = \int x^2 e^{x^3}\, dx = \int e^{x^3} .\, x^2\, dx$

$$= \int \frac{e^t}{3}\, dt = \frac{1}{3} \int e^t\, dt = \frac{1}{3}\, e^t + C = \frac{1}{3}\, e^{x^3} + C,$$

where C is the constant of integration, so-called **guide factor**.

The case b)

Integration by Parts can be applied to the integration of a product of multiple differentiable functions. One has to apply the formula for Integration by Parts that reads

$$uv = \int u\, dv + \int v\, du \tag{3.4}$$

u and v being two differentiable functions. The proper choice of the first function to be integrated is to some extent a matter of practice. In some cases of integration we have to use the formula several times in a process in order to get at the final results.

Example Find the integral of $\int x^2 \, Ln\, x \, dx$.

Let us assume *Ln x* as the first function and $x^2\,dx$ as the second and put $Ln\,x = u$ and $x^2\,dx = dv$. On differentiating the first function and integrating the second we obtain

$$\frac{1}{x}\,dx = \text{du} \quad \text{and} \quad \frac{1}{3}\,x^3 = v.$$

Now if we apply the formula (3.4) selecting as assumed we find

$$I = \int x^2\, Ln\, x\, dx = \frac{1}{3}\,x^3\, Ln\, x - \frac{1}{3}\int x^3.\,\frac{1}{x}\,dx = \frac{1}{3}\,x^3\, Ln\, x - \frac{1}{3}\int x^2\, dx$$

We can apply the formula again by considering the integral $\int x^2\,dx$ as the product of the function given and unity and choosing unity as the first function. The final solution of the integral is

$$I = \frac{1}{3}\,x^3\, Ln\, x. - \frac{1}{9}\,x^3 + C.$$

As a matter of fact, the evaluation of definite integral from the practical viewpoint is regardless of concerning the basic rules and the guide factor *C*, constant of integration, that are remained in the open. The evaluation from the practical viewpoint is meant for a computerised solution of a mathematical problem by means of a computer software that I wish to lay out.

The software layout for the determination of numerical solution of definite integrals is nothing but the program named **INTGSIMP** built in programming language C++. This program used to determine the approximate solution of definite integrals has been described in chapter ten (section 10.1)

The program instructions have been designed by the computer language C++ (Turbo) applying the mathematical formula from Simpson and is executed on any MS-DOS operating system (version 6.0) with an appropriate C++ (version 3.0) compiler from BORLAND International.

3.2. Integration of Functions with Finite Limits

To solve a definite integral I apply the mathematical formula according to the extended SIMPSONS'S rule with states

$$I = \frac{w\,[y_0 + 4(y_1 + y_3 + \ldots + y_{m-1}) + 2(y_2 + y_4 + \ldots + y_{m-2}) + y_m]}{3}$$

where m = total number of divisions, w = width of each division and $y_0, y_1, y_2, \ldots$ are the values of y, i.e., the ordinates at points $x_0, x_1, x_2, \ldots$ on the x-axis.

Here I limit myself to the concise presentation of the rule from Simpson without a detailed consideration of the formula. If you want to make much of it, it is then advisable to look at the literatures on analysis. To approximate the definite integral by means of C++ program INTGSIMP the following two steps should be performed before start:

1) The DEFINITION Block of *IC*, a section of the program, will be provided with the initial conditions, i.e., the lower limit *L*1, the upper limit *U*1 and the superscript *K* for number of divisions. Moreover, the exact solution (*ES*) will be put.

2) The FUNCTION Block *Fx* will be furnished with the integrand function.

The estimated value thus obtained, can be eventually compared with the exact value determined simultaneously by the program in order to find out the error for approximation.

Example 1

$DI : \int_0^1 xe^x \, dx$

ES : 1.0

W : 0.015625, K : 6, M : 64

Now the integrand function xe^x in the definite integral (*DI*) will be put in the FUNCTION block *Fx* of the program as mentioned before. The integrand xe^x in C++ conversion will be, thus, $x * \exp(x)$. some conversions gas been given at the end of Chapter 1. In the DEFINITION Block of *IC*, the lower and upper limits 0 & 1 for *L*1 & *U*1, the superscript 6 for *K*, and the value 1.0 for *ES* will be inserted. After the execution of the program we get the results as follows :

Estimated solution of the integral : 1.00000000

Exact solution of the integral : 1.00000000

Error for estimation : –2.60697e-09

f we have a look at the results, we see that the values for estimation and xact are correct to 8 decimal places. The amount of error indicates that the rror begins at the 9th place after decimal. The approximation in this case is ccurate to within this value. e-09 reads usually as 10^{-09}.

xample 2

DI : $\displaystyle\int_{1}^{7.38905609} \frac{1}{x(1 + Ln\,x)^2}\,dx$

ES : $\dfrac{2}{3}$

W : 0.024957, K : 8, M : 256

Estimated solution of the integral : 0.66666686

Exact solution of the integral : 0.66666666

Error for approximation : –1.95158e-07

he significant digit of the error is at the 7th decimal place.

he approximation is correct to within the amount of error.

xample 3

DI : $\displaystyle\int_{0}^{1} \frac{Ln(1 + x)}{(1 + x^2)}\,dx$

ES : $\dfrac{\pi\, Ln\, 2}{8}$

W : 0.003906, K : 8, M : 256

Estimated solution of the integral : 0.27219826

Exact solution of the integral : 0.27219826

Error for approximation : –3.17823e-10

ne significant digit of the error is at the 10th decimal place.

ne approximation is correct to within the amount of error.

xample 4

DI : $\displaystyle\int_{2}^{3} \frac{1}{\sqrt{(x-1)(5-x)}}\,dx$

ES : $\frac{\pi}{6}$

W : 0.03125, *K* : 5, *M* : 32

Estimated solution of the integral : 0.52359878

Exact solution of the integral : 0.52359878

Error for approximation : –5.34768e-09

The significant digit of the error is at the 9th decimal place.

The approximation is correct to within the amount of error.

Example 5

DI : $\int_0^{0.5} \frac{1}{[(1-2x^2)\sqrt{(1-x^2)}]}\,dx$

ES : $\frac{Ln(2+\sqrt{3})}{2}$

W : 0.003906, *K* : 7, *M* : 128

Estimated solution of the integral : 0.65847895

Exact solution of the integral : 0.65847895

Error for approximation : –2.0906e-09

The significant digit of the error is at the 9th decimal place.

The approximation is correct to within the amount of error.

Example 6

DI : $\int_0^{1} n\ Ln(1+2x)\,dx$

ES : $\frac{3\ Ln\ 3}{8}$

W : 0.015625, *K* : 6, *M* : 64

Estimated solution of the integral : 0.41197961

Exact solution of the integral : 0.41197961

Error for approximation : –3.72378e-09

The significant digit of the error is at the 9th decimal place.

The approximation is correct to within the amount of error.

Example 7

$$DI : \int_0^{Ln\,2} \frac{e^x}{(1+e^x)}\,dx$$

$$ES : Ln\left(\frac{3}{2}\right)$$

W : 0.01083, K : 6, M : 64

Estimated solution of the integral : 0.40546511

Exact solution of the integral : 0.40546511

Error for approximation : –3.89283e-12

The significant digit of the error is at the 12th decimal place.

The approximation is correct to within the amount of error.

Example 8

$$DI : \int_2^{e} [1 / Ln\,x - 1 / (Ln\,x)^2]\,dx$$

$$ES : e - \frac{2}{Ln\,2}$$

W : 0.011223, K : 6, M : 64

Estimated solution of the integral : –0.16710826

Exact solution of the integral : –0.16710826

Error for approximation : –6.48702e-09

The significant digit of the error is at the 9th decimal place.

The approximation is correct to within the amount of error.

Example 9

$$DI : \int_0^{4} \sqrt{(1+\sqrt{x})}\,dx$$

ES : 6.07586788

W : 0.007813, K : 9, M : 512

Estimated solution of the integral : 6.07586789

Exact solution of the integral : 6.07586788

Error for approximation : –1.1909e-08

The significant digit of the error is at the 8th decimal place.

The approximation is correct to within the amount of error.

Example 10

$$DI : \int_0^1 x \, Ln\left(1 + \frac{x}{2}\right) dx$$

$$ES : \frac{3[1 - 2\, Ln\,(3/2)]}{4}$$

W : 0.03125, K : 5, M : 32

Estimated solution of the integral : 0.14180234

Exact solution of the integral : 0.14180234

Error for approximation : –2.59905e-09

The significant digit of the error is at the 9th decimal place.

The approximation is correct to within the amount of error.

Example 11

$$DI : \int_{1.0}^{1.414214} \frac{(x^2 + 1)}{(x^4 + 1)} dx$$

$$ES : \frac{\frac{\pi}{2} - \tan^{-1} 2}{\sqrt{2}}$$

W : 0.012944, K : 5, M : 32

Estimated solution of the integral : 0.32784863

Exact solution of the integral : 0.32784837

Error for approximation : –2.61947e-07

The significant digit of the error is at the 7th decimal place.

The approximation is correct to within the amount of error.

Example 12

DI : $$\int_{1.5}^{2.5} \frac{1}{\sqrt{(x-1)(3-x)}}\,dx$$

ES : $\frac{\pi}{3}$

W : 0.015625, K : 6, M : 64

Estimated solution of the integral : 1.04719756

Exact solution of the integral : 1.04719755

Error for approximation : –1.06954e-08

The significant digit of the error is at the 8th decimal place.

The approximation is correct to within the amount of error.

Example 13

DI : $$\int_{0}^{1} \frac{1}{(1-x+x^2)}\,dx$$

ES : $\frac{2\pi}{3\sqrt{3}}$

W : 0.001953, K : 9, M : 512

Estimated solution of the integral : 1.20919958

Exact solution of the integral : 1.20919957

Error for approximation : –1.38268e-09

The significant digit of the error is at the 9th decimal place.

The approximation is correct to within the amount of error.

Example 14

DI : $$\int_{0}^{1} \frac{1}{(x^2-2x+2)^3}\,dx$$

ES : $\frac{3\pi+8}{32}$

W : 0.03125, K : 5, M : 32

Estimated solution of the integral : 0.5445243

Exact solution of the integral : 0.54452431

Error for approximation : 1.55718e-08

The significant digit of the error is at the 8th decimal place.

The approximation is correct to within the amount of error.

Example 15

$$DI : \int_{0}^{\pi/2} Ln\,(1 + x)\,dx$$

ES : 0.85658994

W : 0.024544, K : 6, M : 64

Estimated solution of the integral : 0.85658994

Exact solution of the integral : 0.85658994

Error for approximation : 4.37542e-09

The significant digit of the error is at the 9th decimal place.

The approximation is correct to within the amount of error.

Example 16

$$DI : \int_{-5}^{-3} \sqrt{(x^2 - 4)}\,dx$$

$$ES : 8.10233722 - 2\,Ln\,\frac{(3 - \sqrt{5})}{(5 - \sqrt{21})}$$

W : 0.0625, K : 5, M : 32

Estimated solution of the integral : 6.89358605

Exact solution of the integral : 6.89358605

Error for approximation : 6.95035e-10

The significant digit of the error is at the 10th decimal place.

The approximation is correct to within the amount of error.

Example 17

$$DI : \int_{0}^{1.414214} x^3 e^{x^2}\,dx$$

ES : 4.19452800

W : 0.005524, *K* : 8, *M* : 256

Estimated solution of the integral : 4.19452806

Exact solution of the integral : 4.194528

Error for approximation : –6.35782e-08

The significant digit of the error is at the 8th decimal place.

The approximation is correct to within the amount of error.

Example 18

DI : $\int_{1}^{2} \frac{1}{x(1+2x)^2} dx$

ES : $Ln\left(\frac{6}{5}\right) - \frac{2}{15}$

W : 0.03125, *K* : 5, *M* : 32

Estimated solution of the integral : 0.04898824

Exact solution of the integral : 0.04898823

Error for approximation : –1.32284e-08

The significant digit of the error is at the 8th decimal place.

The approximation is correct to within the amount of error.

Example 19

DI : $\int_{2}^{3} \frac{2x}{(1+x^2)} dx$

ES : *Ln* 2

W : 0.015625, *K* : 6, *M* : 64

Estimated solution of the integral : 0.69314718

Exact solution of the integral : 0.69314718

Error for approximation : 5.56145e-11

The significant digit of the error is at the 11th decimal place.

The approximation is correct to within the amount of error.

Example 20

DI : $\int_0^5 \frac{(x^2-3)}{(x+2)(x+1)^2}\,dx$

ES : $Ln\left(\frac{7}{2}\right)-\frac{5}{3}$

W : 0.019531, K : 8, M : 256

Estimated solution of the integral : –0.41390374

Exact solution of the integral : –0.41390369

Error for approximation : 4.5113e-08

The significant digit of the error is at the 8th decimal place.

The approximation is correct to within the amount of error.

Example 21

DI : $\int_1^2 \frac{x-3}{x^2(x+1)}\,dx$

ES : $4Ln\left(\frac{4}{3}\right)-\frac{3}{2}$

W : 0.015625, K : 6, M : 64

Estimated solution of the integral : –0.34927173

Exact solution of the integral : –0.34927172

Error for approximation : 6.02869e-09

The significant digit of the error is at the 9th decimal place.

The approximation is correct to within the amount of error.

Example 22

DI : $\int_0^2 \frac{x}{\sqrt{(25-4x^2)}}\,dx$

ES : 0.50000001

W : 0.03125, K : 6, M : 64

Estimated solution of the integral : 0.50000006

Exact solution of the integral : 0.50000001

Error for approximation : –5.37134e-08

The significant digit of the error is at the 8th decimal place.

The approximation is correct to within the amount of error.

3.3. Integration Of Particular Trigonometric Functions

Before I enter upon the evaluation process for the approximate solution of definite integrals containing trigonometric functions, I wish to discuss on some standard indefinite integrals involving trigonometric functions or transcendental functions or related functions.

I shall now consider the trigonometric differentials that are integrated by transformation method without any difficulty.

Example Find the integral of $\int \text{Sin}^2 x \cos^5 x\, dx$

$$I = \int \text{Sin}^2 x \cos^5 x\, dx = \int \sin^2 x \cos^4 x \cos x\, dx \tag{3.5}$$

As we know from Trigonometry, $\sin^2 x + \cos^2 x = 1$ and putting it in (3.5) for $\cos^2 x$ we obtain a simplified form

$$I = \int \sin^2 x(1 - \sin^2 x)^2 \cos x\, dx$$

$$= \int \sin^2 x(1 - 2\sin^2 x + \sin^4 x) \cos x\, dx$$

$$= \int (\sin^2 x - 2\sin^4 x + \sin^6 x) \cos x\, dx$$

The substitution $\sin x = u$ yields on differentiation $\cos x\, dx = du$. By means of this transformation we have

$$I = \int (u^2 - 2u^4 + u^6)\, du$$

On integrating and rearranging we get

$$I = \frac{1}{3}u^3 - \frac{2}{5}u^5 + \frac{1}{7}u^7 + C$$

$$= \frac{1}{3}\sin^3 x - \frac{2}{5}\sin^5 x + \frac{1}{7}\sin^7 x + C$$

$$= \frac{\sin^3 x\,(35 - 42\sin^2 x + 15\sin^4 x)}{105} + C$$

where C, the guide factor that can be found out when the limits of integration are known.

Let us consider another illustrative example applying the formula for integration by parts stated in equation (3.4) in section (3.1).

Example Integrate $\int e^{2x} \sin 3x \, dx$.

Let $u = e^{2x}$ and $dv = \sin 3x \, dx$

then $du = 2e^{2x} \, dx$ and $v = \frac{-1}{3} \cos 3x$.

Applying the formula for integration by parts we get

$$\int e^{2x} \sin 3x \, dx = \frac{-1}{3} e^{2x} \cos 3x + \frac{2}{3} \int e^{2x} \cos 3x \, dx \qquad (\alpha)$$

Again let $u = e^{2x}$ and $dv = \cos 3x \, dx$,

then $du = 2e^{2x} \, dx$ and $v = \frac{1}{3} \sin 3x$.

Hence, by the equation (3.4)

$$\int e^{2x} \cos 3x \, dx = \frac{1}{3} e^{2x} \sin 3x - \frac{2}{3} \int e^{2x} \sin 3x \, dx \qquad (\beta)$$

Substitution (β) in (α) and rearranging we get finally

$$\int e^{2x} \sin 3x \, dx = \frac{e^{2x}}{13} (2 \sin 3x - 3 \cos 3x) + C$$

Example Integrate $\int \tan^4 \theta \, d\theta$.

From Trigonometry we know $\text{Sec}^2 \theta - \text{Tan}^2 \theta = 1$.

Arranging the integral properly and putting the trigonometric formula we obtain

$$\int \tan^4 \theta \, d\theta = \int \tan^2 \theta \, . \, \tan^2 \theta \, d\theta = \int \tan^2 \theta \, (\sec^2 \theta - 1) d\theta$$

$$= \int \tan^2 \theta \, . \, \sec^2 \theta \, d\theta - \int \tan^2 \theta \, d\theta$$

$$= \frac{1}{3} \tan^3 \theta - \int (\sec^2 \theta - 1) \, d\theta$$

$$= \frac{1}{3} \tan^3 \theta - \tan \theta + \theta + C$$

is the general solution of the integral.

Now to solve a definite integral I employ the mathematical formula according to the Simpson's rule that has been defined in section (3.2).

Example 1

DI : $\int_{0}^{\pi/2} x^2 \sin x \, dx$

ES : $\pi - 2$

W : 0.012272, K : 7, M : 128

Here the integrand $x^2 \sin x$ in example 1 will be inserted in the FUNCTION Block Fx of the program INTGSIMP. The C++ conversion of $x^2 \sin x$ is x*x* sin(x). As I have already mentioned in section (3.2), the conversion table in C++ has been provided at the end of chapter 1. The lower and upper limits : 0 & $\frac{\pi}{2}$, the superscript 7 and the quantity $\pi - 2$ for ES are put in the DEFINITION Block. After program execution we obtain the following data:

Estimated solution of the integral	:	1.14159265
Exact solution of the integral	:	1.14159265
Error for approximation	:	2.78252e-09

From the computerised approximation it can be seen that the values for estimation and exact are correct to 8 decimal places. The error for estimation amounts to, in this case, 2.78252e-09. The significant digit of the error is at the 9th place after decimal. The approximation is correct to within this value.

Example 2

DI : $\int_{0}^{\pi} \frac{x}{(1 + \cos^2 x)} \, dx$

ES : $\frac{\pi^2}{(2\sqrt{2})}$

W : 0.098175, K : 5, M : 32

Estimated solution of the integral	:	3.48943209
Exact solution of the integral	:	3.48943209
Error for approximation	:	–2.33436e-09

The significant digit of the error is at the 9th decimal place.

The approximation is correct to within the amount of error.

Example 3

DI : $\displaystyle\int_0^{\pi/2} \frac{1}{(5\cos x + 3)}\, dx$

ES : $\dfrac{Ln\ 3}{4}$

W : 0.024544, K : 6, M : 64

Estimated solution of the integral : 0.27465309

Exact solution of the integral : 0.27465307

Error for approximation : –1.68876e-08

The significant digit of the error is at the 8th decimal place.

The approximation is correct to within the amount of error.

Example 4

DI : $\displaystyle\int_0^{\pi/4} \text{Tan}^6 x\, dx$

ES : $\dfrac{13}{15} - \dfrac{\pi}{4}$

W : 0.003068, K : 8, M : 256

Estimated solution of the integral : 0.0812685

Exact solution of the integral : 0.0812685

Error for approximation : –5.74571e-09

The significant digit of the error is at the 9th decimal place.

The approximation is correct to within the amount of error.

Example 5

DI : $\displaystyle\int_0^{\pi/2} \text{Cos}^2 x\, dx$

ES : $\dfrac{\pi}{4}$

W : 0.049087, K : 5, M : 32

Estimated solution of the integral : 0.78539816

Exact solution of the integral : 0.78539816

Error for approximation : –8.97449e-10

The significant digit of the error is at the 10th decimal place.

The approximation is correct to within the amount of error.

Example 6

$$DI : \int_{\pi/6}^{\pi/3} \frac{1}{\sin(2x)} dx$$

ES : $Ln(\sqrt{3})$

W : 0.008181, K : 6, M : 64

Estimated solution of the integral : 0.54930615

Exact solution of the integral : 0.54930614

Error for approximation : –1.16636e-09

The significant digit of the error is at the 9th decimal place.

The approximation is correct to within the amount of error.

Example 7

$$DI : \int_{0}^{\pi/4} \tan x \, dx$$

$$ES : \frac{Ln\ 2}{2}$$

W : 0.012272, K : 6, M : 64

Estimated solution of the integral : 0.34657359

Exact solution of the integral : 0.34657359

Error for approximation : –8.65419e-10

The significant digit of the error is at the 10th decimal place.

The approximation is correct to within the amount of error.

Example 8

$$DI : \int_{0}^{\pi/4} \frac{\sin(2x)}{(\sin^4 x + \cos^4 x)} dx$$

$$ES : \frac{\pi}{4}$$

W : 0.012272, K : 6, M : 64

Estimated solution of the integral : 0.78539816

Exact solution of the integral : 0.78539816

Error for approximation : 2.91336e-09

The significant digit of the error is at the 9th decimal place.

The approximation is correct to within the amount of error.

Example 9

DI : $\displaystyle\int_0^{\pi} \frac{x \sin x}{(1+\cos^2 x)}\, dx$

ES : $\dfrac{\pi^2}{4}$

W : 0.024544, K : 7, M : 128

Estimated solution of the integral : 2.46740109

Exact solution of the integral : 2.46740109

Error for approximation : 6.94338e-10

The significant digit of the error is at the 10th decimal place.

The approximation is correct to within the amount of error.

Example 10

DI : $\displaystyle\int_0^{\pi} \frac{x \tan x}{(\sec x + \tan x)}\, dx$

ES : $\dfrac{\pi(\pi-2)}{2}$

W : 0.024544, K : 7, M : 128

Estimated solution of the integral : 1.79320952

Exact solution of the integral : 1.79320954

Error for approximation : 2.39515e-08

The significant digit of the error is at the 8th decimal place.

The approximation is correct to within the amount of error.

Example 11

DI : $\displaystyle\int_0^{\pi/2} \frac{\sin^2 x}{(\sin x + \cos x)}\,dx$

ES : $\dfrac{Ln\,(\sqrt{2} + 1)}{\sqrt{2}}$

W : 0.024544, K : 6, M : 64

Estimated solution of the integral : 0.62322526

Exact solution of the integral : 0.62322524

Error for approximation : –2.0329e-08

The significant digit of the error is at the 8th decimal place.

The approximation is correct to within the amount of error.

Example 12

DI : $\displaystyle\int_0^{\pi/2} \frac{\sqrt{(\sin x)}}{\sqrt{\sin x} + \sqrt{\cos x}}\,dx$

ES : $\dfrac{\pi}{4}$

W : 0.001534, K : 10, M : 1024

Estimated solution of the integral : 0.78539814

Exact solution of the integral : 0.78539816

Error for approximation : 2.25162e-08

The significant digit of the error is at the 8th decimal place.

The approximation is correct to within the amount of error.

Example 13

DI : $\displaystyle\int_0^{2.35619446} \frac{\sin x}{(1 + \cos^2 x)}\,dx$

ES : $\dfrac{\pi}{4} + \tan^{-1}\dfrac{1}{\sqrt{2}}$

W : 0.036816, K : 6, M : 64

Estimated solution of the integral : 1.40087785

Exact solution of the integral : 1.40087787

Error for approximation : 1.77284e-08

The significant digit of the error is at the 8th decimal place.

The approximation is correct to within the amount of error.

Example 14

DI : $\int_0^{\pi/4} x \sqrt{(\tan x)}\, dx$

ES : 0.23318157

W : 0.012272, *K* : 6, *M* : 64

Estimated solution of the integral : 0.23318159

Exact solution of the integral : 0.23318157

Error for approximation : –1.6132e-08

The significant digit of the error is at the 8th decimal place.

The approximation is correct to within the amount of error.

Example 15

DI : $\int_0^{2\pi} e^{-x} \sin (10\, x)\, dx$

ES : 0.09882513

W : 0.012272, *K* : 9, *M* : 512

Estimated solution of the integral : 0.09882513

Exact solution of the integral : 0.09882513

Error for approximation : 2.13575e-09

The significant digit of the error is at the 9th decimal place.

The approximation is correct to within the amount of error.

Example 16

DI : $\int_0^{1} (\cos^{-1} x)^2\, dx$

ES : $\pi - 2.0$

W : 0.015625, K : 6, M : 64

Estimated solution of the integral : 1.14159265

Exact solution of the integral : 1.14159265

Error for approximation : –4.45322e-09

The significant digit of the error is at the 9th decimal place.

The approximation is correct to within the amount of error.

Example 17

DI : $\int_0^1 \tan^{-1} x \, dx$

ES : $\frac{\pi}{4} - \frac{Ln\ 2}{2}$

W : 0.015625, K : 6, M : 64

Estimated solution of the integral : 0.43882457

Exact solution of the integral : 0.43882457

Error for approximation : –1.72555e-09

The significant digit of the error is at the 9th decimal place.

The approximation is correct to within the amount of error.

Example 18

DI : $\int_0^{\pi/2} \text{Sin}\ x\ Ln\ (\sin x)\ dx$

ES : – 0.30611106

W : 0.098175, K : 4, M : 16

Estimated solution of the integral : –0.30611105

Exact solution of the integral : –0.30611106

Error for approximation : –8.83164e-09

The significant digit of the error is at the 9th decimal place.

The approximation is correct to within the amount of error.

Example 19

DI : $\int_0^{\pi/4} x \cos x \cos (3x)\ dx$

ES : $\frac{(\pi - 3)}{16}$

W : 0.012272, K : 6, M : 64

Estimated solution of the integral : 0.00884955

Exact solution of the integral : 0.00884954

Error for approximation : –7.77958e-09

The significant digit of the error is at the 9th decimal place.

The approximation is correct to within the amount of error.

Example 20

DI : $\int_0^{\pi/2} \sin^6 x \cos^2 x \, dx$

ES : $\frac{5\pi}{256}$

W : 0.024544, K : 6, M : 64

Estimated solution of the integral : 0.06135923

Exact solution of the integral : 0.06135923

Error for approximation : –7.01134e-11

The significant digit of the error is at the 11th decimal place.

The approximation is correct to within the amount of error.

Example 21

DI : $\int_0^{\pi/4} \frac{1}{\cos x} dx$

ES : $Ln(\sqrt{2} + 1)$

W : 0.012272, K : 6, M : 64

Estimated solution of the integral : 0.88137359

Exact solution of the integral : 0.88137359

Error for approximation : –6.89749e-10

The significant digit of the error is at the 10th decimal place.

The approximation is correct to within the amount of error.

Example 22

$$DI : \int_0^{\pi/2} \frac{\cos x}{(1+\sin x)(2+\sin x)}\, dx$$

$$ES : Ln\, \frac{4}{3}$$

W : 0.024544, K : 6, M : 64

Estimated solution of the integral : 0.28768208

Exact solution of the integral : 0.28768207

Error for approximation : –7.28552e-09

The significant digit of the error is at the 9th decimal place.

The approximation is correct to within the amount of error.

Example 23

$$DI : \int_0^{2\pi/3} \frac{1}{(4\cos x + 5)}\, dx$$

$$ES : \frac{\pi}{9}$$

W : 0.032725, K : 6, M : 64

Estimated solution of the integral : 0.34906586

Exact solution of the integral : 0.34906585

Error for approximation : –6.96421e-09

The significant digit of the error is at the 9th decimal place.

The approximation is correct to within the amount of error.

Example 24

$$DI : \int_0^{\pi/2} x^3 \sin 3x\, dx$$

$$ES : \frac{2}{27} - \frac{\pi^2}{12}$$

W : 0.003068, K : 9, M : 512

Estimated solution of the integral : –0.74839295

Exact solution of the integral : –0.74839296

Error for approximation : –9.24651e-09

The significant digit of the error is at the 9th decimal place.

The approximation is correct to within the amount of error.

Example 25

DI : $\int_0^{\pi} x \cos^4 x \, dx$

ES : $\dfrac{3\pi^2}{16}$

W : 0.012272, K : 8, M : 256

Estimated solution of the integral : 1.85055081

Exact solution of the integral : 1.85055082

Error for approximation : 7.04854e-09

The significant digit of the error is at the 9th decimal place.

The approximation is correct to within the amount of error.

Example 26

DI : $\int_0^{\pi} \sqrt{2(1 + \cos x)} \, dx$

ES : 4.0

W : 0.049087, K : 6, M : 64

Estimated solution of the integral : 4.00000001

Exact solution of the integral : 4.0

Error for approximation : –8.06455e-09

The significant digit of the error is at the 9th decimal place.

The approximation is correct to within the amount of error.

Chapter 4

Computing Areas

4.1. Estimation of Areas of Plane Curves

Let us consider two fixed points, $x = \alpha$ and $x = \beta$ on an interval $[\alpha, \beta]$ in Cartesian Coordinates System. Consider again a curve, defined by the equation

$$y = \phi(x)$$

that is supposed to be finite and continuous on this interval $[\alpha, \beta]$, accepting $\beta > \alpha$. The area of the figure formed by the curve, by two vertical lines (ordinates) at the points $x = \alpha$ and $x = \beta$ and by a segment of the base (x-axis) is given by the formula

$$\textbf{Area} = \int_{\alpha}^{\beta} \phi(x)\, dx = \psi(x) \Big|_{\alpha}^{\beta} = \psi(\beta) - \psi(\alpha) \tag{4.1}$$

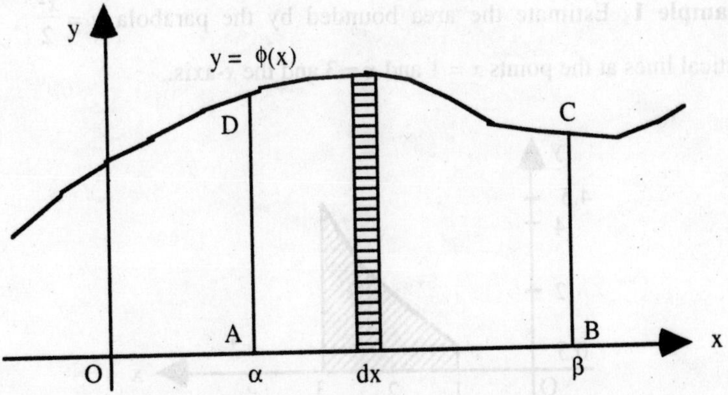

Hence, the **area** is, in general the outcome of indefinite integral with finite limits, which has been explained in chapter 3 (section 3.1) and by definition it is the definite integral having the same numerical measure as in equation (3.2). About more consideration of the matter regarding areas of plane curves I refer to the standard text mentioned in the reference.

The estimation process for evaluation of areas of curves can be performed by the program INTGAREA and the sequence of events follows its proper course according to the instructions presented next.

The program just mentioned that I use here to approximate the definite integral arisen from the problem of area of plane curve is designed by the programming language C++ applying the method of extended SIMPSON'S formulas already described in section 3.2.

Before we process the data of a problem by running the program the two steps should be carried out as follows :

1. The initial conditions of the problem: the lower and the upper limits $L1$ and $U1$ and the superscript K for number of divisions will be given to the section of the program titled DEFINITION Block of IC. In addition to that the exact solution (ES) will be supplied.
2. The FUNCTION Block Fx will be furnished with the new integrand function.

The results of the processing is the approximated solution of the integral. At the same time we get the data of error for approximation.

Example 1 Estimate the area bounded by the parabola $y = \frac{x^2}{2}$, two vertical lines at the points $x = 1$ and $x = 3$ and the x-axis.

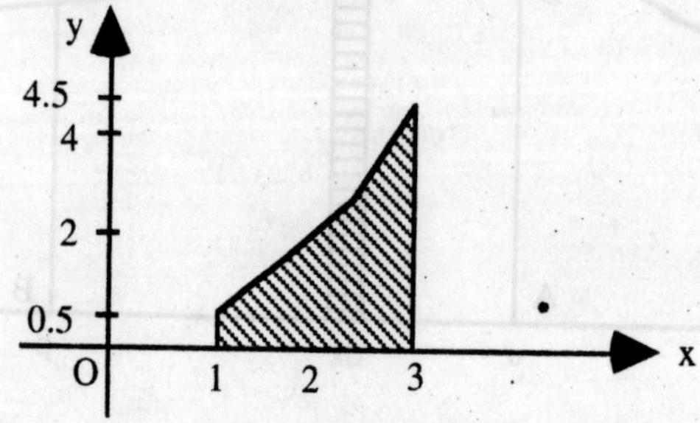

Figure 1

$DI : \int_1^3 \frac{x^2}{2}\, dx$

$ES : 4\frac{1}{3}$

W : 0.03125, K : 6, M : 64

The integrand function $x^2/2$ furnishes now the FUNCTION Block Fx of the program INTGAREA and the DEFINITION Block of IC will get the values 1 & 3 for lower and upper limits, $L1$ & $U1$ respectively; 6 for K and for ES the value $4\frac{1}{3}$. The program supplies the results as follows:

Estimated solution of the integral : 4.33333333

Exact solution of the integral : 4.33333333

Error for approximation : –3.33333e-09

The significant digit of the error is at the 9th decimal place.

The approximation is correct to within the amount of error.

Example 2 Evaluate the area bounded by the curve $y = 2 - x - x^2$ and the x-axis.

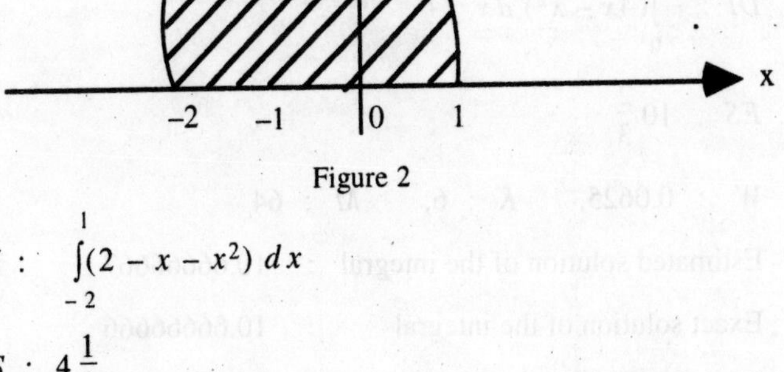

Figure 2

$DI : \int_{-2}^{1} (2 - x - x^2)\, dx$

$ES : 4\frac{1}{2}$

W : 0.046875, K : 6, M : 64

Estimated solution of the integral : 4.5

Exact solution of the integral : 4.5

Error for approximation : 0.0

There is no significant digit of the error. The approximation is correct to within the amount of error.

Example 3 Compute the area bounded by the parabola $y = 4x - x^2$ and the x-axis, the limits of integration being (0.4).

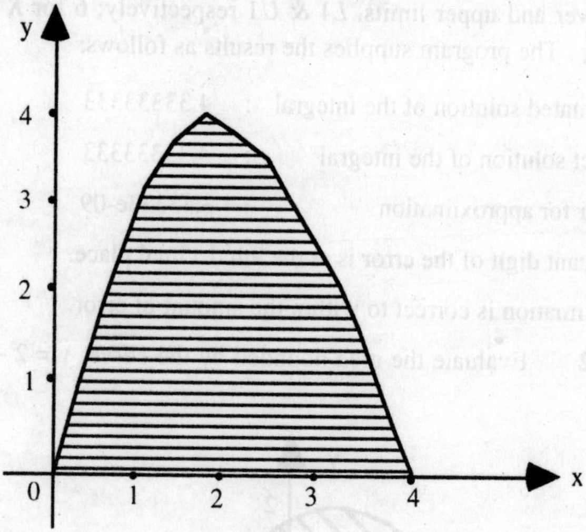

Figure 3

DI : $\int_0^4 (4x - x^2)\, dx$

ES : $10\frac{2}{3}$

W : 0.0625, K : 6, M : 64

Estimated solution of the integral : 10.66666667

Exact solution of the integral : 10.66666666

Error for approximation : –6.66667e-09

The significant digit of the error is at the 9th decimal place.

The approximation is correct to within the amount of error.

Example 4 Compute the area bounded by the curved surface $y = Ln\ x$, the x-axis and the straight line at the point $x = e$.

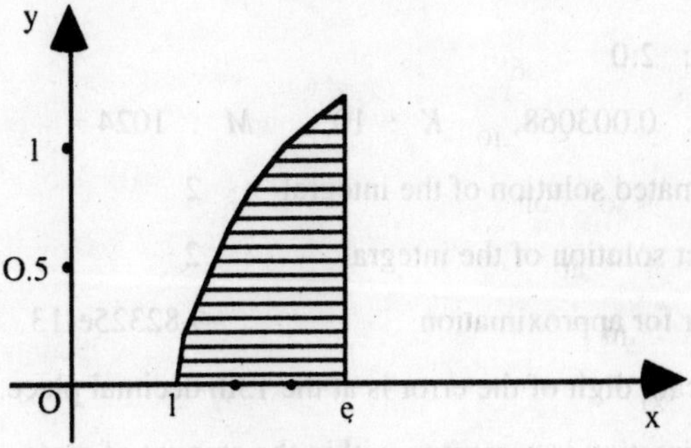

Figure 4

$$DI : \int_1^e Ln\ x\, dx$$

ES : 1.0

W : 0.026848, K : 6, M : 64

Estimated solution of the integral : 0.99999999

Exact solution of the integral : 1.00000000

Error for approximation : 1.39389e-08

The significant digit of the error is at the 8th decimal place.

The approximation is correct to within the amount of error.

Example 5 Compute the area bounded by a single half-wave of the Sine curve represented by $y = \sin x$ and the x-axis. The limits of integration are $(0, \pi)$.

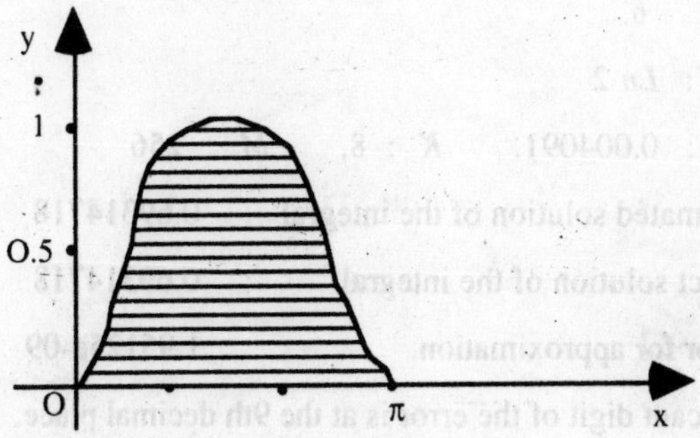

Figure 5

DI : $\int_0^{\pi} \sin x \, dx$

ES : 2.0

W : 0.003068, *K* : 10, *M* : 1024

Estimated solution of the integral : 2

Exact solution of the integral : 2

Error for approximation : –9.82325e-13

The significant digit of the error is at the 13th decimal place.

The approximation is correct to within the amount of error.

Example 6 Find the area held between the curve by $y = \text{Tan } x$, the x-axis and the straight line at $x = \pi/3$.

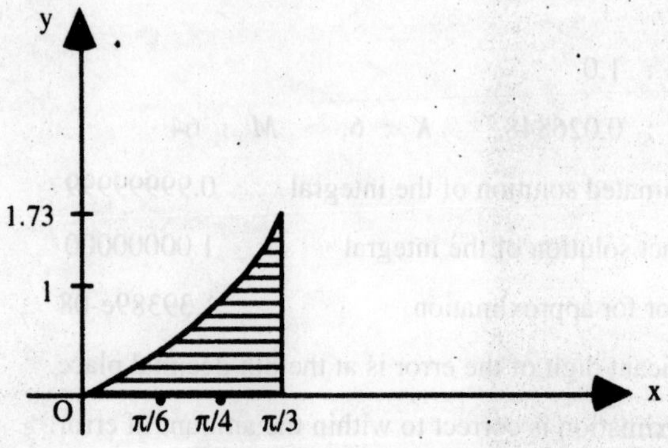

Figure 6

DI : $\int_0^{\pi/3} \text{Tan } x \, dx$

ES : *Ln* 2

W : 0.004091, *K* : 8, *M* : 256

Estimated solution of the integral : 0.69314718

Exact solution of the integral : 0.69314718

Error for approximation : 1.95125e-09

The significant digit of the error is at the 9th decimal place.

The approximation is correct to within the amount of error.

Example 7 Find the area contained between the line $y = 3x$, the x-axis and the straight line at $x = 2$.

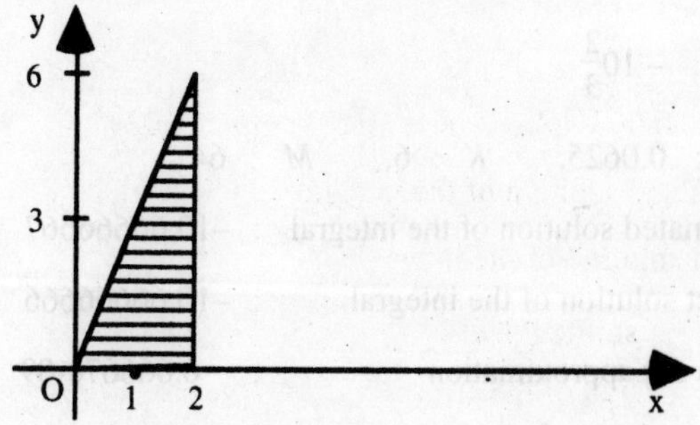

Figure 7

DI : $\int_0^2 3x\, dx$

ES : 6.0

W : 0.03125, K : 6, M : 64

Estimated solution of the integral : 6

Exact solution of the integral : 6

Error for approximation : 0

There is no significant digit of the error.

The approximation is correct to within the amount of error.

Example 8 Compute the area of a segment cut off by the straight line $y = 3 - 2x$ from the parabola $y = x^2$.

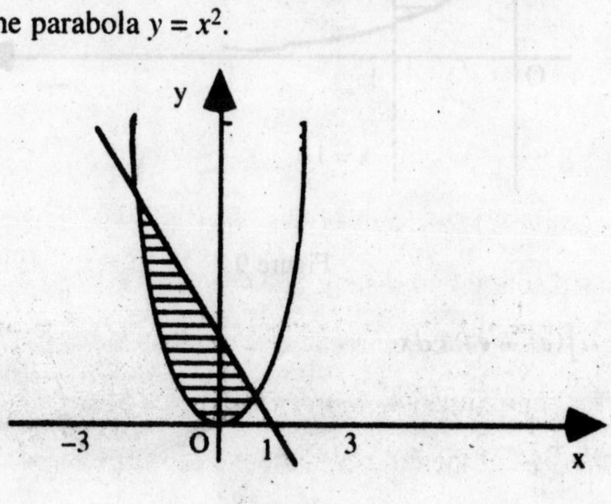

Figure 8

DI : $\int_{-3}^{1}(x^2 + 2x - 3)\,dx$

ES : $-10\frac{2}{3}$

W : 0.0625, K : 6, M : 64

Estimated solution of the integral : –10.66666667

Exact solution of the integral : –10.66666666

Error for approximation : 6.66667e-09

The significant digit of the error is at the 9th decimal place.

The approximation is correct to within the amount of error.

Example 9 Find the area bounded by the curves $y = e^x$ and $y = e^{-x}$ and the straight line at $x = 1$.

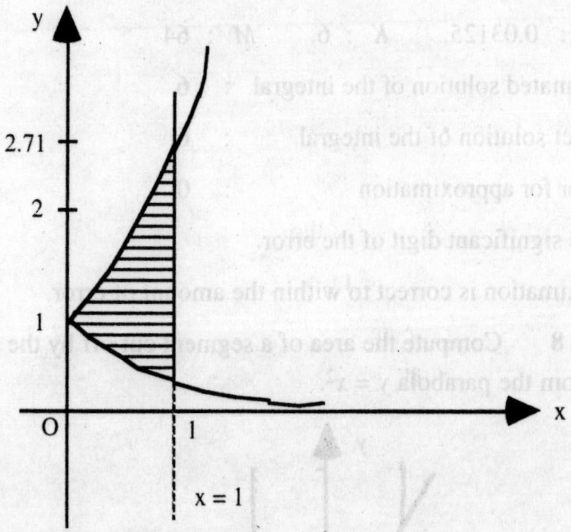

Figure 9

DI : $\int_{0}^{1}(e^x - e^{-x})\,dx$

ES : $e + \frac{1}{e} - 2$

W : 0.015625, K : 6, M : 64

Estimated solution of the integral : 1.08616127

Exact solution of the integral : 1.08616126

Error for approximation : –7.6739e-09

The significant digit of the error is at the 9th decimal place.

The approximation is correct to within the amount of error.

Example 10 Calculate the area contained between the curves $y = 2 - x^2$ and $y^3 = x^2$. The limits of integration are (–1, 1)

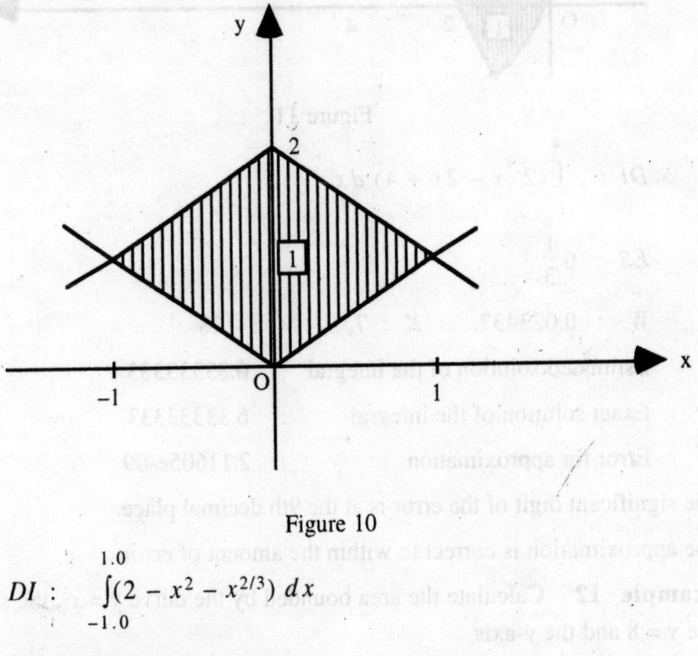

Figure 10

DI : $\int_{-1.0}^{1.0} (2 - x^2 - x^{2/3})\, dx$

ES : 2.13333333

W : 0.000488, K : 12, M : 4096

Estimated solution of the integral : 2.13333359

Exact solution of the integral : 2.13333333

Error for approximation : –2.57037e-07

The significant digit of the error is at the 7th decimal place.

The approximation is correct to within the amount of error.

Example 11 Calculate the finite area bounded by the pair of curves $y^2 - 4x = 0$ and $2x - y = 4$.

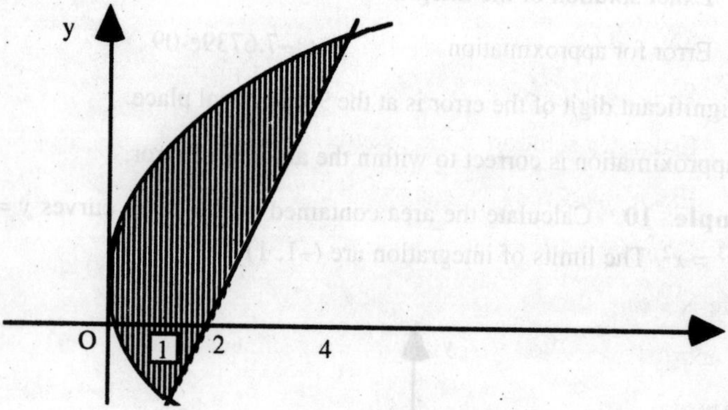

Figure 11

DI : $\int_1^4 (2\sqrt{x} - 2x + 4)\, dx$

ES : $6\frac{1}{3}$

W : 0.023437, K : 7, M : 128

Estimated solution of the integral	:	6.33333333
Exact solution of the integral	:	6.33333333
Error for approximation	:	2.11605e-09

The significant digit of the error is at the 9th decimal place.

The approximation is correct to within the amount of error.

Example 12 Calculate the area bounded by the curve $y = x^3$, the straight line $y = 8$ and the y-axis.

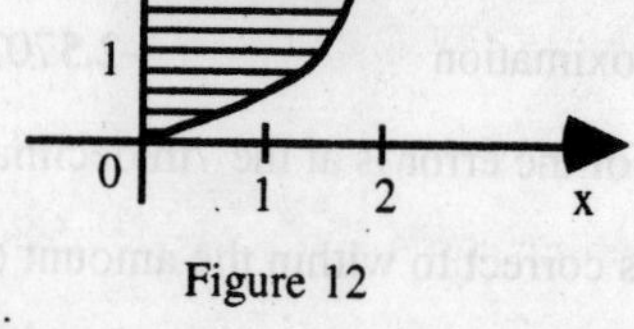

Figure 12

DI : $\int_0^2 (8 - x^3)\,dx$

ES : 12.0

W : 0.03125, K : 6, M : 64

Estimated solution of the integral : 12

Exact solution of the integral : 12

Error for approximation : 0

There is no significant digit of the error.

The approximation is correct to within the amount of error.

Example 13 Find the area bounded by the parabola $y^2 = 2x$ and the circle $x^2 + y^2 = 4x$, the limits of integration being (0, 2).

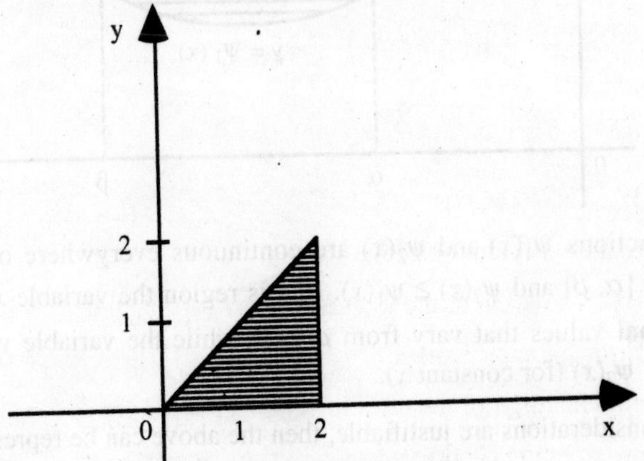

Figure 13

DI : $\int_0^2 [\sqrt{4x - x^2} - \sqrt{2x}\,]\,dx$

ES : $4\left(\frac{\pi}{4} - \frac{2}{3}\right)$

W : 0.000488, K : 12, M : 4096

Estimated solution of the integral : 0.47492547

Exact solution of the integral : 0.47492601

Error for approximation : 5.36214e-07

The significant digit of the error is at the 7th decimal place.

The approximation is correct to within the amount of error.

4.2. Integrals In 2-Dimensional Space

Let us consider a bounded closed region R on the xy-plane surrounded by the curves $y = \psi_1(x)$ and $y = \psi_2(x)$. The region of integration R is bounded by the lines $x = \alpha$ and $x = \beta$ $(\beta > \alpha)$.

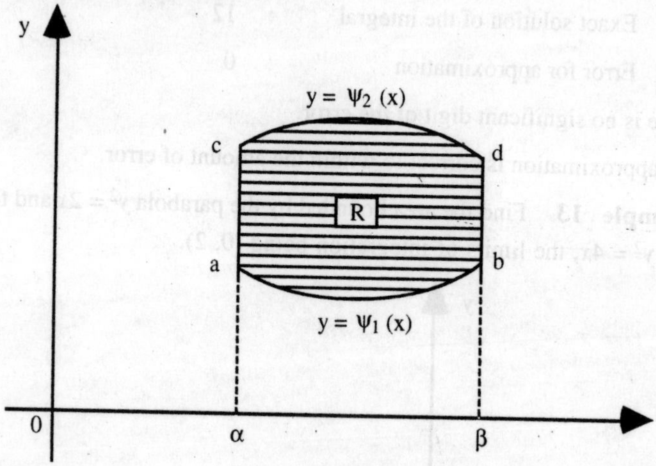

The functions $\psi_1(x)$ and $\psi_2(x)$ are continuous everywhere on the closed interval $[\alpha, \beta]$ and $\psi_2(x) \geq \psi_1(x)$. In this region the variable x has a set of functional values that vary from α to β, while the variable y varies from $\psi_1(x)$ to $\psi_2(x)$ (for constant x).

If the considerations are justifiable, then the above can be represented by the expression

$$\iint_R g(x, y)\, dx\, dy = \int_{\psi_1(x)}^{\psi_2(x)} dy \int_{\alpha}^{\beta} g(x, y)\, dx = \int_{\psi_1(x)}^{\psi_2(x)} \left[\int_{\alpha}^{\beta} g(x, y)\, dx \right] dy \tag{4.20}$$

and is called the **definite double integral** of the function $g(x, y)$ over the region R. The double integral (4.20) is also known as the repeated integral.

The procedure for evaluating a definite double integral such as (4.20) is to first integrate the inner function with respect to the variable x taking y as a constant and then to integrate the obtained result with respect to the variable y. The order of integration is immaterial provided certain conditions are fulfilled.

Example Evaluate the integral $\int_0^2 dx \int_x^{x\sqrt{3}} \frac{x}{x^2+y^2}\,dy.$

Integrating first with respect to the variable y gives

$$\int_0^2 dx \left[\tan^{-1}\left(\frac{y}{x}\right)\right]\Big|_x^{x\sqrt{3}} = [\tan^{-1}(\sqrt{3}) - \tan^{-1}(1)]\int_0^2 dx$$
$$= 0.26179938(x)\,\Big|_0^2$$
$$= 0.26179938\ x\ 2$$
$$= 0.52355987.$$

Example Evaluate the double integral $\iint_R \frac{x^2}{y^2}\,dx\,dy$, if the region of integration R is bounded by the lines $y = x$, $y = \frac{1}{x}$ and $x = 1$, $x = 2$.

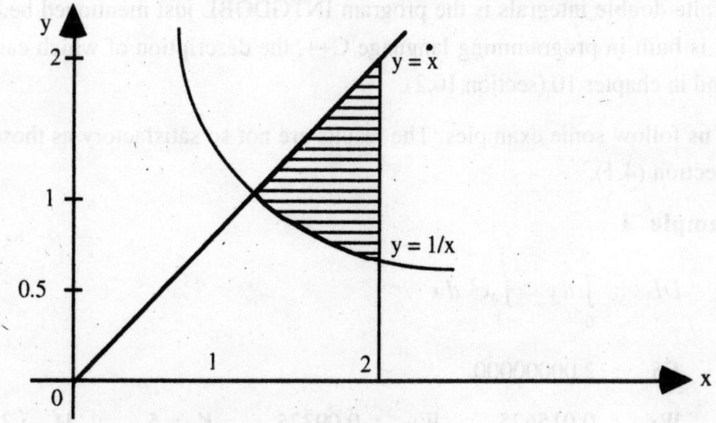

According to the formula (4.20) we can write

$$\psi_1(x) = \frac{1}{x}\ ,\ \psi_2(x) = x,\ \alpha = 1,\ \beta = 2.$$

Therefore, the definite double integral

$$I = \iint_R \frac{x^2}{y^2}\,dx\,dy = \int_1^2 dx\left(\int_{1/x}^{x} \frac{x^2}{y^2}\,dy\right) = \int_1^2 x^2\left(-\frac{1}{y}\right)\Big|_{1/x}^{x} dx$$

$$= \int_1^2 x^2\left(\frac{-1}{x} + x\right)dx = \int_1^2 (x^3 - x)\,dx = \left(\frac{1}{4}x^4 - \frac{1}{2}x^2\right)\Big|_1^2 = 2\frac{1}{4}$$

Now, for the numerical evaluation of the definite double integral the same techniques can be applied. For this type of integral we start as before by employing the composite Simpson's formula with respect to the variables x and y in the program named INTGDOBL designed in C++ (Turbo).

The step size for the variable x is $Wx = (U1x - L1x)/m$ and the step size for y is $Wy = (U1y - L1y)/m$, where $U1x$ and $U1y$ are the upper limits for x & y, $L1x$ and $L1y$ are the lower limits for x & y respectively and m is the total number of divisions dependent on the choice of the superscript K.

The number of functional evaluations required for the approximation is so large that the processing takes much time. If we choose $K = 8$ so that m becomes $2^8 = 256$. The number needed for functional operations is, in this case, $256 \times 256 = 65536 = 2^{16}$.

The software layout for the determination of numerical approximation of definite double integrals is the program INTGDOBL just mentioned before, that is built in programming language C++, the description of which can be found in chapter 10 (section 10.2).

Let us follow some examples. The results are not so satisfactory as those of in section (4.1).

Example 1

$$DI \; : \; \int_0^3 dy \int_{-1}^1 x^2 \, dx$$

ES : 2.00000000

Wx : 0.015625, Wy : 0.09375, K : 5, M : 32

Estimated solution of the integral : 2

Exact solution of the integral : 2

Error for approximation : 4.440892e-16

The significant digit of the error is at the 16th place.

The approximation is correct to within the amount of error.

Example 2

$$DI \; : \; \int_{-0.1}^{0.1} dy \int_{1.3}^{1.5} \sqrt{x} \, y^2 \, dx$$

ES : 0.00015775

Wx : 0.000781, *Wy* : 0.000781, *K* : 8, *M* : 256

Estimated solution of the integral : 0.00015775

Exact solution of the integral : 0.00015775

Error for approximation : 2.226094e-09

The significant digit of the error is at the 9th place.

The approximation is correct to within the amount of error.

Example 3

$$DI \ : \int_0^1 dy \int_1^2 1 \, dx$$

ES : 1

Wx : 0.015625, *Wy* : 0.015625, *K* : 6, *M* : 64

Estimated solution of the integral : 1

Exact solution of the integral : 1

Error for approximation : 0

There is no significant digit of the error.

The approximation is correct to within the amount of error.

Example 4

$$DI \ : \int_{-1}^{1} dy \int_0^3 \text{Cos} \frac{\pi x}{2} \text{Cos} \frac{\pi y}{2} dx$$

$ES \ : \dfrac{-8}{\pi^2}$

Wx : 0.011719, *Wy* : 0.007813, *K* : 8, *M* : 256

Estimated solution of the integral : –0.81057039

Exact solution of the integral : –0.81056946

Error for approximation : 9.34158e-07

The significant digit of the error is at the 7th place.

The approximation is correct to within the amount of error.

Example 5

$$DI : \int_{0}^{0.1} dy \int_{0}^{0.1} e^{y-x}\, dx$$

ES : 0.01000830

Wx : 0.000195, Wy : 0.000195, K : 9, M : 512

Estimated solution of the integral : 0.01000638

Exact solution of the integral : 0.01000830

Error for approximation : 1.91724e-06

The significant digit of the error is at the 6th place.

The approximation is correct to within the amount of error.

Example 6

$$DI : \int_{3}^{4} dy \int_{1}^{2} \frac{1}{(y+x)^2}\, dx$$

ES : 0.04082190

Wx : 0.001953, Wy : 0.001953, K : 9, M : 512

Estimated solution of the integral : 0.04085454

Exact solution of the integral : 0.04082190

Error for approximation : –3.26376e-05

The significant digit of the error is at the 5th place.

The approximation is correct to within the amount of error.

Example 7

$$DI : \int_{1.3}^{1.4} dy \int_{2.1}^{2.2} xy^2\, dx$$

ES : 0.03920166

Wx : 0.000195, Wy : 0.000195, K : 9, M : 512

Estimated solution of the integral : 0.03919034

Exact solution of the integral : 0.03920166

Error for approximation : 1.13233e-05

The significant digit of the error is at the 5th place.

The approximation is correct to within the amount of error.

Example 8

$DI \ : \int_1^2 dy \int_1^2 \frac{1}{(x+y)} dx$

ES : 0.33979807

Wx : 0.001953, Wy : 0.001953, K : 9, M : 512

Estimated solution of the integral : 0.34002807

Exact solution of the integral : 0.33979807

Error for approximation : –0.00023

The significant digit of the error is at the 4th place.

The approximation is correct to within the amount of error.

Example 9

$DI \ : \int_0^1 dy \int_0^1 (x+y)\, dx$

ES : 1.0

Wx : 0.001953, Wy : 0.001953, K : 9, M : 512

Estimated solution of the integral : 0.99804815

Exact solution of the integral : 1

Error for approximation : 0.00195

The significant digit of the error is at the 3rd place.

The approximation is correct to within the amount of error.

Example 10

$DI \ : \int_0^1 dy \int_0^1 e^{x+y}\, dx$

ES : $(e-1)^2$

Wx : 0.001953, Wy : 0.001953, K : 9, M : 512

Estimated solution of the integral : 2.94673367

Exact solution of the integral : 2.95249244

Error for approximation : 0.00576

The significant digit of the error is at the 3rd place.

The approximation is correct to within the amount of error.

Example 11

$$DI \;:\; \int_{0}^{0.5} dy \int_{0}^{0.5} \frac{\text{Sin}\,(xy)}{(1 + xy)}\, dx$$

ES : 0.01406353

Wx : 0.000977, Wy : 0.000977, K : 9, M : 512

Estimated solution of the integral : 0.01401245

Exact solution of the integral : 0.01406353

Error for approximation : 5.10813e-05

The significant digit of the error is at the 5th place.

The approximation is correct to within the amount of error.

Chapter 5

Initial-Valued First-Order Differential Equations

5.1. Introduction

Let us consider a functional equation

$$G(x, y, y') = 0$$

or explicitly

$$y' = f(x, y) \tag{5.10}$$

The equation (5.10) signifies a relation involving the differentials with the variables, independent and dependent, and the desired function $y(x)$. As the relation in (5.10) depends only on a single independent variable, it is called an **ordinary** differential equation. The differential equation containing partial differentials with two or more independent variables is termed as **partial** differential equation.

Let us now keep in view some differential equations :

a) $\dfrac{dy}{dx} = x + y$

b) $\left(\dfrac{d^2y}{dx^2}\right)^2 = e^y \dfrac{dy}{dx}$

c) $\dfrac{(1 + x^2)d^2y}{dx^2} - \dfrac{2x\ dy}{dx} + 6y = 0$

d) $\left(\dfrac{dy}{dx}\right)^2 = mx^2 + nx + p$

e) $4x\ dy - y\ dx - x^2\ dy = 0$

f) $$\frac{x\,\partial t}{\partial x} + \frac{\partial t}{\partial y} = 0$$

g) $$\frac{\partial^2 x}{\partial^2 u} + \frac{\partial^2 x}{\partial^2 v} = 0$$

It is evident that the differential equations a) through e) are ordinary and f) through g) are partial.

The method of solving a differential equation depends upon the order and degree of the differential equation to be solved.

The **order** of a differential equation is the same as the order of the highest derivative it contains. The **degree** of the equation is the power to which the highest derivative is raised after the differential equation is in rational form.

Now in view of the above the equations a), e) and f) are of first order and first degree; equation d) is of first order, but second degree; equations c) and g) are of second order and first degree and finally, equation b) is of second order and second degree.

We shall consider in this chapter only ordinary differential equations of the first order having different forms. It is useful now to review at this stage some Standard forms of differential equations of the first order. They have been classified as

I. The equation of the form

$M\,dx + N\,dy = 0$ **(Separation of Variables)**

A first order differential equation is separable when it can be expressed in the form

$$\frac{dy}{dx} = -\frac{M(x)}{N(y)}$$

where M(x) is a function of x only and $N(y)$ is a function of y only. In differential form it can be written as

$$M(x)\,dx + N(y)\,dy = 0$$

Example $(y^2 + 1)dx + (x^2 + 1)dy = 0$

This can easily be solved when the variables are separated. The equation can be written in differential form

$$\frac{dx}{(x^2 + 1)} + \frac{dy}{(y^2 + 1)} = 0$$

which on integrating both sides we obtain

$\int \frac{1}{(x^2+1)}dx + \int \frac{1}{(y^2+1)}dy = C1$, $C1$ being the constant of integration.

The general solution is

$$\tan^{-1}x + \tan^{-1}y = C1 = \tan^{-1}C$$

or $\frac{(x+y)}{(1-xy)} = C \quad [1 - xy > 0]$

or $x + y = C(1 - xy)$.

The discussion on computed solution with particular values applying the initial conditions is postponed to section (5.3) in this chapter.

II. The equation of the form

$d\mu = M(x, y)dx + N(x, y)dy$ **(Exact form)**

A differential equation

$$M(x, y)dx + N(x, y)dy = 0$$

is a said to be **exact**, if there exist a function $\mu(x, y)$ such that

$$d\mu(x, y) = M(x, y)dx + N(x, y)dy$$

If the functions $M(x, y)$ and $N(x, y)$ are continuous and have partial derivatives of order 1, also continuous, on some rectangular system of the (x, y) plane, then the differential equation

$$M(x, y)dx + N(x, y)dy = 0$$

is exact if and only if

$$\frac{\partial M(x, y)}{\partial y} = \frac{\partial N(x, y)}{\partial x}$$

This is the condition for exactness.

Example $ye^{xy}dx + xe^{xy}dy = 0$

The condition for exactness stating $\frac{\partial M(x, y)}{\partial y} = \frac{\partial N(x, y)}{\partial x}$ is in this case achieved, which amounts to

$$e^{xy}(1 + xy)$$

The differential equation may be rewritten in differential form

$$e^{xy}d(xy) = 0$$

which on integration yields

$e^{xy} = C$ as general solution.

The computed solutions for exact differential equations will be discussed in section (5.4).

III. The equation of the form

$M(x, y)dx + N(x, y)dy = 0$ **(Use of Substitution)**

Method of substitution reduces a differential equation to the form that is readily solvable. In order to bring into conformity with a standard form we need proper setting, that means, the choice of introducing the new variables.

Example $\dfrac{xy\,dy}{dx} = x^2 + y^2$

The substitution $y = xu$ transforms the equation to a simplified form I. On integration we obtain

$$Ln\, x - \frac{1}{2}u^2 = C1$$

that may be written explicity for y

$y^2 = x^2\,(Ln\, x^2 + C)$ as general solution accepting $C = -2C_1$.

For more differential equations of such type with computed solutions vide section (5.5).

A **general solution** of an ordinary differential equation of type (5.10) can be defined as a relation

$$y = \psi(x, C) \tag{5.11}$$

The parameter C is the arbitrary constant, so-called guide factor. The number of constant factors that is furnished with the general solution is, by hypothesis, equal to the order of the differential equation. The equation (5.11) as solution is without doubt complete for theoretical faculty, but the practical understanding retards. Hence, the guide factor, C, must be found out by imposing some conditions on the variables

$$y(x_0) = y_0 \tag{5.12}$$

where x_0 and y_0 are the starting values, called the **Initial Conditions**. The differential equation (5.10) together with the initial conditions (5.12) is defined as the first-order **Initial Value Problem**. Let us elaborate the differential equations and put them to practical use.

5.2. Methods for Solution

The present chapter has the concern only with the first-order initial value problems of different forms. Many of the numerical methods for the approximation of the solution to initial value problems had been proposed and some of them had been accepted as standard methods because of precision and accuracy. I want to outline some of the standards next. For readers having great interest on the development of the standard methods, I wish to request them to consult the textbooks mentioned in the reference.

Euler's Improved Method

The Euler's formula for the approximation is represented by the equation

$$y_{m+1} = y_m + \frac{w[f(x_m, y_m) + f(x_m + w, y_m + wf(x_m, y_m))]}{2} \tag{5.20}$$

where y_m is the m-th approximation at $x = x_m$; $f(x_m, y_m)$ is the functional relation at the m-th approximation; $m = 0, 1, 2, \ldots$ and w is the width.

In order to approximate a differential equation let us use the modified formula.

Example $\dfrac{dy}{dx} = -2xy^2$ (5.21)

We accept the initial conditions for $y_0 = 1.0$ when $x_0 = 0$ bounded on [0, 2].

Here we can formulate the problem

$f(x_m, y_m) = -2x_m\, y_m{}^2$ where $m = 0, 1, 2, \ldots, 9$.

We calculate $w = \dfrac{(2-0)}{10} = 0.2$ and $x_0 = 0, y_0 = 1.0$

The first approximation results from the equation (5.20) (when $m = 0$)

$$y_1 = y_0 + \frac{w[f(x_0, y_0) + f(x_0 + w, y_0 + wf(x_0, y_0))]}{2}$$

Now $f(x_0, y_0) = -2*0*(1,0)^2 = 0$ (putting the values of x_0 & y_0)

$f(x_0 + w, y_0 + wf(x_0, y_0)) = -2*0.2*(1.0 + 0.2*0)^2 = -0.4$

Hence $y_1 = 1 + \dfrac{0.2[0 - 0.4]}{2} = 0.96$

Similarly, the second approximation yields (when $m = 1$)

$$y_2 = y_1 + \frac{w[f(x_1, y_1) + f(x_1 + w, y_1 + wf(x_1, y_1))]}{2}$$

$$= 0.96 + \frac{0.2[-0.36864 - 0.62838]}{2} = 0.86029.$$

Proceeding in this manner the other approximations of the differential equation can be found out easily. The exact solution of the differential equation is

$$y(x) = \frac{1}{(1 + x^2)} \tag{5.22}$$

The difference between the results of the actual values obtained from (5.22) and the approximate values obtained from (5.20) yields the ERROR at each step. This is the simplest method and is not so useful in the field of practical numerical analysis.

Picard's Method

It is a process of successive approximations. The successive approximations $y_m(x)$ are determined from the formula

$$y_{m+1}(x) = y_0 + \int_{x_0}^{x} f(x, y_m(x))\, dx \tag{5.23}$$

where $m = 0, 1, 2, \ldots$

The second term on the right side is a simple integral that can be determined by the process of integration. For each approximation we need the determined (approximate) value of y every time. The method can be employed to find out the approximations of the diferential equation (5.21) using the same initial conditions as taken before.

As the first approximation we have

$$y_1 = 1 + \int_{0}^{0.2} [-2x*(1.0)^2]\, dx = 0.96$$

The other approximate values for y can be obtained as usual.

Heun's Method

The approximation process can be performed applying the formula

$$y_{m+1} = y_m + \frac{w\left[f(x_m, y_m) + 3f\left(x_m + \frac{2w}{3}, y_m + \frac{2wf(x_m, y_m)}{3}\right)\right]}{4} \tag{5.24}$$

where $m = 0, 1, 2, \ldots, M-1$ and M = number of divisions. The approximation is qualitatively better than that of Euler's.

Milne's Method

The formula according to Milne reads

$$y_{m+1} = y_{m-3} + \frac{4w[2f(x_m, y_m) - f(x_{m-1}, y_{m-1}) + 2f(x_{m-2}, y_{m-2})]}{3} \tag{5.25}$$

where $m = 0, 1, 2, \ldots, M-1$ and M = number of equal parts.

Simpson's Method

For approximation Simpson has proposed the following equation

$$y_{m+1} = y_{m-1} + \frac{w[f(x_{m+1}, y_{m+1}) + 4f(x_m, y_m) + f(x_{m-1}, y_{m-1})]}{3} \tag{5.26}$$

where $m = 0, 1, 2, \ldots, M-1$. The formulas of Milne and Simpson are reasonably acceptable.

Runge-Kutta Method

The classical method from *C*. Runge was later developed by W. Kutta, both being german applied mathematicians.

The main mathematical achievement in employing Runge-kutta method involves the function evaluations of F. Each estimation of F is the result of definite mathematical calculations. The algebraic technique of evaluation for the formula needs more operations, but the final representation of the formula is simple which states

$$y_{m+1} = y_m + \frac{(F1 + 2F2 + 2F3 + F4)}{6} \tag{5.27}$$

where $m = 0, 1, 2, \ldots$ and

$$\begin{aligned} F1 &= wf(x_m, y_m) \\ F2 &= wf\left(x_m + \frac{w}{2}, y_m + \frac{F1}{2}\right) \\ F3 &= wf\left(x_m + \frac{w}{2}, y_m + \frac{F2}{2}\right) \\ F4 &= wf(x_m + w, y_m + F3) \end{aligned} \tag{5.28}$$

As we see from formula (5.27) that each approximation requires four function evaluations. That means, we consider the function $f(x, y)$ four times for a single integration process. In view of this consideration the method is known as the **fourth-order method**.

Example Returning to the initial-value problem considered in Euler's method

$$\frac{dy}{dx} = -2xy^2$$

with the initial conditions $x_0 = 0$, $y_0 = 1.0$, and accepting the auxiliary conditions $w = 0.2$ and $m = 0, 1, 2, \ldots, 9$

We have for the first approximation the following function evaluations from (5.28) (when $m = 0$)

$$F1 = wf(x_0, y_0) = 0.2*(-2*0*1^2) = 0$$

$$F2 = wf\left(x_0 + \frac{w}{2}, y_0 + \frac{F1}{2}\right) = 0.2*(-2*0.1*1^2) = -0.04$$

$$F3 = wf\left(x_0 + \frac{w}{2}, y_0 + \frac{F2}{2}\right) = 0.2*(-2*0.1*(0.98)^2) = -0.038416$$

$$F4 = wf(x_0 + w, y_0 + F3) = 0.2*(-2*0.2*(0.961584)^2) = -0.0739715$$

Hence

$$y_1 = y_0 + \frac{(F1 + 2F2 + 2F3 + F4)}{6}$$

$$= 1 - 0.0384$$

$$= 0.9615327$$

Similarly, for second approximation (when $m = 1$) we have

$$F1 = wf(x_1, y_1) = 0.2(-2*0.2*(0.9615327)^2) = -0.073963$$

$$F2 = wf\left(x_1 + \frac{w}{2}, y_1 + \frac{F1}{2}\right) = 0.2(-2*0.3*(0.9245508)^2)$$

$$= -0.102575$$

$$F3 = wf\left(x_1 + \frac{w}{2}, y_1 + \frac{F2}{2}\right) = 0.2(-2*0.3*(0.910245)^2)$$

$$= -0.099425$$

$$F4 = wf(x_1 + w, y_1 + F3) = 0.2(-2*0.4*(0.832107)^2) = -0.118916$$

Hence

$$y_2 = y_1 + \frac{(F1 + 2F2 + 2F3 + F4)}{6}$$

$$= 0.9615327 - 0.099479 = 0.8620528$$

If we carry on the procedure with the laborious algebraic operations we determine the other approximate values of y that ascertain the estimate of error after a comparison with the actual values obtained from the equation (5.22) imposing the corresponding increments of x.

In order to avoid this tedious algebraic process we attack the differential equation with an appropriate numerical method that runs on a computer program. The approximate values obtained by applying the Runge-Kutta method to the initial-value problems, are reasonably accurate upto 8 places after decimal point and I think, this extent is acceptable with content. In view of that I employ the classical Runge-Kutta method of order 4 for the approximate solutions to the initial value problems using throughout the constant value 0.01 for computational width, w.

The fourth-order Runge-Kutta method yields considerably better results correct to 8 places after decimal for a fixed width of 0.01 as mentioned before. The Runge-kutta method of order 4 is clearly a more efficient method that can be used for the approximation of ordinary differential equation.

The method was very popular in U.S.A. and also in Germany. The application of this method was very extensive for this purpose. It can be taken as a standard method because of the stable and accurate results and it is very friendly to a computer program.

5.3. Separation of Variables

I have already introduced this particular form of differential equation in section (5.1) defining as standard form I and have obtained the theoretical result containing the constant of integration, C. The computational achievement in finding the practical solution with the help of initial conditions needs a real software, a **program**.

The program IVPD1SES used to approximate the solution of initial value problems of the type, when the variables are separated, is described in chapter 10 (section 10.3). This program has been employed, also for the approximations of other different problems that are considered in sections 5.4 and 5.5 in this chapter.

The program instructions have been designed by the programming language C++ (Turbo) using the classical Runge-Kutta method described in previous section and the complete program has been executed on any MS-DOS operating system (version 6.0) furnished with an appropriate Turbo C++ (version 3.0) compiler from BORLAND International.

Example 1

$$DE : \frac{dy}{dx} - \frac{y}{\text{Tan } x} = \text{Cot } x \qquad \text{(Sev)}$$

$$PS : y(x) = \text{Sin } x - 1$$

$$IC : y\left(\frac{\pi}{6}\right) = -0.5$$

$$w : 0.01$$

Before we put the differential equation (*DE*) with the initial conditions (*IC*) into the program IVPD1SEV, the equation should be rearranged in differential form with the variables separated, namely,

$$\text{Tan } x \, dy = (1 + y)dx \qquad (5.30)$$

that I term computer equation (*CE*) and this is the first requirement for the solution of the problem. The particular solution (*PS*) is clearly the exact solution when we remove the constant of integration from the general solution imposing initial conditions $x_0 = \frac{\pi}{6}$ and $y_0 = -0.5$. The value of the width (*w*) at each step size is considered constant for each problem amounting to 0.01. The short form : Sev stands for separation of variables.

Now to approximate the initial value problem by means of C++ program IVPD1SES the following three steps should be carried out:

a) The DEFINITION Block of *IC*, a section of the program, will be provided with the initial conditions, i.e. the starting values of *x* and *y*.

b) The MEMBER FUNCTION *SetACT* will be furnished with the function of *y*(*x*) for the particular solution which is the exact solution of the differential equation. In example 1 it amounts to sin(*x*) – 1.

c) The associated terms of the differentials *dx* and *dy* of the computer equation are to be put to the MEMBER FUNCTION *SetDE*. In equation (5.30) the term (1 + *y*) is associated with the differential *dx* and the term tan(*x*) is associated with the differential *dy*.

The program IVPD1SES determines simultaneously the actual values of *y*(*x*) with the corresponding increments of the independent variable *x* in order to find out the errors caused by the approximations.

During the execution of the program you have the possibility for a modification of the data. The answer with a negation at this stage means there is nothing to alter and the following results for the initial value problem in example 1 will be appeared on the screen:

The Computer Solution of the IVP of order 1

[y (0.52359878) = – 0.5 , Width: 0.01]

x-value		Approx value	Exact Value	Error
y (0.53359878)	:	– 0.49136489	– 0.49136489	– 5.31010e-10
y (0.54359878)	:	– 0.48278064	– 0.48278064	– 5.43717e-10
y (0.55359878)	:	– 0.47424812	– 0.47424812	– 5.56266e-10
y (0.56359878)	:	– 0.46576817	– 0.46576817	– 5.68660e-10
y (0.57359878)	:	– 0.45734164	– 0.45734164	– 5.80907e-10
y (0.58359878)	:	– 0.44896938	– 0.44896938	– 5.93005e-10
y (0.59359878)	:	– 0.44065222	– 0.44065222	– 6.04958e-10
y (0.60359878)	:	– 0.43239099	– 0.43239099	– 6.16768e-10
y (0.61359878)	:	– 0.42418653	– 0.42418653	– 6.28440e-10
y (0.62359878)	:	– 0.41603964	– 0.41603964	– 6.39973e-10

Type (e) to exit :

Now, if we throw a glance at the results, we get a general conception of the initial value problem in example 1 that is represented here by the numerical values with 8 digits after decimal. In this case, for the correseponding increments of x the exact values and the approximate values are the same.

The graphical figure that can be drawn with the aid of numerical data from the exact solution has no degree of variation with the graphical representation of the approximations. The errors that arise from the approximate values have also been displayed.

The amount of error in the first case is equal to – 5.3101e-10. In floating-point decimal conversion it can be expressed as – 0.0000000053101 that indicates the first significant digit at the 10th place after decimal. In view of that we can conclude that the approximate solution for the initial value problem is correct to 9 places after decimal.

For the sake of convenience, I have confined myself to exhibiting only the first ten values of approximations. If you wish to have more from the development of approximation process, you are recommended to increase the value of *m* in the program. In the present case, *m* has been given the value 10.

Example 2

$$DE : \frac{Dy}{dx} = xy^{1/3}$$

$$CE : dy = xy^{1/3}dx$$

$$PS : y(x) = \left[\frac{(x^2 + 2)}{3}\right]^{3/2}$$

$$IC : y(1) = 1, \quad \text{Width} : 0.01$$

The Computer Solution of the IVP of Order 1

x-value		*Approx value*	*Exact Value*	*Error*
y (1.01)	:	1.01006681	1.01006681	1.94245e-12
y (1.02)	:	1.02026785	1.02026785	7.33302e-12
y (1.03)	:	1.03060401	1.03060401	1.62839e-11
y (1.04)	:	1.04107619	1.04107619	2.89107e-11
y (1.05)	:	1.05168530	1.05168530	4.53286e-11
y (1.06)	:	1.06243224	1.06243224	6.56561e-11
y (1.07)	:	1.07331792	1.07331792	9.00118e-11
y (1.08)	:	1.08434326	1.08434326	1.18517e-10
y (1.09)	:	1.09550918	1.09550918	1.51291e-10
y (1.10)	:	1.10681661	1.10681661	1.88461e-10

The significant digit of the error starts up at 12th decimal position and ends in 10th decimal position. The field of errors confines to the range [1.94245e-12, 1.88461e-10]. The approximations are correct to within this domain.

Example 3

$$DE : \frac{Dy}{dx} - \sqrt{1 - y^2} = 0$$

$$CE : dy = \sqrt{1 - y^2}\, dx$$

PS : $y(x) = \text{Sin } x$

IC : $y(0) = 0$, Width : 0.01

The Computer Solution of the IVP of Order 1

x-value		*Approx value*	*Exact Value*	*Error*
y (0.01)	:	0.00999983	0.00999983	3.12543e-13
y (0.02)	:	0.01999867	0.01999867	6.25403e-13
y (0.03)	:	0.02999550	0.02999550	9.38895e-13
y (0.04)	:	0.03998933	0.03998933	1.25336e-12
y (0.05)	:	0.04997917	0.04997917	1.56911e-12
y (0.06)	:	0.05996401	0.05996401	1.88648e-12
y (0.07)	:	0.06994285	0.06994285	2.20579e-12
y (0.08)	:	0.07991469	0.07991469	2.52739e-12
y (0.09)	:	0.08987855	0.08987855	2.85161e-12
y (0.10)	:	0.09983342	0.09983342	3.17880e-12

The significant digit of the error starts up at 13th decimal position and ends in 12th decimal position. The field of errors confines to the range [3.12543e-13, 3.17880e-12]. The approximations are correct to within this domain.

Example 4

DE : $e^y \dfrac{dy}{dx} - x(1 + e^y) = 0$

CE : $e^y dy = x(1 + e^y)\, dx$

PS : $y(x) = Ln\,[2e^{(x^2 - 1)/2} - 1]$

IC : $y(1) = 0$, Width : 0.01

The Computer Solution of the IVP of Order 1

x-value		*Approx value*	*Exact Value*	*Error*
y (1.01)	:	0.02000000	0.02000000	5.49560e-15
y (1.02)	:	0.04000003	0.04000003	2.15591e-14
y (1.03)	:	0.06000013	0.06000013	4.77812e-14
y (1.04)	:	0.08000041	0.08000041	8.34055e-14

x-value		*Approx value*	*Exact Value*	*Error*
y (1.05)	:	0.10000099	0.10000099	1.28009e-13
y (1.06)	:	0.12000204	0.12000204	1.81202e-13
y (1.07)	:	0.14000374	0.14000374	2.42639e-13
y (1.08)	:	0.16000631	0.16000631	3.11612e-13
y (1.09)	:	0.18001001	0.18001001	3.88162e-13
y (1.10)	:	0.20001512	0.20001512	4.71428e-13

The significant digit of the error starts up at 15th decimal position and ends in 13th decimal position. The field of errors confines to the range [5.49560e-15, 4.71428e-13]. The approximations are correct to within this domain.

Example 5

DE : $\text{Cos}^2 x \dfrac{dy}{dx} + \text{Sin}\, x\, \text{Cos}^2 y = 0$

CE : $-\text{Cos}^2 x\, dy = \text{Sin}\, x\, \text{Cos}^2 y\, dx$

PS : $y(x) = \text{Tan}^{-1}\left[1 - \dfrac{1}{\text{Cos}\, x}\right]$

IC : $y(0) = 0$, Width : 0.01

The Computer Solution of the IVP of Order 1

x-value		*Approx value*	*Exact Value*	*Error*
y (0.01)	:	– 5.00220834e-05	– 5.00020834e-05	1.74272e-16
y (0.02)	:	– 0.00020003	– 0.00020003	6.92399e-16
y (0.03)	:	– 0.00045017	– 0.00045017	1.52775e-15
y (0.04)	:	– 0.00080053	– 0.00080053	2.62789e-15
y (0.05)	:	– 0.00125130	– 0.00125130	3.91570e-15
y (0.06)	:	– 0.00180270	– 0.00180270	5.28787e-15
y (0.07)	:	– 0.00245501	– 0.00245501	6.61450e-15
y (0.08)	:	– 0.00320854	– 0.00320854	7.73817e-15
y (0.09)	:	– 0.00406369	– 0.00406369	8.47326e-15
y (0.10)	:	– 0.00502088	– 0.00502088	8.60163e-13

The significant digit of the error starts up at 16th decimal position and ends in 15th decimal position. The field of errors confines to the range [1.74272e-16, 8.60163e-15]. The approximations are correct to within this domain.

Example 6

DE : $2x^3 \dfrac{dy}{dx} = y^2(3x+1)$

CE : $2x^3 dy = y^2(3x+1)dx$

PS : $y(x) = \dfrac{4x^2}{(1 + 6x - 3x^2)}$

IC : $y(1) = 1$, Width : 0.01

The Computer Solution of the IVP of Order 1

x-value		*Approx value*	*Exact Value*	*Error*
y (1.01)	:	1.02017651	1.02017651	1.85555e-10
y (1.02)	:	1.04071221	1.04071221	3.80775e-10
y (1.03)	:	1.06161659	1.06161659	5.86197e-10
y (1.04)	:	1.08289948	1.08289948	8.02385e-10
y (1.05)	:	1.10457107	1.10457107	1.02994e-09
y (1.06)	:	1.12664193	1.12664193	1.26948e-09
y (1.07)	:	1.14912303	1.14912303	1.52169e-09
y (1.08)	:	1.17202572	1.17202572	1.78728e-09
y (1.09)	:	1.19536182	1.19536182	2.06697e-09
y (1.10)	:	1.21914357	1.21914358	2.36159e-09

The significant digit of the error starts up at 10th decimal position and ends in 9th decimal position. The field of errors confines to the range [1.85555e-10, 2.36159e-09]. The approximations are correct to within this domain.

Example 7

DE : $\dfrac{Dy}{dx} = e^y \text{Sin } x$

CE : $dy = e^y \text{Sin } x \, dx$

PS : $y(x) = Ln\left(\dfrac{1}{\text{Cos } x}\right)$

IC : $y(0) = 0$, Width : 0.01

The Computer Solution of the IVP of Order 1

x-value		*Approx value*	*Exact Value*	*Error*
y (0.01)	:	– 5.00008334e-05	– 5.00008334e-05	– 5.45281e-15
y (0.02)	:	0.00020001	0.00020001	– 2.15673e-14
y (0.03)	:	0.00045007	0.00045007	– 4.84572e-14
y (0.04)	:	0.00080021	0.00080021	– 8.62896e-14
y (0.05)	:	0.00125052	0.00125052	– 1.34921e-13
y (0.06)	:	0.00180108	0.00180108	– 1.94359e-13
y (0.07)	:	0.00245200	0.00245200	– 2.64886e-13
y (0.08)	:	0.00320342	0.00320342	– 3.46553e-13
y (0.09)	:	0.00405548	0.00405548	– 4.39368e-13
y (0.10)	:	0.00500836	0.00500836	– 5.43327e-13

The significant digit of the error starts up at 15th decimal position and ends in 13th decimal position. The field of errors confines to the range [– 5.45281e-15, – 5.43327e-13]. The approximations are correct to within this domain.

Example 8

$DE : \dfrac{Dy}{dx} = e^{3x-2y}$

$CE : e^{2y}\, dy = e^{3x}\, dx$

$PS : y(x) = 0.5\, Ln \left[\dfrac{2e^{3x} + 1}{3}\right]$

$IC : y(0) = 0,$ Width : 0.01

The Computer Solution of the IVP of Order 1

x-value		*Approx value*	*Exact Value*	*Error*
y (0.01)	:	0.01004983	0.01004983	– 1.20970e-11
y (0.02)	:	0.02019865	0.02019865	– 2.40142e-11
y (0.03)	:	0.03044540	0.03044540	– 3.74180e-11
y (0.04)	:	0.04078903	0.04078903	– 4.72711e-11
y (0.05)	:	0.05122842	0.05122842	– 5.85935e-11

x-value		*Approx value*	*Exact Value*	*Error*
y (0.06)	:	0.06176248	0.06176248	– 6.97006e-11
y (0.07)	:	0.07239004	0.07239004	– 8.05847e-11
y (0.08)	:	0.08310996	0.08310996	– 9.12383e-11
y (0.09)	:	0.09392105	0.09392105	– 1.01654e-10
y (0.10)	:	0.10482210	0.10482210	– 1.11826e-10

The significant digit of the error starts up at 11th decimal position and ends in 10th decimal position. The field of errors confines to the range [– 1.20970e-11, – 1.11826e-10]. The approximations are correct to within this domain.

Example 9

$$DE : (x^2 - 1)\frac{dy}{dx} + 2xy^2 = 0$$

$$CE : (x^2 - 1)dy = -2xy^2\, dx$$

$$PS : y(x) = \frac{1}{[Ln\ (1 - x^2) + 1]}$$

$IC : y(0) = 1,$ Width : 0.01

The Computer Solution of the IVP of Order 1

x-value		*Approx value*	*Exact Value*	*Error*
y (0.01)	:	1.00010002	1.00010002	– 1.25011e-13
y (0.02)	:	1.00040024	1.00040024	– 5.00711e-13
y (0.03)	:	1.00090122	1.00090122	– 1.12998e-12
y (0.04)	:	1.00160385	1.00160385	– 2.01772e-12
y (0.05)	:	1.00250941	1.00250941	– 3.17213e-12
y (0.06)	:	1.00361955	1.00361955	– 4.60232e-12
y (0.07)	:	1.00493629	1.00493629	– 6.32117e-12
y (0.08)	:	1.00646206	1.00646206	– 8.34399e-12
y (0.09)	:	1.00819967	1.00819967	– 1.06894e-11
y (0.10)	:	1.01015237	1.01015237	– 1.33782e-11

The significant digit of the error starts up at 13th decimal position and ends in 11th decimal position. The field of errors confines to the range [– 1.25011e-13, – 1.33782e-11]. The approximations are correct to within this domain.

Example 10

DE : $\text{Cot}\, x \dfrac{dy}{dx} - y^2 + 1 = 0$

CE : $\text{Cos}\, x\, dy = (y^2 - 1)\, \text{Sin}\, x\, dx$

PS : $y(x) = \dfrac{-\text{Sin}^2 x}{(1 + \text{Cos}^2 x)}$

IC : $y(0) = 0$, Width : 0.01

The Computer Solution of the IVP of Order 1

x-value		*Approx value*	*Exact Value*	*Error*
y (0.01)	:	– 5.00008333e-05	– 5.00008333e-05	– 7.63889e-15
y (0.02)	:	– 0.00020001	– 0.00020001	– 3.05623e-14
y (0.03)	:	– 0.00045007	– 0.00045007	– 6.87957e-14
y (0.04)	:	– 0.00080021	– 0.00080021	– 1.22384e-13
y (0.05)	:	– 0.00125052	– 0.00125052	– 1.91393e-13
y (0.06)	:	– 0.00180108	– 0.00180108	– 2.75906e-13
y (0.07)	:	– 0.00245200	– 0.00245200	– 3.76030e-13
y (0.08)	:	– 0.00320341	– 0.00320341	– 4.91860e-13
y (0.09)	:	– 0.00405546	– 0.00405546	– 6.23220e-13
y (0.10)	:	– 0.00500831	– 0.00500831	– 7.71400e-13

The significant digit of the error starts up at 15th decimal position and ends in 13th decimal position. The field of errors confines to the range [– 7.63889e-15, – 7.7140e-13]. The approximations are correct to within this domain.

Example 11

DE : $(1 + x^2) \dfrac{dy}{dx} + (1 + y^2) = 0$

CE : $(1 + x^2)dy = -(1 + y^2)dx$

$$PS : y(x) = \frac{(1-x)}{(1+x)}$$

$IC : y(1) = 0,$ Width : 0.01

The Computer Solution of the IVP of Order 1

x-value		*Approx value*	*Exact Value*	*Error*
y (1.01)	:	– 0.00497512	– 0.00497512	1.30834e-13
y (1.02)	:	– 0.00990099	– 0.00990099	2.59104e-13
y (1.03)	:	– 0.01477833	– 0.01477833	3.84923e-13
y (1.04)	:	– 0.01960784	– 0.01960784	5.08395e-13
y (1.05)	:	– 0.02439024	– 0.02439024	6.29618e-13
y (1.06)	:	– 0.02912621	– 0.02912621	7.48679e-13
y (1.07)	:	– 0.03381643	– 0.03381643	8.65655e-13
y (1.08)	:	– 0.03846154	– 0.03846154	9.80639e-13
y (1.09)	:	– 0.04306220	– 0.04306220	1.09368e-12
y (1.10)	:	– 0.04761905	– 0.04761905	1.20486e-12

The significant digit of the error starts up at 13th decimal position and ends in 12th decimal position. The field of errors confines to the range [1.30834e-13, 1.20486e-12]. The approximations are correct to within this domain.

Example 12

$$DE : 4y\, Ln\, y \frac{dx}{dy} + x = 0$$

$$CE : -x\, dy = 4y\, Ln\, y\, dx$$

$$PS : y(x) = e^{Ln2/x^4}$$

$IC : y(1) = 2,$ Width : 0.01

The Computer Solution of the IVP of Order 1

x-value		*Approx value*	*Exact Value*	*Error*
y (1.01)	:	1.94663223	1.94663223	– 5.44190e-09
y (1.02)	:	1.89716536	1.89716535	– 9.66414e-09
y (1.03)	:	1.85123373	1.85123372	– 1.29173e-08

x-value		*Approx value*	*Exact Value*	*Error*
y (1.04)	:	1.80851329	1.80851328	– 1.53986e-08
y (1.05)	:	1.76871609	1.76871607	– 1.72641e-08
y (1.06)	:	1.73158556	1.73158555	– 1.86377e-08
y (1.07)	:	1.69689257	1.69689255	– 1.96181e-08
y (1.08)	:	1.66443193	1.66443191	– 2.02839e-08
y (1.09)	:	1.63401953	1.63401951	– 2.06985e-08
y (1.10)	:	1.60548977	1.60548975	– 2.09127e-08

The significant digit of the error starts up at 9th decimal position and ends in 8th decimal position. The field of errors confines to the range [– 5.44190e-09, – 2.09127e-08]. The approximations are correct to within this domain.

Example 13

$$DE : \sqrt{(1 + x^2)}\, \frac{dy}{dx} + xy = 0$$

$$CE : \sqrt{(1 + x^2)}\, dy = -xy \;\; dx$$

$$PS : y\,(x) = exp\,[\, - \sqrt{(1 + x^2)}\,]$$

$$IC : y(0) = \frac{1}{e}, \quad \text{Width} : 0.01$$

The Computer Solution of the IVP of Order 1

x-value		*Approx value*	*Exact Value*	*Error*
y (0.01)	:	0.36786105	0.36786105	– 1.14475e-09
y (0.02)	:	0.36780588	0.36780588	– 1.14457e-09
y (0.03)	:	0.36771397	0.36771397	– 1.14427e-09
y (0.04)	:	0.36758537	0.36758537	– 1.14385e-09
y (0.05)	:	0.36742017	0.36742017	– 1.14331e-09
y (0.06)	:	0.36721845	0.36721845	– 1.14265e-09
y (0.07)	:	0.36698034	0.36698034	– 1.14187e-09
y (0.08)	:	0.36670598	0.36670598	– 1.14098e-09
y (0.09)	:	0.36639554	0.36639554	– 1.13996e-09
y (0.10)	:	0.36604919	0.36604919	– 1.13883e-09

The significant digit of the error starts up at 9th decimal position and ends in 9th decimal position. The field of errors confines to the range [– 1.14475e-09, – 1.13883e-09]. The approximations are correct to within this domain.

Example 14

DE : $y(1 + x^2) \dfrac{dy}{dx} + x(4 + y^2) = 0$

CE : $y(1 + x^2)\, dy = -x(4 + y^2)dx$

PS : $y(x) = 2\sqrt{\dfrac{(3 - x^2)}{(x^2 + 1)}}$

IC : $y(1) = 2,$ Width : 0.01

The Computer Solution of the IVP of Order 1

x-value		Approx value	Exact Value	Error
y (1.01)	:	1.97999999	1.97999999	2.22045e-16
y (1.02)	:	1.95999992	1.95999992	1.11022e-15
y (1.03)	:	1.93999959	1.93999959	4.21885e-15
y (1.04)	:	1.91999872	1.91999872	1.11022e-14
y (1.05)	:	1.89999687	1.89999687	2.30926e-14
y (1.06)	:	1.87999351	1.87999351	4.15223e-14
y (1.07)	:	1.85998796	1.85998796	6.86118e-14
y (1.08)	:	1.83997945	1.83997945	1.05471e-13
y (1.09)	:	1.81996705	1.81996705	1.54543e-13
y (1.10)	:	1.79994972	1.79994972	2.18048e-13

The significant digit of the error starts up at 16th decimal position and ends in 13th decimal position. The field of errors confines to the range [2.22045e-16, 2.18048e-13]. The approximations are correct to within this domain.

Example 15

DE : $y' \operatorname{Cos} y - \operatorname{Sin} x \operatorname{Sin} y = \operatorname{Sin} x$

CE : $\operatorname{Cos} y\, dy = \operatorname{Sin} x(1 + \operatorname{Sin} y)\, dx$

PS : $y(x) = \operatorname{Sin}^{-1}(e^{1-\operatorname{Cos} x} - 1)$

IC : $y(0) = 0,$ Width : 0.01

The Computer Solution of the IVP of Order 1

x-value		*Approx value*	*Exact Value*	*Error*
y (0.01)	:	5.00008334e-05	5.00008334e-05	– 5.38214e-15
y (0.02)	:	0.00020001	0.00020001	– 2.15356e-14
y (0.03)	:	0.00045007	0.00045007	– 4.84854e-14
y (0.04)	:	0.00080021	0.00080021	– 8.62755e-14
y (0.05)	:	0.00125052	0.00125052	– 1.34970e-13
y (0.06)	:	0.00180108	0.00180108	– 1.94650e-13
y (0.07)	:	0.00245200	0.00245200	– 2.65419e-13
y (0.08)	:	0.00320342	0.00320342	– 3.47400e-13
y (0.09)	:	0.00405548	0.00405548	– 4.40736e-13
y (0.10)	:	0.00500836	0.00500836	– 5.45587e-13

The significant digit of the error starts up at 15th decimal position and ends in 13th decimal position. The field of errors confines to the range [– 5.38214e-15, – 5.45587e-13]. The approximations are correct to within this domain.

Example 16

DE : $y(1 + e^x)\, y' - e^x = 0$

CE : $y(1 + e^x)\, dy = e^x\, dx$

PS : $y(x) = \sqrt{2Ln\left(\dfrac{\sqrt{e}(1 + e^x)}{2}\right)}$

IC : $y(0) = 1$, Width : 0.01

The Computer Solution of the IVP of Order 1

x-value		*Approx value*	*Exact Value*	*Error*
y (0.01)	:	1.00500000	1.00500000	– 2.22045e-16
y (0.02)	:	1.01000000	1.01000000	– 2.22045e-16
y (0.03)	:	1.01500000	1.01500000	– 4.44080e-16
y (0.04)	:	1.01999999	1.01999999	– 6.66134e-16
y (0.05)	:	1.02499997	1.02499997	– 1.11022e-15

x-value		*Approx value*	*Exact Value*	*Error*
y (0.06)	:	1.02999993	1.02999993	– 1.33227e-15
y (0.07)	:	1.03499988	1.03499988	– 1.77636e-15
y (0.08)	:	1.03999979	1.03999979	– 2.22045e-15
y (0.09)	:	1.04499967	1.04499967	– 2.88658e-15
y (0.10)	:	1.04999950	1.04999950	– 3.77476e-15

The significant digit of the error starts up at 16th decimal position and ends in 15th decimal position. The field of errors confines to the range [– 2.22045e-16, – 3.77476e-15]. The approximations are correct to within this domain.

Example 17

$$DE : 3\frac{dy}{dx} + y(3y^3 - 1)\ \text{Sin}\ x = 0$$

$$CE : \frac{3}{y}\,dy = (1 - 3y^3)\ \text{Sin}\ x\ dx$$

$$PS : y(x) = \left[\frac{1}{3 - 2e^{\cos x}}\right]^{1/3}$$

$$IC : y\left(\frac{\pi}{2}\right) = 1, \qquad \text{Width} : 0.01$$

The Computer Solution of the IVP of Order 1

x-value		*Approx value*	*Exact Value*	*Error*
y (1.58079633)	:	0.99345333	0.99345333	1.79060e-09
y (1.59079633)	:	0.98713808	0.98713808	2.36197e-09
y (1.60079633)	:	0.98104211	0.98104211	2.91185e-09
y (1.61079633)	:	0.97515419	0.97515419	3.44132e-09
y (1.62079633)	:	0.96946386	0.96946386	3.95140e-09
y (1.63079633)	:	0.96396142	0.96396142	4.44303e-09
y (1.64079633)	:	0.95863781	0.95863782	4.91712e-09
y (1.65079633)	:	0.95348461	0.95348461	5.37450e-09
y (1.66079633)	:	0.94849392	0.94849393	5.81596e-09
y (1.67079633)	:	0.94365838	0.94365838	6.24225e-09

The significant digit of the error starts up at 9th decimal position and ends in 9th decimal position. The field of errors confines to the range [1.79060e-09, 6.24225e-09]. The approximations are correct to within this domain.

Example 18

$DE \ : \ \dfrac{Dy}{dx} = \text{Cos } y$

$CE \ : \ Dy = \text{Cos } y \ dx$

$PS \ : \ y\,(x) = 2\ \text{Tan}{-1}\ (e^x) - \dfrac{\pi}{2}$

$IC \ : \ y(0) = 0,$ Width : 0.01

The Computer Solution of the IVP of Order 1

x-value		*Approx value*	*Exact Value*	*Error*
y (0.01)	:	0.00999983	0.00999984	1.79507e-09
y (0.02)	:	0.01999867	0.01999867	1.79524e-09
y (0.03)	:	0.02999550	0.02999550	1.79542e-09
y (0.04)	:	0.03998934	0.03998934	1.79559e-09
y (0.05)	:	0.04997918	0.04997918	1.79577e-09
y (0.06)	:	0.05996403	0.05996403	1.79594e-09
y (0.07)	:	0.06994290	0.06994291	1.79612e-09
y (0.08)	:	0.07991480	0.07991480	1.79630e-09
y (0.09)	:	0.08987875	0.08987875	1.79647e-09
y (0.10)	:	0.09983375	0.09983375	1.79665e-09

The significant digit of the error starts up at 9th decimal position and ends in 9th decimal position. The field of errors confines to the range [1.79507e-09, 1.79507e-09]. The approximations are correct to within this domain.

Example 19

$DE \ : \ \dfrac{Dy}{dx} = 2x(1 + y)$

$CE \ : \ Dy = 2x(1 + y)\ dx$

$PS \ : \ y\,(x) = e^{x^2} - 1$

$IC \ : \ y(0) = 0,$ Width : 0.01

The Computer Solution of the IVP of Order 1

x-value		*Approx value*	*Exact Value*	*Error*
y (0.01)	:	0.00010001	0.00010001	4.17418e-18
y (0.02)	:	0.00040008	0.00040008	4.16876e-17
y (0.03)	:	0.00090041	0.00090041	1.46150e-16
y (0.04)	:	0.00160128	0.00160128	3.52149e-16
y (0.05)	:	0.00250313	0.00250313	6.95624e-16
y (0.06)	:	0.00360649	0.00360649	1.21561e-15
y (0.07)	:	0.00491202	0.00491202	1.95503e-15
y (0.08)	:	0.00642052	0.00642052	2.96291e-15
y (0.09)	:	0.00813289	0.00813289	4.29691e-15
y (0.10)	:	0.01005017	0.01005017	6.02990e-15

The significant digit of the error starts up at 18th decimal position and ends in 15th decimal position. The field of errors confines to the range [4.17418e-18, 6.02990e-15]. The approximations are correct to within this domain.

Example 20

$$DE : \frac{Dy}{dx} \text{ Sin } x = y \text{ Ln } y$$

$$CE : \text{Sin } x \, dy = y \text{ Ln } y \, dx$$

$$PS : y(x) = e^{\text{Sin } x/(1+\text{Cos } x)}$$

$$IC : y\left(\frac{\pi}{2}\right) = e, \qquad \text{Width} : 0.01$$

The Computer Solution of the IVP of Order 1

x-value		*Approx value*	*Exact Value*	*Error*
y (1.58079633)	:	2.74573921	2.74573921	3.67577e-09
y (1.59079633)	:	2.77375694	2.77375694	3.77479e-09
y (1.60079633)	:	2.80235229	2.80235230	3.87721e-09
y (1.61079633)	:	2.83154324	2.83154324	3.98321e-09
y (1.62079633)	:	2.86134847	2.86134848	4.09295e-09
y (1.63079633)	:	2.89178745	2.89178745	4.20661e-09

x-value		*Approx value*	*Exact Value*	*Error*
y (1.64079633)	:	2.92288039	2.92288040	4.32440e-09
y (1.65079633)	:	2.95464839	2.95464840	4.44652e-09
y (1.66079633)	:	2.98711339	2.98711340	4.57318e-09
y (1.67079633)	:	3.02029826	3.02029826	4.70463e-09

The significant digit of the error starts up at 9th decimal position and ends in 9th decimal position. The field of errors confines to the range [3.675773-09, 4.70463e-09]. The approximations are correct to within this domain.

5.4. Exact Differential Equations

This particular form of differential equation has been defined in section (5.1) and classified as standard form II.

The same program IVPD1SES used to approximate the solution of initial value problems of the type, when the forms are exact, is described in Chapter 10 (Section 10.3). The program has been written in computer language C++ using the Runge-Kutta method described earlier in this Chapter and the execution of this program has been performed on any MS-DOS operating System furnished with an appropriate C++ (version 3.0) compiler.

Example 1

$$DE \;:\; x^y \, Ln\, x \frac{dy}{dx} + yx^{y-1} = 0$$

$$CE \;:\; yx^{y-1}\, dx = -\, x^y \, Ln\, x\, dy$$

$$PS \;:\; y(x) = \frac{1}{Ln\; x}$$

$$IC \;:\; y(e) = 1.0, \qquad \text{Width} \;:\; 0.01$$

The initial value problem, that is, the differential equation (*DE*) together with the initial condition (*IC*) is the mathematical problem. The differential equation is rearranged in differntial form for the input of computer equation (*CE*). A detailed description on the treatment of mathematical problem has been given in section (5.3). The excution of the program provides the following results:

The Computer Solution of the IVP of Order 1

x-value		*Approx value*	*Exact Value*	*Error*
y (2.72828182)	:	0.99634139	0.99634139	3.10057e-09
y (2.73828182)	:	0.99272269	0.99272270	3.08935e-09

x-value		*Approx value*	*Exact Value*	*Error*
y (2.74828182)	:	0.98914324	0.98914324	3.07826e-09
y (2.75828182)	:	0.98560236	0.98560236	3.06728e-09
y (2.76828182)	:	0.98209942	0.98209942	3.05642e-09
y (2.77828182)	:	0.97863379	0.97863380	3.04568e-09
y (2.78828182)	:	0.97520486	0.97520486	3.03505e-09
y (2.79828182)	:	0.97181201	0.97181202	3.02452e-09
y (2.80828182)	:	0.96845467	0.96845468	3.01411e-09
y (2.81828182)	:	0.96513226	0.96513227	3.00381e-09

The significant digit of the error starts up at 9th decimal position and ends in 9th decimal position. The field of errors confines to the range [3.10057e-09, 3.00381e-09]. The approximations are correct to within this domain.

Example 2

$DE\ :\ \dfrac{Dy}{dx} = \dfrac{y(3x^2 - y^2)}{x(3y^2 - x^2)}$

$CE\ :\ x(3y^2 - x^2)dy = y(3x^2 - y^2)dx$

$PS\ :\ y\ (x) = x$

$IC\ :\ y(1) = 1,$ Width : 0.01

The Computer Solution of the IVP of Order 1

x-value		*Approx value*	*Exact Value*	*Error*
y (1.01)	:	1.01	1.01	0
y (1.02)	:	1.02	1.02	0
y (1.03)	:	1.03	1.03	0
y (1.04)	:	1.04	1.04	0
y (1.05)	:	1.05	1.05	0
y (1.06)	:	1.06	1.06	0
y (1.07)	:	1.07	1.07	0
y (1.08)	:	1.08	1.08	0
y (1.09)	:	1.09	1.09	0
y (1.10)	:	1.10	1.10	0

The is no significant digit of the error. The field of errors confines to the range [0, 0]. The approximations are correct to within this domain.

Example 3

$$DE : \frac{Dy}{dx} = \frac{(e^x \text{Cos} y + 3x^2)}{e^x \text{ Sin } y}$$

$$CE : e^x \text{ Sin } y\, dy = (e^x \text{ Cos } y + 3x^3)dx$$

$$PS : y(x) = \cos^{-1}\left(\frac{-x^3}{e^x}\right)$$

IC : $y(0) = 1.57079633$, Width : 0.01

The Computer Solution of the IVP of Order 1

x-value		*Approx value*	*Exact Value*	*Error*
y (0.01)	:	1.57079732	1.57079732	1.77703e-09
y (0.02)	:	1.57080417	1.57080417	1.75929e-09
y (0.03)	:	1.57082253	1.57082253	1.74170e-09
y (0.04)	:	1.57085782	1.57085782	1.72424e-09
y (0.05)	:	1.57091523	1.57091523	1.70692e-09
y (0.06)	:	1.57099975	1.57099975	1.68974e-09
y (0.07)	:	1.57111614	1.57111614	1.67270e-09
y (0.08)	:	1.57126896	1.57126896	1.65580e-09
y (0.09)	:	1.57146258	1.57146258	1.63903e-09
y (0.10)	:	1.57170116	1.57170116	1.62240e-09

The significant digit of the error starts up at 9th decimal position and ends in 9th decimal position. The field of errors confines to the range [1.77703e-09, 1.62240e-09]. The approximations are correct to within this domain.

Example 4

$$DE : \frac{Dy}{dx} = \frac{(x^2 - y \text{ Cos} y)}{(y + \text{Sin } x)}$$

$$CE : (y + \text{Sin } x)\, dy = (x^2 - y \text{ Cos } x)\, dx$$

$$PS : y(x) = \left(\frac{\frac{x^3}{3} - \frac{y^2}{2} + 0.5}{\text{Sin } x}\right)$$

IC : $y(0) = 1$, Width : 0.01

The Computer Solution of the IVP of Order 1

x-value		*Approx value*	*Exact Value*	*Error*
y (0.01)	:	0.99005050	0.99005050	– 3.34396e-11
y (0.02)	:	0.98020395	0.98020395	– 3.52083e-11
y (0.03)	:	0.97046326	0.97046326	– 3.70561e-11
y (0.04)	:	0.96083124	0.96083124	– 3.89869e-11
y (0.05)	:	0.95131062	0.95131062	– 4.10005e-11
y (0.06)	:	0.94190409	0.94190409	– 4.30971e-11
y (0.07)	:	0.93261422	0.93261422	– 4.52756e-11
y (0.08)	:	0.92344351	0.92344351	– 4.75348e-11
y (0.09)	:	0.91439440	0.91439440	– 4.98727e-11
y (0.10)	:	0.90546921	0.90546921	– 5.22886e-11

The significant digit of the error starts up at 11th decimal position and ends in 11th decimal position. The field of errors confines to the range [– 3.34396-11, – 5.22886e-11]. The approximations are correct to within this domain.

Example 5

$$DE : \frac{Dy}{dx} = -\frac{(e^y + 2xy)}{x(x + e^y)}$$

$$CE : x(x + e^y)\, dy = -(e^y + 2xy)\, dx$$

$$PS : y(x) = \left(\frac{-(x^2 + x) + \sqrt{(x^4 + 2x^3 - x^2 + 2x)}}{x}\right)$$

$$IC : y(1) = 0, \qquad \text{Width} : 0.01$$

The Computer Solution of the IVP of Order 1

x-value		*Approx value*	*Exact Value*	*Error*
y (1.01)	:	– 0.00493191	– 0.00493192	– 9.96218e-09
y (1.02)	:	– 0.00973021	– 0.00973029	– 7.61969e-08
y (1.03)	:	– 0.01439871	– 0.01439895	– 2.45962e-07
y (1.04)	:	– 0.01894108	– 0.01894163	– 5.57748e-07

x-value		*Approx value*	*Exact Value*	*Error*
y (1.05)	:	– 0.02336088	– 0.02336192	– 1.04235e-06
y (1.06)	:	– 0.02766158	– 0.02766330	– 1.72381e-06
y (1.07)	:	– 0.03184653	– 0.03184915	– 2.62031e-06
y (1.08)	:	– 0.03591899	– 0.03592274	– 3.74487e-06
y (1.09)	:	– 0.03988212	– 0.03988723	– 5.10610e-06
y (1.10)	:	– 0.04373897	– 0.04374568	– 6.70880e-06

The significant digit of the error starts up at 9th decimal position and ends in 6th decimal position. The field of errors confines to the range [– 9.96218e-09, – 6.70880e-06]. The approximations are correct to within this domain.

Example 6

$$DE : \frac{Dy}{dx} = \frac{y(x \text{ Sin } x - \text{Cos } x)}{(x \text{ Cos } x - 2y)}$$

$$CE : (x \text{ Cos } x - 2y)\, dy = y(x \text{ Sin } x - \text{Cos } x)\, dx$$

$$PS : y(x) = \frac{x \text{ Cos } x + \sqrt{(x^2 \text{ Cos}^2 x + 4)}}{2}$$

IC : y(0) = 1, Width : 0.01

The Computer Solution of the IVP of Order 1

x-value		*Approx value*	*Exact Value*	*Error*
y (0.01)	:	1.00501225	1.00501225	3.79696e-14
y (0.02)	:	1.01004798	1.01004798	6.50591e-14
y (0.03)	:	1.01510564	1.01510564	8.10463e-14
y (0.04)	:	1.02018366	1.02018366	8.59313e-14
y (0.05)	:	1.02528043	1.02528043	7.92699e-14
y (0.06)	:	1.03039430	1.03039430	6.15064e-14
y (0.07)	:	1.03552360	1.03552360	3.21965e-14
y (0.08)	:	1.04066664	1.04066664	– 8.88178e-15
y (0.09)	:	1.04582169	1.04582169	– 6.17284e-14
y (0.10)	:	1.05098699	1.05098699	– 1.26121e-13

The significant digit of the error starts up at 14th decimal position and ends in 13th decimal position. The field of errors confines to the range [3.79696e-14, – 1.26121e-13]. The approximations are correct to within this domain.

Example 7

$DE : \frac{Dy}{dx} + \frac{3x^2 + 2xy^2}{2x^2y} = 0$

$CE : 2x^2y\, dy = -(3x^2 + 2xy^2)\, dx$

$PS : y(x) = \frac{\sqrt{44 - x^3}}{x}$

$IC : y(2) = 3.$ Width : 0.01

The Computer Solution of the IVP of Order 1

x-value		Approx value	Exact Value	Error
y (2.01)	:	2.98007039	2.98007039	1.50102e-13
y (2.02)	:	2.96027981	2.96027981	2.95319e-13
y (2.03)	:	2.94062565	2.94062565	4.36540e-13
y (2.04)	:	2.92110537	2.92110537	5.71987e-13
y (2.05)	:	2.90171645	2.90171645	7.03437e-13
y (2.06)	:	2.88245642	2.88245642	8.30003e-13
y (2.07)	:	2.86332284	2.86332284	9.53015e-13
y (2.08)	:	2.84431333	2.84431333	1.07114e-12
y (2.09)	:	2.82542554	2.82542554	1.18483e-12
y (2.10)	:	2.80665713	2.80665713	1.29452e-12

The significant digit of the error starts up at 13th decimal position and ends in 12th decimal position. The field of errors confines to the range [1.50102e-13, 1.29452e-12]. The approximations are correct to within this domain.

Example 8

$DE : \frac{Dy}{dx} + \frac{2x - ye^{-x}}{e^{-x}} = 0$

$CE : e^{-x}dy = (ye^{-x} - 2x)\, dx$

$PS : y(1) = e^x(1 - x^2)$

$IC : y(1) = 0,$ Width : 0.01

The Computer Solution of the IVP of Order 1

x-value		Approx value	Exact Value	Error
y (1.01)	:	– 0.05518658	– 0.05518658	– 1.23164e-11
y (1.02)	:	– 0.11203707	– 0.11203707	– 2.50126e-11
y (1.03)	:	– 0.17058491	– 0.17058491	– 3.80965e-11
y (1.04)	:	– 0.23086411	– 0.23086411	– 5.15766e-11
y (1.05)	:	– 0.29290924	– 0.29290924	– 6.54614e-11
y (1.06)	:	– 0.35675545	– 0.35675545	– 7.97595e-11
y (1.07)	:	– 0.42243849	– 0.42243849	– 9.44795e-11
y (1.08)	:	– 0.48999468	– 0.48999468	– 1.09631e-10
y (1.09)	:	– 0.55946095	– 0.55946095	– 1.25222e-10
y (1.10)	:	– 0.63087486	– 0.63087487	– 1.41262e-10

The significant digit of the error starts up at 11th decimal position and ends in 10th decimal position. The field of errors confines to the range [– 1.23164e-11, – 1.41262e-10]. The approximations are correct to within this domain.

Example 9

$$DE : \frac{Dy}{dx} - \frac{2x\,(1 + \sqrt{x^2 - y})}{\sqrt{x^2 - y}} = 0$$

$$CE : \sqrt{x^2 - y}\; dy = 2x(1 + \sqrt{x^2 - y}\,)\, dx$$

$$PS : y(x) = x^2 - \left[\frac{(5 - 3x^2)}{2}\right]^{2/3}$$

IC : $y(1) = 0$, Width : 0.01

The Computer Solution of the IVP of Order 1

x-value		Approx value	Exact Value	Error
y (1.01)	:	0.04030238	0.04030238	– 2.59435e-10
y (1.02)	:	0.08121943	0.08121943	– 5.27222e-10
y (1.03)	:	0.12276698	0.12276698	– 8.04774e-10
y (1.04)	:	0.16496224	0.16496224	– 1.09387e-09

x-value		*Approx value*	*Exact Value*	*Error*
y (1.05)	:	0.20782400	0.20782400	– 1.39678e-09
y (1.06)	:	0.25137284	0.25137284	– 1.71640e-09
y (1.07)	:	0.29563142	0.29563141	– 2.05648e-09
y (1.08)	:	0.34062471	0.34062471	– 2.42193e-09
y (1.09)	:	0.38638046	0.38638046	– 2.81924e-09
y (1.10)	:	0.43292957	0.43292957	– 3.25708e-09

The significant digit of the error starts up at 10th decimal position and ends in 9th decimal position. The field of errors confines to the range [– 2.59435e-10, – 3.25708e-09]. The approximations are correct to within this domain.

Example 10

$$DE : \frac{Dy}{dx} = \frac{1 + y^2 \operatorname{Sin}(2x)}{2y \operatorname{Cos}^2 x}$$

$$CE : 2y \operatorname{Cos}^2 x \, dy = [1 + y^2 \operatorname{Sin}(2x)] \, dx$$

$$PS : y(x) = \frac{\sqrt{x + 1}}{\operatorname{Cos} x}$$

IC : $y(0) = 1$, Width : 0.01

The Computer Solution of the IVP of Order 1

x-value		*Approx value*	*Exact Value*	*Error*
y (0.01)	:	1.00503781	1.00503781	1.05915e-13
y (0.02)	:	1.01015252	1.01015252	1.99840e-13
y (0.03)	:	1.01534603	1.01534603	2.80886e-13
y (0.04)	:	1.02062029	1.02062029	3.49276e-13
y (0.05)	:	1.02597728	1.02597728	4.03899e-13
y (0.06)	:	1.03141901	1.03141901	4.44755e-13
y (0.07)	:	1.03694753	1.03694753	4.71179e-13
y (0.08)	:	1.04256491	1.04256491	4.82725e-13
y (0.09)	:	1.04827329	1.04827329	4.78284e-13
y (0.10)	:	1.05407483	1.05407483	4.57634e-13

The significant digit of the error starts up at 13th decimal position and ends in 13th decimal position. The field of errors confines to the range [1.05915e-13, 4.57634e-13]. The approximations are correct to within this domain.

Example 11

$$DE : \frac{Dy}{dx} + \frac{yx^{y-1}}{x^y \, Ln\, x} = 0$$

$$CE : -x^y \, Ln\, x\, dy = yx^{y-1}\, dx$$

$$PS : y(x) = \frac{Ln\, 2}{Ln\, x}$$

$IC : y(2) = 1,$ Width : 0.01

The Computer Solution of the IVP of Order 1

x-value		*Approx value*	*Exact Value*	*Error*
y (2.01)	:	0.99285590	0.99285590	6.44373e-13
y (2.02)	:	0.98584787	0.98584787	1.25011e-12
y (2.03)	:	0.97897195	0.97897195	1.81966e-12
y (2.04)	:	0.97222437	0.97222437	2.35523e-12
y (2.05)	:	0.96560150	0.96560150	2.85916e-12
y (2.06)	:	0.95909982	0.95909982	3.33344e-12
y (2.07)	:	0.95271597	0.95271597	3.77975e-12
y (2.08)	:	0.94644671	0.94644671	4.19997e-12
y (2.09)	:	0.94028889	0.94028889	4.59555e-12
y (2.10)	:	0.93423951	0.93423951	4.96814e-12

The significant digit of the error starts up at 13th decimal position and ends in 12th decimal position. The field of errors confines to the range [6.44373e-13, 4.96814e-12]. The approximations are correct to within this domain.

Example 12

$$DE : \frac{Dy}{dx} - \frac{2\text{Sin}\, y(x + 2\text{Sin}\, y)}{(x^2 + 1)\, \text{Cos}\, y} = 0$$

$$CE : (x^2 + 1)\, \text{Cos}\, y\, dy = 2\text{Sin}\, y(x + 2\text{Sin}\, y)\, dx$$

$$PS : y(x) = \text{Sin}^{-1} \frac{(x^2 + 1)}{(8 - 4x)}$$

IC : $y(1) = \dfrac{\pi}{6}$ Width : 0.01

The Computer Solution of the IVP of Order 1

x-value		*Approx value*	*Exact Value*	*Error*
y (1.01)	:	0.53533158	0.53533158	6.67642e-10
y (1.02)	:	0.54744837	0.54744837	7.42313e-10
y (1.03)	:	0.55996884	0.55996884	8.22592e-10
y (1.04)	:	0.57291433	0.57291433	9.08715e-10
y (1.05)	:	0.58630808	0.58630808	1.00085e-09
y (1.06)	:	0.60017541	0.60017541	1.09903e-09
y (1.07)	:	0.61454401	0.61454401	1.20313e-09
y (1.08)	:	0.62944431	0.62944431	1.31273e-09
y (1.09)	:	0.64490982	0.64490982	1.42697e-09
y (1.10)	:	0.66097764	0.66097764	1.54436e-09

The significant digit of the error starts up at 10th decimal position and ends in 9th decimal position. The field of errors confines to the range [6.67642e-10, 1.54436e-09]. The approximations are correct to within this domain.

Example 13

DE : $x\dfrac{dy}{dx} = (x^2 + y^2)\left(\dfrac{y}{x^2 + y^2} - 1\right)$

CE : $\dfrac{x}{x^2 + y^2}\,dy = \left(\dfrac{y}{x^2 + y^2} - 1\right)dx$

PS : $y(x) = x \operatorname{Tan}(3.00388482 - x)$

IC : $y(2) = \pi$ Width : 0.01

The Computer Solution of the IVP of Order 1

x-value		*Approx value*	*Exact Value*	*Error*
y (2.01)	:	3.08868143	3.08868142	– 9.00110e-09
y (2.02)	:	3.03717480	3.03717480	– 8.74895e-09
y (2.03)	:	2.98699710	2.98699709	– 8.50940e-09
y (2.04)	:	2.93807758	2.93807757	– 8.28181e-09

x-value		*Approx value*	*Exact Value*	*Error*
y (2.05)	:	2.89035004	2.89035003	– 8.06553e-09
y (2.06)	:	2.84375246	2.84375245	– 7.85996e-09
y (2.07)	:	2.79822664	2.79822663	– 7.66452e-09
y (2.08)	:	2.75371794	2.75371793	– 7.47866e-09
y (2.09)	:	2.71017499	2.71017498	– 7.30184e-09
y (2.10)	:	2.66754945	2.66754944	– 7.13358e-09

The significant digit of the error starts up at 9th decimal position and ends in 9th decimal position. The field of errors confines to the range [– 9.00110e-09, – 7.13358e-09]. The approximations are correct to within this domain.

5.5. Evaluation By Use of Substitutions

This form of differential equation has already been introduced in section (5.1) characterising as standard form III. The program IVPD1SES has been applied to approximate the solution of initial value problems of the form, when the variables are separable by the method of substitution. The program in C++ that you want to retain in a storage device, is provided in chapter 10.

Example 1

$DE\ :\ \frac{Dy}{dx} + 1 = \frac{(x+y)}{2}$

$CE\ :\ 2dy = (x + y - 2)dx$

$PS\ :\ y(x) = e^{x/2} - x$

$IC\ :\ y(0) = 1,$ Width : 0.01

The Computer Solution of the IVP of Order 1

x-value		*Approx value*	*Exact Value*	*Error*
y (0.01)	:	0.99501252	0.99501252	2.60902e-14
y (0.02)	:	0.99005017	0.99005017	5.24025e-14
y (0.03)	:	0.98511306	0.98511306	7.90479e-14
y (0.04)	:	0.98020134	0.98020134	1.05915e-13
y (0.05)	:	0.97531512	0.97531512	1.33005e-13
y (0.06)	:	0.97045453	0.97045453	1.60427e-13

x-value		Approx value	Exact Value	Error
y (0.07)	:	0.96561971	0.96561971	1.88072e-13
y (0.08)	:	0.96081077	0.96081077	2.16049e-13
y (0.09)	:	0.95602786	0.95602786	2.44249e-13
y (0.10)	:	0.95127110	0.95127110	2.72671e-13

The significant digit of the error starts up at 14th decimal position and ends in 13th decimal position. The field of errors confines to the range [2.60902e-14, 2.72671e-13]. The approximations are correct to within this domain.

Example 2

DE : $\dfrac{Dy}{dx} = 4e^{-y}\,\text{Sin}\,x - 1.0$

CE : $Dy = (4e^{-y}\,\text{Sin} - 1.0)dx$

PS : $y(x) = Ln\,[2(\text{Sin}\,x - \text{Cos}\,x) + 3e^{-x}]$

IC : $y(0) = 0$, Width : 0.01

The Computer Solution of the IVP of Order 1

x-value		Approx value	Exact Value	Error
y (0.01)	:	– 0.00979868	– 0.00979868	– 3.91577e-13
y (0.02)	:	– 0.01918961	– 0.01918961	– 1.50503e-12
y (0.03)	:	– 0.02816541	– 0.02816541	– 3.40447e-12
y (0.04)	:	– 0.03671920	– 0.03671920	– 6.15136e-12
y (0.05)	:	– 0.04484456	– 0.04484456	– 9.80337e-12
y (0.06)	:	– 0.05253561	– 0.05253561	– 1.44130e-11
y (0.07)	:	– 0.05978700	– 0.05978700	– 2.00269e-11
y (0.08)	:	– 0.06659395	– 0.06659395	– 2.66848e-11
y (0.09)	:	– 0.07295228	– 0.07295228	– 3.44187e-11
y (0.10)	:	– 0.07885842	– 0.07885842	– 4.32521e-11

The significant digit of the error starts up at 13th decimal position and ends in 11th decimal position. The field of errors confines to the range [– 3.91577e-13, – 4.32521e-11]. The approximations are correct to within this domain.

Example 3

$$DE : \frac{Dy}{dx} = \frac{2\text{Sin } x - 2x - y}{x + y}$$

$$CE : Dy = \frac{2\text{Sin } x - 2x - y}{x + y} dx$$

$$PS : y(x) = \sqrt{(8 - 4\text{Cos } x - x^2)} - x$$

IC : $y(0) = 2$, Width : 0.01

The Computer Solution of the IVP of Order 1

x-value		*Approx value*	*Exact Value*	*Error*
y (0.01)	:	1.99002500	1.99002500	– 4.44089e-16
y (0.02)	:	1.98009999	1.98009999	– 1.99840e-15
y (0.03)	:	1.97022495	1.97022495	– 4.44089e-15
y (0.04)	:	1.96039985	1.96039985	– 7.99361e-15
y (0.05)	:	1.95062464	1.95062464	– 1.24345e-14
y (0.06)	:	1.94089926	1.94089926	– 1.79856e-14
y (0.07)	:	1.93122363	1.93122363	– 2.44249e-14
y (0.08)	:	1.92159766	1.92159766	– 3.19744e-14
y (0.09)	:	1.91202125	1.91202125	– 4.01901e-14
y (0.10)	:	1.90249428	1.90249428	– 4.95159e-14

The significant digit of the error starts up at 16th decimal position and ends in 14th decimal position. The field of errors confines to the range [– 4.44089e-16, – 4.95159e-14]. The approximations are correct to within this domain.

Example 4

$$DE : \frac{Dy}{dx} = \frac{y^2 - 2}{x^2}$$

$$CE : dy = (x^2y^2 - 2)\, dx$$

$$PS : y(x) = \frac{1}{x} - \frac{6x^2}{2x^3 + 1}$$

IC : $y(1) = -1$, Width : 0.01

The Computer Solution of the IVP of Order 1

x-value		Approx value	Exact Value	Error
y (1.01)	:	– 1.00970364	– 1.00970364	– 8.67995e-11
y (1.02)	:	– 1.01882896	– 1.01882896	– 1.67848e-10
y (1.03)	:	– 1.02739710	– 1.02739710	– 2.43369e-10
y (1.04)	:	– 1.03542867	– 1.03542867	– 3.13584e-10
y (1.05)	:	– 1.04294368	– 1.04294368	– 3.78718e-10
y (1.06)	:	– 1.04996161	– 1.04996161	– 4.38992e-10
y (1.07)	:	– 1.05650136	– 1.05650136	– 4.94625e-10
y (1.08)	:	– 1.06258128	– 1.06258128	– 5.45834e-10
y (1.09)	:	– 1.06821918	– 1.06821918	– 5.92830e-10
y (1.10)	:	– 1.07343230	– 1.07343230	– 6.35823e-10

The significant digit of the error starts up at 11th decimal position and ends in 10th decimal position. The field of errors confines to the range [– 8.67995e-11, – 6.35823e-10]. The approximations are correct to within this domain.

Example 5

$$DE : \frac{Dy}{dx} = 2 + xy^{1/2}$$

$$CE : Dy = (2 + xy^{1/2})\, dx$$

$$PS : y(x) = 2x + \frac{2^{3/2}x^{5/2}}{5} + \frac{x^4}{20}$$

IC : $y(0) = 0$, Width : 0.01

The Computer Solution of the IVP of Order 1

x-value		Approx value	Exact Value	Error
y (0.01)	:	0.02000569	0.02000566	– 3.35047e-08
y (0.02)	:	0.04003204	0.04003201	– 3.45694e-08
y (0.03)	:	0.06008826	0.06008822	– 3.48742e-08
y (0.04)	:	0.08018118	0.08018115	– 3.50284e-08
y (0.05)	:	0.10031658	0.10031654	– 3.51503e-08

x-value		Approx value	Exact Value	Error
y (0.06)	:	0.12049951	0.12049948	– 3.52953e-08
y (0.07)	:	0.14073460	0.14073457	– 3.55154e-08
y (0.08)	:	0.16102608	0.16102605	– 3.58763e-08
y (0.09)	:	0.18137793	0.18137790	– 3.64672e-08
y (0.10)	:	0.20179389	0.20179385	– 3.74072e-08

The significant digit of the error starts up at 8th decimal position and ends in 8th decimal position. The field of errors confines to the range [– 3.35047e-08, – 3.74072e-08]. The approximations are correct to within this domain.

Example 6

$DE : \dfrac{Dy}{dx} = xy^2 + 1$

$CE : Dy = (xy^2 + 1)\, dx$

$PS : y = x + \dfrac{x^4}{4} + \dfrac{x^7}{14} + \dots$

$IC : y(0) = 0,$ Width : 0.01

The Computer Solution of the IVP of Order 1

x-value		Approx value	Exact Value	Error
y (0.01)	:	0.01	0.01	1.94289e-16
y (0.02)	:	0.02000004	0.02000004	1.42941e-15
y (0.03)	:	0.03000020	0.03000020	4.52416e-15
y (0.04)	:	0.04000064	0.04000064	1.01377e-14
y (0.05)	:	0.05000156	0.05000156	1.77081e-14
y (0.06)	:	0.06000324	0.06000324	2.10248e-14
y (0.07)	:	0.07000600	0.07000600	– 5.63438e-15
y (0.08)	:	0.08001024	0.08001024	– 1.43191e-13
y (0.09)	:	0.09001641	0.09001641	– 6.07042e-13
y (0.10)	:	0.10002501	0.10002501	– 1.90556e-12

The significant digit of the error starts up at 16th decimal position and ends in 12th decimal position. The field of errors confines to the range [1.94289e-16. – 1.90556e-12]. The approximations are correct to within this domain.

Example 7

$DE : \frac{Dy}{dx} = (xy)^{1/3} + 1$

$CE : Dy = [(xy)^{1/3} + 1]\, dx$

$PS : y = x(1 + \frac{3}{5}x^{2/3} + \frac{3}{35}x^{4/3} - \frac{2}{525}x^2 + \ldots)$

$IC : y(0) = 0,$ Width : 0.01

The Computer Solution of the IVP of Order 1

x-value		*Approx value*	*Exact Value*	*Error*
y (0.01)	:	0.01027399	0.01028034	6.34906e-06
y (0.02)	:	0.02088698	0.02089344	6.46747e-06
y (0.03)	:	0.03175520	0.03176175	6.54499e-06
y (0.04)	:	0.04284711	0.04285372	6.61047e-06
y (0.05)	:	0.05414342	0.05415009	6.66895e-06
y (0.06)	:	0.06563068	0.06563741	6.72206e-06
y (0.07)	:	0.07729871	0.07730548	6.77044e-06
y (0.08)	:	0.08913946	0.08914627	6.81424e-06
y (0.09)	:	0.10114632	0.10115317	6.85337e-06
y (0.10)	:	0.11331376	0.11332065	6.88756e-06

The significant digit of the error starts up at 6th decimal position and ends in 6th decimal position. The field of errors confines to the range [6.34906e-06, 6.88756e-06]. The approximations are correct to within this domain.

Example 8

$DE : \frac{Dy}{dx} = \frac{y(x - y)}{x(x + y)}$

$CE : x(x + y)\, dy = y(x - y)\, dx$

PS : $x - y = y\,Ln\,(xy)$

IC : $y(1) = 1$, Width : 0.01

The Computer Solution of the IVP of Order 1

x-value		*Approx value*	*Exact Value*	*Error*
y (1.01)	:	1.00002471	1.00002471	– 1.51371e-10
y (1.02)	:	1.00009772	1.00009771	– 2.36253e-09
y (1.03)	:	1.00021737	1.00021736	– 1.16377e-08
y (1.04)	:	1.00038211	1.00038208	– 3.57898e-08
y (1.05)	:	1.00059043	1.00059034	– 8.50410e-08
y (1.06)	:	1.00084087	1.00084070	– 1.71667e-07
y (1.07)	:	1.00113206	1.00113175	– 3.09680e-07
y (1.08)	:	1.00146266	1.00146215	– 5.14549e-07
y (1.09)	:	1.00183140	1.00183060	– 8.02946e-07
y (1.10)	:	1.00223705	1.00223586	– 1.19253e-06

The significant digit of the error starts up at 10th decimal position and ends in 6th decimal position. The field of errors confines to the range [– 1.51371e-10, – 1.19253e-06]. The approximations are correct to within this domain.

Example 9

DE : $\dfrac{Dy}{dx} = (x + y + 2)(x + y)$

CE : $\dfrac{Dy}{x + y} = (x + y + 2)\,dx$

PS : $y = \dfrac{1}{1 - x} - x - 1$

IC : $y(0) = 0$, Width : 0.01

The Computer Solution of the IVP of Order 1

x-value		*Approx value*	*Exact Value*	*Error*
y (0.01)	:	0.00010101	0.00010101	4.33656e-12
y (0.02)	:	0.00040816	0.00040816	9.03349e-12

x-value		Approx value	Exact Value	Error
y (0.03)	:	0.00092784	0.00092784	1.41201e-11
y (0.04)	:	0.00166667	0.00166667	1.96284e-11
y (0.05)	:	0.00263158	0.00263158	2.55931e-11
y (0.06)	:	0.00382979	0.00382979	3.20523e-11
y (0.07)	:	0.00526882	0.00526882	3.90474e-11
y (0.08)	:	0.00695652	0.00695652	4.66237e-11
y (0.09)	:	0.00890110	0.00890110	5.48308e-11
y (0.10)	:	0.01111111	0.01111111	6.37228e-11

The significant digit of the error starts up at 12th decimal position and ends in 11th decimal position. The field of errors confines to the range [4.33656e-12, 6.37228e-11]. The approximations are correct to within this domain.

Example 10

$DE : \dfrac{Dy}{dx} = \dfrac{y}{x} - 2x^2 \text{ Tan } \dfrac{y}{x}$

$CE : Dy = \left[\dfrac{x}{y} - 2x^2 \text{ Tan } \dfrac{y}{x} \right] dx$

$PS : y = x \text{ Sin}^{-1}[2.28735543\ exp(-x^2)]$

$IC : y(1) = 1,$ Width : 0.01

The Computer Solution of the IVP of Order 1

x-value		Approx value	Exact Value	Error
y (1.01)	:	0.97941518	0.97941527	9.50837e-08
y (1.02)	:	0.95982974	0.95982983	9.22514e-08
y (1.03)	:	0.94108644	0.94108653	8.92078e-08
y (1.04)	:	0.92306256	0.92306265	8.61649e-08
y (1.05)	:	0.90566056	0.90566065	8.32191e-08
y (1.06)	:	0.88880177	0.88880185	8.04105e-08
y (1.07)	:	0.87242191	0.87242199	7.77519e-08
y (1.08)	:	0.85646796	0.85646804	7.52425e-08

x-value		*Approx value*	*Exact Value*	*Error*
y (1.09)	:	0.84089575	0.84089582	7.28753e-08
y (1.10)	:	0.82566823	0.82566830	7.06405e-08

The significant digit of the error starts up at 8th decimal position and ends in 8th decimal position. The field of errors confines to the range [9.50837e-08, 7.06405e-08]. The approximations are correct to within this domain.

Example 11

$$DE : x\frac{dy}{dx} = y \, Ln \frac{y}{x}$$

$$CE : x \, dy = y \, Ln \frac{y}{x} dx$$

$$PS : y = x \, e^{1-x}$$

IC : $y(1) = 1$, Width : 0.01

The Computer Solution of the IVP of Order 1

x-value		*Approx value*	*Exact Value*	*Error*
y (1.01)	:	0.99995033	0.99995033	– 6.21625e-12
y (1.02)	:	0.99980265	0.99980265	– 1.21728e-11
y (1.03)	:	0.99955890	0.99955890	– 1.78831e-11
y (1.04)	:	0.99922102	0.99922102	– 2.33599e-11
y (1.05)	:	0.99879090	0.99879090	– 2.86146e-11
y (1.06)	:	0.99827041	0.99827041	– 3.36585e-11
y (1.07)	:	0.99766139	0.99766139	– 3.85021e-11
y (1.08)	:	0.99696565	0.99696565	– 4.31551e-11
y (1.09)	:	0.99618499	0.99618499	– 4.76270e-11
y (1.10)	:	0.99532116	0.99532116	– 5.19265e-11

The significant digit of the error starts up at 12th decimal position and ends in 11th decimal position. The field of errors confines to the range [– 6.21625e-12, – 5.19265e-11]. The approximations are correct to within this domain.

Example 12

$DE : xy' - y = \sqrt{x^2 + y^2}$

$CE : x\,dy = [y + \sqrt{x^2 + y^2}\,]\,dx$

$PS : y = \dfrac{x^2 - 1}{2}$

$IC : y(1) = 0,$ Width : 0.01

The Computer Solution of the IVP of Order 1

x-value		*Approx value*	*Exact Value*	*Error*
y (1.01)	:	0.01005	0.01005	5.33660e-13
y (1.02)	:	0.02020	0.02020	1.09262e-12
y (1.03)	:	0.03045	0.03045	1.67636e-12
y (1.04)	:	0.04080	0.04080	2.28439e-12
y (1.05)	:	0.05125	0.05125	2.91620e-12
y (1.06)	:	0.06180	0.06180	3.57130e-12
y (1.07)	:	0.07245	0.07245	4.24920e-12
y (1.08)	:	0.08320	0.08320	4.94943e-12
y (1.09)	:	0.09405	0.09405	5.67152e-12
y (1.10)	:	0.10500	0.10500	6.41498e-12

The significant digit of the error starts up at 13th decimal position and ends in 12th decimal position. The field of errors confines to the range [5.33660e-13, 6.41498e-12]. The approximations are correct to within this domain.

Chapter 6

Extensive First-Order Initial-Value Problems

6.1. Second Round Discussion On Methods

Returning to the discussion on standard forms of differential equations of the first order, that have already been considered in chapter 5 (section 5.1), I want to introduce here some other forms.

IV. The equation of the form (***Linear form***)

$$\frac{dy}{dx} + P(x)y = Q(x) \tag{6.10}$$

A first order differential equation is said to be linear, since it is of the first degree in the unknown function y and its derivative $\frac{dy}{dx}$ presenting the form (6.10). $P(x)$ and $Q(x)$ denote the integrable functions of x.

On account of

$$\frac{d}{dx}\left(ye^{\int P(x)dx}\right) = \frac{dy}{dx}e^{\int P(x)dx} + P(x)ye^{\int P(x)dx}$$

$$= e^{\int P(x)dx}\left[\frac{dy}{dx} + P(x)y\right]$$

the factor $e^{\int P(x)dx}$ is called an **integrating factor** of the equation (6.10). Multiplying the equation by the integrating factor we obtain a simplified form that can be readily solvable. Such type of differential equations have been often encountered in different branches of physics and technics.

Example Solve $\frac{dy}{dx} + \frac{y}{x} = x^2$.

Here I.F. $= e^{\int P(x)dx} = e^{\int 1/x \, dx} = e^{Lnx} = x$

Multiplying both sides of the equation by x yields

$$x\frac{dy}{dx} + x.\frac{y}{x} = x.x^2$$

or $$\frac{d}{dx}(xy) = x^3$$

On integrating we have the required general solution

$$xy = \frac{1}{4}x^4 + C_1$$

or $4xy = x^4 + C$, setting $C = 4C_1$

For the other standard forms I will come back again in later sections.

6.2. Linear Homogeneous Equations

For $Q(x) = 0$ the equation (6.10) takes the form

$$\frac{dy}{dx} + P(x)y = 0$$

that is called a **linear homogeneous** equation.

We have now an equation with variables separated and the general solution can be had easily in y

$$y = Ce^{\int P(x)dx}$$

with the arbitrary constant C and the integrating factor $e^{\int P(x)dx}$.

Example Integrate $y' - 3x^2y = 0$

Here $P(x) = -3x^2$, I.F. $= e^{-3\int x^2 dx} = e^{-x^3}$

Multiplying the differential equation by e^{-x^3} we get

$$e^{-x^3}y' - 3x^2ye^{-x^3} = 0$$

or $$\frac{d}{dx}(ye^{-x^3}) = 0$$

Integrating gives $ye^{-x^3} = C$ or $y = Ce^{x^3}$ as general solution.

To find the approximate solutions of linear **homogeneous equations** I use the program named IVPD1LIN described in Chapter 10. The steps of the procedure how to run the C++ Program by means of the appropriate method have been outlined in section 5.3.

Let us determine the approximations of linear differential equations with the aid of this program.

Example 1

$$DE : \frac{Dy}{dx} = \frac{y}{x\ (4 - x)}$$

$$CE : x(4 - x)dy = y\ dx$$

$$PS : y(x) = \left[\frac{x}{5(x - 4)}\right]^{1/4}$$

IC : $y(5) = 1$, Width : 0.01

The Computer Solution of the IVP of Order 1

x-value		*Approx value*	*Exact Value*	*Error*
y (5.01)	:	0.99801389	0.99801389	2.02727e-13
y (5.02)	:	0.99605515	0.99605515	3.94795e-13
y (5.03)	:	0.99412315	0.99412315	5.77094e-13
y (5.04)	:	0.99221731	0.99221731	7.49956e-13
y (5.05)	:	0.99033703	0.99033703	9.14047e-13
y (5.06)	:	0.98848176	0.98848176	1.06981e-12
y (5.07)	:	0.98665096	0.98665096	1.21791e-12
y (5.08)	:	0.98484410	0.98484410	1.35858e-12
y (5.09)	:	0.98306067	0.98306067	1.49225e-12
y (5.10)	:	0.98130016	0.98130016	1.61937e-12

The significant digit of the error starts up at 13th decimal position and ends in 12th decimal position. The field of errors confines to the range [1.61937e-12, 2.02727e-13]. The approximations are correct to within this domain.

Example 2

$$DE : \frac{Dy}{dx} = \frac{-2xy}{1 + x^2}$$

$$CE : (1 + x^2)\ dy = -2xy\ dx$$

$$PS : y(x) = \frac{1}{1 + x^2}$$

IC : $y(0) = 1$, Width : 0.01

The Computer Solution of the IVP of Order 1

x-value		*Approx value*	*Exact Value*	*Error*
y (0.01)	:	0.99990001	0.99990001	4.16334e-14
y (0.02)	:	0.99960016	0.99960016	1.66422e-13
y (0.03)	:	0.99910081	0.99910081	3.73812e-13
y (0.04)	:	0.99840256	0.99840256	6.62581e-13
y (0.05)	:	0.99750623	0.99750623	1.03140e-12
y (0.06)	:	0.99641291	0.99641291	1.47815e-12
y (0.07)	:	0.99512389	0.99512389	2.00073e-12
y (0.08)	:	0.99364070	0.99364070	2.59637e-12
y (0.09)	:	0.99196508	0.99196508	3.26195e-12
y (0.10)	:	0.99009901	0.99009901	3.99392e-12

The significant digit of the error starts up at 14th decimal position and ends in 12th decimal position. The field of errors confines to the range [3.99392e-12, 4.16334e-14]. The approximations are correct to within this domain.

Example 3

$$DE : \frac{Dy}{dx} - y \text{ Cos } x = 0$$

$$CE : Dy = y \text{ Cos } x\, dx$$

$$PS : y(x) = e^{\sin x}$$

$$IC : y(0) = 1, \qquad \text{Width} : 0.01$$

The Computer Solution of the IVP of Order 1

x-value		*Approx value*	*Exact Value*	*Error*
y (0.01)	:	1.01005000	1.01005000	8.04024e-13
y (0.02)	:	1.02019998	1.02019998	1.62359e-12
y (0.03)	:	1.03044990	1.03044990	2.45892e-12
y (0.04)	:	1.04079967	1.04079967	3.30935e-12
y (0.05)	:	1.05124920	1.05124920	4.17488e-12
y (0.06)	:	1.06179833	1.06179833	5.05551e-12

x-value		*Approx value*	*Exact Value*	*Error*
y (0.07)	:	1.07244689	1.07244689	5.95057e-12
y (0.08)	:	1.08319466	1.08319466	6.86007e-12
y (0.09)	:	1.09404140	1.09404140	7.78355e-12
y (0.10)	:	1.10498683	1.10498683	8.72102e-12

The significant digit of the error starts up at 13th decimal position and ends in 12th decimal position. The field of errors confines to the range [8.72102e-12, 8.04024e-13]. The approximations are correct to within this domain.

Example 4

$$DE : \frac{Dy}{dx} + \frac{2xy}{1 + x^2} = 0$$

$$CE : (1 + x^2)dy = -2xy\,dx$$

$$PS : y(x) = \frac{-1}{1 + x^2}$$

IC : $y(0) = -1$, Width : 0.01

The Computer Solution of the IVP of Order 1

x-value		*Approx value*	*Exact Value*	*Error*
y (0.01)	:	– 0.99990001	– 0.99990001	– 4.16334e-14
y (0.02)	:	– 0.99960016	– 0.99960016	– 1.66422e-13
y (0.03)	:	– 0.99910081	– 0.99910081	– 3.73812e-13
y (0.04)	:	– 0.99840256	– 0.99840256	– 6.62581e-13
y (0.05)	:	– 0.99750623	– 0.99750623	– 1.03140e-12
y (0.06)	:	– 0.99641291	– 0.99641291	– 1.47815e-12
y (0.07)	:	– 0.99512389	– 0.99512389	– 2.00073e-12
y (0.08)	:	– 0.99364070	– 0.99364070	– 2.59637e-12
y (0.09)	:	– 0.99196508	– 0.99196508	– 3.26195e-12
y (0.10)	:	– 0.99009901	– 0.99009901	– 3.99392e-12

The significant digit of the error starts up at 14th decimal position and ends in 12th decimal position. The field of errors confines to the range [– 4.16334e-14, – 3.99392e-12]. The approximations are correct to within this domain.

Example 5

$DE : \dfrac{Dy}{dx} + \dfrac{2xy}{1 + x^2} = 0$

$CE : (1 + x^2)dy = -2xy\ dx$

$PS : y(x) = \dfrac{15}{1 + x^2}$

$IC : y(2) = 3,$ Width : 0.01

The Computer Solution of the IVP of Order 1

x-value		*Approx value*	*Exact Value*	*Error*
y (2.01)	:	2.97613143	2.97613143	– 8.69971e-13
y (2.02)	:	2.95252342	2.95252342	– 1.71241e-12
y (2.03)	:	2.92917261	2.92917261	– 2.52820e-12
y (2.04)	:	2.90607564	2.90607564	– 3.31779e-12
y (2.05)	:	2.88322922	2.88322922	– 4.08207e-12
y (2.06)	:	2.86063010	2.86063010	– 4.82192e-12
y (2.07)	:	2.83827509	2.83827509	– 5.53735e-12
y (2.08)	:	2.81616101	2.81616101	– 6.23013e-12
y (2.09)	:	2.79428476	2.79428476	– 6.89981e-12
y (2.10)	:	2.77264325	2.77264325	– 7.54818e-12

The significant digit of the error starts up at 13th decimal position and ends in 12th decimal position. The field of errors confines to the range [– 8.69971e-13, – 7.54818e-12]. The approximations are correct to within this domain.

Example 6

$DE : y' + 2xy = 0$

$CE : Dy = -2xy\ dx$

$PS : y(x) = 3e^{4-x^2}$

$IC : y(-2) = 3;$ Width : 0.01

The Computer Solution of the IVP of Order 1

x-value		*Approx value*	*Exact Value*	*Error*
y (– 1.99)	:	3.12212009	3.12212009	2.54706e-09
y (– 1.98)	:	3.24856151	3.24856152	5.23512e-09
y (– 1.97)	:	3.37944767	3.37944768	8.06852e-09
y (– 1.96)	:	3.51490425	3.51490426	1.10516e-08
y (– 1.95)	:	3.65505918	3.65505919	1.41889e-08
y (– 1.94)	:	3.80004263	3.80004264	1.74848e-08
y (– 1.93)	:	3.94998698	3.94998700	2.09438e-08
y (– 1.92)	:	4.10502685	4.10502687	2.45706e-08
y (– 1.91)	:	4.26529899	4.26529902	2.83697e-08
y (– 1.90)	:	4.43094235	4.43094238	3.23459e-08

The significant digit of the error starts up at 9th decimal position and ends in 8th decimal position. The field of errors confines to the range [3.23459e-08, 2.54706e-09]. The approximations are correct to within this domain.

Example 7

DE : $y' + (x - 1)y = 0$

CE : $\frac{1}{y} dy = (1 - x)\, dx$

PS : $y(x) = \frac{e^{x - x^2/2}}{e^{0.5}}$

IC : $y(1) = 1$, Width : 0.01

The Computer Solution of the IVP of Order 1

x-value		*Approx value*	*Exact Value*	*Error*
y (1.01)	:	0.99995000	0.99995000	0
y (1.02)	:	0.99980002	0.99980002	0
y (1.03)	:	0.99955010	0.99955010	0
y (1.04)	:	0.99920032	0.99920032	0
y (1.05)	:	0.99875078	0.99875078	0
y (1.06)	:	0.99820162	0.99820162	0

x-value		*Approx value*	*Exact Value*	*Error*
y (1.07)	:	0.99755300	0.99755300	1.11022e-16
y (1.08)	:	0.99680511	0.99680511	2.22045e-16
y (1.09)	:	0.99595819	0.99595819	2.22045e-16
y (1.10)	:	0.99501248	0.99501248	3.33067e-16

The significant digit of the error starts up at 0th decimal position and ends in 16th decimal position. The field of errors confines to the range [0, 3.33067e-16]. The approximations are correct to within this domain.

Example 8

DE : $\frac{Dy}{dx} + (x^2 + 1)y = 0$

CE : $Dy = -y(1 + x^2)\, dx$

PS : $y(x) = e^{-(x^3+3x+4)/3}$

IC : $y(-1) = 1.0$, Width : 0.01

The Computer Solution of the IVP of Order 1

x-value		*Approx value*	*Exact Value*	*Error*
y (– 0.99)	:	0.98029637	0.98029637	– 2.58108e-11
y (– 0.98)	:	0.96117127	0.96117127	– 4.93757e-11
y (– 0.97)	:	0.94260402	0.94260402	– 7.08702e-11
y (– 0.96)	:	0.92457479	0.92457479	– 9.04564e-11
y (– 0.95)	:	0.90706455	0.90706455	– 1.08284e-10
y (– 0.94)	:	0.89005502	0.89005502	– 1.24490e-10
y (– 0.93)	:	0.87352867	0.87352867	– 1.39202e-10
y (– 0.92)	:	0.85746864	0.85746864	– 1.52538e-10
y (– 0.91)	:	0.84185878	0.84185878	– 1.64606e-10
y (– 0.90)	:	0.82668353	0.82668353	– 1.75506e-10

The significant digit of the error starts up at 11th decimal position and ends in 10th decimal position. The field of errors confines to the range [– 2.58108e-11, – 1.75506e-10]. The approximations are correct to within this domain.

6.3. Nonhomogeneous Equations

The equation (6.10) in the standard form is of **nonhomogeneous** type. It is very important equation and is extensively used in the branches of mathematics, physics and engineering. The method we use here to solve the equation has already been described partly in section 6.1.

The first step is to find an elementary differentiable function, the derivative of which with respect to x is $P(x)$. That means, the **elementary function** $\varphi(x)$ can be written as

$$\varphi(x) = \int P(x)\, dx$$

Now, if the equation (6.10) stated as

$$\frac{dy}{dx} + P(x)y = Q(x)$$

is multiplied by the integrating factor $e^{\varphi(x)}$, it becomes

$$e^{\varphi(x)}\frac{dy}{dx} + e^{\varphi(x)}P(x)y = e^{\varphi(x)}Q(x)$$

$$\text{or} \quad \frac{d}{dx}(ye^{\varphi(x)}) = e^{\varphi(x)}Q(x)$$

Integrating yields

$$ye^{\varphi(x)} = \int e^{\varphi(x)}Q(x)dx + C$$

$$\text{or} \quad y = e^{-\varphi(x)}[\int e^{-\varphi(x)}Q(x)dx + C]$$

is the required solution.

The integrating factor $e^{\varphi(x)} = e^{\int P(x)\, dx}$ has been introduced in section 6.1.

Example Solve $\dfrac{dy}{dx} - y \text{ Cos } x = - \text{Cos } x.$

Here, $\int P(x)\, dx = -\int \cos x\, dx = -\sin x$, I.F. $= e^{-\sin x}$

Multiplying by the factor gives $\quad e^{-\sin x}\dfrac{dy}{dx} - ye^{-\sin x}\cos x = -\cos x\, e^{-\sin x}$

On integrating we obtain $\quad y\, e^{-\sin x} = -\int \cos x\, e^{-\sin x}\, dx + C = e^{-\sin x} + C$

or $\quad y = 1 + Ce^{\sin x}$.

We want to treat now the initial value problems of nonhomogeneous character in other way. This is the way in which the approximated solutions of the initial value problems are determined. As regards computerised solution I employ the program IVPD1LIN. The methods of procedure are remained unaltered as mentioned in section 6.2. For the problems considered in sections 6.4 and 6.5 the same program has been applied as for the previous one.

Example 1

$DE \ : \ \dfrac{Dy}{dx} - x + y = 0$

$CE \ : \ Dy = (x - y)\, dx$

$PS \ : \ y(x) = x - 1 + 3e^{-x}$

$IC \ : \ y(0) = 2, \qquad$ Width : 0.01

The Computer Solution of the IVP of Order 1

x-value		*Approx value*	*Exact Value*	*Error*
y (0.01)	:	1.98014950	1.98014950	– 2.49600e-12
y (0.02)	:	1.96059602	1.96059602	– 4.94205e-12
y (0.03)	:	1.94133660	1.94133660	– 7.33924e-12
y (0.04)	:	1.92236832	1.92236832	– 9.68825e-12
y (0.05)	:	1.90368827	1.90368827	– 1.19897e-11
y (0.06)	:	1.88529360	1.88529360	– 1.42446e-11
y (0.07)	:	1.86718146	1.86718146	– 1.64533e-11
y (0.08)	:	1.84934904	1.84934904	– 1.86164e-11
y (0.09)	:	1.83179356	1.83179356	– 2.07352e-11
y (0.10)	:	1.81451225	1.81451225	– 2.28100e-11

The significant digit of the error starts up at 12th decimal position and ends in 11th decimal position. The field of errors confines to the range [– 2.49600e-12, – 2.28100e-11]. The approximations are correct to within this domain.

Example 2

$DE \ : \ \dfrac{Dy}{dx} = x + y + \text{Sin } x$

$CE \ : \ Dy = (x + y + \text{Sin } x)\, dx$

$PS \ : \ y(x) = 2e^{x} - x - 1 - \dfrac{(\text{Cos } x + \text{Sin } x)}{2}$

IC : $y(0) = 0.5$, Width : 0.01

The Computer Solution of the IVP of Order 1

x-value		*Approx value*	*Exact Value*	*Error*
y (0.01)	:	0.50512542	0.50512542	1.94811e-12
y (0.02)	:	0.51050334	0.51050334	3.93841e-12
y (0.03)	:	0.51613630	0.51613630	5.97156e-12
y (0.04)	:	0.52202683	0.52202683	8.04812e-12
y (0.05)	:	0.52817748	0.52817748	1.01685e-11
y (0.06)	:	0.53459082	0.53459082	1.23336e-11
y (0.07)	:	0.54126944	0.54126944	1.45438e-11
y (0.08)	:	0.54821594	0.54821594	1.67998e-11
y (0.09)	:	0.55543293	0.55543293	1.91019e-11
y (0.10)	:	0.56292305	0.56292305	2.14511e-11

The significant digit of the error starts up at 12th decimal position and ends in 11th decimal position. The field of errors confines to the range [2.14511e-11, 1.94811e-12]. The approximations are correct to within this domain.

Example 3

$$DE : y' - \frac{y}{x} = \frac{Ln \frac{1}{x}}{x}$$

$$CE : x\,dy = \left[y + Ln \frac{1}{x} \right] dx$$

$$PS : y(x) = Ln\, x + x + 1$$

IC : $y(0.5) = 0.80685282$, Width : 0.01

The Computer Solution of the IVP of Order 1

x-value		*Approx value*	*Exact Value*	*Error*
y (0.51)	:	0.83665545	0.83665545	– 7.34327e-10
y (0.52)	:	0.86607353	0.86607353	– 8.96663e-10
y (0.53)	:	0.89512173	0.89512173	– 1.04827e-09
y (0.54)	:	0.92381386	0.92381386	– 1.19032e-09

x-value		*Approx value*	*Exact Value*	*Error*
y (0.55)	:	0.95216300	0.95216300	– 1.32381e-09
y (0.56)	:	0.98018151	0.98018150	– 1.44964e-09
y (0.57)	:	1.00788108	1.00788108	– 1.56859e-09
y (0.58)	:	1.03527283	1.03527282	– 1.68135e-09
y (0.59)	:	1.06236726	1.06236726	– 1.78854e-09
y (0.60)	:	1.08917438	1.08917438	– 1.89070e-09

The significant digit of the error starts up at 10th decimal position and ends in 9th decimal position. The field of errors confines to the range [– 7.34327e-10, – 1.89070e-09]. The approximations are correct to within this domain.

Example 4

DE : $\dfrac{Dy}{dx} - \text{Sin } 2x - y \text{ Tan } x = 0$

CE : $Dy = (\text{Sin } 2x + y \text{ Tan } x)\ dx$

PS : $y(x) = \text{Sec } x - \dfrac{2\text{Cos}^2 x}{3}$

IC : $y(0) = \dfrac{1}{3}$, Width : 0.01

The Computer Solution of the IVP of Order 1

x-value		*Approx value*	*Exact Value*	*Error*
y (0.01)	:	0.33345000	0.33345000	3.33347e-09
y (0.02)	:	0.33379999	0.33379999	3.33389e-09
y (0.03)	:	0.33438332	0.33438332	3.33459e-09
y (0.04)	:	0.33519996	0.33519996	3.33556e-09
y (0.05)	:	0.33624991	0.33624991	3.33682e-09
y (0.06)	:	0.33753316	0.33753316	3.33836e-09
y (0.07)	:	0.33904968	0.33904968	3.34018e-09
y (0.08)	:	0.34079946	0.34079946	3.34228e-09
y (0.09)	:	0.34278248	0.34278248	3.34467e-09
y (0.10)	:	0.34499872	0.34499873	3.34734e-09

The significant digit of the error starts up at 9th decimal position and ends in 9th decimal position. The field of errors confines to the range [3.34734e-09, 3.33347e-09]. The approximations are correct to within this domain.

Example 5

DE : $Dy + y \text{ Sin } x\, dx = \text{Sin } x\, dx$

CE : $Dy = \text{Sin } x(1 - y)\, dx$

PS : $y(x) = 1 + e^{\cos x - 1}$

IC : $y(0) = 2$, Width : 0.01

The Computer Solution of the IVP of Order 1

x-value		*Approx value*	*Exact Value*	*Error*
y (0.01)	:	1.99995000	1.99995000	2.22045e-16
y (0.02)	:	1.99980003	1.99980003	6.66134e-16
y (0.03)	:	1.99955013	1.99955013	1.55431e-15
y (0.04)	:	1.99920043	1.99920043	2.66454e-15
y (0.05)	:	1.99875104	1.99875104	4.21885e-15
y (0.06)	:	1.99820216	1.99820216	6.21725e-15
y (0.07)	:	1.99755400	1.99755400	8.43769e-15
y (0.08)	:	1.99680682	1.99680682	1.11022e-14
y (0.09)	:	1.99596091	1.99596091	1.39888e-14
y (0.10)	:	1.99501662	1.99501662	1.73195e-14

The significant digit of the error starts up at 16th decimal position and ends in 14th decimal position. The field of errors confines to the range [1.73195e-14, 2.22045e-16]. The approximations are correct to within this domain.

Example 6

DE : $\dfrac{Dy}{dx} + y = e^x$

CE : $Dy = (e^x - y)\, dx$

PS : $y = \dfrac{e^x}{2} + e^{-x}$

IC : $y(0) = 1.5$, Width : 0.01

The Computer Solution of the IVP of Order 1

x-value		*Approx value*	*Exact Value*	*Error*
y (0.01)	:	1.49507492	1.49507492	– 1.63225e-12
y (0.02)	:	1.49029934	1.49029934	– 3.24807e-12
y (0.03)	:	1.48567280	1.48567280	– 4.84768e-12
y (0.04)	:	1.48119483	1.48119483	– 6.43152e-12
y (0.05)	:	1.47686497	1.47686497	– 7.99982e-12
y (0.06)	:	1.47268281	1.47268281	– 9.55303e-12
y (0.07)	:	1.46864791	1.46864791	– 1.10911e-11
y (0.08)	:	1.46475988	1.46475988	– 1.26150e-11
y (0.09)	:	1.46101833	1.46101833	– 1.41245e-11
y (0.10)	:	1.45742288	1.45742288	– 1.56199e-11

The significant digit of the error starts up at 12th decimal position and ends in 11th decimal position. The field of errors confines to the range [– 1.63225e-12, – 1.56199e-11]. The approximations are correct to within this domain.

Example 7

DE : $\dfrac{Dy}{dx} + y \text{ Tan } x = \text{Cos}^2 x$

CE : $Dy = (\text{Cos}^2 x - y \text{ Tan } x)\, dx$

PS : $y = (1 + \text{Sin } x)\text{Cos } x$

IC : $y(0) = 1$, Width : 0.01

The Computer Solution of the IVP of Order 1

x-value		*Approx value*	*Exact Value*	*Error*
y (0.01)	:	1.00994933	1.00994933	8.36220e-13
y (0.02)	:	1.01979467	1.01979467	1.67844e-12
y (0.03)	:	1.02953204	1.02953204	2.52687e-12
y (0.04)	:	1.03915745	1.03915745	3.38218e-12
y (0.05)	:	1.04866697	1.04866697	4.24416e-12
y (0.06)	:	1.05805664	1.05805664	5.11391e-12

x-value		*Approx value*	*Exact Value*	*Error*
y (0.07)	:	1.06732256	1.06732256	5.99121e-12
y (0.08)	:	1.07646081	1.07646081	6.87672e-12
y (0.09)	:	1.08546752	1.08546752	7.77090e-12
y (0.10)	:	1.09433883	1.09433883	8.67395e-12

The significant digit of the error starts up at 13th decimal position and ends in 12th decimal position. The field of errors confines to the range [8.67395e-12, 8.36220e-13]. The approximations are correct to within this domain.

Example 8

DE : $\dfrac{Dy}{dx} + y = x$

CE : $Dy = (x - y)\,dx$

PS : $y(x) = x + 1 + 3e^{-x}$

IC : $y(0) = 2$, Width : 0.01

The Computer Solution of the IVP of Order 1

x-value		*Approx value*	*Exact Value*	*Error*
y (0.01)	:	1.98014950	1.98014950	– 2.49600e-12
y (0.02)	:	1.96059602	1.96059602	– 4.94205e-12
y (0.03)	:	1.94133600	1.94133660	– 7.33924e-12
y (0.04)	:	1.92236832	1.92236832	– 9.68825e-12
y (0.05)	:	1.90368827	1.90368827	– 1.19897e-11
y (0.06)	:	1.88529360	1.88529360	– 1.42446e-11
y (0.07)	:	1.86718146	1.86718146	– 1.64533e-11
y (0.08)	:	1.84934904	1.84934904	– 1.86164e-11
y (0.09)	:	1.83179356	1.83179356	– 2.07352e-11
y (0.10)	:	1.81451225	1.81451225	– 2.28100e-11

The significant digit of the error starts up at 12th decimal position and ends in 11th decimal position. The field of errors confines to the range [– 2.49600e-12, – 2.28100e-11]. The approximations are correct to within this domain.

Example 9

DE : $\dfrac{Dy}{dx} + y \text{ Cot } x = 2\text{Sec } x$

CE : $Dy = (2\text{Sec } x - y \text{ Cot } x)\, dx$

PS : $y \text{ Sin } x + Ln\,(\text{Cos}^2 x) = -\ 1.23125292$

IC : $y(1) = 0,$ Width : 0.01

The Computer Solution of the IVP of Order 1

x-value		*Approx value*	*Exact Value*	*Error*
y (1.01)	:	0.03719075	0.03719077	2.44973e-08
y (1.02)	:	0.07475079	0.07475081	2.43111e-08
y (1.03)	:	0.11271150	0.11271150	2.41261e-08
y (1.04)	:	0.15110534	0.15110537	2.39420e-08
y (1.05)	:	0.18996598	0.18996601	2.37583e-08
y (1.06)	:	0.22932840	0.22932843	2.35743e-08
y (1.07)	:	0.26922905	0.26922907	2.33895e-08
y (1.08)	:	0.30970596	0.30970598	2.32032e-08
y (1.09)	:	0.35079894	0.35079896	2.30146e-08
y (1.10)	:	0.39254974	0.39254976	2.28227e-08

The significant digit of the error starts up at 08th decimal position and ends in 08th decimal position. The field of errors confines to the range [2.44973e-08, 2.28227e-08]. The approximations are correct to within this domain.

Example 10

DE : $\text{Sin } 2x\ dy = 2(y + \text{Cos } x)\, dx$

CE : $\text{Sin } 2x\ dy = 2(y + \text{Cos } x)\, dx$

PS : $y(x) = \dfrac{\text{Sin} x - 1}{\text{Cos } x}$

IC : $y\left(\dfrac{\pi}{2}\right) = 0,$ Width : 0.01

The Computer Solution of the IVP of Order 1

x-value	*Approx value*	*Exact Value*	*Error*
y (1.58079633) :	0.00499999	0.00500004	5.55594e-08
y (1.59079633) :	0.01000030	0.01000033	2.77763e-08
y (1.60079633) :	0.01500111	0.01500112	1.85137e-08
y (1.61079633) :	0.02000265	0.02000267	1.38813e-08
y (1.62079633) :	0.02500520	0.02500521	1.11010e-08
y (1.63079633) :	0.03000899	0.03000900	9.24664e-09
y (1.64079633) :	0.03501429	0.03501430	7.92148e-09
y (1.65079633) :	0.04002134	0.04002135	6.92704e-09
y (1.66079633) :	0.04503039	0.04503040	6.15309e-09
y (1.67079633) :	0.05004170	0.05004171	5.53347e-09

The significant digit of the error starts up at 8th decimal position and ends in 9th decimal position. The field of errors confines to the range [5.55594e-08, 5.53347e-09]. The approximations are correct to within this domain.

Example 11

DE : $xy' - y = x^3 \text{ Cos } x \, dx$

CE : $x \, dy = (x^3 \text{Cos } x + y) \, dx$

PS : $y(x) = x(1 + x \text{ Sin } x + \text{Cos } x)$

IC : $y(\pi) = 0.$ Width : 0.01

The Computer Solution of the IVP of Order 1

x-value	*Approx value*	*Exact Value*	*Error*
y (3.15159265) :	– 0.09916613	– 0.09916609	3.55425e-08
y (3.16159265) :	– 0.19926774	– 0.19926770	3.56553e-08
y (3.17159265) :	– 0.30029763	– 0.30029759	3.57680e-08
y (3.18159265) :	– 0.40224837	– 0.40224834	3.58807e-08
y (3.19159265) :	– 0.50511234	– 0.50511230	3.59935e-08
y (3.20159265) :	– 0.60888165	– 0.60888162	3.61062e-08

x-value	Approx value	Exact Value	Error
y (3.21159265) :	– 0.71354823	– 0.71354820	3.62190e-08
y (3.22159265) :	– 0.81910377	– 0.81910374	3.63317e-08
y (3.23159265) :	– 0.92553974	– 0.92553971	3.64445e-08
y (3.24159265) :	– 1.03284738	– 1.03284735	3.65573e-08

The significant digit of the error starts up at 8th decimal position and ends in 8th decimal position. The field of errors confines to the range [3.65573e-08, 3.55425e-08]. The approximations are correct to within this domain.

Example 12

DE : $(x^2+1)\,y' = 4xy + (x^2+1)^2$

CE : $(x^2+1)dy = [4xy + (x^2+1)^2]\,dx$

PS : $y = (x^2+1)^2\,(1 + \text{Tan}^{-1} x)$

IC : $y(0) = 1$, Width : 0.01

The Computer Solution of the IVP of Order 1

x-value	Approx value	Exact Value	Error
y (0.01) :	1.01020168	1.01020168	1.15792e-11
y (0.02) :	1.02081350	1.02081350	2.29659e-11
y (0.03) :	1.03184582	1.03184582	3.41374e-11
y (0.04) :	1.04330928	1.04330928	4.50717e-11
y (0.05) :	1.05521475	1.05521475	5.57465e-11
y (0.06) :	1.06757337	1.06757337	6.61426e-11
y (0.07) :	1.08039657	1.08039657	7.62399e-11
y (0.08) :	1.09369604	1.09369604	8.60214e-11
y (0.09) :	1.10748376	1.10748376	9.54710e-11
y (0.10) :	1.12177199	1.12177199	1.04574e-10

The significant digit of the error starts up at 11th decimal position and ends in 10th decimal position. The field of errors confines to the range [1.04574e-10, 1.15792e-11]. The approximations are correct to within this domain.

Example 13

DE : $(x + 1) y' + y(2 + x) = 2\text{Sin } x$

CE : $(x + 1)dy = [2\text{Sin } x - (2 + x)y]\, dx$

PS : $y = \dfrac{\text{Sin } x - \text{Cos } x + 3e^{-x}}{x + 1}$

IC : $y(0) = 2$, Width : 0.01

The Computer Solution of the IVP of Order 1

x-value		*Approx value*	*Exact Value*	*Error*
y (0.01)	:	1.96059340	1.96059340	– 6.04883e-11
y (0.02)	:	1.92234773	1.92234773	– 1.17095e-10
y (0.03)	:	1.88522531	1.88522531	– 1.70050e-10
y (0.04)	:	1.84918995	1.84918995	– 2.19565e-10
y (0.05)	:	1.81420684	1.81420684	– 2.65843e-10
y (0.06)	:	1.78024252	1.78024252	– 3.09071e-10
y (0.07)	:	1.74726477	1.74726477	– 3.49424e-10
y (0.08)	:	1.71524262	1.71524262	– 3.87069e-10
y (0.09)	:	1.68414621	1.68414621	– 4.22160e-10
y (0.10)	:	1.65394682	1.65394682	– 4.54844e-10

The significant digit of the error starts up at 11th decimal position and ends in 10th decimal position. The field of errors confines to the range [– 6.04883e-10, – 4.54844e-10]. The approximations are correct to within this domain.

Example 14

DE : $\dfrac{Dy}{dx} + y \text{ Tan } x = \text{Sec } x$

CE : $\text{Cos } x\, dy = (1 - y \text{ Sin } x)\, dx$

PS : $y(x) = \text{Sin } x + \text{Cos } x$

IC : $y(0) = 1$, Width : 0.01

The Computer Solution of the IVP of Order 1

x-value		Approx value	Exact Value	Error
y (0.01)	:	1.00994983	1.00994983	3.15303e-13
y (0.02)	:	1.01979867	1.01979867	6.36602e-13
y (0.03)	:	1.02954553	1.02954553	9.63674e-13
y (0.04)	:	1.03918944	1.03918944	1.29718e-12
y (0.05)	:	1.04872943	1.04872943	1.63713e-12
y (0.06)	:	1.05816455	1.05816455	1.98375e-12
y (0.07)	:	1.06749385	1.06749385	2.33769e-12
y (0.08)	:	1.07671640	1.07671640	2.69873e-12
y (0.09)	:	1.08583128	1.08583128	3.06732e-12
y (0.10)	:	1.09483758	1.09483758	3.44369e-12

The significant digit of the error starts up at 13th decimal position and ends in 12th decimal position. The field of errors confines to the range [3.44369e-12, 3.15303e-13]. The approximations are correct to within this domain.

Example 15

DE : $\dfrac{Dy}{dx} + \dfrac{y}{x} = x^3$

CE : $x\,dy = (x^4 - y)\,dx$

PS : $5y = x^4 + \dfrac{9}{x}$

IC : $y(1) = 2$, Width : 0.01

The Computer Solution of the IVP of Order 1

x-value		Approx value	Exact Value	Error
y (1.01)	:	1.99029902	1.99029902	– 8.24896e-13
y (1.02)	:	1.98119231	1.98119231	– 1.63403e-12
y (1.03)	:	1.97267458	1.97267458	– 2.42717e-12
y (1.04)	:	1.96474094	1.96474094	– 3.20499e-12
y (1.05)	:	1.95738696	1.95738696	– 3.96816e-12
y (1.06)	:	1.95060860	1.95060860	– 4.71689e-12

x-value		*Approx value*	*Exact Value*	*Error*
y (1.07)	:	1.94440219	1.94440219	– 5.45164e-12
y (1.08)	:	1.93876446	1.93876446	– 6.17284e-12
y (1.09)	:	1.93369247	1.93369247	– 6.88072e-12
y (1.10)	:	1.92918364	1.92918364	– 7.57572e-12

The significant digit of the error starts up at 13th decimal position and ends in 12th decimal position. The field of errors confines to the range [– 8.24896e-13, – 7.57572e-12]. The approximations are correct to within this domain.

Example 16

DE : $\text{Cot}\, x \dfrac{dy}{dx} + y = 2$

CE : $Dy = (2 - y)\, \text{Tan}\, x\, dx$

PS : $y(x) = 2 - 3\text{Cos}\, x$

IC : $y(0) = -1$, Width : 0.01

The Computer Solution of the IVP of Order 1

x-value		*Approx value*	*Exact Value*	*Error*
y (0.01)	:	– 0.99985000	– 0.99985000	– 8.32667e-15
y (0.02)	:	– 0.99940002	– 0.99940002	– 3.34177e-14
y (0.03)	:	– 0.99865010	– 0.99865010	– 7.50511e-14
y (0.04)	:	– 0.99760032	– 0.99760032	– 1.33671e-13
y (0.05)	:	– 0.99625078	– 0.99625078	– 2.08944e-13
y (0.06)	:	– 0.99460162	– 0.99460162	– 3.01204e-13
y (0.07)	:	– 0.99265300	– 0.99265300	– 4.10671e-13
y (0.08)	:	– 0.99040512	– 0.99040512	– 5.37237e-13
y (0.09)	:	– 0.98785820	– 0.98785820	– 6.81011e-13
y (0.10)	:	– 0.98501250	– 0.98501250	– 8.42437e-13

The significant digit of the error starts up at 15th decimal position and ends in 13th decimal position. The field of errors confines to the range [– 8.32667e-15, – 8.42437e-13]. The approximations are correct to within this domain.

Example 17

$$DE : \frac{Dy}{dx} + y \text{ Cot } x = \text{Cos } x$$

$$CE : Dy = \left(\text{Cos } x - \frac{y}{\text{Tan } x}\right)dx$$

$$PS : y(x) = 0.5\frac{\text{Sin}^2 x + 1}{\text{Sin } x}$$

$$IC : y\left(\frac{\pi}{2}\right) = 1, \quad \text{Width : } 0.01$$

The Computer Solution of the IVP of Order 1

x-value	*Approx value*	*Exact Value*	*Error*
y (1.58079633) :	1.00000000	1.00000000	2.66454e-15
y (1.59079633) :	1.00000002	1.00000002	1.06581e-14
y (1.60079633) :	1.00000010	1.00000010	2.37588e-14
y (1.61079633) :	1.00000032	1.00000032	4.19664e-14
y (1.62079633) :	1.00000078	1.00000078	6.52811e-14
y (1.63079633) :	1.00000162	1.00000162	9.37028e-14
y (1.64079633) :	1.00000301	1.00000301	1.27454e-13
y (1.65079633) :	1.00000513	1.00000513	1.66311e-13
y (1.66079633) :	1.00000822	1.00000822	2.10054e-13
y (1.67079633) :	1.00001245	1.00001245	2.58904e-13

The significant digit of the error starts up at 15th decimal position and ends in 13th decimal position. The field of errors confines to the range [2.58904e-13, 2.66454e-15]. The approximations are correct to within this domain.

Example 18

$$DE : \frac{Dy}{dx} = \frac{y}{x} + x^2 + 3x - 2$$

$$CE : Dy = \left(\frac{y}{x} + x^2 + 3x - 2\right)dx$$

$$PS : y(x) = 0.5(x^3 + 6x^2 - 4x \, Ln \, x - 5x)$$

$$IC : y(1) = 1, \quad \text{Width : } 0.01$$

The Computer Solution of the IVP of Order 1

x-value		*Approx value*	*Exact Value*	*Error*
y (1.01)	:	1.03035083	1.03035083	9.81104e-12
y (1.02)	:	1.06140664	1.06140664	1.95346e-11
y (1.03)	:	1.09317237	1.09317237	2.91722e-11
y (1.04)	:	1.12565292	1.12565292	3.87252e-11
y (1.05)	:	1.15885316	1.15885316	4.81946e-11
y (1.06)	:	1.19277791	1.19277791	5.75815e-11
y (1.07)	:	1.22743199	1.22743199	6.68876e-11
y (1.08)	:	1.26282015	1.26282015	7.61140e-11
y (1.09)	:	1.29894712	1.29894712	8.52620e-11
y (1.10)	:	1.33581760	1.33581760	9.43332e-11

The significant digit of the error starts up at 12th decimal position and ends in 11th decimal position. The field of errors confines to the range [9.43332e-11, 9.81104e-12]. The approximations are correct to within this domain.

Example 19

$$DE : \frac{Dy}{dx} = \frac{1}{x + 2y}$$

$$CE : (x + 2y)\, dy = dx$$

$$PS : y(x) = -0.5(x + 2)$$

IC : $y(0) = -1$, Width : 0.01

The Computer Solution of the IVP of Order 1

x-value		*Approx value*	*Exact Value*	*Error*
y (0.01)	:	– 1.005	– 1.005	0
y (0.02)	:	– 1.010	– 1.010	– 2.22045e-16
y (0.03)	:	– 1.015	– 1.015	– 2.22045e-16
y (0.04)	:	– 1.020	– 1.020	– 4.44089e-16
y (0.05)	:	– 1.025	– 1.025	– 4.44089e-16
y (0.06)	:	– 1.030	– 1.030	– 6.66134e-16

x-value		*Approx value*	*Exact Value*	*Error*
y (0.07)	:	– 1.035	– 1.035	– 6.66134e-16
y (0.08)	:	– 1.040	– 1.040	– 8.88178e-16
y (0.09)	:	– 1.045	– 1.045	– 8.88178e-16
y (0.10)	:	– 1.050	– 1.050	– 1.11022e-15

The significant digit of the error starts up at 0th decimal position and ends in 15th decimal position. The field of errors confines to the range [0, –1.11022e-15]. The approximations are correct to within this domain.

Example 20

$DE : \dfrac{Dy}{dx} = \dfrac{x+y}{x}$

$CE : x\,dy = (x + y)dx$

$PS : y(x) = x(1 + Ln\ x)$

$IC : y\ (0.36787944) = 0,$ Width : 0.01

The Computer Solution of the IVP of Order 1

x-value		*Approx value*	*Exact Value*	*Error*
y (0.37787944)	:	0.01013470	0.01013470	– 1.03141e-09
y (0.38787944)	:	0.02053406	0.02053406	– 9.04080e-10
y (0.39787944)	:	0.03119127	0.03119127	– 7.87950e-10
y (0.40787944)	:	0.04209983	0.04209983	– 6.81558e-10
y (0.41787944)	:	0.05325359	0.05325359	– 5.83894e-10
y (0.42787944)	:	0.06464668	0.06464668	– 4.93927e-10
y (0.43787944)	:	0.07627349	0.07627349	– 4.10802e-10
y (0.44787944)	:	0.08812870	0.08812870	– 3.33775e-10
y (0.45787944)	:	0.10020721	0.10020721	– 2.62196e-10
y (0.46787944)	:	0.11250413	0.11250413	– 1.95499e-10

The significant digit of the error starts up at 9th decimal position and ends in 10th decimal position. The field of errors confines to the range [– 1.95499e-10, – 1.03141e-09]. The approximations are correct to within this domain.

Example 21

$DE : \dfrac{Dy}{dx} = -5e^{-x} + 4y$

$CE : e^{x}\,dy = (4ye^{x} - 5)dx$

$PS : y(x) = e^{-x}$

$IC : y(0) = 1,$ Width : 0.01

The Computer Solution of the IVP of Order 1

x-value		*Approx value*	*Exact Value*	*Error*
y (0.01)	:	0.99004983	0.99004983	7.28236e-11
y (0.02)	:	0.98019867	0.98019867	1.47894e-10
y (0.03)	:	0.97044553	0.97044553	2.25312e-10
y (0.04)	:	0.96078944	0.96078944	3.05178e-10
y (0.05)	:	0.95122942	0.95122942	3.87601e-10
y (0.06)	:	0.94176453	0.94176453	4.72691e-10
y (0.07)	:	0.93239382	0.93239382	5.60565e-10
y (0.08)	:	0.92311635	0.92311635	6.51342e-10
y (0.09)	:	0.91393118	0.91393119	7.45148e-10
y (0.10)	:	0.90483742	0.90483742	8.42114e-10

The significant digit of the error starts up at 11th decimal position and ends in 10th decimal position. The field of errors confines to the range [8.42114e-10, 7.28236e-11]. The approximations are correct to within this domain.

Example 22

$DE : \dfrac{Dy}{dx} = \dfrac{Ln\ x + 2y}{x\ Ln\ x}$

$CE : x\ Ln\ x\ dy = (2y + Ln\ x)dx$

$PS : y(x) = Ln\ x(2\ Ln\ x - 1)$

$IC : y(e) = 1,$ Width : 0.01

The Computer Solution of the IVP of Order 1

x-value		*Approx value*	*Exact Value*	*Error*
y (2.72828182)	:	1.01104310	1.01104309	– 9.40410e-09
y (2.73828182)	:	1.02209944	1.02209943	– 9.47249e-09

x-value	*Approx value*	*Exact Value*	*Error*
y (2.74828182) :	1.03316872	1.03316871	– 9.54088e-09
y (2.75828182) :	1.04425067	1.04425066	– 9.60927e-09
y (2.76828182) :	1.05534498	1.05534497	– 9.67767e-09
y (2.77828182) :	1.06645140	1.06645139	– 9.74607e-09
y (2.78828182) :	1.07756964	1.07756963	– 9.81448e-09
y (2.79828182) :	1.08869944	1.08869943	– 9.88288e-09
y (2.80828182) :	1.09984052	1.09984501	– 9.95128e-09
y (2.81828182) :	1.11099264	1.11099263	– 1.00197e-08

The significant digit of the error starts up at 9th decimal position and ends in 8th decimal position. The field of errors confines to the range [-- 9.4041e-09, – 1.00197e-08]. The approximations are correct to within this domain.

Example 23

DE : $\dfrac{Dy}{dx} = 3(2x + y) + 1$

CE : $Dy = [3(y + 2x) + 1]dx$

PS : $y(x) = e^{3x} - 2x - 1$

IC : $y(0) = 0$, Width : 0.01

The Computer Solution of the IVP of Order 1

x-value	*Approx value*	*Exact Value*	*Error*
y (0.01) :	0.01045453	0.01045453	2.03517e-10
y (0.02) :	0.02183655	0.02183655	4.19430e-10
y (0.03) :	0.03417428	0.03417428	6.48305e-10
y (0.04) :	0.04749685	0.04749685	8.90732e-10
y (0.05) :	0.06183424	0.06183424	1.14732e-09
y (0.06) :	0.07721736	0.07721736	1.41872e-09
y (0.07) :	0.09367806	0.09367806	1.70558e-09
y (0.08) :	0.11124915	0.11124915	2.00859e-09
y (0.09) :	0.12996445	0.12996445	2.32849e-09
y (0.10) :	0.14985880	0.14985881	2.66600e-09

The significant digit of the error starts up at 10th decimal position and ends in 9th decimal position. The field of errors confines to the range [2.66600e-09, 2.03517e-10]. The approximations are correct to within this domain.

6.4. Equations in Bernoulli Form

There are some differential equations that are not directly belonged to the linear form as they explicitly appear. One of such type of equation is a classic example as represented below:

$$\frac{dy}{dx} + P(x)y = Q(x)y^n \tag{6.40}$$

in which n is a constant quantity different from 0 and 1. $P(x)$ and $Q(x)$ are functions of x or constants. This form (6.40) is known as **Bernoulli's equation** that can be transformed to a linear form on appropriate setting of the dependent variable y.

If we put $n = 0$ in the equation, we obtain a **linear nonhomogeneous** form. When $n = 1$, the equation reduces to a **linear homogeneous** form.

Dividing both sides of the equation by y^n and setting $u = y^{-n+1}$ we get another equation in reduced form that can be readily solved. Let us illustrate an example.

Example Solve $\dfrac{dy}{dx} - xy = -y^3e^{-x^2}$.

According to the method of solution just mentioned we divide the equation by y^3 in order to approach the linearity.

The equation now becomes

$$y^{-3}\frac{dy}{dx} - xy^{-2} = -e^{-x^2} \tag{A}$$

Setting a new variable u for y, $u = y^{-2}$ yields on differentiation

$$\frac{du}{dx} = -2y^{-3}\frac{dy}{dx}$$

The equation (A) is now reduced to a linear homogeneous form on substituting these values

$$\frac{du}{dx} + 2xu = 2e^{-x^2}$$

Multiplying by the I.F. $e^{\int 2x\,dx}$ and integrating we obtain the general solution of the equation

$$y^{-2} = (2x + C)e^{-x^2} \quad \text{or} \quad y^2 = \frac{e^{x^2}}{2x + C}$$

Let us determine the approximations of the differential equations of Bernoulli type with the help of the computer technique. The same rules apply as for the previous one.

Example 1

DE : $y' + xy = y^3 e^{x^2}$

CE : $Dy = (y^3 e^{x^2} - xy)dx$

PS : $y(x) = \sqrt{\dfrac{1}{2e^{x^2}(2 - x)}}$

IC : $y(0) = 0.5$, Width : 0.01

The Computer Solution of the IVP of Order 1

x-value		*Approx value*	*Exact Value*	*Error*
y (0.01)	:	0.50122965	0.50122965	– 4.18776e-13
y (0.02)	:	0.50241841	0.50241841	– 8.43436e-13
y (0.03)	:	0.50356607	0.50356607	– 1.27376e-12
y (0.04)	:	0.50467237	0.50467237	– 1.70963e-12
y (0.05)	:	0.50573712	0.50573712	– 2.15084e-12
y (0.06)	:	0.50676009	0.50676009	– 2.59726e-12
y (0.07)	:	0.50774111	0.50774111	– 3.04856e-12
y (0.08)	:	0.50867998	0.50867998	– 3.50475e-12
y (0.09)	:	0.50957654	0.50957654	– 3.96538e-12
y (0.10)	:	0.51043063	0.51043063	– 4.43057e-12

The significant digit of the error starts up at 13th decimal position and ends in 12th decimal position. The field of errors confines to the range [– 4.18776e-13, – 4.43057e-12]. The approximations are correct to within this domain.

Example 2

DE : $y' = y - \dfrac{2x}{y}$

CE : $y\,dy = (y^2 - 2x)dx$

$PS : y(x) = \sqrt{2x + 1}$

$IC : y(0) = 1,$ Width : 0.01

The Computer Solution of the IVP of Order 1

x-value		*Approx value*	*Exact Value*	*Error*
y (0.01)	:	1.00995049	1.00995049	– 4.16667e-12
y (0.02)	:	1.01980390	1.01980390	– 8.22076e-12
y (0.03)	:	1.02956301	1.02956301	– 1.21774e-11
y (0.04)	:	1.03923048	1.03923048	– 1.60489e-11
y (0.05)	:	1.04880885	1.04880885	– 1.98472e-11
y (0.06)	:	1.05830052	1.05830052	– 2.35822e-11
y (0.07)	:	1,06770783	1.06770783	– 2.72631e-11
y (0.08)	:	1.07703296	1.07703296	– 3.08977e-11
y (0.09)	:	1.08627805	1.08627805	– 3.44933e-11
y (0.10)	:	1.09544512	1.09544512	– 3.80562e-11

The significant digit of the error starts up at 12th decimal position and ends in 11th decimal position. The field of errors confines to the range [4.16667e-12, – 3.80562e-11]. The approximations are correct to within this domain.

Example 3

$DE : 2x^2y' = y^3 + xy$

$CE : 2x^2\,dy = y(y^2 + x)dx$

$PS : y(x) = \sqrt{\dfrac{x}{1 - Ln\ x}}$

$IC : y(1) = 1,$ Width : 0.01

The Computer Solution of the IVP of Order 1

x-value		*Approx value*	*Exact Value*	*Error*
y (1.01)	:	1.01002517	1.01002517	2.95408e-12
y (1.02)	:	1.02010134	1.02010134	6.00386e-12
y (1.03)	:	1.03022954	1.03022954	9.15068e-12

x-value		*Approx value*	*Exact Value*	*Error*
y (1.04)	:	1.04041080	1.04041080	1.23965e-11
y (1.05)	:	1.05064617	1.05064617	1.57427e-11
y (1.06)	:	1.06093671	1.06093671	1.91918e-11
y (1.07)	:	1.07128350	1.07128350	2.27454e-11
y (1.08)	:	1.08168763	1.08168763	2.64055e-11
y (1.09)	:	1.09215021	1.09215021	3.01752e-11
y (1.10)	:	1.10267237	1.10267237	3.40563e-11

The significant digit of the error starts up at 12th decimal position and ends in 11th decimal position. The field of errors confines to the range [3.40563e-11, 2.95408e-12]. The approximations are correct to within this domain.

Example 4

$DE : \dfrac{1}{y}\dfrac{dy}{dx} = x(y+2)$

$CE : \dfrac{1}{y}dy = x(y+2)dx$

$PS : y(x) = \dfrac{2}{3e^{-x^2} - 1}$

$IC : y(0) = 1,$ Width : 0.01

The Computer Solution of the IVP of Order 1

x-value		*Approx value*	*Exact Value*	*Error*
y (0.01)	:	1.00015002	1.00015002	– 9.37028e-14
y (0.02)	:	1.00060024	1.00060024.	– 3.75033e-13
y (0.03)	:	1.00135122	1.00135122	– 8.45102e-13
y (0.04)	:	1.00240385	1.00240385	– 1.50613e-12
y (0.05)	:	1.00375940	1.00375940	– 2.36167e-12
y (0.06)	:	1.00541950	1.00541950	– 3.41593e-12
y (0.07)	:	1.00738618	1.00738618	– 4.67493e-12
y (0.08)	:	1.00966180	1.00966180	– 6.14553e-12
y (0.09)	:	1.01224915	1.01224915	– 7.83573e-12
y (0.10)	:	1.01515139	1.01515139	– 9.75486e-12

The significant digit of the error starts up at 14th decimal position and ends in 12th decimal position. The field of errors confines to the range [– 9.37028e-14, – 9.75486e-12]. The approximations are correct to within this domain.

Example 5

$DE : 2x^3 \dfrac{dy}{dx} = y(2x^2 - y^2)$

$CE : 2x^3\, dy = y(2x^2 - y^2)dx$

$PS : y(x) = x(Ln\ x + 1)^{-1/2}$

$IC : y(1) = 1,$ Width : 0.01

The Computer Solution of the IVP of Order 1

x-value		*Approx value*	*Exact Value*	*Error*
y (1.01)	:	1.00501227	1.00501227	9.72555e-13
y (1.02)	:	1.01004822	1.01004822	1.86806e-12
y (1.03)	:	1.01510659	1.01510659	2.69385e-12
y (1.04)	:	1.02018619	1.02018619	3.45635e-12
y (1.05)	:	1.02528593	1.02528593	4.16134e-12
y (1.06)	:	1.03040474	1.03040474	4.81393e-12
y (1.07)	:	1.03554164	1.03554164	5.41855e-12
y (1.08)	:	1.04069570	1.04069570	5.97966e-12
y (1.09)	:	1.04586603	1.04586603	6.50080e-12
y (1.10)	:	1.05105181	1.05105181	6.98508e-12

The significant digit of the error starts up at 13th decimal position and ends in 12th decimal position. The field of errors confines to the range [6.98508e-12, 9.72555e-13]. The approximations are correct to within this domain.

Example 6

$DE : 2x^2y \dfrac{dy}{dx} = 1 - xy^2$

$CE : 2x^2y\, dy = (1 - xy^2)dx$

$PS\ :\ y(x) = \sqrt{\dfrac{Ln\ x + 1}{x}}$

$IC\ :\ y(1) = 1,$ Width : 0.01

The Computer Solution of the IVP of Order 1

x-value		*Approx value*	*Exact Value*	*Error*
y (1.01)	:	0.99997541	0.99997541	– 6.57252e-13
y (1.02)	:	0.99990324	0.99990324	– 1.26077e-12
y (1.03)	:	0.99978580	0.99978580	– 1.81555e-12
y (1.04)	:	0.99962527	0.99962527	– 2.32581e-12
y (1.05)	:	0.99942372	0.99942372	– 2.79453e-12
y (1.06)	:	0.99918311	0.99918311	– 3.22775e-12
y (1.07)	:	0.99890531	0.99890531	– 3.62599e-12
y (1.08)	:	0.99859208	0.99859208	– 3.99303e-12
y (1.09)	:	0.99824511	0.99824511	– 4.33142e-12
y (1.10)	:	0.99786599	0.99786599	– 4.64351e-12

The significant digit of the error starts up at 13th decimal position and ends in 12th decimal position. The field of errors confines to the range [– 6.57252e-13, – 4.64351e-12]. The approximations are correct to within this domain.

Example 7

$DE\ :\ x\dfrac{dy}{dx} = 2\sqrt{xy} - y$

$CE\ :\ x\,dy = [2\sqrt{xy} - y]dx$

$PS\ :\ y(x) = \dfrac{(x+1)^2}{x}$

$IC\ :\ y(0.5) = 4.5,$ Width : 0.01

The Computer Solution of the IVP of Order 1

x-value		*Approx value*	*Exact Value*	*Error*
y (0.51)	:	4.47078431	4.47078431	7.54357e-11
y (0.52)	:	4.44307692	4.44307692	1.42177e-10

x-value		*Approx value*	*Exact Value*	*Error*
y (0.53)	:	4.41679245	4.41679245	2.01298e-10
y (0.54)	:	4.39185185	4.39185185	2.53723e-10
y (0.55)	:	4.36818182	4.36818182	3.00254e-10
y (0.56)	:	4.34571429	4.34571429	3.41586e-10
y (0.57)	:	4.32438596	4.32438596	3.78326e-10
y (0.58)	:	4.30413793	4.30413793	4.10999e-10
y (0.59)	:	4.28491525	4.28491525	4.40068e-10
y (0.60)	:	4.26666667	4.26666667	4.65933e-10

The significant digit of the error starts up at 11th decimal position and ends in 10th decimal position. The field of errors confines to the range [4.65933e-10, 7.54357e-11]. The approximations are correct to within this domain.

Example 8

$$DE : \frac{Dy}{dx} = y(y^3 \text{ Cos } x + \text{Tan } x)$$

$$CE : \frac{dy}{y} = (y^3 \text{ Cos } x + \text{Tan } x)\, dx$$

$$PS : y(x) = \left[\frac{1}{\text{Cos}^2 x\,(\text{Cos } x - 3\text{Sin } x)}\right]^{1/3}$$

IC : $y(0) = 1$, Width : 0.01

The Computer Solution of the IVP of Order 1

x-value		*Approx value*	*Exact Value*	*Error*
y (0.01)	:	1.01025565	1.01025565	– 1.48680e-10
y (0.02)	:	1.02104640	1.02104640	– 3.11181e-10
y (0.03)	:	1.03241101	1.03241101	– 4.89377e-10
y (0.04)	:	1.04439273	1.04439273	– 6.85489e-10
y (0.05)	:	1.05704002	1.05704002	–9.02158e-10
y (0.06)	:	1.07040741	1.07040741	– 1.14255e-09
y (0.07)	:	1.08455651	1.08455651	– 1.41048e-09
y (0.08)	:	1.09955723	1.09955723	– 1.71056e-10

x-value		*Approx value*	*Exact Value*	*Error*
y (0.09)	:	1.11548935	1.11548935	– 2.04841e-09
y (0.10)	:	1.13244436	1.13244436	– 2.43092e-09

The significant digit of the error starts up at 10th decimal position and ends in 9th decimal position. The field of errors confines to the range [– 1.48680e-10, – 2.43092e-09]. The approximations are correct to within this domain.

Example 9

$DE : \dfrac{Dy}{dx} = y + xe^{y}$

$CE : Dy = (y + xe^{y})\, dx$

$PS : y(x) = \dfrac{x^2}{2} + \dfrac{x^3}{6} + \dfrac{x^4}{6} + \ldots$

$IC : y(0) = 0,$ Width : 0.01

The Computer Solution of the IVP of Order 1

x-value		*Approx value*	*Exact Value*	*Error*
y (0.01)	:	0.00005016	0.00005016	– 6.29711e-12
y (0.02)	:	0.00020136	0.00020136	– 2.16316e-10
y (0.03)	:	0.00045464	0.00045463	– 1.66286e-09
y (0.04)	:	0.00081110	0.00081109	– 7.07453e-09
y (0.05)	:	0.00127190	0.00127188	– 2.17886e-08
y (0.06)	:	0.00183821	0.00183816	– 5.47119e-08
y (0.07)	:	0.00251129	0.00251117	– 1.19332e-07
y (0.08)	:	0.00329239	0.00329216	– 2.34779e-07
y (0.09)	:	0.00418286	0.00418243	– 4.26945e-07
y (0.10)	:	0.00518406	0.00518333	– 7.29656e-07

The significant digit of the error starts up at 12th decimal position and ends in 7th decimal position. The field of errors confines to the range [– 6.29711e-12, – 7.29656e-07]. The approximations are correct to within this domain.

Example 10

$$DE : x\frac{dy}{dx} = y(x^2 + 3Ln\ y)$$

$$CE : x\,dy = y(x^2 + 3Ln\ y)\,dx$$

$$PS : y(x) = e^{x^2(x-1)}$$

IC : $y(1) = 1$, Width : 0.01

The Computer Solution of the IVP of Order 1

x-value		*Approx value*	*Exact Value*	*Error*
y (1.01)	:	1.01025321	1.01025321	2.23220e-10
y (1.02)	:	1.02102600	1.02102600	4.63971e-10
y (1.03)	:	1.03233889	1.03233890	7.23738e-10
y (1.04)	:	1.04421353	1.04421353	1.00414e-09
y (1.05)	:	1.05667269	1.05667269	1.30694e-09
y (1.06)	:	1.06974040	1.06974040	1.63407e-09
y (1.07)	:	1.08344199	1.08344199	1.98764e-09
y (1.08)	:	1.09780419	1.09780420	2.36994e-09
y (1.09)	:	1.11285524	1.11285524	2.78350e-09
y (1.10)	:	1.12862491	1.12862491	3.23107e-09

The significant digit of the error starts up at 10th decimal position and ends in 09th decimal position. The field of errors confines to the range [3.23107e-09, 2.23220e-10]. The approximations are correct to within this domain.

Example 11

$$DE : (1 - x^2)\frac{dy}{dx} = xy(1 + 2y)$$

$$CE : (1 - x^2)\,dy = xy(1 + 2y)\,dx$$

$$PS : y(x) = \frac{1}{1.73205081\sqrt{(x^2 - 1)} - 2}$$

IC : $y(2) = 1$, Width : 0.01

The Computer Solution of the IVP of Order 1

x-value		Approx value	Exact Value	Error
y (2.01)	:	0.98040807	0.98040807	– 4.09875e-09
y (2.02)	:	0.96159929	0.96159929	– 3.98992e-09
y (2.03)	:	0.94352713	0.94352713	– 3.88449e-09
y (2.04)	:	0.92614867	0.92614867	– 3.78252e-09
y (2.05)	:	0.90942430	0.90942429	– 3.68404e-09
y (2.06)	:	0.89331734	0.89331734	– 3.58902e-09
y (2.07)	:	0.87779385	0.87779385	– 3.49742e-09
y (2.08)	:	0.86282231	0.86282231	– 3.40917e-09
y (2.09)	:	0.84837347	0.84837346	– 3.32417e-09
y (2.10)	:	0.83442008	0.83442008	– 3.24233e-09

The significant digit of the error starts up at 9th decimal position and ends in 9th decimal position. The field of errors confines to the range [– 3.24233e-09, – 4.09875e-09]. The approximations are correct to within this domain.

Example 12

$$DE : \frac{x}{2}\frac{dy}{dx} = \sqrt{y}\,\text{Cos}\,x - y$$

$$CE : \frac{x}{2}\,dy = (\sqrt{y}\,\text{Cos}\,x - y)\,dx$$

$$PS : y(x) = \frac{(\text{Sin}\,x + 0.57079632)^2}{x^2}$$

$$IC : y\left(\frac{\pi}{2}\right) = 1, \qquad \text{Width} : 0.01$$

The Computer Solution of the IVP of Order 1

x-value		Approx value	Exact Value	Error
y (1.58079633)	:	0.98732531	0.98732530	– 6.28764e-09
y (1.59079633)	:	0.97476516	0.97476516	– 6.21016e-09
y (1.60079633)	:	0.96231830	0.96231830	– 6.13375e-09
y (1.61079633)	:	0.94998352	0.94998351	– 6.05837e-09
y (1.62079633)	:	0.93775963	0.93775963	– 5.98402e-09

x-value	*Approx value*	*Exact Value*	*Error*
y (1.63079633) :	0.92564552	0.92564551	– 5.91066e-09
y (1.64079633) :	0.91364009	0.91364008	– 5.83828e-09
y (1.65079633) :	0.90174228	0.90174227	– 5.76687e-09
y (1.66079633) :	0.88995108	0.88995107	– 5.69640e-09
y (1.67079633) :	0.87826551	0.87826550	– 5.62685e-09

The significant digit of the error starts up at 9th decimal position and ends in 9th decimal position. The field of errors confines to the range [– 5.62685e-09, – 6.28764e-09]. The approximations are correct to within this domain.

Example 13

$$DE : y^2 \frac{dy}{dx} = \frac{y^3 \text{ Cos } x}{\text{Sin } x} - x^2 \text{ Sin}^3 x$$

$$CE : y^2 \, dy = \left(\frac{y^3 \text{ Cos } x}{\text{Sin } x} - x^2 \text{ Sin}^3 x \right) dx$$

PS : $y(x) = \text{Sin } x(2.67835 - x^3)^{1/3}$

IC : $y(1) = 1$, Width : 0.01

The Computer Solution of the IVP of Order 1

x-value	*Approx value*	*Exact Value*	*Error*
y (1.01) :	1.00027765	1.00027762	– 2.57027e-08
y (1.02) :	1.00017820	1.00017817	– 2.60664e-08
y (1.03) :	0.99969066	0.99969063	– 2.64404e-08
y (1.04) :	0.99880338	0.99880335	– 2.68254e-08
y (1.05) :	0.99750394	0.99750391	– 2.72222e-08
y (1.06) :	0.99577910	0.99577908	– 2.76316e-08
y (1.07) :	0.99361470	0.99361467	– 2.80543e-08
y (1.08) :	0.99099550	0.99099547	– 2.84913e-08
y (1.09) :	0.98790514	0.98790511	– 2.89433e-08
y (1.10) :	0.98432592	0.98432589	– 2.94112e-08

The significant digit of the error starts up at 8th decimal position and ends in 8th decimal position. The field of errors confines to the range [– 2.57027e-08, – 2.94112e-08]. The approximations are correct to within this domain.

Example 14

$DE\ :\ x\dfrac{dy}{dx} + y(x^4y + 1) = 0$

$CE\ :\ x\,dy = -\,y(x^4y + 1)\,dx$

$PS\ :\ y(x) = \dfrac{6}{x(2x^3 + 5)}$

$IC\ :\ y(-1) = -2,$ Width : 0.01

The Computer Solution of the IVP of Order 1

x-value	*Approx value*	*Exact Value*	*Error*
y (– 0.99) :	– 1.98097735	– 1.98097735	– 4.50995e-10
y (– 0.98) :	– 1.96382395	– 1.96382395	– 8.40270e-10
y (– 0.97) :	– 1.94842241	– 1.94842241	– 1.17737e-09
y (– 0.96) :	– 1.93466826	– 1.93466826	– 1.47029e-09
y (– 0.95) :	– 1.92246845	– 1.92246845	– 1.72577e-09
y (– 0.94) :	– 1.91174001	– 1.91174001	– 1.94949e-09
y (– 0.93) :	– 1.90240897	– 1.90240897	– 2.14623e-09
y (– 0.92) :	– 1.89440936	– 1.89440936	– 2.32004e-09
y (– 0.91) :	– 1.8876824	– 1.88768241	– 2.47435e-09
y (– 0.90) :	– 1.88217579	– 1.8821758	– 2.61208e-09

The significant digit of the error starts up at 10th decimal position and ends in 9th decimal position. The field of errors confines to the range [– 4.50995e-10, – 2.61208e-09]. The approximations are correct to within this domain.

Example 15

$DE\ :\ \dfrac{1}{x}\dfrac{dy}{dx} = 6\sqrt{y} - y$

$CE\ :\ \dfrac{1}{x}\,dy = (6\sqrt{y} - y)\,dx$

$PS\ :\ y(x) = 36(1 - e^{-x^2/4})^2$

$IC\ :\ y(1) = 1.7614474,$ Width : 0.01

The Computer Solution of the IVP of Order 1

x-value		*Approx value*	*Exact Value*	*Error*
y (1.01)	:	1.82416698	1.82416695	– 3.17605e-08
y (1.02)	:	1.88829676	1.88829672	– 3.20336e-08
y (1.03)	:	1.95384463	1.95384459	– 3.23053e-08
y (1.04)	:	2.02081802	2.02081799	– 3.25757e-08
y (1.05)	:	2.08922388	2.08922385	– 3.28444e-08
y (1.06)	:	2.15906865	2.15906861	– 3.31114e-08
y (1.07)	:	2.23035827	2.23035824	– 3.33765e-08
y (1.08)	:	2.30309820	2.30309817	– 3.36397e-08
y (1.09)	:	2.37729338	2.37729335	– 3.39006e-08
y (1.10)	:	2.45294824	2.45294820	– 3.41592e-08

The significant digit of the error starts up at 8th decimal position and ends in 8th decimal position. The field of errors confines to the range [– 3.176005e-08, – 3.41592e-08]. The approximations are correct to within this domain.

6.5. Equations in Riccati Form

The differential equation

$$\frac{dy}{dx} = P(x) + Q(x) + R(x)y^2 \tag{6.50}$$

is known as **Riccati** equation. Fundamentally is was first considered by J. Bernoulli whose concepts had been further developed.

This equation (6.50) can be transformed to a Bernoulli equation with the substitution

$$y = y_1(x) + \frac{1}{u}$$

when the particular solution $y_1(x)$ satisfies the original equation. Then we have

$$P + Qy_1 + Ry_1^2 - \frac{1}{u^2}\frac{du}{dx} = \frac{dy_1}{dx} - \frac{1}{u^2}\frac{du}{dx}$$

$$= \frac{dy}{dx}$$

$$= \mathrm{P} + Q\left(y_1 + \frac{1}{u}\right) + R\left(y_1 + \frac{1}{u}\right)^2$$

Hence, by equating both sides we have

$$\frac{du}{dx} + (Q + 2Ry_1)u = -R$$

Integrating factor in this case is $e^{\int(Q+2Ry_1)dx}$ and we find the solution in u

$$ue^{\int(Q+2Ry_1)dx} = C - Re^{\int(Q+2Ry_1)dx}\, dx$$

The substitution of the value of u in the expression for y provides the general value of y that satisfies the equation (6.50).

Example Solve the differential equation

$$\frac{dy}{dx} = 1 - xy - y^2$$

It is a Riccati form where $P(x) = 1$, $Q(x) = -x$, $R(x) = -1$

A particular soultion is, by inference, given by $y = \frac{1}{x}$ that satisfies the equation.

Therefore, we can set $y = \frac{1}{x} + \frac{1}{u}$

that converts the equation in u as follows

$$\frac{dy}{dx} = -\frac{1}{x^2} - \frac{1}{u^2}\frac{du}{dx} = 1 - x\left(\frac{1}{x} + \frac{1}{u}\right) - \left(\frac{1}{x} + \frac{1}{u}\right)^2$$

Equating and rearranging we have

$$\frac{du}{dx} = u\left(x + \frac{2}{x}\right) + 1$$

or $$\frac{du}{dx} - \left(x + \frac{2}{x}\right)u = 1 .$$

This is a linear nonhomogeneous equation having the I.F.

$$e^{-\int(x+2/x)dx} = \frac{1}{x^2}\, e^{-x^2/2}$$

The solution of the equation is

$$\frac{u}{x^2}\, e^{-x^2/2} = C + \int \frac{e^{-x^2/2}}{x^2}\, dx \qquad \text{(A1)}$$

By means of the series expansion we have

$$e^{-x^2/2} = 1 - \frac{x^2}{2} + \frac{x^4}{8} - \frac{x^6}{48}$$ (only 4 terms of the series are considered)

Now, $\dfrac{e^{-x^2/2}}{x^2}\,dx = \displaystyle\int\left(x^{-2} - \frac{1}{2} + \frac{x^2}{8} - \frac{x^4}{48}\right)dx = -x^{-1} - \frac{x}{2} + \frac{x^3}{24} - \frac{x^5}{240}$

Hence, the equation (A1) takes the form

$$\frac{u}{x^2}e^{-x^2/2} = C - \frac{1}{x} - \frac{x}{2} + \frac{x^3}{24} - \frac{x^5}{240}$$

Transforming in y and rearranging yields

$$\frac{x}{xy-1} = e^{x^2/2}\left[Cx^2 - x - \frac{x^3}{2} + \frac{x^5}{24} - \frac{x^7}{240}\right]$$

For the approximations of the initial value problems of Riccati type applying the classical Runge-Kutta method I use the same rules as described before. Some examples are given for elaboration as follows:

Example 1

DE : $x^2\dfrac{dy}{dx} = (1 - xy - x^2y^2)$

CE : $x^2\,dy = (1 - xy - x^2y^2)\,dx$

PS : $y(x) = -\dfrac{1}{x}$

IC : $y(1) = -1$, Width : 0.01

The Computer Solution of the IVP of Order 1

x-value		*Approx value*	*Exact Value*	*Error*
y (1.01)	:	– 0.99009901	– 0.99009901	– 1.21112e-11
y (1.02)	:	– 0.98039216	– 0.98039216	– 2.36439e-11
y (1.03)	:	– 0.97087379	– 0.97087379	– 3.46367e-11
y (1.04)	:	– 0.96153846	– 0.96153846	– 4.51251e-11
y (1.05)	:	– 0.95238095	– 0.95238095	– 5.51423e-11
y (1.06)	:	– 0.94339623	– 0.94339623	– 6.47186e-11
y (1.07)	:	– 0.93457944	– 0.93457944	– 7.38823e-11
y (1.08)	:	– 0.92592593	– 0.92592593	– 8.26595e-11
y (1.09)	:	– 0.91743119	– 0.91743119	– 9.10749e-11
y (1.10)	:	– 0.90909091	– 0.90909091	– 9.91508e-11

The significant digit of the error starts up at 11th decimal position and ends in 11th decimal position. The field of errors confines to the range [– 1.21112e-11, – 9.91508e-11]. The approximations are correct to within this domain.

Example 2

$$DE : x\frac{dy}{dx} = x^2 + y^2 + y$$

$$CE : x\,dy = (x^2 + y^2 + y)\,dx$$

$$PS : y(x) = x\,\text{Tan}\left(x + \frac{\pi}{4} - 2\right)$$

$$IC : y(2) = 2, \qquad \text{Width} : 0.01$$

The Computer Solution of the IVP of Order 1

x-value		*Approx value*	*Exact Value*	*Error*
y (2.01)	:	2.05060743	2.05060742	– 3.66590e-09
y (2.02)	:	2.10246020	2.10246020	– 3.74240e-09
y (2.03)	:	2.15560586	2.15560586	– 3.81922e-09
y (2.04)	:	2.21009451	2.21009450	– 3.89587e-09
y (2.05)	:	2.26597896	2.26597896	– 3.97208e-09
y (2.06)	:	2.32331495	2.32331495	– 4.04741e-09
y (2.07)	:	2.38216132	2.38216132	– 4.12138e-09
y (2.08)	:	2.44258025	2.44258025	– 4.19340e-09
y (2.09)	:	2.50463750	2.50463750	– 4.26281e-09
y (2.10)	:	2.56840265	2.56840264	– 4.32882e-09

The significant digit of the error starts up at 9th decimal position and ends in 9th decimal position. The field of errors confines to the range [– 3.66590e-09, – 4.32882e-09]. The approximations are correct to within this domain.

Example 3

$$DE : \frac{Dy}{dx} = 1 + \frac{y}{x} + \left(\frac{y}{x}\right)^2$$

$$CE : dy = \left[1 + \frac{y}{x} + \left(\frac{y}{x}\right)^2\right] dx$$

PS : $y(x) = x \text{ Tan } (Ln\, x)$

IC : $y(1) = 0$, Width : 0.01

The Computer Solution of the IVP of Order 1

x-value		*Approx value*	*Exact Value*	*Error*
y (1.01)	:	0.01005017	0.01005017	– 2.01127e-12
y (1.02)	:	0.02020132	0.02020132	– 3.92257e-12
y (1.03)	:	0.03045444	0.03045444	– 5.73754e-12
y (1.04)	:	0.04081047	0.04081047	– 7.45960e-12
y (1.05)	:	0.05127036	0.05127036	– 9.09198e-12
y (1.06)	:	0.06183504	0.06183504	– 1.06378e-11
y (1.07)	:	0.07250542	0.07250542	– 1.20998e-11
y (1.08)	:	0.08328242	0.08328242	– 1.34807e-11
y (1.09)	:	0.09416692	0.09416692	– 1.47832e-11
y (1.10)	:	0.10515982	0.10515982	– 1.60096e-11

The significant digit of the error starts up at 12th decimal position and ends in 11th decimal position. The field of errors confines to the range [– 1.60096e-11, 2.01127e-12]. The approximations are correct to within this domain.

Example 4

$$DE : \frac{Dy}{dx} = \frac{x^2 + y - 2xy^2}{x(1 - x^3)}$$

$$CE : x(1 - x^3)dy = (x^2 + y - 2xy^2)\, dx$$

$$PS : y(x) = x^2 + \frac{x - x^4}{x^2 + 1}$$

IC : $y(-1) = 0$, Width : 0.01

The Computer Solution of the IVP of Order 1

x-value		*Approx value*	*Exact Value*	*Error*
y (– 0.99)	:	– 0.00499975	– 0.00499975	– 1.31512e-12
y (– 0.98)	:	– 0.00999796	– 0.00999796	– 2.65598e-12
y (– 0.97)	:	– 0.01499304	– 0.01499304	– 4.02201e-12

x-value		*Approx value*	*Exact Value*	*Error*
y (– 0.96)	:	– 0.01998335	– 0.01998335	– 5.41258e-12
y (– 0.95)	:	– 0.02496715	– 0.02496715	– 6.82699e-12
y (– 0.94)	:	– 0.02994266	– 0.02994266	– 8.26448e-12
y (– 0.93)	:	– 0.03490804	– 0.03490804	– 9.72425e-12
y (– 0.92)	:	– 0.03986135	– 0.03986135	– 1.12055e-11
y (– 0.91)	:	– 0.04480061	– 0.04480061	– 1.27072e-11
y (– 0.90)	:	– 0.04972376	– 0.04972376	– 1.42286e-11

The significant digit of the error starts up at 12th decimal position and ends in 11th decimal position. The field of errors confines to the range [– 1.31512e-12, – 1.42286e-11]. The approximations are correct to within this domain.

Example 5

DE : $x \dfrac{dy}{dx} = y^2 - 3y + 2$

CE : $x\,dy = (y^2 - 3y + 2)\,dx$

PS : $y(x) = \dfrac{2(x-1)}{2x-1}$

IC : $y(1) = 0$, Width : 0.01

The Computer Solution of the IVP of Order 1

x-value		*Approx value*	*Exact Value*	*Error*
y (1.01)	:	0.01960784	0.01960784	1.33454e-11
y (1.02)	:	0.03846154	0.03846154	2.44767e-11
y (1.03)	:	0.05660377	0.05660377	3.37495e-11
y (1.04)	:	0.07407407	0.07407407	4.14588e-11
y (1.05)	:	0.09090909	0.09090909	4.78507e-11
y (1.06)	:	0.10714286	0.10714286	5.31303e-11
y (1.07)	:	0.12280702	0.12280702	5.74696e-11
y (1.08)	:	0.13793103	0.13793103	6.10129e-11
y (1.09)	:	0.15254237	0.15254237	6.38816e-11
y (1.10)	:	0.16666667	0.16666667	6.61780e-11

The significant digit of the error starts up at 11th decimal position and ends in 11th decimal position. The field of errors confines to the range [6.6178e-11, 1.33454e-11]. The approximations are correct to within this domain.

Example 6

$$DE : \frac{Dy}{dx} = x^2 - y^2$$

$$CE : Dy = (x^2 - y^2)\, dx$$

$$PS : y(x) = \frac{x^3}{3} - \frac{x^7}{63} - \frac{2x^{11}}{2079} - \ldots$$

$IC : y(0) = 0,$ Width : 0.01

The Computer Solution of the IVP of Order 1

x-value		*Approx value*	*Exact Value*	*Error*
y (0.01)	:	3.33333333e-07	3.33333333e-07	– 2.48017e-18
y (0.02)	:	2.66666665e-06	2.66666665e-06	5.50595e-16
y (0.03)	:	8.99999965e-06	8.99999965e-06	2.49252e-15
y (0.04)	:	2.13333307e-05	2.13333307e-05	6.65593e-15
y (0.05)	:	4.16666543e-05	4.16666543e-05	1.38671e-14
y (0.06)	:	7.19999555e-05	7.19999556e-05	2.49152e-14
y (0.07)	:	0.00011433	0.00011433	4.04352e-14
y (0.08)	:	0.00017067	0.00017067	6.05486e-14
y (0.09)	:	0.00024300	0.00024300	8.36973e-14
y (0.10)	:	0.00033333	0.00033333	1.05730e-13

The significant digit of the error starts up at 18th decimal position and ends in 13th decimal position. The field of errors confines to the range [1.0573e-13, – 2.48017e-18]. The approximations are correct to within this domain.

Example 7

$$DE : \frac{Dy}{dx} = \frac{y^2 - 3y + 2}{x^2 - 3x + 2}$$

$$CE : (x^2 - 3x + 2)dy = (y^2 - 3y + 2)\, dx$$

$$PS : y(x) = x$$

$IC : y(0) = 0,$ Width : 0.01

The Computer Solution of the IVP of Order 1

x-value		*Approx value*	*Exact Value*	*Error*
y (0.01)	:	0.01	0.01	0
y (0.02)	:	0.02	0.02	0
y (0.03)	:	0.03	0.03	0
y (0.04)	:	0.04	0.04	0
y (0.05)	:	0.05	0.05	0
y (0.06)	:	0.06	0.06	0
y (0.07)	:	0.07	0.07	0
y (0.08)	:	0.08	0.08	0
y (0.09)	:	0.09	0.09	0
y (0.10)	:	0.10	0.10	0

The significant digit of the error starts up at 0th decimal position and ends in 0th decimal position. The field of errors confines to the range [0, 0]. The approximations are correct to within this domain.

Example 8

$$DE \; : \; \frac{Dy}{dx} = x^2y^2 - 1$$

$$CE \; : \; Dy = (x^2y^2 - 1)\, dx$$

$$PS \; : \; y(x) = 1 - x + \frac{x^3}{3} - \frac{x^4}{2} + \frac{x^5}{5} + \ldots$$

IC : $y(0) = 1$, Width : 0.01

The Computer Solution of the IVP of Order 1

x-value		*Approx value*	*Exact Value*	*Error*
y (0.01)	:	0.99000033	0.99000033	– 9.35585e-13
y (0.02)	:	0.98000259	0.98000259	– 8.46578e-12
y (0.03)	:	0.97000860	0.97000860	– 7.83927e-11
y (0.04)	:	0.96002007	0.96002007	– 4.20564e-10
y (0.05)	:	0.95003861	0.95003860	– 1.56107e-09
y (0.06)	:	0.94006568	0.94006568	– 4.55174e-09

x-value		*Approx value*	*Exact Value*	*Error*
y (0.07)	:	0.93010268	0.93010266	– 1.12174e-08
y (0.08)	:	0.92015087	0.92015084	– 2.44322e-08
y (0.09)	:	0.91021142	0.91021138	– 4.84157e-08
y (0.10)	:	0.90028542	0.90028533	– 8.90433e-08

The significant digit of the error starts up at 13th decimal position and ends in 8th decimal position. The field of errors confines to the range [– 9.35585e-13, – 8.90433e-08]. The approximations are correct to within this domain.

Chapter 7

Second-Order Initial-Value Problems

7.1. Preliminary Concepts

The present chapter contains an account of fundamentals and applications involving the differential equations of second order. The second order differential equation can be represented in compact form

$$G(x, y, y', y'') = 0$$

or explicitly

$$y'' = \phi(x, y, y') \tag{7.10}$$

The equation (7.10) describes a relationship involving the differentials of the first and second order with the variables, dependent and independent, and the function $y(x)$.

Let us consider a functional polynomial of $\frac{dy}{dx}$ that can be expressed as

$$\frac{d^m y}{dx^m} + \frac{P_1 d^{m-1} y}{dx^{m-2}} + \frac{P_2 d^{m-2} y}{dx^{m-2}} + \dots + \frac{P_{m-1} dy}{dx} + P_m y = Q \tag{7.11}$$

where $P_1, P_2, \dots, P_m$ and Q are functions of x or constants.

The equation (7.11) is the general form of a **linear differential equation of the m-th order**. If we put $m = 1$ in equation (7.11) we obtain a relation

$$\frac{dy}{dx} + P_1 y = Q$$

which is equivalent to the first-order linear form (6.10) described in chapter 6 ([illegible] 6.1). The relation (7.11) furnishes another equation by putting $m = 2$

$$\frac{d^2y}{dx^2} + P_1 \frac{dy}{dx} + P_2 y = Q \tag{7.12}$$

that is the required linear differential equation of order 2.

Linear differential equations of second order are extremely important in many branches of mathematics, mathematical physics and engineering.

There exist various types of second order linear differential equations. But this chapter concerns only with three types of equations. The second order linear homogeneous and linear nonhomogeneous differential equations that include the equations from Euler, Bessel, Lagrange, Abel and the nonlinear differential equations which include the equations from Van der Pol have been dealt with next.

7.2. Linear Homogeneous Type

By putting $Q = 0$ in equation (7.12) we get a new equation

$$\frac{d^2y}{dx^2} + P_1 \frac{dy}{dx} + P_2 y = 0 \tag{7.20}$$

in which the right side is free of function and is of linear homogeneous type.

There are several methods by which the equation of type (7.20) can be readily solved. As the simplest possible method we accept a trial solution of (7.20) for which we set $y = e^{\lambda x}$, λ is a constant quantity.

Putting $y = e^{\lambda x}$ in (7.20) yields

$e^{\lambda x}(\lambda^2 + P_1 \lambda + P_2) = 0$, the factor $e^{\lambda x}$ being common to all.

Hence, $\lambda^2 + P_1 \lambda + P_2 = 0$, since $e^{\lambda x}$ can never be zero.

This equation is called the auxiliary or characteristic equation of (7.20) and has two roots, namely λ_1 and λ_2.

Obviously, $y = C_1 e^{\lambda_1 x}$ and $y = C_2 e^{\lambda_2 x}$ are the solutions of (7.20) and as the general solution we have the expression

$$y = C_1 e^{\lambda_1 x} + C_2 e^{\lambda_2 x} \tag{7.21}$$

containing two arbitrary constants according to the order of the equation. The general solution is dependent on the nature of the roots λ_1 and λ_2.

In the case of real and distinct roots the solution (7.21) satisfies the original differential equation (7.20).

If $\lambda_1 = \lambda_2$ (equal roots), The equation (7.21) takes the shape as

$$y = e^{\mu x}(C_1 + C_2) = Ce^{\mu x},\ C = C_1 + C_2 \text{ and } \mu = \lambda_1 = \lambda_2,$$

that is not the general solution because it contains only one constant.

The general solution will be, thus, $y = (C_1 + C_2x)e^{\mu x}$

if we accept $y = e^{\mu x}u$ as a trial solution, where u is a function of x.

If $\lambda_1 = \alpha + i\beta$ and $\lambda_2 = \alpha - i\beta$ (complex roots),

then the general solution of (7.20) is

$$y = C_1e^{(\alpha+i\beta)x} + C_2e^{(\alpha-i\beta)x}$$

Using the trigonometric relations we get another form

$$y = e^{\alpha x}(C_3\text{Cos } \beta x + C_4\text{Sin } \beta x).$$

Example Solve $\frac{d^2y}{dx^2} - \frac{dy}{dx} - 2y = 0$

If $y = e^{\lambda x}$ is a solution for some value of λ, then we get

$$\frac{d^2y}{dx^2} - \frac{dy}{dx} - 2y = e^{\lambda x}(\lambda^2 - \lambda - 2) = 0$$

which is satisfied when $\lambda = -1$ or 2 (real and distinct roots)

Hence, the general solution is

$$y = C_1e^{-x} + C_2e^{2x}.$$

Example Solve $y'' - 2y' + y = 0$

By setting $y = e^{\lambda x}$ we obtain

$$y'' - 2y' + y = e^{\lambda x}(\lambda^2 - 2\lambda + 1) = 0$$

which is satisfied when $x = 1$ twice

Here, the characteristic equation $\lambda^2 - 2\lambda + 1 = 0$ has repeated roots and the general solution is

$$y = e^x(C_1 + C_2x).$$

Example $\frac{d^2y}{dx^2} + 4\frac{dy}{dx} + 13y = 0$

As a trial solution let us write $y = e^{\lambda x}$

Then $\frac{d^2y}{dx^2} + 4\frac{dy}{dx} + 13y = e^{\lambda x}(\lambda^2 + 4\lambda + 13) = 0$

yields $\lambda = -2 \pm 3i$ (complex roots).

According to the theoretical discussion

$$y = e^{-2x}(C_1 \text{ Cos } 3x + C_2 \text{ Sin } 3x)$$

is the general solution.

As in the case of initial-valued first-order differential equations there are many numerical methods for the approximation of the solution to initial value problem of order 2 available. Some of them have already been mentioned in section 5.2.

In this section I confine myself to discussing about the classical **Runge-Kutta** method of order 4, which is definitely a more efficient method that can be applied for the approximation of ordinary linear differential equation of the second order.

The main mathematical achievement in using the fourth-order Runge-Kutta method involves the function evaluations of G. The technique of evaluation for the formula presented here requires more operations.

$$y_{v+1} = y_v + wy'_v + \frac{w(G_1 + G_2 + G_3)}{6} \tag{7.22}$$

$$y'_{v+1} = y'_v + \frac{G_1 + 2G_2 + 2G_3 + G_4}{6} \tag{7.23}$$

where $v = 0, 1, 2, \ldots$. Taking w as width the functions are defined by

$$G_1 = wG(x_v, y_v, y'_v)$$

$$G_2 = wG\left(x_v + \frac{w}{2}, y_v + \frac{wy'_v}{2}, y'_v + \frac{G_1}{2}\right)$$

$$G_3 = wG\left(x_v + \frac{w}{2}, y_v + \frac{wy'_v}{2} + \frac{G_1}{4}, y'_v + \frac{G_2}{2}\right)$$

$$G_4 = wG\left(x_v + w, y_v + wy'_v + \frac{wG_2}{2}, y'_v + G_3\right)$$

Now to approximate the initial value problem of order 2 by means of C++ program named IVPD2LIN applying the method from Runge-Kutta the following steps should be performed.

a) The initial conditions of the methematical problem, i.e. the starting values of x, y, y' will be put in the DEFINITION Block of IC.

b) The exact solutions for $y(x)$ and $y'(x)$ will be inserted in the MEMBER FUNCTION SetACT.

c) The MEMBER FUNCTION SetDE will be furnished with the right side expression of the Computer equation (CE) of the initial value problem given in each example. y' or $\frac{dy}{dx}$ is replaced by $y1$.

After processing the program calculates simultaneously the exact values of $y(x)$ and $y'(x)$ with the corresponding increments of the independent variable x, so that the errors caused by the approximations can be found out.

Example 1

DE : $y'' + 3y' + 2y = 0$

CE : $y'' = -3y' - 2y$

PS : $y(x) = e^{-x}, y' = -e^{-x}$

IC : $y(0) = 1, \quad y'(0) = -1,$ Width : 0.01

The Computer Solution of the IVP of Order 2

x-value	*y-Approx*	*y-Exact*	*Error*	*y'-Approx*	*y'-Exact*	*Error*
0.01	0.99004983	0.99004983	–8.319e-13	–0.99004983	–0.99004983	–8.319e-13
0.02	0.98019867	0.98019867	–8.267e-10	–0.98019859	–0.98019867	–8.126e-08
0.03	0.97044554	0.97044553	–2.445e-09	–0.97044537	–0.97044553	–1.593e-07
0.04	0.96078944	0.96078944	–4.823e-09	–0.96078920	–0.96078944	–2.342e-07
0.05	0.95122943	0.95122942	–7.931e-09	–0.95122912	–0.95122942	–3.060e-07
0.06	0.94176455	0.94176453	–1.174e-08	–0.94176416	–0.94176453	–3.749e-07
0.07	0.93239384	0.93239382	–1.622e-08	–0.93239338	–0.93239382	–4.408e-07
0.08	0.92311637	0.92311635	–2.133e-08	–0.92311584	–0.92311635	–5.040e-07
0.09	0.91393121	0.91393119	–2.707e-08	–0.91393062	–0.91393119	–5.644e-07
0.10	0.90483745	0.90483742	–3.339e-08	–0.90483680	–0.90483742	–6.221e-07

The field of errors in y-approximation confines to the range [– 8.319e-13, – 3.339e-08) and the field of errors in y'-approximation is limited to the range [– 8.319e-13, – 6.221e-07]. The approximations are accurate to within these confines.

Example 2

DE : $y'' + y = 0$

CE : $y'' = -y$

PS : $y = \text{Sin } x, y' = \text{Cos } x$

IC : $y(0) = 0, \quad y'(0) = 1,$ Width : 0.01

The Computer Solution of the IVP of Order 2

x-value	*y-Approx*	*y-Exact*	*Error*	*y'-Approx*	*y'-Exact*	*Error*
0.01	0.00999983	0.00999983	8.333e-13	0.99995000	0.99995000	−1.443e-15
0.02	0.01999867	0.00999867	5.833e-12	0.99980001	0.99980001	4.166e-10
0.03	0.02999550	0.02999550	6.666e-12	0.99955003	0.99955003	−1.237e-13
0.04	0.03998933	0.03998933	−5.003e-12	0.99920011	0.99920011	−1.250e-09
0.05	0.04997917	0.04997917	−3.750e-11	0.99875026	0.99875026	−3.333e-09
0.06	0.05996401	0.05996401	−9.916e-11	0.99820055	0.99820054	−6.249e-09
0.07	0.06994285	0.06994285	−1.983e-10	0.99755101	0.99755100	−9.996e-09
0.08	0.07991469	0.07991469	−3.432e-10	0.99680172	0.99680171	−1.457e-08
0.09	0.08987855	0.08987855	−5.422e-10	0.99595275	0.99595273	−1.998e-08
0.10	0.09983342	0.09983342	−8.037e-10	0.99500419	0.99500417	−2.622e-08

The field of errors in y-approximation confines to the range [8.333e-13, − 8.037e-10] and the field of errors in y'-approximation is limited to the range [− 1.443e-15, − 2.622e-08]. The approximations are accurate to within these confines.

Example 3

DE : $y'' + y' - 6y = 0$

CE : $y'' = -y' + 6y$

PS : $y = \dfrac{e^{2x} + 4e^{-3x}}{5}, \; y' = \dfrac{2(e^{2x} - 6e^{-3x})}{5}$

IC : $y(0) = 1, \quad y'(0) = 2,$ Width : 0.01

The Computer Solution of the IVP of Order 2

x-value	*y-Approx*	*y-Exact*	*Error*	*y'-Approx*	*y'-Exact*	*Error*
0.01	0.98039670	0.98039669	−1.558e-10	−1.92098875	−1.92098874	4.943e-10
0.02	0.96157384	0.96157378	−5.747e-08	−1.84390488	−1.84391057	−5.689e-06
0.03	0.94351243	0.94351226	−1.699e-07	−1.76868905	−1.76870023	−1.117e-05
0.04	0.92619410	0.92619376	−3.353e-07	−1.69527776	−1.69529422	−1.646e-05
0.05	0.90960112	0.90960056	−5.520e-07	−1.62360922	−1.62363078	−2.156e-05

x-value	*y-Approx*	*y-Exact*	*Error*	*y'-Approx*	*y'-Exact*	*Error*
0.06	0.89371636	0.89371554	-8.180e-07	-1.55362329	-1.55364977	-2.648e-05
0.07	0.87852329	0.87852216	-1.132e-06	-1.48526144	-1.48529267	-3.123e-05
0.08	0.86400595	0.86400446	-1.491e-06	-1.41846669	-1.41850252	-3.583e-05
0.09	0.85014896	0.85014707	-1.896e-06	-1.35318357	-1.35322384	-4.027e-05
0.10	0.83693747	0.83693513	-2.343e-06	-1.28935806	-1.28940263	-4.457e-05

The field of errors in y-approximation confines to the range [–1.558e-10, – 2.343e-06] and the field of errors in y'-approximation is limited to the range [4.943e-10, – 4.457e-05]. The approximations are accurate to within these confines.

Example 4

DE : $y'' + 8y = 0$ (Harmonic oscillator)

CE : $y'' = -8y$

PS : $y = \dfrac{\text{Cos}(2\sqrt{2}x)}{2}$, $y' = -\sqrt{2}\,\text{Sin}(2\sqrt{2}x)$

IC : $y(0) = 0.5$, $y'(0) = 0$, Width : 0.01

The Computer Solution of the IVP of Order 2

x-value	*y-Approx*	*y-Exact*	*Error*	*y'-Approx*	*y'-Exact*	*Error*
0.01	0.49980001	0.49980001	-3.555e-13	-0.03999467	-0.03999467	-2.133e-10
0.02	0.49920024	0.49920021	-2.667e-08	-0.07995467	-0.07995734	-2.666e-06
0.03	0.49820116	0.49820108	-7.998e-08	-0.11985072	-0.11985605	-5.329e-06
0.04	0.49680357	0.49680341	-1.599e-07	-0.15965090	-0.15965889	-7.984e-06
0.05	0.49500859	0.49500833	-2.662e-07	-0.19932337	-0.19933400	-1.063e-05
0.06	0.49281766	0.49281726	-3.989e-07	-0.23883640	-0.23884966	-1.325e-05
0.07	0.49023253	0.49023197	-5.578e-07	-0.27815839	-0.27817425	-1.586e-05
0.08	0.48725526	0.48725452	-7.425e-07	-0.31725787	-0.31727632	-1.844e-05
0.09	0.48388824	0.48388729	-9.529e-07	-0.35610358	-0.35612458	-2.100e-05
0.10	0.48013417	0.48013298	-1.189e-06	-0.39466444	-0.39468796	-2.352e-05

The field of errors in y-approximation confines to the range [–3.555e-13, – 1.189e-06] and the field of errors in y'-approximation is limited to the range [–2.133e-10, – 2.352e-05]. The approximations are accurate to within these confines.

Example 5

DE : $y'' + 2y' + 5y = 0$

CE : $y'' = -2y' - 5y$

PS : $y = \dfrac{e^{-x}\text{Sin}(2x)}{4}, y' = \dfrac{e^{-x}[2\text{Cos}(2x) - \text{Sin}(2x)]}{4}$

IC : $y(0) = 0$, $y'(0) = 0.5$, Width : 0.01

The Computer Solution of the IVP of Order 2

x-value	*y-Approx*	*y-Exact*	*Error*	*y'-Approx*	*y'-Exact*	*Error*
0.01	0.00494992	0.00494992	–7.932e-12	0.48997600	0.48997600	–9.070e-12
0.02	0.00979938	0.00979937	–5.005e-09	0.47990843	0.47990794	–4.939e-07
0.03	0.01454797	0.01454795	–1.481e-08	0.46980265	0.46980168	–9.698e-07
0.04	0.01919533	0.01919530	–2.925e-08	0.45966441	0.45966298	–1.428e-06
0.05	0.02374117	0.02374112	–4.814e-08	0.44949937	0.44949750	–1.868e-06
0.06	0.02818525	0.02818518	–7.130e-08	0.43931309	0.4331080	–2.291e-06
0.07	0.03252738	0.03252728	–9.856e-08	0.42911105	0.42910835	–2.695e-06
0.08	0.03676744	0.03676731	–1.297e-07	0.41889859	0.41889551	–3.083e-06
0.09	0.04090534	0.04090518	–1.646e-07	0.40868099	0.40867754	–3.452e-06
0.10	0.04494106	0.04494086	–2.031e-07	0.39846340	0.39845959	–3.805e-06

The field of errors in y-approximation confines to the range [– 7.932e-12, – 2.031e-07] and the field of errors in y'-approximation is limited to the range [– 9.070e-12, – 3.805e-06]. The approximations are accurate to within these confines.

Example 6

DE : $2y'' + y' - y = 0$

CE : $y'' = \dfrac{(-y' + y)}{2}$

PS : $y = 9e^{x/2} - 4e^{-x}$, $y' = \dfrac{9e^{x/2}}{2} + 4e^{-x}$

IC : $y(\text{Ln } 4) = 17$, $y'(\text{Ln } 4) = 10$, Width : 0.01

The Computer Solution of the IVP of Order 2

x-value	*y-Approx*	*y-Exact*	*Error*	*y'-Approx*	*y'-Exact*	*Error*
1.3963	17.10017554	17.10017554	–1.300e-12	10.03516252	10.03516252	–5.986e-13
1.4063	17.20070433	17.20070433	-9.483e-11	10.07065019	10.07065018	-9.718e-09

x-value	y-Approx	y-Exact	Error	y'-Approx	y'-Exact	Error
1.4163	17.30158963	17.30158963	−3.009e-10	10.10646314	10.10646312	−2.068e-08
1.4263	17.40283468	17.40283468	−6.293e-10	10.14260153	10.1426015	−3.289e-08
1.4363	17.50444275	17.50444274	−1.092e-09	10.17906556	10.17906551	−4.631e-08
1.4463	17.60641708	17.60641708	−1.702e-09	10.21585540	10.21585534	−6.095e-08
1.4563	17.70876094	17.70876094	−2.471e-09	10.25297128	10.25297120	−7.680e-08
1.4663	17.81147759	17.81147759	−3.410e-09	10.29041341	10.29041331	−9.383e-08
1.4763	17.91457030	17.91457029	−4.532e-09	10.32818204	10.32818192	−1.121e-07
1.4863	18.01804232	18.01804232	−5.848e-09	10.36627742	10.36627729	−1.314e-07

The field of errors in y-approximation confines to the range [−1.300e-12, − 5.848e-09] and the field of errors in y'-approximation is limited to the range [−5.986e-13, − 1.314e-07]. The approximations are accurate to within these confines.

Example 7

DE : $y'' - 2y' - 15y = 0$

CE : $y'' = 2y' + 15y$

PS : $y = \dfrac{4e^{5x}}{5} - 2e^{-3x}$, $y' = 4e^{5x} + 6e^{-3x}$

IC : $y(0) = -1.2$, $y'(0) = 10$, Width : 0.01

The Computer Solution of the IVP of Order 2

x-value	y-Approx	y-Exact	Error	y'-Approx	y'-Exact	Error
0.01	−1.09987419	−1.09987419	2.504e-09	10.02775758	10.02775759	9.295e-09
0.02	−0.99939207	−0.99939233	−2.668e-07	10.07129834	10.07127087	−2.747e-05
0.03	−0.89839414	−0.89839498	−8.389e-07	10.13098218	10.13092408	−5.810e-05
0.04	−0.79671692	−0.79671867	−1.747e-06	10.20722575	10.20713365	−9.210e-05
0.05	−0.69419259	−0.69419562	−3.026e-06	10.30047921	10.30034953	−0.000012
0.06	−0.59064866	−0.59065338	−4.714e-06	10.41122760	10.41105650	−0.000017
0.07	−0.48590760	−0.48591445	−6.851e-06	10.53999228	10.53977567	−0.000021
0.08	−0.37978648	−0.37979596	−9.480e-06	10.68733243	10.68706596	−0.000026
0.09	−0.27209659	−0.27210924	−1.265e-05	10.85384671	10.85352571	−0.000032
0.10	−0.16264303	−0.16265942	−1.640e-05	11.04017491	11.03979441	−0.000038

The field of errors in y-approximation confines to the range [2.504e-09, – 1.640e-05] and the field of errors in y'-approximation is limited to the range [9.295e-09, – 0.00038]. The approximations are accurate to within these confines.

Example 8

DE : $y'' + 2y' + 4y = 0$

CE : $y'' = -2y' - 4y$

PS : $y = e^{-x}[\sqrt{3} \text{ Sin } \sqrt{3}x + 3 \text{ Cos } \sqrt{3}x]$, $y' = -4\sqrt{3}e^{-x} \text{ Sin } \sqrt{3}x$

IC : $y(0) = 3$, $y'(0) = 0$, Width : 0.01

The Computer Solution of the IVP of Order 2

x-value	*y-Approx*	*y-Exact*	*Error*	*y'-Approx*	*y'-Exact*	*Error*
0.01	2.99940400	2.99940400	–7.973e-11	–0.11880004	–0.11880004	1.600e-10
0.02	2.99763200	2.99763200	–5.523e-10	–0.23520060	–0.23520063	–3.888e-08
0.03	2.99470798	2.99470798	–6.176e-10	–0.34920320	–0.34920320	1.279e-09
0.04	2.99065592	2.99065592	4.924e-10	–0.46081019	–0.46081008	1.175e-07
0.05	2.98549975	2.98549975	3.514e-09	–0.57002481	–0.57002450	3.066e-07
0.06	2.97926338	2.97926339	9.154e-09	–0.67685116	–0.67685060	5.654e-07
0.07.	2.97197067	2.97197069	1.809e-08	–0.78129424	–0.78129335	8.911e-07
0.08.	2.96364542	2.96364545	3.095e-08	–0.88335988	–0.88335860	1.280e-06
0.09	2.95431137	2.95431142	4.837e-08	–0.98305473	–0.98305300	1.730e-06
0.10	2.94399220	2.94399227	7.093e-08	–1.08038625	–1.08038401	2.238e-06

The field of errors in y-approximation confines to the range [–7.973e-11, 7.093e-08] and the field of errors in y'-approximation is limited to the range [1.600e-10, 2.238e-06]. The approximations are accurate to within these confines.

Example 9

DE : $y'' - 2y' + y = 0$

CE : $y'' = 2y' - y$

PS : $y = e^{x-2}(7 - 3x)$, $y' = e^{x-2}(4 - 3x)$

IC : $y(2) = 1$, $y'(2) = -2$, Width : 0.01

The Computer Solution of the IVP of Order 2

x-value	*y-Approx*	*y-Exact*	*Error*	*y'-Approx*	*y'-Exact*	*Error*
2.01	0.97974866	0.97974866	−1.169e-11	−2.05040184	−2.05040184	−1.419e-11
2.02	0.95898925	0.95898926	9.176e-09	−2.10161569	−2.10161476	9.292e-07
2.03	0.93771360	0.93771363	2.787e-08	−2.15365186	−2.15364998	1.889e-06
2.04	0.91591342	0.91591348	5.637e-08	−2.20652172	−2.20651884	2.880e-06
2.05	0.89358034	0.89358043	9.500e-08	−2.26023676	−2.26023286	3.903e-06
2.06	0.87070582	0.87070597	1.441e-07	−2.31480863	−2.31480367	4.958e-06
2.07	0.84728126	0.84728146	2.039e-07	−2.37024913	−2.37024308	6.046e-06
2.08	0.82329790	0.82329817	2.749e-07	−2.4265702	−2.42656303	7.169e-06
2.09	0.79874687	0.79874723	3.574e-07	−2.48378395	−2.48377562	8.326e-06
2.10	0.77361919	0.77361964	4.516e-07	−2.54190263	−2.54189311	9.519e-06

The field of errors in *y*-approximation confines to the range [−1.169e-11, 4.516e-07] and the field of errors in *y*'-approximation is limited to the range [−1.419e-11, 9.519e-06]. The approximations are accurate to within these confines.

Example 10

$DE \ : \ (1 + x^2)y'' - 2xy' = 0$

$CE \ : \ y'' = \dfrac{2xy'}{(1 + x^2)}$

$PS \ : \ y = x(x^2 + 3), \ y' = 3(x^2 + 1)$

$IC \ : \ y(0) = 0, \qquad y'(0) = 3,$ Width : 0.01

The Computer Solution of the IVP of Order 2

x-value	*y-Approx*	*y-Exact*	*Error*	*y'-Approx*	*y'-Exact*	*Error*
0.01	0.03000100	0.030001	6.245e-16	3.00030000	3.0003	−1.248e-13
0.02	0.06000800	0.060008	−7.500e-11	3.00120001	3.0012	−7.502e-09
0.03	0.09002700	0.090027	−3.750e-10	3.00270003	3.0027	−3.001e-08
0.04	0.12006400	0.120064	−1.050e-09	3.00480007	3.0048	−6.752e-08
0.05	0.15012500	0.150125	−2.250e-09	3.00750012	3.0075	−1.200e-07
0.06	0.18021600	0.180216	−4.125e-09	3.01080019	3.0108	−1.876e-07
0.07	0.21034301	0.210343	−6.824e-09	3.01470027	3.0147	−2.701e-07

x-value	*y-Approx*	*y-Exact*	*Error*	*y'-Approx*	*y'-Exact*	*Error*
0.08	0.24051201	0.240512	−1.050e-08	3.01920037	3.0192	−3.677e-07
0.09	0.27072902	0.270729	−1.530e-08	3.02430048	3.0243	−4.803e-07
0.10	0.30100002	0.301000	−2.137e-08	3.03000061	3.0300	−6.079e-07

The field of errors in *y*-approximation confines to the range [6.245e-16, – 2.137e-08] and the field of errors in *y*′-approximation is limited to the range [−1.248e-13, – 6.079e-07]. The approximations are accurate to within these confines.

Example 11

DE : $(1 + x^2)y'' - 2y = 0$

CE : $y'' = \dfrac{2y}{(1+x^2)}$

PS : $y = \dfrac{\operatorname{Tan}^{-1}x(x^2+1)}{2} + x^2 + \dfrac{x}{2} + 1.\ y' = 1 + 2x + x\operatorname{Tan}^{-1} x$

IC : $y(0) = 1$, $y'(0) = 1$, Width : 0.01

The Computer Solution of the IVP of Order 2

x-value	*y-Approx*	*y-Exact*	*Error*	*y'-Approx*	*y'-Exact*	*Error*
0.01	1.01010033	1.01010033	1.667e-12	1.02010000	1.02010000	8.366e-12
0.02	1.02040267	1.02040267	−5.005e-09	1.04040045	1.04039995	−5.009e-07
0.03	1.03090901	1.03090900	−1.510e-08	1.06090074	1.06089973	−1.010e-06
0.04	1.04162136	1.04162133	−3.038e-08	1.08160068	1.08159915	−1.528e-06
0.05	1.05254170	1.05254165	−5.091e-08	1.10249997	1.10249792	−2.054e-06
0.06	1.06367203	1.06367195	−7.678e-08	1.12359828	1.12359569	−2.588e-06
0.07	1.07501433	1.07501422	−1.081e-07	1.14489515	1.14489202	−3.131e-06
0.08	1.08657059	1.08657045	−1.449e-07	1.16639008	1.6638640	−3.681e-06
0.09	1.09834279	1.09834261	−1.873e-07	1.18808248	1.18807824	−4.240e-06
0.10	1.11033290	1.11033267	−2.353e-07	1.20997167	1.20996687	−4.807e-06

The field of errors in *y*-approximation confines to the range [1.667e-12, – 2.353e-07] and the field of errors in *y*′-approximation is limited to the range [8.366e-12, – 4.807e-06]. The approximations are accurate to within these confines.

Example 12

$$DE : \frac{D^2y}{dx^2} + 2\frac{dy}{dx} + 2y = 0$$

$$CE : \frac{D^2y}{dx^2} = -2\frac{dy}{dx} - 2y$$

$$PS : y = e^{-x}(3\text{Sin } x - 2\text{Cos } x), \frac{dy}{dx} = e^{-x}(5\text{Cos } x - \text{Sin } x)$$

$$IC : y(0) = -2, \quad y'(0) = 5, \quad \text{Width} : 0.01$$

The Computer Solution of the IVP of Order 2

x-value	*y-Approx*	*y-Exact*	*Error*	*y'-Approx*	*y'-Exact*	*Error*
0.01	–1.95029966	–1.95029966	–1.663e-11	4.94010132	4.94010133	1.999e-11
0.02	–1.90119727	–1.90119728	–6.716e-09	4.88041120	4.88041053	–6.615e-07
0.03	–1.85269071	–1.85269073	–1.980e-08	4.82093662	4.82093533	–1.293e-06
0.04	–1.80477779	–1.80477783	–3.897e-08	4.76168512	4.76168322	–1.896e-06
0.05	–1.75745624	–1.75745630	–6.395e-08	4.70266399	4.70266152	–2.471e-06
0.06	–1.71072371	–1.71072381	–9.446e-08	4.64388037	4.64387735	–3.018e-06
0.07	–1.66457781	–1.66457794	–1.302e-07	4.58534120	4.58533766	–3.538e-06
0.08	–1.61901605	–1.61901622	–1.710e-07	4.52705322	4.52704919	–4.031e-06
0.09	–1.57403588	–1.57403610	–2.165e-07	4.46902300	4.46901850	–4.499e-06
0.10	–1.52963470	–1.52963497	–2.664e-07	4.41125693	4.41125199	–4.941e-06

The field of errors in y-approximation confines to the range [–1.663e-11, – 2.664e-07] and the field of errors in y'-approximation is limited to the range [1.999e-11, – 4.941e-06]. The approximations are accurate to within these confines.

Example 13

$$DE : \frac{D^2y}{dx^2} - 6\frac{dy}{dx} + 9y = 0$$

$$CE : \frac{D^2y}{dx^2} = 6\frac{dy}{dx} - 9y$$

$$PS : y = 2xe^{3x}, \frac{dy}{dx} = 2e^{3x}(3x + 1)$$

$$IC : y(0) = 0, \quad y'(0) = 2, \quad \text{Width} : 0.01$$

The Computer Solution of the IVP of Order 2

x-value	*y-Approx*	*y-Exact*	*Error*	*y'-Approx*	*y'-Exact*	*Error*
0.01	0.02060909	0.02060909	6.791e-10	2.12273634	2.12273634	2.444e-09
0.02	0.04247364	0.04247346	–1.806e-07	2.25111222	2.25109348	–1.874e-05
0.03	0.06565102	0.06565046	–5.619e-07	2.38533927	2.38529994	–3.934e-05
0.04	0.09020091	0.09019975	–1.162e-06	2.52565485	2.52559295	–6.190e-05
0.05	0.11618543	0.11618342	–2.003e-06	2.67230532	2.67221876	–8.656e-05
0.06	0.14366919	0.14366608	–3.104e-06	2.82554644	2.82543298	–1.134e-04
0.07	0.17271942	0.17271493	–4.491e-06	2.98564364	2.98550091	–1.427e-04
0.08	0.20340605	0.20339986	–6.186e-06	3.15287243	3.15269789	–1.745e-04
0.09	0.23580182	0.23579360	–8.217e-06	3.32751872	3.32730970	–2.090e-04
0.10	0.26998237	0.26997176	–1.061e-05	3.50987924	3.50963290	–2.463e-04

The field of errors in y-approximation confines to the range [6.791e-10, – 1.061e-05] and the field of errors in y'-approximation is limited to the range [2.444e-09, – 2.463e-04]. The approximations are accurate to within these confines.

Example 14

$$DE : \frac{D^2y}{dx^2} + 9y = 0$$

$$CE : \frac{D^2y}{dx^2} = -9y$$

$$PS : y = 3\text{Cos}(3x) - \frac{5\text{Sin}(3x)}{3},\ y' = -9\ \text{Sin}3x - 5\text{Cos}3x$$

$$IC : y(0) = 3, \quad y'(0) = -5, \quad \text{Width} : 0.01$$

The Computer Solution of the IVP of Order 2

x-value	*y-Approx*	*y-Exact*	*Error*	*y'-Approx*	*y'-Exact*	*Error*
0.01	2.94865760	2.94865760	–3.405e-10	–5.26770967	–5.26770967	–1.817e-09
0.02	2.89466181	2.89466161	–2.049e-07	–5.53065834	–5.53067876	–2.041e-05
0.03	2.83806123	2.83806062	–6.100e-07	–5.78863015	–5.78867061	–4.046e-05
0.04	2.77890677	2.77890556	–1.212e-06	–6.04139294	–6.04145304	–6.010e-05
0.05	2.71725169	2.71724968	–2.006e-06	–6.28871927	–6.28879858	–7.931e-05
0.06	2.65315144	2.65314846	–2.988e-06	–6.53038657	–6.53048462	–9.805e-05

x-value	*y-Approx*	*y-Exact*	*Error*	*y'-Approx*	*y'-Exact*	*Error*
0.07	2.58666373	2.58665958	−4.153e-06	−6.76617739	−6.76629367	−1.162e-04
0.08	2.51784838	2.51784288	−5.496e-06	−6.99587953	−6.99601351	−1.339e-04
0.09	2.44676730	2.44676029	−7.010e-06	−7.21928630	−7.21943741	−1.511e-04
0.10	2.37348448	2.37347579	−8.691e-06	−7.43619667	−7.43636431	−1.676e-04

The field of errors in y-approximation confines to the range [−3.405e-10, − 8.691e-06] and the field of errors in y'-approximation is limited to the range [−1.817e-09, −1.676e-04]. The approximations are accurate to within these confines.

Example 15

DE : $y'' + 4y' + 4y = 0$

CE : $y'' = -4y' - 4y$

PS : $y = (7 + 5x)e^{-2(x+1)}$, $y' = -(9 + 10x)e^{-2(x+1)}$

IC : $y(-1) = 2$, $y'(-1) = 1$, Width : 0.01

The Computer Solution of the IVP of Order 2

x-value	*y-Approx*	*y-Exact*	*Error*	*y'-Approx*	*y'-Exact*	*Error*
−0.99	2.00940728	2.00940728	2.788e-10	0.88217881	0.88217881	−6.906e-10
−0.98	2.01765772	2.01765782	1.065e-07	0.76862117	0.76863155	1.038e-05
−0.97	2.02479344	2.02479375	3.116e-07	0.65921510	0.65923517	2.008e-05
−0.96	2.03085535	2.03085596	6.091e-07	0.55384068	0.55386981	2.912e-05
−0.95	2.03588320	2..03588419	9.926e-07	0.45238116	0.45241871	3.754e-05
−0.94	2.03991555	2.03991700	1.456e-06	0.35472281	0.35476817	4.537e-05
−0.93	2.04298986	2.04299185	1.994e-06	0.26075485	0.26080747	5.262e-05
−0.92	2.04514249	2.04514509	2.600e-06	0.17036942	0.17042876	5.933e-05
−0.91	2.04640875	2.04641202	3.269e-06	0.08346150	0.08352702	6.552e-05
−0.90	2.04682289	2.04682688	3.997e-06	0.07121844	0.07271789	9.945e-05

The field of errors in y-approximation confines to the range [2.788e-10, 3.997e-06] and the field of errors in y'-approximation is limited to the range [−6.906e-10, 9.945e-05]. The approximations are accurate to within these confines.

7.3. Linear Nonhomogeneous Type

The equation (7.12) in section 7.1 is a linear nonhomogeneous differential equation of order 2. The general solution of a linear nonhomogeneous differential equation.

$$\frac{d^2y}{dx^2} + P_1\frac{dy}{dx} + P_2y = Q$$

may be expressed as $y = y_c + y_p$ (7.30)

where y_c is the general solution of the linear homogeneous form

$$\frac{d^2y}{dx^2} + P_1\frac{dy}{dx} + P_2y = 0$$

that has already been introduced in section 7.2 and y_p is a particular solution of the equation (7.12). y_c is also called the complementary solution. The function y_p can be found out by the method of undetermined coefficients in the particular cases when the right side function Q contains the following expressions :

A) The right side contains exponentials

B) The right side contains polynomial with exponentials

C) The right side contains trigonometric functions

D) The right side contains a combination of terms

Let us discuss on the cases with examples.

Case A) Solve $y'' - y' - 2y = e^{3x}$.

The auxiliary equation $\lambda^2 - \lambda - 2 = 0$ has two roots $\lambda_1 = -1$ and $\lambda_2 = 2$ that are real and distinct.

Hence, $y_c = C_1e^{-x} + C_2e^{2x}$

Let us assume a particular solution $y_p = C_0e^{3x}$.

Substituting y_p and the derivatives of y_p into the differential equation yields

$$9C_0e^{3x} - 3C_0e^{3x} - 2C_0e^{3x} = e^{3x}$$

or $$4C_0e^{3x} = e^{3x},\ C_0 = \frac{1}{4}.$$

The general solution is $y = C_1e^{-x} + C_2e^{2x} + \dfrac{e^{3x}}{4}$.

Case B) Solve $y'' - y' - 2y = (6x^2 + 8x + 7)e^x$.

$y_c = C_1e^{-x} + C_2e^{2x}$ as before.

We try a particular solution $y_p = (C_3x^2 + C_4x + C_5)e^x$.

Differentiating we get $\quad y'_p = (C_3x^2 + 2C_3x + C_4x + C_4 + C_5)e^x$ and

$$y''_p = (C_3x^2 + 4C_3x + C_4x + 2C_3 + 2C_4 + C_5)\, e^x$$

Substituting y_p and the derivatives into the differential equation and equating the coefficients of like powers of x, we obtain

$$-2C_3 = 6 \quad \text{or } C_3 = -3$$

$$2C_3 - 2C_4 = 8 \quad \text{or } C_4 = -7$$

$$2C_3 + C_4 - 2C_5 = 7 \quad \text{or } C_5 = -10$$

Hence, according to the equation (7.30) the general solution is

$$y = C_1e^{-x} + C_2e^{2x} - (3x^2 + 7x + 10)e^x.$$

Case C) $\quad$ Solve $\dfrac{d^2y}{dx^2} + 4\dfrac{dy}{dx} + 5y = 2(\cos x - \sin x)$

The complementary solution of the equation

$$y_c = e^{-2x}(C_1\cos x + C_2\sin x).$$

We take a particular form, such as,

$$y_p = C_3 \sin x + C_4 \cos x.$$

Putting the values of y_p, y'_p and y''_p into the given differential equation and with some arrangement we get

$$(4C_3 - 4C_4)\sin x + (4C_3 + 4C_4)\cos x = -2\sin x + 2\cos x$$

Equating the coefficients of like terms yields

$$4C_3 - 4C_4 = -2$$

and $\quad 4C_3 + 4C_4 = 2$

A simple calculation gives $C_3 = 0$, $C_4 = \dfrac{1}{2}$.

Thus, the general solution is $y = e^{-2x}(C_1\cos x + C_2\sin x) + \dfrac{1}{2}\cos x$.

Case D) $\quad$ Solve $y'' + 2y' + 4y = 8x^2 + 12e^{-x}$.

Now, $y_c = e^{-x}(C_1\cos\sqrt{3}\,x + C_2\sin\sqrt{3}\,x)$.

In order to obtain a particular solution we take

$$y_p = C_3x^2 + C_4x + C_5 + C_6e^{-x}$$

corresponding to the polynomial

$8x^2$ and to $12e^{-x}$.

Substituting, rearranging and equating we get the values for the constants

$$C_3 = 2,\ C_4 = -2,\ C_5 = 0,\ C_6 = 4$$

that furnish the particular solution in the form $y_p = 2x^2 - 2x + 4e^{-x}$.

The general solution is obtained accordingly as (7.30).

The computerised solutions of the second order initial value problems of the type just discussed we apply the same rules and regulations as for the previous section.

Example 1

DE : $y'' + 4y = \text{Sin}x$

CE : $y'' = \text{Sin}x - 4y$

PS : $y = \text{Cos}2x + \dfrac{\text{Sin}x + \text{Sin}2x}{3}$, $y' = -2\text{Sin}2x + \dfrac{\text{Cos}x + 2\text{Cos}2x}{3}$

IC : $y(0) = 1$, $y'(0) = 1$, Width : 0.01

The Computer Solution of the IVP of Order 2

x-value	*y-Approx*	*y-Exact*	*Error*	*y'-Approx*	*y'-Exact*	*Error*
0.01	1.00979951	1.00979951	9.772e-12	0.95085267	0.95985267	–5.340e-11
0.02	1.01919612	1.01919611	–1.327e-08	0.91942273	0.91942140.	–1.328e-06
0.03	1.02818708	1.02818704	–3.993e-08	0.87872502	0.87872236	–2.666e-06
0.04	1.03676980	1.03676972	–8.006e-08	0.83777580	0.83777179	–4.013e-06
0.05	1.04494183	1.04494169	–1.337e-07	0.79659140	0.79658603	–5.367e-06
0.06	1.05270091	1.05270071	–2.010e-07	0.75518825	0.75518152	–6.727e-06
0.07	1.06004493	1.06004465	–2.820e-07	0.71358286	0.71357477	–8.093e-06
0.08	1.06697196	1.06697158	–3.767e-07	0.67179181	0.67178234	–9.463e-06
0.09	1.07348022	1.07347973	–4.851e-07	0.62983173	0.62982089	–1.084e-05
0.10	1.07956810	1.07956749	–6.074e-07	0.58771932	0.58770711	–1.221e-05

The field of errors in y-approximation confines to the range [9.772e-12, – 6.074e-07] and the field of errors in y'-approximation is limited to the range [– 5.340e-11, –1.221e-05]. The approximations are accurate to within these confines.

Example 2

$DE\ :\ y'' - 2y' = e^{2x} + x^2 - 1$

$CE\ :\ y'' = e^{2x} + x^2 - 1 + 2y'$

$PS\ :\ y = e^{2x}(4x+1)/8 - x^3/6 - x^2/4 + x/4,\ y' = e^{2x}(4x+1)/4 + e^{2x}/2 - x^2/2 - x/2 + 1/4$

$IC\ :\ y(0) = 0.125, \qquad y'(0) = 1, \qquad$ Width : 0.01

The Computer Solution of the IVP of Order 2

x-value	*y-Approx*	*y-Exact*	*Error*	*y'-Approx*	*y'-Exact*	*Error*
0.01	0.13510101	0.13510101	1.871e-10	1.02030302	1.02030302	3.687e-11
0.02	0.14540813	0.14540812	–7.444e-09	1.04122505	1.04122430	–7.557e-07
0.03	0.15592764	0.15592762	–2.281e-08	1.06278406	1.06278251	–1.554e-06
0.04	0.16666600	0.16666596	–4.651e-08	1.08499918	1.08499678	–2.396e-06
0.05	0.17762988	0.17762980	–7.901e-08	1.10789002	1.10788673	–3.284e-06
0.06	0.18882613	0.18882601	–1.208e-07	1.13147667	1.13147245	–4.219e-06
0.07	0.20026181	0.20026164	–1.723e-07	1.15577972	1.15577452	–5.204e-06
0.08	0.21194419	0.21194396	–2.340e-07	1.18082026	1.18081402	–6.239e-06
0.09	0.22388076	0.22388045	–3.065e-07	1.20661991	1.20661259	–7.326e-06
0.10	0.23607921	0.23607882	–3.903e-07	1.23320081	1.23319234	–8.468e-06

The field of errors in y-approximation confines to the range [0.13510101, – 3.903e-07] and the field of errors in y'-approximation is limited to the range [3.687e-11, –8.468e-06]. The approximations are accurate to within these confines.

Example 3

$DE\ :\ x^2y'' - xy' + y = 2x$

$CE\ :\ y'' = \dfrac{(2x - y + xy')}{x^2}$

$PS\ :\ y = x(\text{Ln}\ x + (\text{Ln}\ x)^2),\ y' = 1 + 3\text{Ln}\ x + (\text{Ln}\ x)^2$

$IC\ :\ y(1) = 0, \qquad y'(1) = 1, \qquad$ Width : 0.01

The Computer Solution of the IVP of Order 2

x-value	*y-Approx*	*y-Exact*	*Error*	*y'-Approx*	*y'-Exact*	*Error*
1.01	0.01014983	0.01014983	−2.883e-12	1.02995000	1.02995000	−4.459e-13
1.02	0.02059866	0.02059867	4.961e-09	1.05979953	1.05980003	4.991e-07
1.03	0.03134549	0.03134550	1.486e-08	1.08954913	1.08955013	9.947e-07
1.04	0.04238931	0.04238934	2.965e-08	1.11919892	1.11920040	1.487e-06
1.05	0.05372913	0.05372918	4.931e-08	1.14874900	1.14875097	1.976e-06
1.06	0.06536395	0.06536402	7.380e-08	1.17819953	1.17820199	2.461e-06
1.07	0.07729278	0.07729289	1.031e-07	1.20755070	1.20755364	2.942e-06
1.08	0.08951463	0.08951477	1.371e-07	1.23680271	1.23680613	3.420e-06
1.09	0.10202850	0.10202868	1.759e-07	1.26595579	1.26595968	3.895e-06
1.10	0.11483341	0.11483363	2.194e-07	1.29501020	1.29501457	4.366e-06

The field of errors in y-approximation confines to the range [−2.883e-12, 2.194e-07] and the field of errors in y'-approximation is limited to the range [− 4.459e-13, 4.366e-06]. The approximations are accurate to within these confines.

Example 4

$$DE : xy'' - 4y' = x^5$$

$$CE : y'' = \frac{(x^5 + 4y')}{x}$$

$$PS : y(x) = \frac{x^6}{6} - x^5 - \frac{1}{6}, y'(x) = x^4(x - 5)$$

$$IC : y(1) = -1, \quad y'(1) = -4, \quad \text{Width} : 0.01$$

The Computer Solution of the IVP of Order 2

x-value	*y-Approx*	*y-Exact*	*Error*	*y'-Approx*	*y'-Exact*	*Error*
1.01	−1.04075669	−1.04075669	−9.889e-10	−4.15201000	−4.1520100	−2.869e-09
1.02	−1.08305391	−1.08305373	1.725e-07	−4.30809778	−4.30808000	1.779e-05
1.03	−1.12693255	−1.12693203	5.283e-07	−4.46830636	−4.46826998	3.638e-05
1.04	−1.17243414	−1.17243307	1.075e-06	−4.63269570	−4.6326990	5.580e-05
1.05	−1.21960078	−1.21959896	1.820e-06	−4.80132575	−4.80124969	7.606e-05
1.06	−1.26847517	−1.26847240	2.772e-06	−4.97425640	−4.97415922	9.718e-05
1.07	−1.31910062	−1.31909668	3.941e-06	−5.15154748	−5.15142832	1.191e-04

x-value	*y-Approx*	*y-Exact*	*Error*	*y'-Approx*	*y'-Exact*	*Error*
1.08	−1.37152103	−1.37151569	5.334e-06	−5.33325876	−5.33311672	1.420e-04
1.09	−1.42578090	−1.42577394	6.961e-06	−5.51944991	−5.51928410	1.658e-04
1.10	−1.48192534	−1.48191651	8.831e-06	−5.71018052	−5.70999000	1.905e-04

The field of errors in y-approximation confines to the range [−9.889e-10, 8.831e-06] and the field of errors in y'-approximation is limited to the range [−2.869e-09, 1.905e-04]. The approximations are accurate to within these confines.

Example 5

DE : $y'' + 12x = 16\text{Sin}x$

CE : $y'' = 16\text{Sin}x - 12x$

PS : $y(x) = 2 + 12x - 2x^3 - 16\text{Sin}x$, $y'(x) = 12 - 6x^2 - 16\text{Cos}x$

IC : $y(0) = 2$, $y'(0) = -4$, Width : 0.01

The Computer Solution of the IVP of Order 2

x-value	*y-Approx*	*y-Exact*	*Error*	*y'-Approx*	*y'-Exact*	*Error*
0.01	1.96000067	1.96000067	−2.222e-12	−3.99980001	−3.99980001	−3.109e-15
0.02	1.92000533	1.92000533	−3.778e-11	−3.99920010	−3.99920011	−3.333e-09
0.03	1.88001800	1.88001800	−1.733e-10	−3.99820053	−3.99820054	−1.333e-08
0.04	1.84004265	1.84004265	−4.755e-10	−3.99680168	−3.99680171	−3.000e-08
0.05	1.80008329	1.80008329	−1.011e-09	−3.99500411	−3.99500417	−5.333e-08
0.06	1.76014390	1.76014390	−1.846e-09	−3.99280856	−3.99280864	−8.332e-08
0.07	1.72022845	1.72022844	−3.048e-09	−3.99021588	−3.99021600	−1.200e-07
0.08	1.68034090	1.68034090	−4.683e-09	−3.98722714	−3.98722730	−1.633e-07
0.09	1.64048522	1.64048521	−6.818e-09	−3.98384351	−3.98384373	−2.132e-07
0.10	1.60066534	1.60066533	−9.518e-09	−3.98006637	−3.98006664	−2.698e-07

The field of errors in y-approximation confines to the range [−2.222e-12, − 9.518e-09] and the field of errors in y'-approximation is limited to the range [−3.109e-15, −2.698e-07]. The approximations are accurate to within these confines.

Example 6

DE : $y'' - 3y' + 2y = e^{-x}$

CE : $y'' = e^{-x} - 2y + 3y'$

PS : $y = -e^{x-2}/2 + e^{2x-3}/3 + e^{-x}/6,\ y' = -e^{x-2}/2 + 2e^{2x-3}/3 - e^{-x}/6$

IC : $y(1) = 0, \quad y'(1) = 0,$ Width : 0.01

The Computer Solution of the IVP of Order 2

x-value	*y-Approx*	*y-Exact*	*Error*	*y'-Approx*	*y'-Exact*	*Error*
1.01	0.00001850	0.00001850	−9.518e-09	0.00371589	0.00371589	4.228e-12
1.02	0.00007457	0.00007457	−1.075e-09	0.00750733	0.00750722	−1.096e-07
1.03	0.00016892	0.00016892	−3.301e-09	0.01137610	0.01137588	−2.261e-07
1.04	0.00030236	0.00030235	−6.745e-09	0.01532415	0.01532380	−3.498e-07
1.05	0.00047568	0.00047567	−1.148e-08	0.01935345	0.01935297	−4.810e-07
1.06	0.00068971	0.00068969	−1.759e-08	0.02346601	0.02346539	−6.198e-07
1.07	0.00094528	0.00094526	−2.514e-08	0.02766388	0.02766311	−7.666e-07
1.08	0.00124328	0.00124324	−3.422e-08	0.03194916	0.03194824	−9.217e-07
1.09	0.00158457	0.00158452	−4.491e-08	0.03632399	0.03632291	−1.085e-06
1.10	0.00197006	0.00197001	−5.731e-08	0.04079056	0.04078930	−1.258e-06

The field of errors in y-approximation confines to the range [−9.518e-09, – 5.731e-08] and the field of errors in y'-approximation is limited to the range [4.228e-12, −1.258e-06]. The approximations are accurate to within these confines.

Example 7

DE : $y'' - y = 2x$

CE : $y'' = 2x + y$

$$PS : y = \frac{\text{Sinh } x}{\text{Sinh } 1} - 2x,\ y' = \frac{\text{Cosh } x}{\text{Sinh } 1} - 2$$

IC : $y(0) = 0, \quad y'(0) = -1.149,$ Width : 0.01

The Computer Solution of the IVP of Order 2

x-value	*y-Approx*	*y-Exact*	*Error*	*y'-Approx*	*y'-Exact*	*Error*
0.01	−0.01148986	−0.01149068	−8.187e-07	−1.14895745	−1.14903933	−8.188e-05
0.02	−0.02297887	−0.02298050	−1.638e-06	−1.14882979	−1.14891168	−8.189e-05
0.03	−0.03446617	−0.03446863	−2.457e-06	−1.14861702	−1.14869893	−8.191e-05
0.04	−0.04595092	−0.04595420	−3.276e-06	−1.14831911	−1.14840105	−8.194e-05
0.05	−0.05743227	−0.05743636	−4.095e-06	−1.14793603	−1.14801800	−8.198e-05

x-value	*y-Approx*	*y-Exact*	*Error*	*y'-Approx*	*y'-Exact*	*Error*
0.06	−0.06890936	−0.06891427	−4.915e-06	−1.14746774	−1.14754976	−8.202e-05
0.07	−0.08038134	−0.08038707	−5.736e-06	−1.14691419	−1.14699627	−8.208e-05
0.08	−0.09184736	−0.09185391	−6.557e-06	−1.14627533	−1.14635748	−8.215e-05
0.09	−0.10330656	−0.10331394	−7.379e-06	−1.14555111	−1.14563333	−8.222e-05
0.10	−0.11475810	−0.11476630	−8.202e-06	−1.14474143	−1.14482373	−8.230e-05

The field of errors in *y*-approximation confines to the range [−8.187e-07, − 8.202e-06] and the field of errors in *y'*-approximation is limited to the range [−8.188e-05, −8.230e-05]. The approximations are accurate to within these confines.

Example 8

DE : $y'' + y = 2x - \pi$

CE : $y'' = 2x - \pi - y$

PS : $y = 2x - \pi\,(1 - \text{Cos}x) + \text{Sin}x,\; y' = 2 - \pi\text{Sin}x + \text{Cos}x$

IC : $y(0) = 0$, $y'(0) = 3$, Width : 0.01

The Computer Solution of the IVP of Order 2

x-value	*y-Approx*	*y-Exact*	*Error*	*y'-Approx*	*y'-Exact*	*Error*
0.01	0.02984276	0.02984276	8.290e-13	2.96853460	2.96853460	−2.619e-12
0.02	0.05937037	0.05937037	−2.612e-09	2.93697260	2.93697234	−2.614e-07
0.03	0.08858190	0.08858189	−7.847e-09	2.90531691	2.90531639	−5.235e-07
0.04	0.11747641	0.11747640	−1.571e-08	2.87357069	2.87356991	−7.864e-07
0.05	0.14605302	0.14605300	−2.621e-08	2.84173712	2.84173607	−1.050e-06
0.06	0.17431088	0.17431084	−3.936e-08	2.80981937	2.80981805	−1.314e-06
0.07	0.20224914	0.20224909	−5.515e-08	2.77782064	2.77781906	−1.579e-06
0.08	0.22986703	0.22986696	−7.360e-08	2.74574413	2.74574229	−1.844e-06
0.09	0.25716378	0.25716368	−9.470e-08	2.71359305	2.71359094	−2.110e-06
0.10	0.28413866	0.28413854	−1.185e-07	2.68137061	2.68136823	−2.377e-06

The field of errors in *y*-approximation confines to the range [8.290e-13, − 1.185e-07] and the field of errors in *y'*-approximation is limited to the range [−2.619e-12, −2.377e-06]. The approximations are accurate to within these confines.

Example 9

$$DE : \frac{D^2y}{dx^2} + 2\frac{dy}{dx} - 3y = 2\text{Cosx} - 4\text{Sinx}$$

$$CE : \frac{D^2y}{dx^2} = 2\text{Cos}x - 4\text{Sin}x - 2\frac{dy}{dx} + 3y$$

$$PS : y(x) = 2e^{-3x} + \text{Sin}x,\ y'(x) = \text{Cos}x - 6e^{-3x}$$

$$IC : y(0) = 2, \quad y'(0) = -5, \quad \text{Width} : 0.01$$

The Computer Solution of the IVP of Order 2

x-value	*y-Approx*	*y-Exact*	*Error*	*y'-Approx*	*y'-Exact*	*Error*
0.01	1.95089090	1.95089090	–4.091e-10	–4.82272320	–4.82272320	1.227e-09
0.02	1.90352787	1.90352773	–1.390e-07	–4.65077352	–4.65078719	–1.368e-05
0.03	1.85785828	1.85785787	–4.089e-07	–4.48401038	–4.48403708	–2.669e-05
0.04	1.81383101	1.81383021	–8.038e-07	–4.32228344	–4.32232251	–3.907e-05
0.05	1.77139644	1.77139512	–1.318e-06	–4.16544676	–4.16549760	–5.084e-05
0.06	1.73050637	1.73050443	–1.944e-06	–4.01335871	–4.01342073	–6.202e-05
0.07	1.69111402	1.69111134	–2.678e-06	–3.86588183	–3.86595448	–7.265e-05
0.08	1.65317393	1.65317042	–3.513e-06	–3.72288272	–3.72296546	–8.274e-05
0.09	1.61664198	1.61663754	–4.446e-06	–3.58423191	–3.58432423	–9.233e-05
0.10	1.58147533	1.58146986	–5.470e-06	–3.44980373	–3.44990516	–1.014e-04

The field of errors in y-approximation confines to the range [–4.091e-10, – 5.470e-06] and the field of errors in y'-approximation is limited to the range [1.227e-09, –1.014e-04]. The approximations are accurate to within these confines.

Example 10

$$DE : \frac{D^2y}{dx^2} + y = 1$$

$$CE : \frac{D^2y}{dx^2} = 1 - y$$

$$PS : y(x) = 1 - \text{Sin}x - \text{Cos}x,\ y'(x) = \text{Sin}x - \text{Cos}x$$

$$IC : y(0) = 0, \quad y'(0) = -1, \quad \text{Width} : 0.01$$

The Computer Solution of the IVP of Order 2

x-value	*y-Approx*	*y-Exact*	*Error*	*y'-Approx*	*y'-Exact*	*Error*
0.01	–0.00994983	–0.00994983	-8.319e-13	–0.98995017	–0.98995017	8.348e-13
0.02	–0.01979867	–0.01979867	8.275e-10	–0.97980142	–0.97980134	8.291e-08

x-value	y-Approx	y-Exact	Error	y'-Approx	y'-Exact	Error
0.03	−0.02954554	−0.02954553	2.493e-09	−0.96955470	−0.96955453	1.666e-07
0.04	−0.03918945	−0.03918944	5.005e-09	−0.95921102	−0.95921077	2.512e-07
0.05	−0.04872944	−0.04872943	8.369e-09	−0.94877143	−0.94877109	3.365e-07
0.06	−0.05816456	−0.05816455	1.260e-08	−0.93823696	−0.93823653	4.226e-07
0.07	−0.06749387	−0.06749385	1.769e-08	−0.92760866	−0.92760815	5.095e-07
0.08	−0.07671642	−0.07671640	2.366e-08	−0.91688761	−0.91688701	5.970e-07
0.09	−0.08583131	−0.08583128	3.051e-08	−0.90607487	−0.90607418	6.853e-07
0.10	−0.09483762	−0.09483758	3.826e-08	−0.89517152	−0.89517075	7.743e-07

The field of errors in y-approximation confines to the range [−8.319e-13, 3.826e-08] and the field of errors in y'-approximation is limited to the range [8.348e-13, 7.743e-07]. The approximations are accurate to within these confines.

Example 11

DE : $xy'' + y' + x = 0$

CE : $y'' = \dfrac{-(x + y1)}{x}$

PS : $y(x) = (\text{Ln}x/2 - x^2/4 + 1/4,\ y'(x) = (1/x - x)/2$

IC : $y(1) = 0$, $y'(1) = 0$, Width : 0.01

The Computer Solution of the IVP of Order 2

x-value	y-Approx	y-Exact	Error	y'-Approx	y'-Exact	Error
1.01	−0.00004938	−0.00004938	1.636e-12	−0.00995050	−0.00995050	−6.939e-18
1.02	−0.00019869	−0.00019869	1.539e-11	−0.01980392	−0.01980392	1.213e-09
1.03	−0.00044560	−0.00044560	4.055e-11	−0.02956311	−0.02956311	2.356e-09
1.04	−0.00078964	−0.00078964	7.646e-11	−0.03923077	−0.03923077	3.433e-09
1.05	−0.00122992	−0.00122992	1.225e-10	−0.04880953	−0.04880952	4.448e-09
1.06	−0.00176555	−0.00176555	1.781e-10	−0.05830189	−0.05830189	5.405e-09
1.07	−0.00239568	−0.00239568	2.427e-10	−0.06771029	−0.06771028	6.306e-09
1.08	−0.00311948	−0.00311948	3.157e-10	−0.07703704	−0.07703704	7.156e-09
1.09	−0.00393615	−0.00393615	3.968e-10	−0.08628441	−0.08628440	7.957e-09
1.10	−0.00484491	−0.00484491	4.854e-10	−0.09545455	−0.09545455	8.712e-09

The field of errors in y-approximation confines to the range [1.636e-12, 4.854e-10] and the field of errors in y'-approximation is limited to the range [–6.939e-18, 8.712e-09]. The approximations are accurate to within these confines.

Example 12

$$DE : y''(1 + \text{Ln}x) + \frac{y'}{x} = \text{Ln}x + 2$$

$$CE : y'' = \frac{\text{Ln}x + 2 - \dfrac{y'}{x}}{1 + \text{Ln}x}$$

$$PS : y(x) = \frac{x^2}{2},\ y'(x) = x$$

$$IC : y(1) = 0.5, \quad y'(1) = 1, \quad \text{Width} : 0.01$$

The Computer Solution of the IVP of Order 2

x-value	*y-Approx*	*y-Exact*	*Error*	*y'-Approx*	*y'-Exact*	*Error*
1.01	0.51005	0.51005	0	1.01	1.01	0
1.02	0.52020	0.52020	0	1.02	1.02	0
1.03	0.53045	0.53045	0	1.03	1.03	0
1.04	0.54080	0.54-80	1.11e-16	1.04	1.04	0
1.05	0.55125	0.55125	1.11e-16	1.05	1.05	0
1.06	0.56180	0.56180	2.22e-16	1.06	1.06	0
1.07	0.57245	0.57245	1.11e-16	1.07	1.07	0
1.08	0.58320	0.58320	1.11e-16	1.08	1.08	0
1.09	0.59405	0.59405	1.11e-16	1.09	1.09	0
1.10	0.60500	0.60500	1.11e-16	1.10	1.10	0

The field of errors in y-approximation confines to the range [0, 1.11e-16] and the field of errors in y'-approximation is limited to the range [0, 0]. The approximations are accurate to within these confines.

Example 13

$$DE : y'' + 4y' + 4y = (x + 1)^2$$

$$CE : y'' = (x + 1)^2 - 4y' - 4y$$

$$PS : y = \frac{[7(1 + 2x)e^{-2x} + 2x^2 + 1]}{8},\ y' = \frac{x(1 - 7e^{-2x})}{2}$$

$$IC : y(0) = 1, \quad y'(0) = 0, \quad \text{Width} : 0.01$$

The Computer Solution of the IVP of Order 2

x-value	*y-Approx*	*y-Exact*	*Error*	*y'-Approx*	*y'-Exact*	*Error*
0.01	0.99985232	0.99985232	1.013e-10	–0.02930695	–0.02930695	–2.574e-10
0.02	0.99941835	0.99941839	3.746e-08	–0.05725891	–0.05725526	3.651e-06
0.03	0.99871150	0.99871160	1.097e-07	–0.08389234	–0.08388528	7.068e-06
0.04	0.99774473	0.99774495	2.145e-07	–0.10924655	–0.10923629	1.026e-05
0.05	0.99653067	0.99653101	3.497e-07	–0.13335978	–0.13334655	1.324e-05
0.06	0.99508151	0.99508203	5.132e-07	–0.15626930	–0.15625329	1.601e-05
0.07	0.99340914	0.99340984	7.030e-07	–0.17801135	–0.17799277	1.858e-05
0.08	0.99152503	0.99152595	9.172e-07	–0.19862123	–0.19860026	2.097e-05
0.09	0.98944034	0.98944149	1.154e-06	–0.21813329	–0.21811012	2.317e-05
0.10	0.98716588	0.98716729	1.411e-06	–0.23658097	–0.23655576	2.521e-05

The field of errors in y-approximation confines to the range [1.013e-10, 1.411e-06] and the field of errors in y'-approximation is limited to the range [–2.574e-10, 2.521e-05]. The approximations are accurate to within these confines.

Example 14

DE : $y'' + 16y = \text{Sin } 4x$

CE : $y'' = \text{Sin } 4x - 16y$

PS : $y = \dfrac{(\text{Sin } 4x - 4x \text{ Cos } 4x)}{32}, \; y' = \dfrac{x \text{ Sin } 4x}{2}$

IC : $y(0) = 0, \quad y'(0) = 0,$ Width : 0.01

The Computer Solution of the IVP of Order 2

x-value	*y-Approx*	*y-Exact*	*Error*	*y'-Approx*	*y'-Exact*	*Error*
0.01	6.66622223e-07	6.66560006e-07	–6.222e-11	0.00019995	0.00019995	8.888e-13
0.02	5.33044489e-06	5.32992078e-06	–5.241e-10	0.00079919	0.00079915	–3.995e-08
0.03	1.79752109e-05	1.79740933e-05	–1.118e-09	0.00179574	0.00179568	–5.309e-08
0.04	4.25591145e-05	4.25575398e-05	–1.575e-09	0.00318640	0.00318636	–3.945e-08
0.05	8.30021047e-05	8.30004758e-05	–1.629e-09	0.00496673	0.00496673	7.868e-10
0.06	0.00014317	0.00014317	–1.017e-09	0.00713101	0.00713108	6.725e-08
0.07	0.00022688	0.00022688	5.177e-10	0.00967229	0.00967245	1.594e-07

x-value	y-Approx	y-Exact	Error	y'-Approx	y'-Exact	Error
0.08	0.00033785	0.00033785	3.227e-09	0.01258239	0.01258266	2.766e-07
0.09	0.00047972	0.00047973	7.354e-09	0.01585192	0.01585234	4.179e-07
0.10	0.00065605	0.00065606	1.313e-08	0.01947033	0.01947092	5.823e-07

The field of errors in y-approximation confines to the range [–6.222e-11, 1.313e-08] and the field of errors in y'-approximation is limited to the range [8.888e-13, 5.823e-07]. The approximations are accurate to within these confines.

Example 15

$$DE : \frac{D^2y}{dx^2} + 2\frac{dy}{dx} + 5y = 8x^2e^{-x}$$

$$CE : \frac{D^2y}{dx^2} = 8x^2e^{-x} - 2\frac{dy}{dx} - 5y$$

$$PS : y = e^{-x}(\text{Cos}\,2x + 2x^2 - 1),\; y' = e^{-x}(4x - 2x^2 + 1 - 2\,\text{Sin}\,2x - \text{Cos}\,2x)$$

IC : $y(0) = 0$, $y'(0) = 0$, Width : 0.01

The Computer Solution of the IVP of Order 2

x-value	y-Approx	y-Exact	Error	y'-Approx	y'-Exact	Error
0.01	6.60024945e-09	6.60024422e-09	-5.2e-15	2.63346633e-06	2.63347984e-06	1.4e-11
0.02	9.79820371e-08	1.04548949e-07	6.6e-09	2.01546123e-05	2.08046833e-05	6.5e-07
0.03	5.04346149e-07	5.23977707e-07	2.0e-08	6.80424114e-05	6.93355248e-05	1.3e-06
0.04	1.60027728e-06	1.63939754e-06	3.9e-08	0.00016035	0.00016228	1.9e-06
0.05	3.89718016e-06	3.96213502e-06	6.5e-08	0.00031040	0.00031296	2.6e-06
0.06	8.03588810e-06	1.32940890e-06	9.7e-08	0.00053076	0.00053393	3.2e-06
0.07	1.47794427e-05	1.49147698e-05	1.4e-07	0.00083329	0.00083708	3.8e-06
0.08	2.50060436e-05	2.51857300e-05	1.8e-07	0.00122918	0.00123356	4.4e-06
0.09	3.97021663e-05	3.99322016e-05	2.3e-07	0.00172889	0.00173387	5.0e-06
0.10	9.99558482e-05	6.02421220e-05	2.9e-07	0.00234228	0.00234784	5.6e-06

The field of errors in y-approximation confines to the range [–5.2e-15, 2.9e-07] and the field of errors in y'-approximation is limited to the range [1.4e-11, 5.6e-06]. The approximations are accurate to within these confines.

Example 16

$$DE : D^2y/dx^2 - 3dy/dx + 2y = x$$

$$CE : \frac{D^2y}{dx^2} = x + 3\frac{dy}{dx} - 2y$$

PS : $y = e^x + x/2 - 3(e^{2x} - 1)/4, y' = e^x + 1/2 - 3e^{2x}/2$

IC : $y(0) = 1, \quad y'(0) = 0,$ Width : 0.01

The Computer Solution of the IVP of Order 2

x-value	*y-Approx*	*y-Exact*	*Error*	*y'-Approx*	*y'-Exact*	*Error*
0.01	0.99989916	0.99989916	–1.923e-11	–0.02025184	–0.02025184	–3.930e-11
0.02	0.99959325	0.99959326	9.169e-09	–0.04101576	–0.04101482	9.345e-07
0.03	0.99907710	0.99907712	2.804e-08	–0.06230220	–0.06230029	1.917e-06
0.04	0.99834542	0.99834547	5.707e-08	–0.08412278	–0.08411983	2.949e-06
0.05	0.99739281	0.99739291	9.679e-08	–0.10648931	–0.10648528	4.033e-06
0.06	0.99621376	0.99621391	1.477e-07	–0.12941390	–0.12940873	5.169e-06
0.07	0.99480262	0.99480283	2.104e-07	–0.15290888	–0.15290252	6.360e-06
0.08	0.99315363	0.99315391	2.853e-07	–0.17698685	–0.17697924	7.609e-06
0.09	0.99126089	0.99126126	3.732e-07	–0.20166068	–0.20165176	8.915e-06
0.10	0.98911837	0.98911885	4.745e-07	–0.22694350	–0.22693322	1.028e-05

The field of errors in *y*-approximation confines to the range [–1.923e-11, 4.745e-07] and the field of errors in *y'*-approximation is limited to the range [–3.930e-11, 1.028e-05]. The approximations are accurate to within these confines.

Example 17

DE : $y'' + y' - 2y = \text{Sin}x$

CE : $y'' = \text{Sin}x - y' + 2y$

PS : $y = e^x/6 - e^{-2x}/15 - (\text{Cos}x + 3\text{Sin}x)/10, \; y' = e^x/6 + 2e^{-2x}/15 - (\text{Sin}x - 3\text{Cos}x)/10$

IC : $y(0) = 0, \quad y'(0) = 0,$ Width : 0.01

The Computer Solution of the IVP of Order 2

x-value	*y-Approx*	*y-Exact*	*Error*	*y'-Approx*	*y'-Exact*	*Error*
0.01	1.66249307e-07	1.72786319e-07	6.537e-09	4.98341674e-05	4.98271029e-05	–7.064e-09
0.02	1.32587545e-06	1.33312491e-06	7.249e-09	0.00019860	0.00019867	7.641e-08
0.03	4.46416274e-06	4.47292942e-06	8.767e-09	0.00044540	0.00044556	1.562e-07
0.04	1.05567861e-05	1.05678383e-05	1.105e-08	0.00078930	0.00078954	2.324e-07
0.05	2.05700013e-05	2.05840718e-05	1.407e-08	0.00122936	0.00122967	3.050e-07

x-value	*y-Approx*	*y-Exact*	*Error*	*y'-Approx*	*y'-Exact*	*Error*
0.06	3.54608319e-05	3.54786185e-05	1.779e-08	0.00176467	0.00176505	3.742e-07
0.07	5.61772516e-05	5.61994182e-05	2.217e-08	0.00239433	0.00239477	4.400e-07
0.08	8.36583640e-05	8.36855414e-05	2.718e-08	0.00311746	0.00311797	5.025e-07
0.09	0.00011883	0.00011887	3.279e-08	0.00393321	0.00393377	5.618e-07
0.10	0.00016263	0.00016267	3.896e-08	0.00484072	0.00484134	6.179e-07

The field of errors in y-approximation confines to the range [6.537e-09, 3.896e-08] and the field of errors in y'-approximation is limited to the range [–7.064e-09, 6.179e-07]. The approximations are accurate to within these confines.

Example 18

$DE \; : \; y'' + 2y' + 5y = e^{-x}\,\text{Sin}x$

$CE \; : \; y'' = e^{-x}\,\text{Sin}x - 2y' - 5y$

$PS \; : \; y = \dfrac{e^{-x}(\text{Sin}x + \text{Sin}2x)}{3},\; y' = \dfrac{e^{-x}(\text{Cos}x - \text{Sin}x + 2\text{Cos}2x - \text{Sin}2x)}{3}$

$IC \; : \; y(0) = 0, \quad y'(0) = 1,$ Width : 0.01

The Computer Solution of the IVP of Order 2

x-value	*y-Approx*	*y-Exact*	*Error*	*y'-Approx*	*y'-Exact*	*Error*
0.01	0.00990000	0.00990000	–1.723e-11	0.98000133	0.98000133	–9.892e-10
0.02	0.01960006	0.01960005	–9.196e-09	0.96001148	0.96001057	–9.078e-07
0.03	0.02910029	0.02910027	–2.721e-08	0.94003731	0.94003552	–1.782e-06
0.04	0.03840090	0.03840084	–5.373e-08	0.92008645	0.92008383	–2.624e-06
0.05	0.04750214	0.04750205	–8.844e-08	0.90016642	0.90016299	–3.434e-06
0.06	0.05640436	0.05640423	–1.310e-07	0.88028458	0.88028037	–4.211e-06
0.07	0.06510799	0.06510781	–1.811e-07	0.86044813	0.86044317	–4.957e-06
0.08	0.07361351	0.07361327	–2.385e-07	0.84066415	0.84065848	–5.671e-06
0.09	0.08192148	0.08192117	–3.027e-07	0.82093955	0.82093320	–6.353e-06
0.10	0.09003253	0.09003215	–3.736e-07	0.80128113	0.80127412	–7.004e-06

The field of errors in y-approximation confines to the range [–1.723e-11, –3.736e-07] and the field of errors in y'-approximation is limited to the range [–9.892e-10, –7.004e-06]. The approximations are accurate to within these confines.

Example 19

DE : $(D^2 - 4D + 4)y = x^2$

CE : $D^2y = x^2 + 4Dy - 4y$

PS : $y = \dfrac{(4xe^{2x} + 2x^2 + 4x + 3)}{8}, \; y' = \dfrac{[x + 1 + e^{2x}(1 + 2x)]}{2}$

IC : $y(0) = 0.375$, $y'(0) = 1$, Width : 0.01

The Computer Solution of the IVP of Order 2

x-value	*y-Approx*	*y-Exact*	*Error*	*y'-Approx*	*y'-Exact*	*Error*
0.01	0.38512601	0.38512601	2.513e-11	1.02530268	1.02530268	5.531e-11
0.02	0.39550812	0.39550811	–1.088e-08	1.05122272	1.05122160	–1.115e-06
0.03	0.40615258	0.40615255	–3.350e-08	1.07777568	1.07777337	–2.310e-06
0.04	0.41706581	0.41706574	–6.865e-08	1.10497860	1.10497502	–3.587e-06
0.05	0.42825439	0.42825427	–1.172e-07	1.13284896	1.13284400	–4.952e-06
0.06	0.43972509	0.43972491	–1.800e-07	1.16140464	1.16139824	–6.407e-06
0.07	0.45148484	0.45148458	–2.580e-07	1.19066402	1.19065607	–7.957e-06
0.08	0.46354079	0.46354043	–3.522e-07	1.22064591	1.22063631	–9.606e-06
0.09	0.47590024	0.47589978	–4.636e-07	1.25136960	1.25135824	–1.136e-05
0.10	0.48857073	0.48857014	–5.932e-07	1.28285487	1.28284165	–1.322e-05

The field of errors in y-approximation confines to the range [2.513e-11, –5.932e-07] and the field of errors in y'-approximation is limited to the range [5.531e-11, –1.322e-05]. The approximations are accurate to within these confines.

Example 20

DE : $(D^2 + 4D + 8)y = \text{Sin}x$

CE : $D^2y = \text{Sin}x - 4Dy - 8y$

PS : $y = \dfrac{e^{-2x}(69\text{Cos}2x + 65.5\text{Sin}2x) + 7\text{Sin}x - 4\text{Cos}x}{65}$

$Dy = \dfrac{e^{-2x}(-7\text{Cos}2x - 269\text{Sin}2x) + 7\text{Cos}x + 4\text{Sin}x}{65}$

IC : $y(0) = 1$, $y'(0) = 0$, Width : 0.01

The Computer Solution of the IVP of Order 2

x-value	*y-Approx*	*y-Exact*	*Error*	*y'-Approx*	*y'-Exact*	*Error*
0.01	0.99960547	0.99960547	7.233e-12	–0.07836133	–0.07836133	4.243e-10
0.02	0.99844349	0.99844355	5.559e-08	–0.15349605	–0.15349061	5.446e-06
0.03	0.99654604	0.99654621	1.645e-07	–0.22546633	–0.22545566	1.066e-05
0.04	0.99394443	0.99394476	3.243e-07	–0.29433982	–0.29432416	1.566e-05
0.05	0.99066929	0.99066982	5.329e-07	–0.36018397	–0.36016355	2.043e-05
0.06	0.98675057	0.98675136	7.880e-07	–0.42306598	–0.42304101	2.497e-05
0.07	0.98221756	0.98221865	1.087e-06	–0.48305273	–0.48302344	2.929e-05
0.08	0.97709889	0.97710032	1.429e-06	–0.54021078	–0.54017738	3.339e-05
0.09	0.97142250	0.97142431	1.810e-06	–0.59460627	–0.59456900	3.728e-05
0.10	0.96521570	0.96521793	2.228e-06	–0.64630497	–0.64626402	4.095e-05

The field of errors in *y*-approximation confines to the range [7.233e-12, 2.228e-06] and the field of errors in *y*'-approximation is limited to the range [4.243e-10, 4.095e-05]. The approximations are accurate to within these confines.

Example 21

DE : $D^2y - \text{Sec}^2x = 0$

CE : $D^2y = \text{Sec}^2x$

PS : $y(x) = -\text{Ln}(\text{Cos}x),\ Dy(x) = \text{Tan}x$

IC : $y(\pi/4) = \dfrac{\text{Ln}2}{2}$, $y'(\pi/4) = 1$, Width : 0.01

The Computer Solution of the IVP of Order 2

x-value	*y-Approx*	*y-Exact*	*Error*	*y'-Approx*	*y'-Exact*	*Error*
0.7954	0.35667426	0.35667428	1.185e-08	1.02020270	1.02020272	2.319e-08
0.8054	0.36697903	0.36697904	1.893e-08	1.04082120	1.04082190	7.068e-07
0.8154	0.37749213	0.37749216	3.320e-08	1.06187341	1.06187483	1.426e-06
0.8254	0.38821799	0.38821805	5.505e-08	1.08337750	1.08337969	2.183e-06
0.8354	0.39916124	0.39916132	8.487e-08	1.10535264	1.10535562	2.981e-06
0.8454	0.41032667	0.41032680	1.231e-07	1.12781900	1.12782282	3.822e-06
0.8554	0.42171932	0.42171949	1.702e-07	1.15079789	1.15080260	4.709e-06

0.8654	0.43334441	0.43334463	2.267e-07	1.17431181	1.17431746	5.646e-06
0.8754	0.44520741	0.44520770	2.931e-07	1.19838454	1.19839118	6.637e-06
0.8854	0.45731403	0.45731440	3.700e-07	1.22304122	1.22304891	7.684e-06

The field of errors in y-approximation confines to the range [1.185e-08, 3.700e-07] and the field of errors in y'-approximation is limited to the range [2.319e-08, 7.684e-06]. The approximations are accurate to within these confines.

Example 22

DE : $D^2y - xe^x = 0$

CE : $D^2y = xe^x$

PS : $y(x) = (x-2)e^x + x + 3,\ Dy(x) = 2e^x(x-1) + 1$

IC : $y(0) = 1, \quad y'(0) = 0, \quad$ Width : 0.01

The Computer Solution of the IVP of Order 2

x-value	*y-Approx*	*y-Exact*	*Error*	*y'-Approx*	*y'-Exact*	*Error*
0.01	1.00000017	1.00000017	4.188e-13	5.03345868e-05	5.03345867e-05	-1.398e-13
0.02	1.00000135	1.00000135	8.404e-10	0.00020260	0.00020269	8.396e-08
0.03	1.00000457	1.00000457	2.533e-09	0.00045893	0.00045910	1.692e-07
0.04	1.00001088	1.00001088	5.090e-09	0.00082140	0.00082166	2.557e-07
0.05	1.00002135	1.00002136	8.526e-09	0.00129211	0.00129246	3.435e-07
0.06	1.00003709	1.00003710	1.285e-08	0.00187321	0.00187365	4.326e-07
0.07	1.00005919	1.00005921	1.808e-08	0.00256687	0.00256739	5.231e-07
0.08	1.00008881	1.00008883	2.423e-08	0.00337528	0.00337590	6.149e-07
0.09	1.00012709	1.00012712	3.132e-08	0.00430069	0.00430140	7.081e-07
0.10	1.00017522	1.00017526	3.934e-08	0.00534537	0.00534617	8.027e-07

The field of errors in y-approximation confines to the range [4.188e-13, 3.934e-08] and the field of errors in y'-approximation is limited to the range [-1.398e-13, 8.027e-07]. The approximations are accurate to within these confines.

7.4. Nonlinear Equations

Nonlinear dif‑ ential equations are the equations that describe the events of interaction. Such equations can be found in quantum physics and electrodynamics. The famous gravitation equation of Newton is such a case. As I mentioned in section 7.1 the nonlinear differential equations include the equations from van der Pol and the singularities.

1) $y'' - 5xy'^4 = e^x + 1$

2) $y''^2 - 3yy' + xy = 0$

These are nonlinear, because the derivatives of the unknown function y are raised to a power other than the first.

Example. Solve $x^2yy'' + (xy' - y)^2 - 3y^2 = 0.$

Simplifying and rearranging the nonlinear equation can be written in exact form

$$\frac{d}{dx}(x^2yy') - 2\frac{d}{dx}(xy^2) = 0.$$

Integrating yields $x^2yy' - 2xy^2 = C$

that can be transformed into a first-order linear form by putting $y^2 = v$.

The transformed linear equation becomes

$$dv/dx - 4v/x = 2C_1/x^2$$

I.F. $= x^{-4}$ and with the help of this we obtain

$$vx^{-4} = 2C_1\int x^{-6}dx = -\frac{2C_1}{5x^5} + C_2$$

Hence, the general solution is

$$y^2 = C_2x^4 - \frac{2C_1}{5x}$$

To solve a nonlinear differential equation the method of power series solution can be applied.

Example. Find a series solution for the equation $y'' = xy^2 - y'$ when the initial conditions are $y(0) = 2$, $y'(0) = 1$.

Let us assume that

$$y = C_0 + C_1x + C_2x^2 + C_3x^3 + \ldots\ldots \quad \text{(A)}$$

is a solution of the given differential equation.

Using the initial conditions we obtain $C_0 = 2$, $C_1 = 1$

The equation (A) takes the form $y = 2 + x + C_2x^2 + C_3x^3 + \ldots\ldots$

If we substitute the series y and its derivatives in the differential equation we get

$$2C_2 + 6C_3x + 12C_4x^2 = x\,(2 + x + C_2x^2 + C_3x^3 + \ldots\ldots)^2 - (1 + 2C_2x + 3C_3x^2 + \ldots\ldots)$$

Rearranging and equating the coefficients of corresponding powers of x one can determine the values

$$2C_2 = -1,\ 6C_3 = 4 - 2C_2,\ 12C_4 = 4 - 3C_3,\ \ldots$$

from which we obtain

$$C_2 = -\frac{1}{2},\ C_3 = \frac{5}{6},\ \ldots$$

Hence, $y = 2 + x - \frac{1}{2}x^2 + \frac{5}{6}x^3 + \ldots$

Example 1

$DE\ :\ y'' - y'^2 + y = 0$

$CE\ :\ y'' = y'^2 - y$

$PS\ :\ y(x) = \frac{x^2}{4} - 0.5,\ \ y'(x) = \frac{x}{2}$

$IC\ :\ y(1) = -0.25,\qquad y'(1) = 0.5,\qquad$ Width : 0.01

The Computer Solution of the IVP of Order 2

x-value	*y-Approx*	*y-Exact*	*Error*	*y'-Approx*	*y'-Exact*	*Error*
1.01	−0.24497500	−0.244975	−5.234e-13	0.50500000	0.505	5.130e-13
1.02	−0.23990000	−0.239900	6.240e-10	0.50999994	0.510	6.282e-08
1.03	−0.23477500	−0.234775	1.880e-09	0.51499987	0.515	1.263e-07
1.04	−0.22960000	−0.229600	3.773e-09	0.51999981	0.520	1.904e-07
1.05	−0.22437501	−0.224375	6.312e-09	0.52499974	0.525	2.552e-07
1.06	−0.21910001	−0.219100	9.501e-09	0.52999968	0.530	3.206e-07
1.07	−0.21377501	−0.213775	1.335e-08	0.53499961	0.535	3.868e-07
1.08	−0.20840002	−0.208400	1.786e-08	0.53999955	0.540	4.536e-07
1.09	−0.20297502	−0.202975	2.304e-08	0.54499948	0.545	5.212e-07
1.10	−0.19750003	−0.197500	2.891e-08	0.54999941	0.550	5.896e-07

The field of errors in y-approximation confines to the range [−5.234e-13, 2.891e-08] and the field of errors in y'-approximation is limited to the range

[5.130e-13, 5.896e-07]. The approximations are accurate to within these confines.

Example 2

DE : $(x+1)y'' + xy'^{\,2} - y' = 0$

CE : $y'' = \dfrac{y'(1-xy')}{x(x+1)}$

PS : $y(x) = 2Ln\, x - \dfrac{2}{x}$, $y'(x) = \dfrac{2}{x} + \dfrac{2}{x^2}$

IC : $y(1) = -2$, $y'(1) = 4$, Width : 0.01

The Computer Solution of the IVP of Order 2

x-value	*y-Approx*	*y-Exact*	*Error*	*y'-Approx*	*y'-Exact*	*Error*
1.01	–1.96029736	–1.96029736	1.689e-10	3.94079012	3.94079012	–2.916e-10
1.02	–1.92117910	–1.92117906	4.511e-08	3.88311747	3.88312188	4.402e-06
1.03	–1.88263010	–1.8826997	1.312e-07	3.82693094	3.82693939	8.450e-06
1.04	–1.84463575	–1.84463550	2.552e-07	3.77217718	3.77218935	1.217e-05
1.05	–1.80718199	–1.80718158	4.138e-07	3.71880527	3.71882086	1.559e-05
1.06	–1.77025524	–1.77025464	6.044e-07	3.66676660	3.66678533	1.873e-05
1.07	–1.73384241	–1.73384158	8.242e-07	3.61601473	3.61603634	2.161e-05
1.08	–1.69793084	–1.69792977	1.071e-06	3.56650525	3.56652949	2.425e-05
1.09	–1.66250833	–1.66250699	1.342e-06	3.51819571	3.51822237	2.666e-05
1.10	–1.62756309	–1.62756146	1.635e-06	3.47104551	3.47107438	2.887e-05

The field of errors in y-approximation confines to the range [1.689e-10, 1.635e-06] and the field of errors in y'-approximation is limited to the range [–2.916e-10, 2.887e-05]. The approximations are accurate to within these confines.

Example 3

DE : $y'' - y'e^{y} = 0$

CE : $y'' = y'e^{y}$

PS : $y(x) = -Ln\,(2e^{-x} - 1)$, $y'(x) = \dfrac{1}{1 - \dfrac{e^{x}}{2}}$

IC : $y(0) = 0$, $y'(0) = 2$, Width : 0.01

The Computer Solution of the IVP of Order 2

x-value	*y-Approx*	*y-Exact*	*Error*	*y'-Approx*	*y'-Exact*	*Error*
0.01	0.02010101	0.02010101	3.129e-11	2.02030440	2.02030440	–3.517e-11
0.02	0.04040818	0.04040818	–1.463e-09	2.04123585	2.04123570	–1.537e-07
0.03	0.06092791	0.06092791	–4.646e-09	2.06282262	2.06282229	–3.237e-07
0.04	0.08166692	0.08166691	–9.697e-09	2.08509483	2.08509431	–5.119e-07
0.05	0.10263220	0.10263219	–1.681e-08	2.10808449	2.10808377	–7.200e-07
0.06	0.12383111	0.12383109	–2.621e-08	2.13182563	2.13182468	–9.502e-07
0.07	0.14527134	0.14527131	–3.814e-08	2.15635446	2.15635325	–1.205e-06
0.08	0.16696096	0.16696091	–5.285e-08	2.18170955	2.18170807	–1.486e-06
0.09	0.18890843	0.18890836	–7.064e-08	2.20793205	2.20793025	–1.797e-06
0.10	0.21112264	0.21112255	–9.184e-08	2.23506584	2.23506370	–2.141e-06

The field of errors in y-approximation confines to the range [3.129e-11, – 9.184e-08] and the field of errors in y'-approximation is limited to the range [– 3.517e-11, – 2.141e-06]. The approximations are accurate to within these confines.

Example 4

DE : $y2 - y1^2 = 1$

CE : $y2 = y1^2 + 1$

PS : $y(x) = Ln(\text{Sec } x)$, $y1(x) = \text{Tan } x$

IC : $y(0) = 0$, $y'(0) = 0$, Width : 0.01

The Computer Solution of the IVP of Order 2

x-value	*y-Approx*	*y-Exact*	*Error*	*y'-Approx*	*y'-Exact*	*Error*
0.01	5.00008334e-05	5:00008334e-05	1.318e-15	0.01000033	0.01000033	8.333e-13
0.02	0.00020001	0.00020001	8.335e-10	0.02000258	0.02000267	8.336e-08
0.03	0.00045007	0.00045007	2.501e-09	0.03000884	0.03000900	1.668e-07
0.04	0.00080021	0.00080021	5.001e-09	0.04002110	0.04002135	2.502e-07
0.05	0.00125051	0.00125052	8.336e-09	0.05004137	0.05004171	3.336e-07
0.06	0.00180107	0.00180108	1.251e-08	0.06007169	0.06007210	4.171e-07
0.07	0.00245199	0.00245200	1.751e-08	0.07011406	0.07011456	5.007e-07
0.08	0.00320340	0.00320342	2.335e-08	0.08017052	0.08017110	5.842e-07

x-value	*y-Approx*	*y-Exact*	*Error*	*y'-Approx*	*y'-Exact*	*Error*
0.09	0.00405545	0.00405548	3.002e-08	0.09024312	0.09024379	6.678e-07
0.10	0.00500832	0.00500836	3.753e-08	0.10033392	0.10033476	7.514e-07

The field of errors in y-approximation confines to the range [1.318e-15, 3.753e-08] and the field of errors in y'-approximation is limited to the range [8.333e-13, 7.514e-07]. The approximations are accurate to within these confines.

Example 5

$$DE : y'' - e^{-2y} = 0$$

$$CE : y'' = e^{-2y}$$

$$PS : y(x) = Ln\left[\text{Cosh}\left(x + \frac{\pi}{2}\right)\right],\ y'(x) = \text{Tanh}\left(x + \frac{\pi}{2}\right)$$

$$IC : y\left(\frac{-\pi}{2}\right) = 0, \quad y'\left(\frac{-\pi}{2}\right) = 0, \quad \text{Width} : 0.01$$

The Computer Solution of the IVP of Order 2

x-value	*y-Approx*	*y-Exact*	*Error*	*y'-Approx*	*y'-Exact*	*Error*
–1.5608	4.99991667e-05	4.99991667e-05	1.472e-15	0.00999967	0.00999967	8.331e-13
–1.5508	0.00019999	0.00019999	1.667e-09	0.01999717	0.01999733	1.667e-07
–1.5408	0.00044993	0.00044993	5.000e-09	0.02999067	0.02999100	3.333e-07
–1.5308	0.00079978	0.00079979	9.998e-09	0.03997818	0.03997868	4.997e-07
–1.5208	0.00124946	0.00124948	1.666e-08	0.04995771	0.04995837	6.660e-07
–1.5108	0.00179890	0.00179892	2.498e-08	0.05992727	0.05992810	8.321e-07
–1.5008	0.00244797	0.00244800	3.497e-08	0.06988489	0.06988589	9.978e-07
–1.4908	0.00319655	0.00319659	4.660e-08	0.07982861	0.07982977	1.163e-06
–1.4808	0.00404448	0.00404454	5.989e-08	0.08975646	0.08975778	1.328e-06
–1.4708	0.00499161	0.00499169	7.482e-08	0.9966650	0.09966799	1.492e-06

The field of errors in y-approximation confines to the range [1.472e-15, 7.482e-08] and the field of errors in y'-approximation is limited to the range [8.331e-13, 1.492e-06]. The approximations are accurate to within these confines.

Example 6

$$DE : yy'' + 3y'^2 = 0$$

$$CE : y'' = \frac{-3y'^2}{y}$$

$$PS : y(x) = 1 + \frac{x}{4} - \frac{3x^2}{32} + \frac{7x^3}{128} - \frac{77x^4}{2048} + \ldots$$

$$y'(x) = \frac{1}{4} - \frac{3x}{16} + \frac{21x^2}{128} - \frac{77x^3}{512} + \ldots$$

$$IC : y(0) = 1, \quad y'(0) = 0.25, \quad \text{Width} : 0.01$$

The Computer Solution of the IVP of Order 2

x-value	*y-Approx*	*y-Exact*	*Error*	*y'-Approx*	*y'-Exact*	*Error*
0.01	1.00249068	1.00249068	–1.943e-12	0.24814126	0.24814126	–1.397e-09
0.02	1.00496293	1.00496293	1.968e-10	0.24631442	0.24631442	6.052e-09
0.03	1.00741707	1.00741707	1.705e-10	0.24451865	0.24451860	–5.610e-08
0.04	1.00985340	1.00985340	–1.149e-09	0.24275314	0.24275288	–2.674e-07
0,05	1.01227223	1.01227223	–5.775e-09	0.24101709	0.24101636	–7.368e-07
0.06.	1.01467384	1.01467383	–1.695e-08	0.23930974	0.23930814	–1.601e-06
0.07	1.01705852	1.01705848	–3.942e-08	0.23763035	0.23762732	–3.025e-06
0.08	1.01942654	1.01942646	–7.971e-08	0.23597820	0.23597300	–5.198e-06
0.09	1.02177817	1.02177803	–1.464e-07	0.23435260	0.23434427	–8.333e-06
0.10	1.02411368	1.02411343	–2.502e-07	0.23275290	0.23274023	–1.267e-05

The field of errors in y-approximation confines to the range [– 1.943e-12, – 2.502e-07] and the field of errors in y'-approximation is limited to the range [– 1.397e-09, – 1.267e-05]. The approximations are accurate to within these confines.

Example 7

$$DE : yy'' + y'^2 = 1$$

$$CE : y'' = \frac{1 - y'^2}{y}$$

$$PS : y(x) = x + 1, \; y'(x) = 1.0$$

$$IC : y(0) = 1, \quad y'(0) = 1, \quad \text{Width} : 0.01$$

The Computer Solution of the IVP of Order 2

x-value	*y-Approx*	*y-Exact*	*Error*	*y'-Approx*	*y'-Exact*	*Error*
0.01	1.01	1.01	0	1	1	0
0.02	1.02	1.02	0	1	1	0
0.03	1.03	1.03	0	1	1	0
0.04	1.04	1.04	0	1	1	0
0.05	1.05	1.05	0	1	1	0
0.06	1.06	1.06	0	1	1	0
0.07	1.07	1.07	0	1	1	0
0.08	1.08	1.08	0	1	1	0
0.09	1.09	1.09	0	1	1	0
0.10	1.10	1.10	0	1	1	0

The field of errors in y-approximation confines to the range [0, 0] and the field of errors in y'-approximation is limited to the range [0, 0]. The approximations are accurate to within these confines.

Example 8

DE : $2yy'' - y'^2 = y^2$

CE : $y'' = \dfrac{y^2 + y'^2}{2y}$,

PS : $y(x) = e^x$, $y'(x) = e^x$

IC : $y(0) = 1$, $y'(0) = 1$, Width : 0.01

The Computer Solution of the IVP of Order 2

x-value	*y-Approx*	*y-Exact*	*Error*	*y'-Approx*	*y'-Exact*	*Error*
0.01	1.01005017	1.01005017	8.347e-13	1.01005017	1.01005017	–8.133e-08
0.02	1.02020134	1.02020134	–8.316e-10	1.02020142	1.02020134	–8.375e-08
0.03	1.03045454	1.03045453	–2.514e-09	1.03045470	1.03045453	–1.692e-07
0.04	1.04081078	1.04081077	–5.064e-09	1.04081103	1.04081077	–2.563e-07
0.05	1.05127110	1.05127110	–8.498e-09	1.05127144	1.05127110	–3.452e-07
0.06	1.06183656	1.06183655	–1.283e-08	1.06183698	1.06183655	–4.358e-07
0.07	1.07250820	1.07250818	–1.809e-08	1.07250871	1.07250818	–5.283e-07
0.08	1.08328709	1.08328707	–2.428e-08	1.08328769	1.08328707	–6.225e-07

x-value	*y-Approx*	*y-Exact*	*Error*	*y'-Approx*	*y'-Exact*	*Error*
0.09	1.09417432	1.09417428	–3.143e-08	1.09417500	1.09417428	–7.186e-07
0.10	1.10517096	1.10517092	–3.955e-08	1.10517173	1.10517092	–8.165e-07

The field of errors in y-approximation confines to the range [8.347e-13, – 3.955e-08] and the field of errors in y'-approximation is limited to the range [– 8.133e-08, – 8.165e-07]. The approximations are accurate to within these confines.

Example 9

$$DE : (y'^2 - 6x)y'' + 2y' = 0$$

$$CE : y'' = \frac{-2y'}{y'^2 - 6x}$$

$$PS : y(x) = \frac{2\sqrt{2}x^{1.5} - 8}{3}, \quad y'(x) = \sqrt{2}x^{0.5}$$

$$IC : y(2) = 0, \quad y'(2) = 2, \quad \text{Width} : 0.01$$

The Computer Solution of the IVP of Order 2

x-value	*y-Approx*	*y-Exact*	*Error*	*y'-Approx*	*y'-Exact*	*Error*
2.01	0.02002498	0.02002498	–6.516-14	2.00499377	2.00499377	–7.061e-14
2.02	0.04009983	0.04009983	1.165e-10	2.00997511	2.00997512	1.169e-08
2.03	0.06022444	0.06022444	3.489e-10	2.01494414	2.01494417	2.330e-08
2.04	0.08039868	0.08039868	6.962e-10	2.01990095	2.01990099	3.482e-08
2.05	0.10062242	0.10062242	1.158e-09	2.02484563	2.02484567	4.626e-08
2.06	0.12089555	0.12089555	1.732e-09	2.02977826	2.02977831	5.762e-08
2.07	0.14121794	0.14121795	2.420e-09	2.03469893	2.03469899	6.889e-08
2.08	0.16158949	0.16158949	3.218e-09	2.03960773	2.03960781	8.008e-08
2.09	0.18201006	0.18201006	4.128e-09	2.04450474	2.04450483	9.120e-08
2.10	0.20247954	0.20247955	5.148e-09	2.04939005	2.04939015	1.022e-07

The field of errors in y-approximation confines to the range [–6.516e-14, 5.148e-09] and the field of errors in y'-approximation is limited to the range [– 7.061e-14, 1.022e-07]. The approximations are accurate to within these confines.

Example 10

$$DE : 2yy'' - 3y'^2 = 4y^2$$

$$CE : y'' = \frac{4y^2 + 3y'^2}{2y}$$

$PS \ : \ y(x) = \dfrac{1}{\text{Cos}^2 x} \ , \ y'(x) = \dfrac{2\text{Tan } x}{\text{Cos}^2 x}$

$IC \ : \ y(0) = 1, \quad y'(0) = 0,$ Width : 0.01

The Computer Solution of the IVP of Order 2

x-value	*y-Approx*	*y-Exact*	*Error*	*y'-Approx*	*y'-Exact*	*Error*
0.01	1.00010001	1.00010001	1.279e-13	0.02000267	0.02000267	1.674e-12
0.02	1.00040011	1.00040011	1.669e-09	0.04002117	0.04002134	1.669e-07
0.03	1.00090054	1.00090054	5.002e-09	0.06007172	0.06007206	3.335e-07
0.04	1.00160170	1.00160171	9.983e-09	0.08017040	0.08017040	4.985e-07
0.05	1.00250416	1.00250417	1.658e-08	0.10033338	0.10033404	6.610e-07
0.06	1.00360863	1.00360866	2.477e-08	0.12057695	0.12057777	8.196e-07
0.07	1.00491602	1.00491605	3.448e-08	0.14091752	0.14091849	9.732e-07
0.08	1.00642736	1.00642741	4.566e-08	0.16137167	0.16137279	1.121e-06
0.09	1.00814388	1.00814394	5.823e-08	0.18195620	0.18195746	1.260e-06
0.10	1.01006697	1.01006705	7.210e-08	0.20268810	0.20268949	1.391e-06

The field of errors in y-approximation confines to the range [1.279e-13, 7.210e-08] and the field of errors in y'-approximation is limited to the range [1.674e-12, 1.391e-06]. The approximations are accurate to within these confines.

Example 11

$DE \ : \ y'' + 2y(1 - y^2) = 0$

$CE \ : \ y'' = -2y(1 - y^2)$

$PS \ : y(x) = \text{Tan } hx \ , \ y'(x) = \dfrac{1}{\text{Cos } h^2 x}$

$IC \ : \ y(0) = 0, \quad y'(0) = 1,$ Width : 0.01

The Computer Solution of the IVP of Order 2

x-value	*y-Approx*	*y-Exact*	*Error*	*y'-Approx*	*y'-Exact*	*Error*
0.01	0.00999967	0.00999967	4.999e-12	0.99990001	0.99990001	1.638e-13
0.02	0.01999733	0.01999733	5.165e-11	0.99960010	0.99960011	4.166e-09
0.03	0.02999100	0.02999100	1.566e-10	0.99910053	0.99910054	9.994e-09
0.04	0.03997868	0.03997868	3.364e-10	0.99840169	0.99840171	1.748e-08
0.05	0.04995837	0.04995837	6.076e-10	0.99750413	0.99750416	2.662e-08

x-value	*y-Approx*	*y-Exact*	*Error*	*y'-Approx*	*y'-Exact*	*Error*
0.06	0.05992810	0.05992810	9.868e-10	0.99640858	0.99640862	3.742e-08
0.07	0.06988589	0.06988589	1.490e-09	0.99511591	0.99511596	4.988e-08
0.08	0.07982977	0.07982977	2.135e-09	0.99362714	0.99362721	6.399e-08
0.09	0.08975778	0.08975778	2.938e-09	0.99194346	0.99194354	7.976e-08
0.10	0.09966799	0.09966799	3.915e-09	0.99006619	0.99006629	9.720e-08

The field of errors in y-approximation confines to the range [4.999e-12, 3.915e-09] and the field of errors in y'-approximation is limited to the range [1.638e-13, 9.720e-08]. The approximations are accurate to within these confines.

Example 12

DE : $yy'' + y'^2 = y'^3$

CE : $y'' = \dfrac{y'^3 - y'^2}{y}$

PS : $y(x) = x + 1$, $y'(x) = 1$

IC : $y(0) = 1$, $y'(0) = 1$, Width : 0.01

The Computer Solution of the IVP of Order 2

x-value	*y-Approx*	*y-Exact*	*Error*	*y'-Approx*	*y'-Exact*	*Error*
0.01	1.01	1.01	0	1	1	0
0.02	1.02	1.02	0	1	1	0
0.03	1.03	1.03	0	1	1	0
0.04	1.04	1.04	0	1	1	0
0.05	1.05	1.05	0	1	1	0
0.06	1.06	1.06	0	1	1	0
0.07	1.07	1.07	0	1	1	0
0.08	1.08	1.08	0	1	1	0
0.09	1.09	1.09	0	1	1	0
0.10	1.10	1.10	0	1	1	0

The field of errors in y-approximation confines to the range [0, 0] and the field of errors in y'-approximation is limited to the range [0, 0]. The approximations are accurate to within these confines.

Example 13

DE : $y'' - y'^2 + y'(y-1) = 0$

CE : $y'' = y'^2 - y'(y-1)$

PS : $y = 2e^x$, $y' = 2e^x$

IC : $y(0) = 2$, $y'(0) = 2$, Width : 0.01

The Computer Solution of the IVP of Order 2

x-value	*y-Approx*	*y-Exact*	*Error*	*y'-Approx*	*y'-Exact*	*Error*
0.01	2.02010033	2.02010033	1.669e-12	2.02010033	2.02010033	1.669e-12
0.02	2.04040268	1.04040268	–1.680e-09	2.04040285	2.04040268	–1.709e-07
0.03	2.06090907	2.06090907	–5.115e-09	2.06090942	2.06090907	–3.488e-07
0.04	2.08162156	2.08162155	–1.037e-08	2.08162208	2.08162155	–5.340e-07
0.05	2.10254221	2.10254219	–1.753e-08	2.10254292	2.10254219	–7.267e-07
0.06	2.12367312	2.12367309	–2.666e-08	2.12367402	2.12367309	–9.273e-07
0.07	2.14501640	2.14501636	–3.784e-08	2.14501750	2.14501636	–1.136e-06
0.08	2.16657419	2.16657414	–5.117e-08	2.16657549	2.16657414	–1.353e-06
0.09	2.18834863	2.18834857	–6.672e-08	2.18835015	2.18834857	–1.579e-06
0.10	2.21034192	2.21034184	–8.458e-08	2.21034365	2.21034184	–1.814e-06

The field of errors in y-approximation confines to the range [1.669e-12, – 8.458e-08] and the field of errors in y'-approximation is limited to the range [1.669e-12, – 1.814e-06]. The approximations are accurate to within these confines.

Example 14

DE : $xy'y'' - y'^2 = x^3$

CE : $y'' = \dfrac{x^3 + y'^2}{xy'}$

PS : $y(x) = 0.4x^2\sqrt{2x} - 3.2$, $y'(x) = x\sqrt{2x}$

IC : $y(2) = 0$, $y'(2) = 4$, Width : 0.01

The Computer Solution of the IVP of Order 2

x-value	*y-Approx*	*y-Exact*	*Error*	*y'-Approx*	*y'-Exact*	*Error*
2.01	0.04015012	0.04015012	8.318e-14	4.030033747	4.03003747	2.398e-14
2.02	0.08060100	0.08060100	–3.114e-10	4.06014978	4.06014975	–3.119e-08

x-value	*y-Approx*	*y-Exact*	*Error*	*y'-Approx*	*y'-Exact*	*Error*
2.03	0.12135337	0.12135337	−9.328e-10	4.09033672	4.09033666	−6.223e-08
2.04	0.16240798	0.16240798	−1.863e-09	4.12059811	4.12059801	−9.311e-08
2.05	0.20376558	0.20376558	−3.099e-09	4.15093375	4.15093363	−1.238e-07
2.06	0.24542690	0.24542690	−4.642e-09	4.18134348	4.18134332	−1.544e-07
2.07	0.28739270	0.28739269	−6.488e-09	4.21182710	4.21182692	−1.849e-07
2.08	0.32966369	0.32966368	−8.637e-09	4.24238445	4.24238424	−2.151e-07
2.09	0.37224063	0.37224062	−1.109e-08	4.27301534	4.27301509	−2.453e-07
2.10	0.41512424	0.41512423	−1.384e-08	4.30371960	4.30371932	−2.753e-07

The field of errors in y-approximation confines to the range [8.318e-14, – 1.384e-08] and the field of errors in y'-approximation is limited to the range [2.398e-14, –2.753e-07]. The approximations are accurate to within these confines.

Example 15

$$DE : (1 + x^2)y'' + y'^2 + 1 = 0$$

$$CE : y'' = -\frac{1 + y'^2}{1 + x^2}$$

$$PS : y(x) = 2Ln(x + 1) - x + 1 , \ y'(x) = \frac{2}{x + 1} - 1$$

$$IC : y(0) = 1, \qquad y'(0) = 1, \qquad \text{Width} : 0.01$$

The Computer Solution of the IVP of Order 2

x-value	*y-Approx*	*y-Exact*	*Error*	*y'-Approx*	*y'-Exact*	*Error*
0.01	1.00990066	1.00990066	1.471e-11	0.98019802	0.98019802	8.588e-12
0.02	1.01960525	1.01960525	4.979e-09	0.96078382	0.96078431	4.902e-07
0.03	1.02911759	1.02911760	1.451e-08	0.94174663	0.94174757	9.426e-07
0.04	1.03844140	1.03844143	2.824e-08	0.92307556	0.92307692	1.360e-06
0.05	1.04758028	1.04758033	4.585e-08	0.90476016	0.90476190	1.744e-06
0.06	1.05653775	1.05653782	6.702e-08	0.88679036	0.88679245	2.097e-06
0.07	1.06531721	1.06531730	9.146e-08	0.86915646	0.86915888	2.422e-06
0.08	1.07392196	1.07392208	1.189e-07	0.85184913	0.85185185	2.720e-06
0.09	1.08235524	1.08235539	1.491e-07	0.83485939	0.83486239	2.993e-06
0.10	1.09062018	1.09062036	1.818e-07	0.81817858	0.81818182	3.242e-06

The field of errors in y-approximation confines to the range [1.471e-11, 1.818e-07] and the field of errors in y'-approximation is limited to the range [8.858e-12, 3.242e-06]. The approximations are accurate to within these confines.

Example 16

$$DE : \operatorname{Cos} y\, y'' + y'^{\,2} \operatorname{Sin} y - y' = 0$$

$$CE : y'' = \frac{y'(1 - y' \operatorname{Sin} y)}{\operatorname{Cos} y}$$

$$PS : y(x) = 2\operatorname{Tan}^{-1}(e^{2(x+1)}) - \frac{\pi}{3},\ y'(x) = \frac{4e^{2(x+1)}}{1 + e^{4(x+1)}}$$

$$IC : y(-1) = 0.52359878, \quad y'(-1) = 2, \quad \text{Width} : 0.01$$

The Computer Solution of the IVP of Order 2

x-value	*y-Approx*	*y-Exact*	*Error*	*y'-Approx*	*y'-Exact*	*Error*
–0.99	0.54359745	0.54359743	–2.317e-08	1.99960007	1.99960007	3.288e-10
–0.98	0.56358813	0.56358810	–3.474e-08	1.99840222	1.99840107	–1.153e-06
–0.97	0.58356285	0.58356279	–5.843e-08	1.99640775	1.99640539	–2.354e-06
–0.96	0.60351366	0.60351356	–9.469e-08	1.99362062	1.99361702	–3.600e-06
–0.95	0.62343265	0.62343251	–1.439e-07	1.99004638	1.99004150	–4.886e-06
–0.94	0.64331200	0.64331179	–2.065e-07	1.98569210	1.98568590	–6.206e-06
–0.93	0.66314394	0.66314366	–2.828e-07	1.98056636	1.98055880	–7.555e-06
–0.92	0.68292080	0.68292043	–3.730e-07	1.97467918	1.97467025	–8.927e-06
–0.91	0.70263504	0.70263456	–4.773e-07	1.96804203	1.96803171	–1.032e-05
–0.90	0.72227920	0.72227861	–5.957e-07	1.96066771	1.96065600	–1.171e-05

The field of errors in y-approximation confines to the range [– 2.317e-08, – 5.957e-07] and the field of errors in y'-approximation is limited to the range [3.288e-10, – 1.171e-05]. The approximations are accurate to within these confines.

Chapter 8

Systems of Differential Equations

8.1. Development of the System

Until this point we have discussed the subject matter only with single differential equations. Let us now consider the systems of simultaneous equations.

The most simple class of the system is that containing only one independent variable and the other two dependent variables. For the sake of restraint we confine ourselves to considering the system of two differential equations which may be written in the form

$$x = f(x, y, t)$$

$$y = g(x, y, t) \tag{8.1}$$

In this system of equations t denotes the independent variable; x and y denoting the dependent variables; $\dot{x}$ stands for $\dfrac{dx}{dt}$ and $\dot{y}$ stands for $\dfrac{dy}{dt}$, usually applied for the velocity range at any instant of time t.

The system of functions $x = F(t)$, $y = G(t)$ (8.2)

is the solution of the original system (8.1) and it represents a particular curve in cartesian coordinates plane, commonly known as xy-plane, being described by the path that moves in a plane and determines the phase of the curve at any instant of time.

The system (8.1) has a dynamic character. If the independent variable, in this case t, does not appear explicitly in the right-hand side of the equations forming the system, we designate the system as **autonomous**, that means independent.

The development of the system (8.1) requires in the beginning a specific definition of the initial conditions :

$$x(t) = \alpha, y(t) = \beta \tag{8.3}$$

which specify the position of the point on the curve at the initial stage and then we proceed to solve the differential equations.

In the simple class of the system, as mentioned earlier, most of the problems of dynamics have been covered. The astronomical problems and the problems from mechanics, a branch of physics, dealing with small vibrations or deviations are also included.

8.2. Software required for solving the system

The program IVPD1SYS designed for the purpose, is the related software for solving the system of differential equations. We need not be concerned in detailed exposition of the complete software here.

As we noted earlier, the program runs on C++ package (version 3.0) from BORLAND International. The execution of the program is performed by the operating system MS-DOS from Microsoft Inc.

If the corresponding, rather to say, compatible package in the computer system with the necessary programming tools is available, it is only then recommendable to run the program on the system, PC or Laptop.

Let us have some indications how to run the program?

The member function setDE in class 'DiffSys' should be provided with new differential equations before start. When the complete program for solution of the system of differential equations begins to run on C++, the member function 'getdata (void)' in class 'DiffSys' shall be furnished with the initial conditions by putting the starting values of t, $x(t)$, and $y(t)$. With these data given, the program proceeds to solve the problem yielding the required results.

8.3. Simultaneous System of First-order Equations

Seeing that we have the necessary tools to solve the systems of differential equations, let us consider the system. We don't outline here the methods for the solutions of the system of differential equations of first-order, which can be found in standard textbooks, some of which have been mentioned in the reference of this text.

We confine ourselves to determining a computerised solution of the mathematical problem with the help of the software mentioned in section (8.2) applying the mathematical formulae from RUNGE-KUTTA, the main features of which had been given in chapter 5. To find a solution of a normal system of two first-order differential equations, for example, a system of the form

$$\frac{dx}{dt} = 3y - x, \quad \frac{dy}{dt} = 4y - 2x + 1.0 \tag{8.4}$$

As we have already discussed in section (8.2) the operation of the program IVPD1SYS can be carried out only with the insertion of new differential equations, that means, with the change of the right-hand side expressions of (8.4). The two system variables SysDx and SysDy in member function setDE of class 'DiffSys' have been furnished with the stated differential equations.

The controlling section of the program reminds you to the insertion before entering into the initial conditions. By putting the initial values of t, x and y, which are 0, 2.0 and 1.0 in this case we have the computational solution of the original equation (8.4) in complete form represented

Example 1

SYS : $\frac{dx}{dt} = 3y - x, \quad \frac{dy}{dt} = 4y - 2x + 1.0$

PS : $x(t) = 0.5[3 + \text{Exp}(2t)], \quad y(t) = 0.5[1 + \text{Exp}(2t)]$

IC : $x(0) = 2.0, y(0) = 1.0$

W : 0.01

Computer solution of the system :

$x(0.01)$	:	2.0101006	$y(0.01)$	:	1.0101007
$x(0.02)$	:	2.0204053	$y(0.02)$	:	1.0204054
$x(0.03)$	:	2.0309181	$y(0.03)$	:	1.0309184
$x(0.04)$	:	2.0416434	$y(0.04)$	:	1.0416436
$x(0.05)$	:	2.0525854	$y(0.05)$	:	1.0525856
$x(0.06)$	:	2.0637484	$y(0.06)$	:	1.0637486
$x(0.07)$	:	2.0751369	$y(0.07)$	:	1.0751371
$x(0.08)$	:	2.0867555	$y(0.08)$	:	1.0867556

$x(0.09)$	:	2.0986087	$y(0.09)$	:	1.0986089
$x(0.10)$	:	2.1107013	$y(0.10)$	:	1.1107016

The first ten estimated values of x and y with the corresponding increments of t have been shown here accepting m = 10 and w = 0.01. With the data just determined we can draw the particular curve to have a clear image on the system of functions.

Finally, one can compare these results with the values obtained from the particular solutions with the help of a calculator. The difference between an approximate value and an exact value amounts to an error estimate that developes the concept of error propagation discussed in chapter 3.

Example 2

SYS : $\frac{dx}{dt} = \frac{2tv}{t^2 - x^2 - y^2}$ $\frac{dy}{dt} = \frac{2ty}{t^2 - x^2 - y^2}$

PS : $t^2 + x^2 + y^2 = 2x,$ $y(t) = x$

IC : $x(0) = 1, y(0) = 1$

W : 0.01

Computer solution of the System :

$x(0.01)$	:	0.99995	$y(0.01)$	:	0.99995
$x(0.02)$	:	0.9998	$y(0.02)$	:	0.9998
$x(0.03)$	:	0.9995498	$y(0.03)$	:	0.9995498
$x(0.04)$	:	0.9991994	$y(0.04)$	:	0.9991994
$x(0.05)$	:	0.9987485	$y(0.05)$	:	0.9987485
$x(0.06)$	:	0.9981968	$y(0.06)$	:	0.9981968
$x(0.07)$	:	0.997544	$y(0.07)$	:	0.997544
$x(0.08)$	:	0.9967897	$y(0.08)$	:	0.9967897
$x(0.09)$	:	0.9959335	$y(0.09)$	:	0.9959335
$x(0.10)$	:	0.9949747	$y(0.10)$	:	0.9949747

Example 3

SYS : $\frac{dx}{dt} = x + 2y,$ $\frac{dy}{dt} = 4y - x$

PS : $x(t) = \text{Exp}(2t)[2 - \exp(t)]$, $y(t) = \text{Exp}(2t)[1 - \exp(t)]$

IC : $x(0) = 1, y(0) = 0$

W : 0.01

Computer solution of the System :

$x(0.01)$	:	1.0099481	$y(0.01)$	:	–0.0102532
$x(0.02)$	:	1.0197850	$y(0.02)$	:	–0.0210258
$x(0.03)$	:	1.0294988	$y(0.03)$	:	–0.0323377
$x(0.04)$	:	1.0390773	$y(0.04)$	:	–0.0442098
$x(0.05)$	:	1.0485076	$y(0.05)$	:	–0.0566633
$x(0.06)$	:	1.0577763	$y(0.06)$	:	–0.0697205
$x(0.07)$	:	1.0668695	$y(0.07)$	:	–0.0834043
$x(0.08)$	:	1.0757725	$y(0.08)$	:	–0.0977383
$x(0.09)$	:	1.0844702	$y(0.09)$	:	–0.1127471
$x(0.10)$	:	1.0929465	$y(0.10)$	:	–0.1284561

Example 4

SYS : $\dfrac{dx}{dt} = x - 2y$, $\dfrac{dy}{dt} = 2y - 3x$

PS : $x(t) = \dfrac{[2\text{Exp}(4t) + 3\text{Exp}(-t)]}{5}$, $y(t) = \dfrac{3[\text{Exp}(-t) - \text{Exp}(4t)]}{5}$

IC : $x(0) = 1, y(0) = 0$

W : 0.01

Computer solution of the System :

$x(0.01)$	:	1.0103542	$y(0.01)$	:	–0.0304566
$x(0.02)$	:	1.0214339	$y(0.02)$	:	–0.0618530
$x(0.03)$	:	1.0332659	$y(0.03)$	:	–0.0942308
$x(0.04)$	:	1.0458779	$y(0.04)$	:	–0.1276329
$x(0.05)$	:	1.0592986	$y(0.05)$	:	–0.1621040
$x(0.06)$	:	1.0735582	$y(0.06)$	:	–0.1976908
$x(0.07)$	:	1.0886880	$y(0.07)$	:	–0.2344416

x(0.08)	:	1.1047207	y(0.08)	:	–0.2724068
x(0.09)	:	1.1216903	y(0.09)	:	–0.3116389
x(0.10)	:	1.1396321	y(0.10)	:	–0.3521923

Example 5

SYS : $\frac{dx}{dt} = t - y - x$ $\qquad \frac{dy}{dt} = t + y + x$

PS : $x(t) = \frac{t**2}{2} - \frac{t**3}{3}$, $\qquad y(t) = \frac{t**2}{2} + \frac{t**3}{3}$

IC : $x(0) = 0$, $y(0) = 0$

W : 0.01

Computer solution of the System :

x(0.01)	:	4.9666665e-05	y(0.01)	:	5.0333329e-05
x(0.02)	:	0.0001973	y(0.02)	:	0.0002027
x(0.03)	:	0.0004410	y(0.03)	:	0.0004590
x(0.04)	:	0.0007787	y(0.04)	:	0.0008213
x(0.05)	:	0.0012083	y(0.05)	:	0.0012917
x(0.06)	:	0.0017280	y(0.06)	:	0.0018720
x(0.07)	:	0.0023357	y(0.07)	:	0.0025643
x(0.08)	:	0.0030293	y(0.08)	:	0.0033707
x(0.09)	:	0.0038070	y(0.09)	:	0.0042930
x(0.10)	:	0.0046667	y(0.10)	:	0.0053333

Example 6

SYS : $Dx = -3y - 3\text{Exp}(t)$, $\qquad Dy = 4y + 6\text{Exp}(t)$

PS : $x = -0.5 + 3\exp(t)[1-0.5\exp(3t)]$, $y = 2\exp(t)[\text{Exp}(3t)-1]$

IC : $x(0) = 1$, $y(0) = 0$

W : 0.01

Computer solution of the System :

x(0.01)	:	0.9689344	y(0.01)	:	0.0615212
x(0.02)	:	0.9356734	y(0.02)	:	0.1261715

$x(0.03)$	:	0.9001184	$y(0.03)$	:	0.1940846
$x(0.04)$	:	0.8621660	$y(0.04)$	:	0.2654002
$x(0.05)$	:	0.8217092	$y(0.05)$	:	0.3402633
$x(0.06)$	:	0.7786359	$y(0.06)$	:	0.4188252
$x(0.07)$	:	0.7328298	$y(0.07)$	:	0.5012432
$x(0.08)$	:	0.6841695	$y(0.08)$	:	0.5876814
$x(0.09)$	:	0.6325287	$y(0.09)$	:	0.6783102
$x(0.10)$	:	0.5777757	$y(0.10)$	:	0.7733075

Example 7

SYS : $Dx = x + y + t,$ $Dy = 2t - 3y - 4x$

PS : $x = -9(1 - \exp(-t)) + t(5 + 4\exp(-t)),$

$y = 14(1 - \text{e xp}(-t)) - 2t(3 + 4\exp(-t))$

IC : $x(0) = 0, y(0) = 0$

W : 0.01

Computer solution of the System :

$x(0.01)$	:	5.0497081e-05	$y(0.01)$	:	9.8340824e-05
$x(0.02)$	:	0.0002040	$y(0.02)$	:	0.0003868
$x(0.03)$	:	0.0004633	$y(0.03)$	:	0.0008556
$x(0.04)$	:	0.0008313	$y(0.04)$	:	0.0014952
$x(0.05)$	:	0.0013107	$y(0.05)$	:	0.0022963
$x(0.06)$	:	0.0019043	$y(0.06)$	:	0.0032496
$x(0.07)$	:	0.0026146	$y(0.07)$	:	0.0043460
$x(0.08)$	:	0.0034443	$y(0.08)$	:	0.0055767
$x(0.09)$	:	0.0043959	$y(0.09)$	:	0.0069330
$x(0.10)$	:	0.0054717	$y(0.10)$	:	0.0084062

Example 8

SYS : $Dx = x + 3y,$ $Dy = 5y - x$

PS : $x(t) = \text{xExp}(2t),$ $y(t) = \text{Exp}(2t)$

IC : $x(0) = 3, y(0) = 1$

W : 0.01

Computer solution of the System :

$x(0.01)$	:	3.0606041	$y(0.01)$	:	1.0202013
$x(0.02)$	:	3.1224325	$y(0.02)$	:	1.0408107
$x(0.03)$	:	3.1855097	$y(0.03)$	:	1.0618365
$x(0.04)$	:	3.2498612	$y(0.04)$	:	1.0832870
$x(0.05)$	:	3.3155129	$y(0.05)$	:	1.1051708
$x(0.06)$	:	3.3824906	$y(0.06)$	:	1.1274967
$x(0.07)$	:	3.4508214	$y(0.07)$	:	1.1502737
$x(0.08)$	:	3.5205326	$y(0.08)$	:	1.1735108
$x(0.09)$	:	3.5916522	$y(0.09)$	:	1.1972172
$x(0.10)$	:	3.6642084	$y(0.10)$	:	1.2214026

Example 9

SYS : $Dx = 4x + y,$ $Dy = 3x + 2y$

PS : $x(t) = \text{Exp}(t)[\text{Exp}(4t) - 2],\ y(t) = \text{Exp}(t)[\text{Exp}(4t) + 6]$

IC : $x(0) = -1, y(0) = 7$

W : 0.01

Computer solution of the System :

$x(0.01)$	:	−0.9688292	$y(0.01)$	:	7.1115723
$x(0.02)$	:	−0.9352317	$y(0.02)$	:	7.2263789
$x(0.03)$	:	−0.8990748	$y(0.03)$	:	7.3445616
$x(0.04)$	:	−0.8602188	$y(0.04)$	:	7.4662676
$x(0.05)$	:	−0.8185167	$y(0.05)$	:	7.5916524
$x(0.06)$	:	−0.7738143	$y(0.06)$	:	7.7208786
$x(0.07)$	:	−0.7259488	$y(0.07)$	:	7.8541174
$x(0.08)$	:	−0.6747494	$y(0.08)$	:	7.9915481

$x(0.09)$	:	–0.6200364	$y(0.09)$	:	8.1333590
$x(0.10)$	:	–0.5616205	$y(0.10)$	:	8.2797480

Example 10

SYS : $Dx = 5x - 2y$, $Dy = 2x + y$

PS : $x(t) = \text{Exp}(3t)(1 + 2t)$, $y(t) = 2t\text{Exp}(3t)$

IC : $x(0) = 1, y(0) = 0$

W : 0.01

Computer solution of the System :

$x(0.01)$	:	1.0510637	$y(0.01)$	:	0.0206091
$x(0.02)$	:	1.1043100	$y(0.02)$	:	0.0424735
$x(0.03)$	:	1.1598247	$y(0.03)$	:	0.0656505
$x(0.04)$	:	1.2176965	$y(0.04)$	:	0.0901997
$x(0.05)$	:	1.2780176	$y(0.05)$	:	0.1161834
$x(0.06)$	:	1.3408834	$y(0.06)$	:	0.1436661
$x(0.07)$	:	1.4063929	$y(0.07)$	:	0.1727149
$x(0.08)$	:	1.4746490	$y(0.08)$	:	0.2033999
$x(0.09)$	:	1.5457580	$y(0.09)$	:	0.2357936
$x(0.10)$	:	1.6198305	$y(0.10)$	:	0.2699718

Example 11

SYS : $Dx = 2x + y$, $Dy = 3x + 4y$

PS : $x(t) = 0.5[\text{Exp}(t) + \text{Exp}(5t)]$, $y(t) = 0.5[3\text{Exp}(5t) - \text{Exp}(t)]$

IC : $x(0) = 1, y(0) = 1$

W : 0.01

Computer solution of the System :

$x(0.01)$	:	1.0306606	$y(0.01)$	:	1.0718815
$x(0.02)$	:	1.0626861	$y(0.02)$	:	1.1476557
$x(0.03)$	:	1.0961443	$y(0.03)$	:	1.2275242

$x(0.04)$	:	1.1311067	$y(0.04)$	:	1.3116988
$x(0.05)$	:	1.1676482	$y(0.05)$	:	1.4004027
$x(0.06)$	:	1.2058476	$y(0.06)$	:	1.4938700
$x(0.07)$	:	1.2457879	$y(0.07)$	:	1.5923473
$x(0.08)$	:	1.2875559	$y(0.08)$	:	1.6960936
$x(0.09)$	:	1.3312433	$y(0.09)$	:	1.8053812
$x(0.10)$	:	1.3769461	$y(0.10)$	:	1.9204965

Example 12

SYS : $Dx = 3y + 6\text{Sin}(t)$, $Dy = -3x$

PS : $x(t) = \dfrac{3\text{Cos}(t) + \text{Cos}(3t)}{4}$, $y(t) = \dfrac{-9\text{Sin}(t) - \text{Sin}(3t)}{4}$

IC : $x(0) = 1, y(0) = 0$

W : 0.01

Computer solution of the System :

$x(0.01)$	:	0.9998500	$y(0.01)$	:	–0.0299985
$x(0.02)$	:	0.9994001	$y(0.02)$	:	–0.0599880
$x(0.03)$	:	0.9986507	$y(0.03)$	:	–0.0899595
$x(0.04)$	:	0.9976023	$y(0.04)$	:	–0.1199040
$x(0.05)$	:	0.9962555	$y(0.05)$	:	–0.1498127
$x(0.06)$	:	0.9946114	$y(0.06)$	:	–0.1796764
$x(0.07)$	:	0.9926710	$y(0.07)$	:	–0.2094864
$x(0.08)$	:	0.9904358	$y(0.08)$	:	–0.2392337
$x(0.09)$	:	0.9879073	$y(0.09)$	:	–0.2689096
$x(0.10)$	:	0.9850873	$y(0.10)$	:	–0.2985052

Example 13

SYS : $Dx = x - y$, $Dy = y - 4x$

PS : $x = \dfrac{3\text{Exp}(-t) + \text{Exp}(3t)}{4}$, $y = \dfrac{3\text{Exp}(-t) - \text{Exp}(3t)}{2}$

IC : $x(0) = 1, y(0) = 1$

W : 0.01

Computer solution of the System :

$x(0.01)$	:	1.0001510	$y(0.01)$	:	0.9698475
$x(0.02)$	:	1.0006082	$y(0.02)$	:	0.9393798
$x(0.03)$	:	1.0013778	$y(0.03)$	:	0.9085812
$x(0.04)$	:	1.0024664	$y(0.04)$	:	0.8774357
$x(0.05)$	:	1.0038807	$y(0.05$	:	0.8459270
$x(0.06)$	:	1.0056279	$y(0.06)$	:	0.8140381
$x(0.07)$	:	1.0077150	$y(0.07)$	:	0.7817517
$x(0.08)$	:	1.0101496	$y(0.08)$	:	0.7490499
$x(0.09)$	:	1.0129396	$y(0.09)$	:	0.7159145
$x(0.10)$	:	1.0160929	$y(0.10)$	:	0.6823267

Example 14

SYS : $4\dfrac{dx}{dt} + 5x - 3y = 4\text{Exp}(t), \quad 4\dfrac{dy}{dt} - 5y + 3x = 4\text{Exp}(t)$

PS : $x = \dfrac{3X}{8} + \dfrac{t\text{Exp}(t)}{4}, y = \dfrac{X}{8} + \dfrac{3t\text{Exp}(t)}{4}$ $[\text{Exp}(t) - \text{Exp}(-t) = X]$

IC : $x(0) = 0, y(0) = 0$

W : 0.01

Computer solution of the System :

$x(0.01)$	:	0.0100253	$y(0.01)$	:	0.0100754
$x(0.02)$	:	0.0201020	$y(0.02)$	:	0.0203034
$x(0.03)$	:	0.0302318	$y(0.03)$	:	0.0306864
$x(0.04)$	:	0.0404161	$y(0.04)$	:	0.0412270
$x(0.05)$	:	0.0506565	$y(0.05)$	:	0.0519279
$x(0.06)$	:	0.0609546	$y(0.06)$	:	0.0627916
$x(0.07)$	:	0.0713118	$y(0.07)$	:	0.0738210
$x(0.08)$	:	0.0817298	$y(0.08)$	:	0.0850186

$x(0.09)$	:	0.0922101	$y(0.09)$	:	0.0963871
$x(0.10)$	:	0.1027543	$y(0.10)$	:	0.1079295

Example 15

SYS : $\frac{dx}{dt} + 3x + y = 10\text{Exp}(-t)$ $\quad \frac{dy}{dt} + 2y + 2x = 4$

PS : $x = \frac{10tX + 14X - Y - 3}{3}$, $y = \frac{-20tX - 8X - Y + 9}{3}$

[$\text{Exp}(-t) = X$, $\text{Exp}(-4t) = Y$]

IC : $x(0) = 3.333333$, $y(0) = 0$

W : 0.01

Computer solution of the System :

$x(0.01)$	:	3.3329709	$y(0.01)$	:	–0.0263994
$x(0.02)$	:	3.3319013	$y(0.02)$	:	–0.0522617
$x(0.03)$	:	3.3301499	$y(0.03)$	:	–0.0775840
$x(0.04)$	:	3.3277411	$y(0.04)$	:	–0.1023636
$x(0.05)$	:	3.3246984	$y(0.05)$	:	–0.1265985
$x(0.06)$	:	3.3210447	$y(0.06)$	:	–0.1502872
$x(0.07)$	:	3.3168018	$y(0.07)$	:	–0.1734285
$x(0.08)$	:	3.3119910	$y(0.08)$	:	–0.1960219
$x(0.09)$	:	3.3066328	$y(0.09)$	:	–0.2180673
$x(0.10)$	:	3.3007472	$y(0.10)$	:	–0.2395647

Example 16

SYS : $Dx + x + 5y = 0$, $\quad Dy - y - x = 0$

PS : $x(t) = \text{Cos}(2t) - 3\text{Sin}(2t)$, $y(t) = \text{Cos}(2t) + \text{Sin}(2t)$

IC : $x(0) = 1$, $y(0) = 1$

W : 0.01

Computer solution of the System :

$x(0.01)$	:	0.9398040	$y(0.01)$	:	1.0197986
$x(0.02)$	:	0.8792321	$y(0.02)$	:	1.0391895

$x(0.03)$	:	0.8183085	$y(0.03)$	:	1.0581646
$x(0.04)$	:	0.7570577	$y(0.04)$	:	1.0767164
$x(0.05)$	:	0.6955040	$y(0.05)$	:	1.0948377
$x(0.06)$	:	0.6336721	$y(0.06)$	:	1.1125209
$x(0.07)$	:	0.5715867	$y(0.07)$	:	1.1297592
$x(0.08)$	:	0.5092727	$y(0.08)$	:	1.1465455
$x(0.09)$	:	0.4467550	$y(0.09)$	:	1.1628733
$x(0.10)$	:	0.3840586	$y(0.10)$	:	1.1787360

Example 17

SYS : $Dx - 5x - 3y = 0,$ $Dy + y + 3x = 0$

PS : $x(t) = \text{Exp}(2t)(1 + 6t),$ $y(t) = \text{Exp}(2t)(1 - 6t)$

IC : $x(0) = 1, y(0) = 1$

W : 0.01

Computer solution of the System :

$x(0.01)$	:	1.0814134	$y(0.01)$	:	0.9589893
$x(0.02)$	:	1.1657081	$y(0.02)$	:	0.9159135
$x(0.03)$	:	1.2529671	$y(0.03)$	:	0.8707060
$x(0.04)$	:	1.3432759	$y(0.04)$	:	0.8232982
$x(0.05)$	:	1.4367222	$y(0.05)$	:	0.7736197
$x(0.06)$	:	1.5333956	$y(0.06)$	:	0.7215980
$x(0.07)$	:	1.6333888	$y(0.07)$	:	0.6671588
$x(0.08)$	:	1.7367960	$y(0.08)$	:	0.6102257
$x(0.09)$	:	1.8437147	$y(0.09)$	:	0.5507200
$x(0.10)$	:	1.9542444	$y(0.10)$	:	0.4885612

Example 18

SYS : $\frac{dx}{dt} - x + y = 0,$ $\frac{dy}{dt} - tx = 0$

PS : $x(t) = \frac{t^{**}2}{2} + t + 1,$ $y(t) = \frac{t^{**}2}{2}$

IC : $x(0) = 1, y(0) = 0$

W : 0.01

Computer solution of the System :

$x(0.01)$	:	1.0100501	$y(0.01)$	:	5.0334580e-05
$x(0.02)$	:	1.0202000	$y(0.02)$	:	0.0002027
$x(0.03)$	:	1.0303500	$y(0.03)$	:	0.0004591
$x(0.04)$	:	1.0407999	$y(0.04)$	:	0.0008217
$x(0.05)$	:	1.0512495	$y(0.05)$	:	0.0012924
$x(0.06)$	:	1.0617989	$y(0.06)$	:	0.0018736
$x(0.07)$	:	1.0724480	$y(0.07)$	:	0.0025673
$x(0.08)$	:	1.0831965	$y(0.08)$	:	0.0033758
$x(0.09)$	:	1.0940443	$y(0.09)$	:	0.0043012
$x(0.10)$	:	1.1049913	$y(0.10)$	:	0.0053458

Example 19

SYS : $\dfrac{dx}{dt} - y = 0, \qquad \dfrac{dy}{dt} - x = \text{Exp}(2t)$

PS : $x = \dfrac{2\text{Exp}(2t) - 3\text{Exp}(t) + \text{Exp}(-t)}{6},$

$$y = \frac{4\text{Exp}(2t) - 3\text{Exp}(t) - \text{Exp}(-t)}{6}$$

IC : $x(0) = 0, y(0) = 0$

W : 0.01

Computer solution of the System :

$x(0.01)$	:	5.0335424e-05	$y(0.01)$	:	0.0101008
$x(0.02)$	:	0.0002027	$y(0.02)$	:	0.0204067
$x(0.03)$	:	0.0004592	$y(0.03)$	:	0.0309228
$x(0.04)$	:	0.0008219	$y(0.04)$	:	0.0416544
$x(0.05)$	:	0.0012930	$y(0.05)$	:	0.0526068
$x(0.06)$	:	0.0018748	$y(0.06)$	:	0.0637855

$x(0.07)$	:	0.0025695	$y(0.07)$	:	0.0751961
$x(0.08)$	:	0.0033795	$y(0.08)$	:	0.0868443
$x(0.09)$	:	0.0043072	$y(0.09)$	:	0.0987359
$x(0.10)$	:	0.0053550	$y(0.10)$	:	0.1108768

Example 20

SYS : $\frac{dx}{dt} - 4x + y = 0, \qquad \frac{dy}{dt} - 2x - y = 0$

PS : $x(t) = \text{Exp}(2t)[1 - \text{Exp}(t)], \quad y(t) = \text{Exp}(2t)[2 - \text{Exp}(t)]$

IC : $x(0) = 0, y(0) = 1$

W : 0.01

Computer solution of the System :

$x(0.01)$	:	–0.0102532	$y(0.01)$	:	1.0099481
$x(0.02)$	:	–0.0210258	$y(0.02)$	:	1.0197850
$x(0.03)$	:	–0.0323377	$y(0.03)$	:	1.0294988
$x(0.04)$	:	–0.0442098	$y(0.04)$	:	1.0390773
$x(0.05)$	:	–0.0566633	$y(0.05)$	:	1.0485076
$x(0.06)$	:	–0.0697205	$y(0.06)$	:	1.0577763
$x(0.07)$	:	–0.0834043	$y(0.07)$	:	1.0668695
$x(0.08)$	:	–0.0977383	$y(0.08)$	:	1.0757725
$x(0.09)$	:	–0.1127471	$y(0.09)$	:	1.0844702
$x(0.10)$	:	–0.1284561	$y(0.10)$	:	1.0929465

Example 21

SYS : $Dx = \frac{\text{Exp}(t)}{3} - x - \frac{2y}{3} \qquad Dy = \frac{4x}{3} + y - t$

PS : $x = \frac{11\text{X}}{2} - \frac{9\text{Y}}{2} - 6t, \qquad y = -11\text{X} + \frac{9\text{Y}}{2} + \frac{\text{Exp}(t)}{2} + 9t + 9$

$\left[\text{Exp}\left(\frac{t}{3}\right) = \text{X}, \text{Exp}\left(\frac{-t}{3}\right) = \text{Y}\right]$

IC : $x(0) = 1, y(0) = 3$

W : 0.01

Computer solution of the System :

$x(0.01)$:	0.9733390	$y(0.01)$:	3.0433223
$x(0.02)$:	0.9466894	$y(0.02)$:	3.0866222
$x(0.03)$:	0.9200516	$y(0.03)$:	3.1298997
$x(0.04)$:	0.8934261	$y(0.04)$:	3.1731548
$x(0.05)$:	0.8668132	$y(0.05)$:	3.2163875
$x(0.06)$:	0.8402133	$y(0.06)$:	3.2595975
$x(0.07)$:	0.8136267	$y(0.07)$:	3.3027852
$x(0.08)$:	0.7870538	$y(0.08)$:	3.3459501
$x(0.09)$:	0.7604950	$y(0.09)$:	3.3890924
$x(0.10)$:	0.7339506	$y(0.10)$:	3.4322119

Example 22

SYS : $Dx = -4x + 2y = 0$ $\quad$ $Dy - 3x + y = 0$

PS : $x = \text{Exp}(t)[3\text{Exp}(t) - 2]$, $\quad$ $y = 3\text{Exp}(t)[\text{Exp}(t) - 1]$

IC : $x(0) = 1, y(0) = 0$

W : 0.01

Computer solution of the System :

$x(0.01)$:	1.0405037	$y(0.01)$:	0.0304535
$x(0.02)$:	1.0820297	$y(0.02)$:	0.0618283
$x(0.03)$:	1.1246006	$y(0.03)$:	0.0941460
$x(0.04)$:	1.1682397	$y(0.04)$:	0.1274289
$x(0.05)$:	1.2129706	$y(0.05)$:	0.1616995
$x(0.06)$:	1.2588176	$y(0.06)$:	0.1969809
$x(0.07)$:	1.3058051	$y(0.07)$:	0.2332969
$x(0.08)$:	1.3539585	$y(0.08)$:	0.2706714
$x(0.09)$:	1.4033035	$y(0.09)$:	0.3091293
$x(0.10)$:	1.4538664	$y(0.10)$:	0.3486955

Example 23

SYS : $Dx - 4x + y = \text{Exp}(t)$, $Dy - 2x - y = 0$

PS : $x = \text{Exp}(2t)[3\text{Exp}(t) - 2]$, $y = \text{Exp}(t)[3\text{Exp}(2t) - 4\text{Exp}(t) + 1]$

IC : $x(0) = 1, y(0) = 0$

W : 0.01

Computer solution of the System :

$x(0.01)$	:	1.0509609	$y(0.01)$	:	0.0206084
$x(0.02)$	:	1.1038880	$y(0.02)$	:	0.0424679
$x(0.03)$	:	1.1588497	$y(0.03)$	:	0.0656312
$x(0.04)$	:	1.2159164	$y(0.04)$	:	0.0901531
$x(0.05)$	:	1.2751609	$y(0.05)$	:	0.1160901
$x(0.06)$	:	1.3366584	$y(0.06)$	:	0.1435012
$x(0.07)$	:	1.4004866	$y(0.07)$	:	0.1724472
$x(0.08)$	:	1.4667257	$y(0.08)$	:	0.2029910
$x(0.09)$	:	1.5354586	$y(0.09)$	:	0.2351982
$x(0.10)$	:	1.6067709	$y(0.10)$	:	0.2691363

Example 24

SYS : $Dx - x + 2y = 0$, $Dy + 3x - 2y = 0$

PS : $x = \text{Exp}(-t)[5 - 2\text{Exp}(5t)]$, $y = \text{Exp}(-t)[5 + 3\text{Exp}(5t)]$

IC : $x(0) = 3, y(0) = 8$

W : 0.01

Computer solution of the System :

$x(0.01)$	:	2.8686275	$y(0.01)$	:	8.0726814
$x(0.02)$	:	2.7344191	$y(0.02)$	:	8.1508541
$x(0.03)$	:	2.5972338	$y(0.03)$	:	8.2347174
$x(0.04)$	:	2.4569254	$y(0.04)$	:	8.3244791
$x(0.05)$	:	2.3133416	$y(0.05)$	:	8.4203548
$x(0.06)$	:	2.1663244	$y(0.06)$	:	8.5225697

$x(0.07)$	:	2.0157094	$y(0.07)$	:	8.6313581
$x(0.08)$	:	1.8613261	$y(0.08)$	:	8.7469645
$x(0.09)$	:	1.7029970	$y(0.09)$	:	8.8696432
$x(0.10)$	:	1.5405376	$y(0.10)$	:	8.9996605

Example 25

SYS : $\frac{dx}{dt} = 4x + y - 36t, \quad \frac{dy}{dt} = -2x + y - 2\text{Exp}(t)$

PS : $x = 10X - Y - Z - 6t - 1,$

$y = -20X + Y + 3Z + 12t + 10$ [$\text{Exp}(2t) = X$, $8\text{Exp}(3t) = Y$, $\text{Exp}(t) = Z$].

IC : $x(0) = 0, y(0) = 1$

W : 0.01

Computer solution of the System :

$x(0.01)$	:	0.00832700	$y(0.01)$	:	0.9897600
$x(0.02)$	:	0.01321400	$y(0.02)$	:	0.9790809
$x(0.03)$	:	0.01451670	$y(0.03)$	:	0.9680269
$x(0.04)$	:	0.01208510	$y(0.04)$	:	0.9566658
$x(0.05)$	:	0.00576420	$y(0.05)$	:	0.9450688
$x(0.06)$	:	−0.00460690	$y(0.06)$	:	0.9333115
$x(0.07)$	:	−0.01919470	$y(0.07)$	:	0.9214730
$x(0.08)$	:	−0.03817150	$y(0.08)$	:	0.9096369
$x(0.09)$	:	−0.06171620	$y(0.09)$	:	0.8978911
$x(0.10)$	:	−0.09001380	$y(0.10)$	:	0.8863280

Example 26

SYS : $\frac{dx}{dt} = 3x - 2y, \quad \frac{dy}{dt} = 4x + 7y$

PS : $x = \text{Exp}(5t)[\text{Cos}(2t) - \text{Sin}(2t)]$, $y = 2\text{Exp}(5t)\text{Sin}(2t)$

IC : $x(0) = 1, y(0) = 0$

W : 0.01

Computer solution of the System :

$x(0.01)$	:	1.0300368	$y(0.01)$	:	0.0420480
$x(0.02)$	:	1.0600919	$y(0.02)$	:	0.0883901
$x(0.03)$	:	1.0900754	$y(0.03)$	:	0.1393365
$x(0.04)$	:	1.1198884	$y(0.04)$	:	0.1952160
$x(0.05)$	:	1.1494220	$y(9.05)$	:	0.2563772
$x(0.06)$	:	1.1785569	$y(0.06)$	:	0.3231891
$x(0.07)$	:	1.2071623	$y(0.07)$	:	0.3960422
$x(0.08)$	:	1.2350951	$y(0.08)$	:	0.4753496
$x(0.09)$	:	1.2621998	$y(0.09)$	:	0.5615485
$x(0.10)$	:	1.2883062	$y(0.10)$	:	0.6551006

Example 27

SYS : $\frac{dx}{dt} = 1 + \frac{2x}{t}$, $\frac{dy}{dt} = x + y - 1 + \frac{2x}{t}$

PS : $x = \frac{t}{3}$, $y = \frac{-t}{3}$

IC : $x(1) = 0.333333, y(1) = -0.333333$

W : 0.01

Computer solution of the System :

$x(1.01)$	:	0.3501330	$y(1.01)$	:	–0.3364652
$x(1.02)$	:	0.3671996	$y(1.02)$	:	–0:3391907
$x(1.03)$	:	0.3845330	$y(1.03)$	:	–0.3415028
$x(1.04)$	:	0.4021330	$y(1.04)$	:	–0.3433945
$x(1.05)$	:	0.4199996	$y(1.05)$	:	–0.3448590
$x(1.06)$	:	0.4381329	$y(1.06)$	:	–0.3458893
$x(1.07)$	:	0.4565329	$y(1.07)$	:	–0.3464784
$x(1.08)$	:	0.4751996	$y(1.08)$	:	–0.3466192
$x(1.09)$	:	0.4941329	$y(1.09)$	:	–0.3463044
$x(1.10)$	:	0.5133329	$y(1.10)$	:	–0.3455269

Example 28

$SYS \quad : \frac{dx}{dt} - \frac{x**2}{y} = 0, \qquad \frac{dy}{dt} + x = 0$

$PS \quad : x = \frac{-1}{2\text{Sqrt}(t)}, \qquad y = \text{Sqrt}(t)$

$IC \quad : x(1) = -0.5, y(1) = 1$

$W \quad : 0.01$

Computer solution of the System :

$x(1.01)$	:	−0.4975186	$y(1.01)$	:	1.0049876
$x(1.02)$	:	−0.4950738	$y(1.02)$	:	1.0099505
$x(1.03)$	:	−0.4926646	$y(1.03)$	:	1.0148892
$x(1.04)$	:	−0.4902903	$y(1.04)$	:	1.0198040
$x(1.05)$	:	−0.4879501	$y(1.05)$	:	1.0246952
$x(1.06)$	:	−0.4856429	$y(1.06)$	:	1.0295631
$x(1.07)$	:	−0.4833682	$y(1.07)$	:	1.0344081
$x(1.08)$	:	−0.4811252	$y(1.08)$	:	1.0392306
$x(1.09)$	:	−0.4789132	$y(1.09)$	:	1.0440308
$x(1.10)$	:	−0.4767313	$y(1.10)$	:	1.0488089

Example 29

$SYS \quad : \frac{dx}{dt} = \frac{x(t+y)}{(t\hat{}2 - xy)}, \qquad \frac{dy}{dt} = \frac{y(y-x)}{(t\hat{}2 - xy)}$

$PS \quad : x(t) = t - y, \qquad y(y - 2t)\hat{}3 = (t - x)\hat{}2$

$IC \quad : x(0) = -1, y(0) = 1$

$W \quad : 0.01$

Computer solution of the System :

$x(0.01)$	:	−1.0100490	$y(0.01)$	:	1.0200490
$x(0.02)$	:	−1.0201921	$y(0.02)$	:	1.0401921
$x(0.03)$	:	−1.0304240	$y(0.03)$	:	1.0604240
$x(0.04)$	:	−1.0407393	$y(0.04)$	:	1.0807393

$x(0.05)$	:	−1.0511332	$y(0.05)$	:	1.1011331
$x(0.06)$	:	−1.0616009	$y(0.06)$	:	1.1216009
$x(0.07)$	:	−1.0721382	$y(0.07)$	:	1.1421381
$x(0.08)$	:	−1.0827408	$y(0.08)$	:	1.1627407
$x(0.09)$	:	−1.0934049	$y(0.09)$	:	1.1834048
$x(0.10)$	:	−1.1041268	$y(0.10)$	:	1.2041267

Example 30

SYS : $\frac{dx}{dt} = \frac{x - t}{y - x}$, $\frac{dy}{dt} = \frac{t - y}{y - x}$

PS : $x + y + t = 0$, $x^2 + y^2 + t^2 = 6$

IC ; $x(1) = -2, y(1) = 1$

W : 0.01

Computer solution of the System :

$x(1.01)$	:	−2.0100167	$y(1.01)$	:	1.0000166
$x(1.02)$	:	−2.0200663	$y(1.02)$	:	1.0000662
$x(1.03)$	:	−2.0301485	$y(1.03)$	:	1.0001484
$x(1.04)$	:	−2.0402632	$y(1.04)$	:	1.0002631
$x(1.05)$	:	−2.0504098	$y(1.05)$	:	1.0004097
$x(1.06)$	:	−2.0605881	$y(1.06)$	:	1.0005881
$x(1.07)$	:	−2.0707979	$y(1.07)$	:	1.0007977
$x(1.08)$	:	−2.0810387	$y(1.08)$	:	1.0010386
$x(1.09)$	:	−2.0913103	$y(1.09)$	:	1.0013101
$x(1.10)$	:	−2.1016121	$y(1.10)$	:	1.0016121

Example 31

SYS : $\frac{dx}{dt} = \frac{t}{y^2}$, $\frac{dy}{dt} = \frac{t}{xy}$

PS : $x - y = 0$, $y^3 - \frac{3t^2}{2} = 1$

IC : $x(0) = 1, y(0) = 1$

W : 0.01

Computer solution of the System :

$x(0.01)$	:	1.0000499	$y(0.01)$	:	1.0000499
$x(0.02)$	:	1.0001999	$y(0.02)$	:	1.0001999
$x(0.03)$	:	1.0004498	$y(0.03)$	:	1.0004498
$x(0.04)$	:	1.0007993	$y(0.04)$	:	1.0007993
$x(0.05)$	:	1.0012484	$y(0.05)$	:	1.0012484
$x(0.06)$	:	1.0017967	$y(0.06)$	:	1.0017967
$x(0.07)$	:	1.0024440	$y(0.07)$	:	1.0024440
$x(0.08)$	:	1.0031898	$y(0.08)$	:	1.0031898
$x(0.09)$	:	1.0040337	$y(0.09)$	:	1.0040337
$x(0.10)$	:	1.0049752	$y(0.10)$	:	1.0049752

Example 32

SYS : $\frac{dx}{dt} = \frac{1.0}{y - t}$, $\frac{dy}{dt} = \frac{x - 1.0}{x}$

PS : $x(t) = \text{Exp}(-t)$ $y(t) = t - \text{Exp}(t)$

IC : $x(0) = 1, y(0) = -1$

W : 0.01

Computer solution of the System :

$x(0.01)$	:	0.9900498	$y(0.01)$	:	−1.0000502
$x(0.02)$	:	0.9801987	$y(0.02)$	:	−1.0002013
$x(0.03)$	:	0.9704455	$y(0.03)$	:	−1.0004545
$x(0.04)$	:	0.9607894	$y(0.04)$	:	−1.0008107
$x(0.05)$	:	0.9512295	$y(0.05)$	:	−1.0012710
$x(0.06)$	:	0.9417645	$y(0.06)$	:	−1.0018364
$x(0.07)$	:	0.9323938	$y(0.07)$	:	−1.0025080
$x(0.08)$	:	0.9231163	$y(0.08)$	:	−1.0032870
$x(0.09)$	:	0.9139312	$y(0.09)$	:	−1.0041742
$x(0.10)$	:	0.9048374	$y(0.10)$	:	−1.0051708

Example 33

$SYS \quad : \quad \dfrac{dx}{dt} = xy + t + 2, \qquad \dfrac{dy}{dt} = tx - 1.0$

$PS \quad : \quad x = t\left(2 + \dfrac{t}{2} - \dfrac{2}{3}t\hat{}2 - \dfrac{1}{8}t\hat{}3 + \ldots\right)$

$y = t\left(-1 + \dfrac{2}{3}t\hat{}2 + \dfrac{1}{8}t\hat{}3 - \dfrac{1}{6}t\hat{}4 + \ldots\right)$

$IC \quad : \quad x(0) = 0, y(0) = 0$

$W \quad : \quad 0.01$

Computer solution of the System :

$x(0.01)$	:	0.0200493	$y(0.01)$	:	–0.0099993
$x(0.02)$	:	0.0401946	$y(0.02)$	:	–0.0199946
$x(0.03)$	:	0.0604319	$y(0.03)$	:	–0.0299819
$x(0.04)$	:	0.0807571	$y(0.04)$	:	–0.0399570
$x(0.05)$	:	0.1011660	$y(0.05)$	:	–0.0499159
$x(0.06)$	:	0.1216547	$y(0.06)$	:	–0.0598545
$x(0.07)$	:	0.1422190	$y(0.07)$	:	–0.0697686
$x(0.08)$	:	0.1628549	$y(0.08)$	:	–0.0796540
$x(0.09)$	:	0.1835582	$y(0.09)$	:	–0.0895066
$x(0.10)$	:	0.2043249	$y(0.10)$	:	–0.0993222

Example 34

$SYS \quad : \quad Dx - xy - 2t = 1.0, \qquad Dy - x\hat{}2 - t = 2.0$

$PS \quad : \quad x = t\left(1 + t + \dfrac{2}{3}t\hat{}2 + \dfrac{5}{8}t\hat{}3 + \ldots\right)$

$y = t\left(2 + \dfrac{t}{2} + \dfrac{1}{3}t\hat{}2 + \dfrac{1}{2}t\hat{}3 + \ldots\right)$

$IC \quad : \quad x(0) = 0, y(0) = 0$

$W \quad : \quad 0.01$

Computer solution of the System :

$x(0.01)$	:	0.0101007	$y(0.01)$	:	0.0200503
$x(0.02)$	:	0.0204054	$y(0.02)$	:	0.0402027
$x(0.03)$	:	0.0309185	$y(0.03)$	:	0.0604594
$x(0.04)$	:	0.0416443	$y(0.04)$	:	0.0808227
$x(0.05)$	:	0.0525874	$y(0.05)$	:	0.1012949
$x(0.06)$	:	0.0637525	$y(0.06)$	:	0.1218789
$x(0.07)$	:	0.0751445	$y(0.07)$	:	0.1425772
$x(0.08)$	:	0.0867685	$y(0.08)$	:	0.1633928
$x(0.09)$	:	0.0986298	$y(0.09)$	:	0.1843288
$x(0.10)$	:	0.1107339	$y(0.10)$	:	0.2053885

Example 35

SYS : $Dx - xy = 1.0, \qquad Dy - x - t = 0$

PS : $x = 1 + 3X + 4X\text{^}2 + \dfrac{16}{3} X\text{^}3 + \ldots$

$y = 2 + 2X + 2X\text{^}2 + \dfrac{4}{3} X\text{^}3 + \ldots \quad [t - 1 = X]$

IC : $x(1) = 1, y(1) = 2$

W : 0.01

Computer solution of the System :

$x(1.01)$	:	1.0304054	$y(1.01)$	:	2.0202014
$x(1.02)$	:	1.0616437	$y(1.02)$	:	2.0408111
$x(1.03)$	:	1.0937494	$y(1.03)$	:	2.0618372
$x(1.04)$	:	1.1267587	$y(1.04)$	:	2.0832889
$x(1.05)$	:	1.1607096	$y(1.05)$	:	2.1051755
$x(1.06)$	:	1.1956422	$y(1.06)$	:	2.1275065
$x(1.07)$	:	1.2315987	$y(1.07)$	:	2.1502919
$x(1.08)$	:	1.2686234	$y(1.08)$	:	2.1735420
$x(1.09)$	:	1.3067628	$y(1.09)$	:	2.1972680
$x(1.10)$	:	1.3460664	$y(1.10)$	:	2.2214811

Example 36

SYS : $Dx - y - t = 2.0$, $Dy - y - x\text{^}2 = 1.0$

PS : $x = 2 + 4X + 3.5X\text{^}2 + \frac{11}{3}X\text{^}3 + \ldots$,

$y = 1 + 6X + 11X\text{^}2 + \frac{41}{3}X\text{^}3 + \ldots \quad [t - 1 = X]$

IC : $x(1) = 2, y(1) = 1$

W : 0.01

Computer solution of the System :

$x(1.01)$	:	2.0403538	$y(1.01)$	:	1.0611138
$x(1.02)$	:	2.0814300	$y(1.02)$	:	1.1245117
$x(1.03)$	:	2.1232519	$y(1.03)$	:	1.1902808
$x(1.04)$	:	2.1658437	$y(1.04)$	:	1.2585123
$x(1.05)$	:	2.2092307	$y(1.05)$	:	1.3293010
$x(1.06)$	:	2.2534387	$y(1.06)$	:	1.4027461
$x(1.07)$	:	2.2984948	$y(1.07)$	:	1.4789509
$x(1.08)$	:	2.3444273	$y(1.08)$	:	1.5580235
$x(1.09)$	:	2.3912654	$y(1.09)$	:	1.6400766
$x(1.10)$	:	2.4390392	$y(1.10)$	:	1.7252282

Example 37

SYS : $Dx - y\text{^}2 - 2t = 1.0$, $Dy - x - t = 2.0$

PS : $x = t\left(1 + t + \frac{4}{3}t\text{^}2 + t\text{^}3 + \ldots\right)$

$y = t\left(2 + t + \frac{1}{3}t\text{^}2 + \frac{1}{3}t\text{^}3 + \ldots\right)$

IC : $x(0) = 0, y(0) = 0$

W : 0.01

Computer solution of the System :

$x(0.01)$	:	0.0101013	$y(0.01)$	:	0.0201003
$x(0.02)$	:	0.0204108	$y(0.02)$	:	0.0404027

x(0.03)	:	0.0309368	y(0.03)	:	0.0609093
x(0.04)	:	0.0416879	y(0.04)	:	0.0816222
x(0.05)	:	0.0526731	y(0.05)	:	0.1025438
x(0.06)	:	0.0639013	y(0.06)	:	0.1236765
x(0.07)	:	0.0753822	y(0.07)	:	0.1450227
x(0.08)	:	0.0871252	y(0.08)	:	0.1665850
x(0.09)	:	0.0991405	y(0.09)	:	0.1883661
x(0.10)	:	0.1114383	y(0.10)	:	0.2103688

Chapter 9

Boundary-Value Problems For Ordinary Differential Equations

9.1. Introduction

In the previous chapters we have discussed on the solutions of differential equations that are of first order and contain one initial condition to satisfy. Later in Chapter 7 the developed techniques for solution would be extended to second-order equations, but using the specified conditions at the endpoints of an interval. These are all the examples of initial value problems.

In this chapter we are concerned only with the differential equations in which the specified conditions are given at different points on the interval. In the case of the first-order initial value problem only one condition, i.e. the starting value is chosen and the approximation process has been developed.

The differential equations having the prescribed conditions at the endpoints have often been encountered in many branches of physics and mathematics, engineering and other related practical sciences. These problems cannot be treated as initial value problems because of the specified boundary. Such problems are known as the **boundary value problems**.

In order to solve a boundary value problem the general solution of the given differential equation will be first found and then a system of equations can be obtained from the prescribed boundary conditions to determine the constants involved in the equations. The general solution of the boundary value problem is thus obtained after evaluating the constants.

Let us consider a two-point boundary value problem

$$y'' = g(x, y, y') \tag{9.10}$$

for $a \le x \le b$. The prime denotes differentiation with respect to the independent variable x, as usual.

We aceept the boundary conditions prescribed for the equation (9.10) by

$$y(a) = \alpha \text{ and } y(b) = \beta$$

for some constant values of α and β.

Such a problem can be solved provided that the function g and its partial derivatives with respect to y and y' are continuous and the boundary conditions exist.

Thus assuming that the boundary value problem has a unique solution we try to determine the solution of the problem.

Example Find the solution of the equation $y'' + y = 1$.

satisfying the boundary conditions $y(0) = y\left(\frac{\pi}{2}\right) = 0$.

The general solution of the above differential equation can be written as

$$y(x) = C_1 \sin x + C_2 \cos x + 1.$$

Applying the above-mentioned conditions we get $C_1 = C_2 = -1$

Hence, the function $y(x) = 1 - \sin x - \cos x$ satisfies the boundary conditions.

The numerical methods for the approximation of the solution to boundary value problems of order 2 can be classified fundamentally in the following two types : The Shooting method and the **Finite Difference** methods.

The Shooting method is not so stable because of round-off error instability often occurred. The methods I want to present here for solving the second-order boundary-value problems are the methods having much stable characters. They need more functional operations in order to get proper accuracy. The methods containing finite differences replace each of the derivatives in the differential equation with the appropriate difference-quotient approximation.

9.2. Linear Boundary Value Problems

A linear two-point boundary value problem for the unknown function y can be represented by

$$y'' = P(x)y' + Q(x)y + R(x) \tag{9.20}$$

for $a \le x \le b$, with the boundary conditions

$$y(a) = \alpha, \; y(b) = \beta$$

If x, $x + w$ and $x - w$ are the points in the interval $[a, b]$, then

$$y'(x) = \frac{y(x+w) - y(x-w)}{2w} \tag{9.21}$$

$$y''(x) = \frac{y(x+w) - 2y(x) + y(x-w)}{w^2} \tag{9.22}$$

are called **finite difference approximations** to the derivatives. Now the derivatives of the function $g(x)$ at any specified point X are required and that the points $X + w$ and $X - w$ lie inside the interval $[a, b]$.

Using **Taylor's series** let us expand

$$g(X+w) = g(X) + wg'(X) + \frac{w^2}{2!}g''(X) + \frac{w^3}{3!}g'''(X) + \ldots$$

$$g(X-w) = g(X) - wg'(X) + \frac{w^2}{2!}g''(X) - \frac{w^3}{3!}g'''(X) + \ldots$$

After rearrangement we can write

$$g'(X) = \frac{g(X+w) - g(X-w)}{2w} - \sum_{k=1}^{\infty} \frac{g^{(2k+1)}(X)}{(2k+1)!} w^{2k} \tag{9.23}$$

$$g''(X) = \frac{g(X+w) - 2g(X) + g(X-w)}{w^2} - \sum_{k=1}^{\infty} \frac{g^{(2k+2)}(X)}{(2k+2)!} w^{2k} \tag{9.24}$$

If it is not possible to obtain an answer to the desired accuracy by decreasing w, the **Richardson extrapolation** technique can be used. The technique combines a sequence of estimates of the derivative to obtain a further estimate which is more accurate.

Expanding the equation (9.23) gives

$$g'(X) = \frac{g(X+w) - g(X-w)}{2w} - \frac{w^2}{6}g^{(3)}(X) - \frac{w^4}{120}g^{(5)}(X) + \ldots \tag{9.25}$$

Replacing w by tw in the equation, where t is any value other then ± 1

we get

$$g'(X) = \frac{g(X+tw) - g(X-tw)}{2tw} - \frac{t^2w^2}{6}g^{(3)}(X) - \frac{t^4w^4}{120}g^{(5)}(X) + \ldots \tag{9.26}$$

Elimination of the term

$$\frac{w^2}{6} g^{(3)}(X) \text{ from (9.25) and (9.26)}$$

and after rearrangement, the equation takes the form

$$g'(X) = \frac{1}{2wt(t^2-1)} [t^3 g(X+w) - g(X+tw) - t^3 g(X-w) + g(X-tw)] + \frac{t^2 w^4}{120} g^{(5)}(X) + \ldots \tag{9.27}$$

Similarly, expansion of the equation (9.24) yields

$$g''(X) = \frac{g(X+w) - 2g(X) + g(X-w)}{w^2} - \frac{w^2}{24} g^{(4)}(X) - \frac{w^4}{720} g^{(6)}(X) + \ldots \tag{9.28}$$

Replacing w by tw we get

$$g''(X) = \frac{g(X+tw) - 2g(X) + g(X-tw)}{w^2} - \frac{t^2 w^2}{24} g^{(4)}(X) - \frac{t^4 w^4}{720} g^{(6)}(X) + \ldots$$

Elimination and rerrangement forms a new equation that reads

$$g''(X) = \frac{1}{w^2(t^2-1)} [t^2 g(X+w) - g(X+tw) + t^2 g(X-w) - g(X-tw)] - \frac{1}{w^2} g(X) + \frac{t^2 w^4}{720} g^{(6)}(X) + \ldots \tag{9.29}$$

At the general point X the differential equation becomes

$$\frac{d^2y}{dx^2}\Big|_{x=X} = P(X) \frac{dy}{dx}\Big|_{x=X} + Q(X)y(X) + R(X) \tag{9.30}$$

The equations (9.27) and (9.29) are called the **centered-difference** formulae for $g'(X)$ and $g''(X)$.

Substituting (9.27) and (9.29) in equation (9.30) we get (taking $m = t^2 - 1$)

$$t^3[2 + wP(X)]g(X+w) - [2t + wP(X)]g(X+tw) + t^3[2 - wP(X)]g(X-w) - [2t - wP(X)]g(X-tw) + 2mt[w^2Q(X) - 1]g(X) = 2mtw^2R(X) - G \tag{9.31}$$

Where $G = \frac{t^2 w^4}{720} [P(X)g^{(5)}(X) + g^{(6)}(X)]$.

The equation can be written in ascending order when $t = 2$

$$-[4 - wP(X)]g(X-2w) + [16 - 8wP(X)]g(X-w) + 12[w^2Q(X) - 1]g(X) + [16 + 8wP(X)]g(X+w) - [4 + wP(X)]g(X+2w) = 12w^2R(X) \tag{9.32}$$

This is the required equation for the approximation.

Example Solve $y'' + x^2y + 2 = 0$

with the boundary conditions $y(-1) = y(1) = 0$ on the interval $[-1, 1]$.

To solve the boundary value problem we use the method of finite differences.

Now dividing the interval into 4 equal parts we have

$$m = 4,\ w = \frac{b - a}{m + 1} = 0.4, \text{ the endpoints } y_0 = 0 \text{ and } y_4 = 0$$

Setting up the system of equations (9.21) and (9.22) we can write

$$y'(x) = \frac{y(x + w) - y(x - w)}{2w} = \frac{y(x_{k+1}) - y(x_{k-1})}{2w} \tag{9.33}$$

$$y''(x) = \frac{(x + w) - 2y(x) + y(x - w)}{w^2} = \frac{y(x_{k+1}) - 2y(x_k) + y(x_{k-1})}{w^2} \tag{9.34}$$

Putting $k = 1, 2, 3$ in order and rearranging the equations we obtain a system of another equations

when $k = 1$,

$$\frac{y_2 - 2y_1 + y_0}{w^2} + w^2 + x^2{}_1y_1 + 2 = 0$$

$$\text{or } (y_2 - 2y_1 + y_0) + 0.0576y_1 + 0.32 = 0$$

$$\text{or } y_2 - 1.9424y_1 + y_0 = -0.32 \tag{9.35}$$

when $k = 2$

$$\frac{y_3 - 2y_2 + y_1}{w^2} + x_2{}^2y_2 + 2 = 0$$

$$\text{or } y_3 - 2y_2 + y_1 + 0.0064y_2 + 0.32 = 0$$

$$\text{or } y_3 - 1.9936y_2 + y_1 = -0.32 \tag{9.36}$$

when $k = 3$

$$\frac{y_4 - 2y_3 + y_2}{w^2} + x_3{}^2y_3 + 2 = 0$$

$$\text{or } y_4 - 2y_3 + y_2 + 0.0064y_3 + 0.32 = 0$$

$$\text{or } y_4 - 1.9936y_3 + y_2 = -0.32 \tag{9.37}$$

Solving the equations (9.35), (9.36) and (9.37)

$$y_1 = 0.5046,\ y_2 = 0.6602,\ y_3 = 0.4917$$

that are the approximations along with $y_0 = y_4 = 0$

Let us now consider the approximations of linear boundary value problems by means of C++ program applying the method of Finite-Difference using fifth-order Taylor series.

Now to approximate the boundary value problem of order 2, I use the program BVPD2LIN and apply the method of Finite Difference.

For the approximation of a BVP the following points should be noted:

a) The initial boundary conditions of the mathematical problem, *xB / xF / yB / yF* are to be put in the DEFINITION Block of BC of the program.

b) The Particular Solution for $y(x)$ given in the example is inserted in the MEMBER FUNCTION setACT.

c) The MEMBER FUNCTION setDE is furnished with the values of P, Q and R mentioned in the example.

After the execution the program calculates simultaneously the exact values of $y(x)$ with the corresponding increments of the independent variable x, so that the errors arisen from the approximations can be found out.

Example 1

BVP : $\frac{xd^2y}{dx^2} - 3\frac{dy}{dx} = 0,$

$$P = \frac{3}{x}, Q = 0.0, R = 0.0$$

PS : $y(x) = x^4$

IC : $y(0) : 0, y(1) : 1, 0 \le x \le 1$

W : 0.01

The Computer Solution of the BVP of Order 2

x-value		*Approx value*	*Exact Value*	*Error*
y (0.01)	:	–1.50037509e-08	1e-08	2.50038e-08
y (0.06)	:	1.20630158e-05	1.296e-05	8.96984e-07
y (0.11)	:	0.00014342	0.00014641	2.98914e-06
y (0.16)	:	0.00064912	0.00065536	6.23772e-06
y (0.21)	:	0.00193427	0.00194481	1.05414e-05
y (0.26)	:	0.00455400	0.00456976	1.57615e-05

x-value		*Approx value*	*Exact Value*	*Error*
y (0.31)	:	0.00921349	0.00923521	2.17216e-05
y (0.36)	:	0.01676795	0.01679616	2.82080e-05
y (0.41)	:	0.02822264	0.02825761	3.49693e-05
y (0.46)	:	0.04473284	0.04477456	4.17168e-05
y (0.51)	:	0.06760389	0.06765201	4.81240e-05
y (0.56)	:	0.09829113	0.09834496	5.38272e-05
y(0.61)	:	0.13839998	0.13845841	5.84250e-05
u(0.66)	:	0.18968588	0.18974736	6.14785e-05
y(0.71)	:	0.25405430	0.25411681	6.25114e-05
y(0.76)	:	0.33356075	0.33362176	6.10098e-05
y(0.81)	:	0.43041079	0.43046721	5.64223e-05
y(0.86)	:	0.54696000	0.54700816	4.81600e-05
y(0.91)	:	0.68571401	0.68574961	3.55965e-05
y(0.96)	:	0.84932849	0.84934656	1.80679e-05

The error field confines to the range [2.50038e-08, 1.80679e-05]. The approximations are correct to within this domain.

Example 2

BVP : $\dfrac{D^2y}{dx^2} - y = 0$

$P = 0,\ Q = 1.0,\ R = 0.0$

PS : $y(x) = \dfrac{\text{Sinh}(x)}{\text{Sinh}(1)}$

IC : $y(0) : 0,\ y(1) : 1,\ 0 \le x \le 1$

W : 0.01

The Computer Solution of the BVP of Order 2

x-value		*Approx value*	*Exact Value*	*Error*
y (0.01)	:	0.00850933	0.00850932	–1.10975e-08
y (0.06)	:	0.05108579	0.05108573	–6.63756e-08
y (0.11)	:	0.09378999	0.09378987	–1.20755e-07

x-value		*Approx value*	*Exact Value*	*Error*
y (0.16)	:	0.13672871	0.13672854	–1.73482e-07
y (0.21)	:	0.18000932	0.18000910	–2.23792e-07
y (0.26)	:	0.22374005	0.22373977	–2.70911e-07
y (0.31)	:	0.26803023	0.26802992	–3.14044e-07
y (0.36)	:	0.31299063	0.31299027	–3.52376e-07
y (0.41)	:	0.35873366	0.35873327	–3.85065e-07
y (0.46)	:	0.40537370	0.40537329	–4.11242e-07
y (0.51)	:	0.45302738	0.45302695	–4.29997e-07
y (0.56)	:	0.50181385	0.50181341	–4.40386e-07
y (0.61)	:	0.55185511	0.55185467	–4.41418e-07
y (0.66)	:	0.60327628	0.60327585	–4.32051e-07
y (0.71)	:	0.65620595	0.65620554	–4.11192e-08
y (0.76)	:	0.71077646	0.71077608	–3.77684e-07
y (0.81)	:	0.76712426	0.76712393	–3.30307e-07
y (0.86)	:	0.82539026	0.82538999	–2.67768e-07
y (0.91)	:	0.88572015	0.88571996	–1.88696e-07
y (0.96)	:	0.94826478	0.94826469	–9.16356e-08

The error field confines to the range [– 1.10975e-08, – 9.16356e-08]. The approximations are correct to within this domain.

Example 3

BVP : $\frac{D^2y}{dx^2} - y(1 + \text{Tan}^2\, x) = 0$

$P = 0$, $Q = 1 + \text{Tan}^2\, x$, $R = 0.0$

PS : $y(x) = \frac{1}{\text{Cos}\, x}$

IC : $y(0) : 1,\ y(1) : \frac{1}{\text{Cos}1},\ 0 \le x \le 1$

W : 0.01

The Computer Solution of the BVP of Order 2

x-value		*Approx value*	*Exact Value*	*Error*
y (0.01)	:	1.00130211	1.00005000	–0.00125
y (0.06)	:	1.00931861	1.00180270	–0.00752
y (0.11)	:	1.01986906	1.00608065	–0.01379
y (0.16)	:	1.03300194	1.01293797	–0.02006
y (0.21)	:	1.04878636	1.02246257	–0.02632
y (0.26)	:	1.06731384	1.03477894	–0.03253
y (0.31)	:	1.08870066	1.05005224	–0.03865
y (0.36)	:	1.11309106	1.06849385	–0.04460
y (0.41)	:	1.14066144	1.09036888	–0.05029
y (0.46)	:	1.17162569	1.11600604	–0.05562
y (0.51)	:	1.20624227	1.14581071	–0.06043
y (0.56)	:	1.24482317	1.18028205	–0.06454
y (0.61)	:	1.28774579	1.22003589	–0.06771
y (0.66)	:	1.33546845	1.26583523	–0.06963
y (0.71)	:	1.38855104	1.31863169	–0.06992
y (0.76)	:	1.44768287	1.37962240	–0.06806
y (0.81)	:	1.51372077	1.45032962	–0.06339
y (0.86)	:	1.58774210	1.53271394	–0.05503
y (0.91)	:	1.67112019	1.62933919	–0.04178
y (0.96)	:	1.76563393	1.74361840	–0.02202

The error field confines to the range [– 0.00125, – 0.02202]. The approximations are correct to within this domain.

Example 4

BVP : $x^2y'' - 2y + x = 0$

$$P = 0,\ Q = \frac{2}{x^2},\ R = \frac{-1}{x}$$

PS : $y(x) = \dfrac{19x^2 - 5x^3 - 36}{38x}$

IC : $y(2) : 0, y(3) : 0, 2 \le x \le 3$

W : 0.01

The Computer Solution of the BVP of Order 2

x-value	*Approx value*	*Exact Value*	*Error*
y (2.01) :	0.00208031	0.00208032	1.50800e-08
y (2.06) :	0.01174391	0.01174400	8.21183e-08
y (2.11) :	0.02020746	0.02020760	1.36464e-07
y (2.16) :	0.02750859	0.02750877	1.79621e-07
y (2.21) :	0.03368156	0.03368177	2.12881e-07
y (2.26) :	0.03875756	0.03875780	2.37362e-07
y (2.31) :	0.04276513	0.04276538	2.54031e-07
y (2.36) :	0.04573033	0.04573060	2.63727e-07
y (2.41) :	0.04767712	0.04767739	2.67182e-07
y (2.46) :	0.04862746	0.04862773	2.65035e-07
y (2.51) :	0.04860160	0.04860186	2.57843e-07
y (2.56) :	0.04761817	0.04761842	2.46095e-07
y (2.61) :	0.04569442	0.04569465	2.30224e-07
y (2.66) :	0.04284625	0.04284646	2.10607e-07
y (2.71) :	0.03908842	0.03908861	1.87578e-07
y (2.76) :	0.03443462	0.03443478	1.61434e-07
y (2.81) :	0.02889755	0.02889769	1.32436e-07
y (2.86) :	0.02248904	0.02248914	1.00815e-07
y (2.91) :	0.01522009	0.01522016	6.67793e-08
y (2.96) :	0.00710097	0.00710100	3.05112e-08

The error field confines to the range [1.50800e-08, 3.05112e-08]. The approximations are correct to within this domain.

Example 5

BVP : $y'' + \frac{1}{x} y' - \frac{1}{x^2} y - 3 = 0$

$$P = \frac{-1}{x}, \; Q = \frac{1}{x^2}, \; R = 3.0$$

PS : $y(x) = x(x-1) + \dfrac{2}{x}$

IC : $y(1) : 2, y(2) : 3, 1 \le x \le 2$

W : 0.01

The Computer Solution of the BVP of Order 2

x-value		*Approx value*	*Exact Value*	*Error*
y (1.01)	:	1.99029838	1.99029802	–3.63306e-07
y (1.06)	:	1.95039432	1.95039245	–1.86548e-06
y (1.11)	:	1.92390474	1.92390180	–2.93561e-06
y (1.16)	:	1.90974160	1.90973793	–3.67290e-06
y (1.21)	:	1.90699671	1.90699256	–4.1517e-06
y (1.26)	:	1.91490602	1.91490159	–4.42859e-06
y (1.31)	:	1.93282210	1.93281756	–4.54657e-06
y (1.36)	:	1.96019277	1.96018824	–4.53905e-06
y (1.41)	:	1.99654415	1.99653972	–4.43199e-06
y (1.46)	:	2.04146726	2.04146301	–4.24574e-06
y (1.51)	:	2.09460731	2.09460331	–3.99638e-06
y (1.56)	:	2.15565498	2.15565128	–3.69664e-06
y (1.61)	:	2.22433938	2.22433602	–3.35673e-06
y (1.66)	:	2.30042226	2.30041928	–2.98479e-06
y (1.71)	:	2.38369323	2.38369064	–2.58740e-06
y (1.76)	:	2.47396581	2.47396364	–2.16988e-06
y (1.81)	:	2.57107411	2.57107238	–1.73655e-06
y (1.86)	:	2.67487011	2.67486882	–1.29091e-06
y (1.91)	:	2.78522125	2.78522042	–8.35809e-07
y (1.96)	:	2.90200854	2.90200816	–3.73597e-07

The error field confines to the range [– 3.63306e-07, – 3.73597e-07]. The approximations are correct to within this domain.

Example 6

BVP : $y'' + xy' - 2y + x = 0$

$P = -x$, $Q = 2.0$, $R = -x$

PS : $y(x) = x^2 + x + 1$

IC : $y(0) : 1, y(1) : 3, 0 \leq x \leq 1$

W : 0.01

The Computer Solution of the BVP of Order 2

x-value		*Approx value*	*Exact Value*	*Error*
y (0.01)	:	1.0101	1.0101	0
y (0.06)	:	1.0636	1.0636	6.66134e-16
y (0.11)	:	1.1221	1.1221	1.11022e-15
y (0.16)	:	1.1856	1.1856	1.33227e-15
y (0.21)	:	1.2541	1.2541	1.99840e-15
y (0.26)	:	1.3276	1.3276	2.66454e-15
y (0.31)	:	1.4061	1.4061	2.88658e-15
y (0.36)	:	1.4896	1.4896	3.33067e-15
y (0.41)	:	1.5781	1.5781	3.99680e-15
y (0.46)	:	1.6716	1.6716	3.99680e-15
y (0.51)	:	1.7701	1.7701	3.77476e-15
y (0.56)	:	1.8736	1.8736	3.55271e-15
y (0.61)	:	1.9821	1.9821	3.55271e-15
y (0.66)	:	2.0956	2.0956	3.55271e-15
y (0.71)	:	2.2141	2.2141	3.10862e-15
y (0.76)	:	2.3376	2.3376	2.66454e-15
y (0.81)	:	2.4661	2.4661	2.22045e-15
y (0.86)	:	2.5996	2.5996	2.22045e-15
y (0.91)	:	2.7381	2.7381	1.33227e-15
y (0.96)	:	2.8816	2.8816	0

Example 7

BVP : $y'' - y' + x + 2e^x = 0$

$P = 0, Q = 1.0, R = -(x + 2e^x)$

PS : $y(x) = x + (1 - x)e^x$

IC : $y(0) : 1, y(1) : 1, 0 \le x \le 1$

W : 0.01

The Computer Solution of the BVP of Order 2

x-value		*Approx value*	*Exact Value*	*Error*
y (0.01)	:	1.00994948	1.00994967	1.83707e-07
y (0.06)	:	1.05812529	1.05812635	1.06419e-06
y (0.11)	:	1.10348560	1.10348748	1.87960e-06
y (0.16)	:	1.14574650	1.14574913	2.62735e-06
y (0.21)	:	1.18460236	1.18460567	3.30438e-06
y (0.26)	:	1.21972436	1.21972826	3.90712e-06
y (0.31)	:	1.25075890	1.25076333	4.43150e-06
y (0.36)	:	1.27732595	1.27733083	4.87289e-06
y (0.41)	:	1.29901727	1.29902249	5.22608e-06
y (0.46)	:	1.31539447	1.31539995	5.48523e-06
y (0.51)	:	1.32598704	1.32599269	5.64386e-06
y (0.56)	:	1.33029021	1.33029590	5.69476e-06
y (0.61)	:	1.32776262	1.32776825	5.62999e-06
y (0.66)	:	1.31782395	1.31782939	5.44082e-06
y (0.71)	:	1.29985235	1.29985747	5.11764e-06
y (0.76)	:	1.27318164	1.27318629	4.64997e-06
y (0.81)	:	1.23709849	1.23710252	4.02634e-06
y (0.86)	:	1.19083926	1.19084250	3.23426e-06
y (0.91)	:	1.13358677	1.13358903	2.26014e-06
y (0.96)	:	1.06446677	1.06446786	1.08919e-06

The error field confines to the range [1.83707e-07, 1.08919e-06]. The approximations are correct to within this domain.

Example 8

BVP : $y'' - 6(x-1) = 0$

$P = 0$, $Q = 1.0$, $R = 6(x-1)$

PS : $y(x) = x\,(2 - 3x + x^2)$

IC : $y(0) : 0$, $y(1) : 0$, $0 \le x \le 1$

W : 0.01

The Computer Solution of the BVP of Order 2

x-value		*Approx value*	*Exact Value*	*Error*
y (0.01)	:	0.019701	0.019701	1.73472e-16
y (0.06)	:	0.109416	0.109416	1.01308e-15
y (0.11)	:	0.185031	0.185031	1.85962e-15
y (0.16)	:	0.247296	0.247296	2.77556e-15
y (0.21)	:	0.296961	0.296961	3.38618e-15
y (0.26)	:	0.334776	0.334776	3.60822e-15
y (0.31)	:	0.361491	0.361491	3.66374e-15
y (0.36)	:	0.377856	0.377856	3.33067e-15
y (0.41)	:	0.384621	0.384621	2.99760e-15
y (0.46)	:	0.382536	0.382536	2.33147e-15
y (0.51)	:	0.372351	0.372351	1.88738e-15
y (0.56)	:	0.354816	0.354816	1.33227e-15
y (0.61)	:	0.330681	0.330681	1.22125e-15
y (0.66)	:	0.300696	0.300696	1.27676e-15
y (0.71)	:	0.265611	0.265611	1.33227e-15
y (0.76)	:	0.226176	0.226176	1.16573e-15
y (0.81)	:	0.183141	0.183141	1.02696e-15
y (0.86)	:	0.137256	0.137256	9.15934e-16

x-value		*Approx value*	*Exact Value*	*Error*
y (0.91)	:	0.089271	0.089271	5.96745e-16
y (0.96)	:	0.039936	0.039936	3.26128e-16

The error field confines to the range [1.73472e-16, 3.26128e-16]. The approximations are correct to within this domain.

Example 9

BVP : $\frac{D^2y}{dx^2} - \pi^2 y = -2\pi^2 \text{Sin}(\pi x)$

$P = 0$, $Q = \pi^2$, $R = -2\pi^2 \text{Sin}(\pi x)$

PS : $y(x) = \text{Sin}(\pi x)$

IC : $y(0) : 0, y(1) : 0, 0 \le x \le 1$

W : 0.01

The Computer Solution of the BVP of Order 2

x-value		*Approx value*	*Exact Value*	*Error*
y (0.01)	:	0.03141205	0.03141076	–1.29172e-06
y (0.06)	:	0.18738902	0.18738131	–7.70575e-06
y (0.11)	:	0.33875185	0.33873792	–1.39300e-05
y (0.16)	:	0.48177348	0.48175367	–1.98113e-05
y (0.21)	:	0.61293226	0.61290705	–2.52048e-05
y (0.26)	:	0.72899860	0.72896863	–2.99776e-05
y (0.31)	:	0.82711459	0.82708057	–3.40123e-05
y (0.36)	:	0.90486426	0.90482705	–3.72094e-05
y (0.41)	:	0.96033318	0.96029369	–3.94903e-05
y (0.46)	:	0.99215550	0.99211470	–4.07988e-05
y (0.51)	:	0.99954766	0.99950656	–4.11027e-05
y (0.56)	:	0.98232765	0.98228725	–4.03944e-05
y (0.61)	:	0.94091946	0.94088077	–3.86915e-05
y (0.66)	:	0.87634272	0.87630668	–3.60357e-05
y (0.71)	:	0.79018751	0.79015501	–3.24927e-05

x-value		Approx value	Exact Value	Error
y (0.76)	:	0.68457526	0.68454711	–2.81494e-05
y (0.81)	:	0.56210649	0.56208338	–2.31130e-05
y (0.86)	:	0.42579680	0.42577929	–1.75073e-05
y (0.91)	:	0.27900258	0.27899111	–1.14704e-05
y (0.96)	:	0.12533839	0.12533324	–5.15100e-06

The error field confines to the range [– 1.29172e-06, – 5.15100e-06]. The approximations are correct to within this domain.

Example 10

BVP : $y'' - 2x = 0$

$P = 0, Q = 0, R = 2x$

PS : $y(x) = \dfrac{x(x^2 - 1)}{3}$

IC : $y(0) : 0, y(1) : 0, 0 \le x \le 1$

W : 0.01

The Computer Solution of the BVP of Order 2

x-value		Approx value	Exact Value	Error
y (0.01)	:	–0.003333	–0.003333	–3.64292e-17
y (0.06)	:	–0.019928	–0.019928	–2.18575e-16
y (0.11)	:	–0.036223	–0.036223	–4.02456e-16
y (0.16)	:	–0.051968	–0.051968	–6.03684e-16
y (0.21)	:	–0.066913	–0.066913	–7.49401e-16
y (0.26)	:	–0.080808	–0.080808	–8.04912e-16
y (0.31)	:	–0.093403	–0.093403	–8.04912e-16
y (0.36)	:	–0.104448	–0.104448	–7.07767e-16
y (0.41)	:	–0.113693	–0.113693	–6.24500e-16
y (0.46)	:	–0.120888	–0.120888	–4.57967e-16
y (0.51)	:	–0.125783	–0.125783	–3.33067e-16
y (0.56)	:	–0.128128	–0.128128	–1.38778e-16

x-value		*Approx value*	*Exact Value*	*Error*
y (0.61)	:	–0.127673	–0.127673	–1.38778e-16
y (0.66)	:	–0.124168	–0.124168	–2.63678e-16
y (0.71)	:	–0.117363	–0.117363	–3.05311e-16
y (0.76)	:	–0.107008	–0.107008	–2.77556e-16
y (0.81)	:	–0.092853	–0.092853	–2.77556e-16
y (0.86)	:	–0.074648	–0.074648	–2.77556e-16
y (0.91)	:	–0.052143	–0.052143	–1.94289e-16
y (0.96)	:	–0.025088	–0.025088	–1.14492e-16

The error field confines to the range [– 3.64292e-17, – 1.14492e-16]. The approximations are correct to within this domain.

Example 11

BVP : $x^2y'' = \text{Sin}(Lnx) - 2xy' + 2y$

$$P = \frac{-2}{x},\ Q = \frac{2}{x^2},\ R = \frac{\text{Sin}(Lnx)}{x^2}$$

PS : $y(x) = 1.139207x - \dfrac{0.039207}{x^2} - \dfrac{3\text{Sin}(Lnx)}{10} - \dfrac{\text{Cos}(Lnx)}{10}$

IC : $y(1) : 1,\ y(2) : 2,\ 1 \le x \le 2$

W : 0.01

The Computer Solution of the BVP of Order 2

x-value		*Approx value*	*Exact Value*	*Error*
y (1.01)	:	1.00918446	1.00918450	3.87004e-08
y (1.06)	:	1.05536407	1.05536426	1.96107e-07
y (1.11)	:	1.10199104	1.10199134	3.04627e-07
y (1.16)	:	1.14907925	1.14907963	3.76290e-07
y (1.21)	:	1.19663204	1.19663246	4.19989e-07
y (1.26)	:	1.24464543	1.24464587	4.42363e-07
y (1.31)	:	1.29311051	1.29311096	4.48419e-07
y (1.36)	:	1.34201505	1.34201550	4.41966e-07
y (1.41)	:	1.39134471	1.39134514	4.25919e-07

x-value	*Approx value*	*Exact Value*	*Error*
y (1.46) :	1.44108385	1.44108425	4.02526e-07
y (1.51) :	1.49121614	1.49121651	3.73530e-07
y (1.56) :	1.54172501	1.54172535	3.40287e-07
y (1.61) :	1.59259394	1.59259424	3.03859e-07
y (1.66) :	1.64380666	1.64380693	2.65078e-07
y (1.71) :	1.69534734	1.69534756	2.24599e-07
y (1.76) :	1.74720062	1.74720080	1.82936e-07
y (1.81) :	1.79935173	1.79925187	1.40495e-07
y (1.86) :	1.85178650	1.85178659	9.75947e-08
y (1.91) :	1.90449138	1.90449144	5.44871e-08
y(1.96) :	1.95745346	1.95745347	1.13683e-08

The error field confines to the range [3.87004e-08, 1.13683e-08]. The approximations are correct to within this domain.

Example 12

BVP : $\frac{D^2y}{dx^2} + x\,\frac{dy}{dx} - 3y = 4.2x$

$P = -x$, $Q = 3$, $R = 4.2x$

PS : $y(x) = x(x^2 + 0.9)$

IC : $y(0) : 0$, $y(1) : 1.9$, $0 \le x \le 1$

W : 0.01

The Computer Solution of the BVP of Order 2

x-value	*Approx value*	*Exact Value*	*Error*
y (0.01) :	0.00900112	0.009001	–1.24986e-07
y (0.06) :	0.05421675	0.054216	–7.47291e-07
y (0.11) :	0.10033236	0.100331	–1.35835e-06
y (0.16) :	0.14809795	0.148096	–1.94878e-06
y (0.21) :	0.19826351	0.198261	–2.50921e-06
y (0.26) :	0.25157903	0.251576	–3.03026e-06

x-value		*Approx value*	*Exact Value*	*Error*
y (0.31)	:	0.30879450	0.308791	–3.50257e-06
y (0.36)	:	0.37065992	0.370656	–3.91675e-06
y (0.41)	:	0.43792526	0.437921	–4.26343e-06
y (0.46)	:	0.51134053	0.511336	–4.53324e-06
y (0.51)	:	0.5916557	0.591651	–4.71680e-06
y (0.56)	:	0.67962080	0.679616	–4.80474e-06
y (0.61)	:	0.77598579	0.775981	–4.78768e-06
y (0.66)	:	0.88150066	0.881496	–4.65624e-06
y (0.71)	:	0.99691540	0.996911	–4.40106e-06
y (0.76)	:	1.12298001	1.122976	–4.01275e-06
y (0.81)	:	1.26044448	1.260441	–3.48194e-06
y (0.86)	:	1.141005880	1.410056	–2.79927e-06
y (0.91)	:	1.57257296	1.572571	–1.95534e-06
y (0.96)	:	1.74873694	1.748736	–9.40788e-07

The error field confines to the range [–1.24986e-07, –9.40788e-07]. The approximations are correct to within this domain.

Example 13

BVP : $\frac{D^2y}{dx^2} + 2\frac{dy}{dx} + y = x$

$P = -2, Q = -1, R = x$

PS : $y(x) = e^{-x}[2 + (e - 2)x] + x - 2$

IC : $y(0) : 0, y(1) : 0, 0 \le x \le 1$

W : 0.01

The Computer Solution of the BVP of Order 2

x-value		*Approx value*	*Exact Value*	*Error*
y (0.01)	:	–0.00278902	–0.00278898	3.99922e-08
y (0.06)	:	–0.01588402	–0.01588379	2.24671e-07
y (0.11)	:	–0.02755136	–0.02755098	3.84092e-07

x-value		*Approx value*	*Exact Value*	*Error*
y (0.16)	:	–0.03778024	–0.03777972	5.18715e-07
y (0.21)	:	–0.04656427	–0.04656364	6.29185e-07
y (0.26)	:	–0.05390114	–0.05390042	7.16301e-07
y (0.31)	:	–0.05979217	–0.05979139	7.80983e-07
y (0.36)	:	–0.06424201	–0.06424119	8.24255e-07
y (0.41)	:	–0.06725830	–0.06725745	8.47214e-07
y (0.46)	:	–0.06885136	–0.06885051	8.51015e-07
y (0.51)	:	–0.06903390	–0.06903306	8.36855e-07
y (0.56)	:	–0.06782079	–0.06781998	8.05954e-07
y (0.61)	:	–0.06522880	–0.06522804	7.59544e-07
y (0.66)	:	–0.06127638	–0.06127568	6.98857e-07
y (0.71)	:	–0.05598347	–0.05598285	6.25116e-07
y (0.76)	:	–0.04937130	–0.04937076	5.39527e-07
y (0.81)	:	–0.04146220	–0.04146176	4.43270e-07
y (0.86)	:	–0.03227949	–0.03227915	3.37493e-07
y (0.91)	:	–0.02184726	–0.02184704	2.23310e-07
y (0.96)	:	–0.01019033	–0.01019023	1.01796e-07

The error field confines to the range [3.99922e-08, 1.01796e-07]. The approximations are correct to within this domain.

Example 14

BVP : $\frac{D^2y}{dx^2} - y - x = 0$

$P = 0, Q = 1, R = x$

PS : $y(x) = \frac{e^1(e^x - e^{-x})}{(e^2 - 1)} - x$

IC : $y(0) : 0,\ y(1) : 0,\ 0 \le x \le 1$

W : 0.01

The Computer Solution of the BVP of Order 2

x-value		Approx value	Exact Value	Error
y (0.01)	:	–0.00149067	–0.00149068	–1.10975e-08
y (0.06)	:	–0.00891421	–0.00891427	–6.63756e-08
y (0.11)	:	–0.01621001	–0.01621013	–1.20755e-07
y (0.16)	:	–0.02327129	–0.02327146	–1.73482e-07
y (0.21)	:	–0.02999068	–0.02999090	–2.23792e-07
y (0.26)	:	–0.03625995	–0.03626023	–2.70911e-07
y (0.31)	:	–0.04196977	–0.04197008	–3.14044e-07
y (0.36)	:	–0.04700937	–0.04700937	–3.52376e-07
y (0.41)	:	–0.05126634	–0.05126673	–3.85065e-07
y (0.46)	:	–0.05462630	–0.05462671	–4.11242e-07
y (0.51)	:	–0.05697262	–0.05697305	–4.29997e-07
y (0.56)	:	–0.05818615	–0.05818659	–4.40386e-07
y (0.61)	:	–0.05814489	–0.05814533	–4.41418e-07
y (0.66)	:	–0.05672372	–0.05672415	–4.32051e-07
y (0.71)	:	–0.05379405	–0.05379446	–4.11192e-07
y (0.76)	:	–0.04922354	–0.04922392	–3.77684e-07
y (0.81)	:	–0.04287574	–0.04287607	–3.30307e-07
y (0.86)	:	–0.03460974	–0.03461001	–2.67768e-07
y (0.91)	:	–0.02427985	–0.02428004	–1.88696e-07
y (0.96)	:	–0.01173522	–0.01173531	–9.16356e-08

The error field confines to the range [– 1.10975e-08, – 9.16356e-08]. The approximations are correct to within this domain.

Example 15

BVP : $\dfrac{D^2y}{dx^2} + \dfrac{dy}{dx} = 2e^x$

$P = -1, Q = 0, R = 2e^x$

PS : $y(x) = e^x$

IC : $y(0) : 1, y(1) : e, 0 \le x \le 1$

W : 0.01

The Computer Solution of the BVP of Order 2

x-value	*Approx value*	*Exact Value*	*Error*
y (0.01) :	1.00018575	1.01005017	0.00986
y (0.06) :	1.00663374	1.06183655	0.05520
y (0.11) :	1.02213812	1.11627807	0.09414
y (0.16) :	1.04652283	1.17351087	0.12699
y (0.21) :	1.07963400	1.23367806	0.15404
y (0.26) :	1.12133959	1.29693009	0.17559
y (0.31) :	1.17152906	1.36342511	0.19190
y (0.36) :	1.23011307	1.43332941	0.20322
y (0.41) :	1.29702328	1.50681779	0.20979
y (0.46) :	1.37221217	1.58407398	0.21186
y (0.51) :	1.45565290	1.66529119	0.20964
y (0.56) :	1.54733930	1.75067250	0.20333
y (0.61) :	1.64728580	1.84043140	0.19315
y (0.66) :	1.75552747	1.93479233	0.17926
y (0.71) :	1.87212015	2.03399126	0.16187
y (0.76) :	1.99714055	2.13827622	0.14114
y (0.81) :	2.13068645	2.24790799	0.11722
y (0.86) :	2.27287695	2.36316069	0.09028
y (0.91) :	2.42385277	2.48432253	0.06047
y (0.96) :	2.58377660	2.61169647	0.02792

The error field confines to the range [0.00986, 0.02792]. The approximations are correct to within this domain.

Example 16

BVP : $\dfrac{D^2y}{dx^2} - y + x + e^x + e^{-x} = 0$

$P = 0, Q = 1.0, R = -x - e^x - e^{-x}$

PS : $y(x) = x + \dfrac{(1-x)(e^{x} - e^{-x})}{2}$

IC : $y(0) : 0,\ y(1) : 1,\ 0 \le x \le 1$

W : 0.01

The Computer Solution of the BVP of Order 2

x-value		*Approx value*	*Exact Value*	*Error*
y (0.01)	:	0.01990001	0.01990017	1.58480e-07
y (0.06)	:	0.11643294	0.11643385	9.01689e-07
y (0.11)	:	0.20809599	0.20809755	1.56480e-06
y (0.16)	:	0.29497202	0.29497417	2.14999e-06
y (0.21)	:	0.37711940	0.37712206	2.65893e-06
y (0.26)	:	0.45457195	0.45457505	3.09277e-06
y (0.31)	:	0.52733901	0.52734246	3.45220e-06
y (0.36)	:	0.59540525	0.59540899	3.73737e-06
y (0.41)	:	0.65873047	0.65873442	3.94796e-06
y (0.46)	:	0.71724931	0.71725339	4.08313e-06
y (0.51)	:	0.77087078	0.77087493	4.14151e-06
y (0.56)	:	0.81947783	0.81948196	4.12122e-06
y (0.61)	:	0.86292668	0.86293070	4.01986e-06
y (0.66)	:	0.90104614	0.90104997	3.83445e-06
y (0.71)	:	0.93363676	0.93364032	3.56144e-06
y (0.76)	:	0.96046998	0.96047318	3.19672e-06
y (0.81)	:	0.98128701	0.98128974	2.73553e-06
y (0.86)	:	0.99579773	0.99579990	2.17249e-06
y (0.91)	:	1.00367942	1.00368092	1.50156e-06
y (0.96)	:	1.00457536	1.00457607	7.15995e-07

The error field confines to the range [1.58480e-07, 7.15995e-07]. The approximations are correct to within this domain.

Example 17

BVP : $\frac{D^2y}{dx^2} + y + x = 0$

$P = 0, Q = -1, R = -x$

PS : $y(x) = \frac{\text{Sin } x}{\text{Sin } 1} - x$

IC : $y(0) : 0, y(1) : 0, 0 \le x \le 1$

W : 0.01

The Computer Solution of the BVP of Order 2

x-value		*Approx value*	*Exact Value*	*Error*
y (0.01)	:	0.00188377	0.00188375	–1.77206e-08
y (0.06)	:	0.01126104	0.01126093	–1.05915e-07
y (0.11)	:	0.02046019	0.02046000	–1.92361e-07
y (0.16)	:	0.02933325	0.02933298	–2.75609e-07
y (0.21)	:	0.03773308	0.03773272	–3.54226e-07
y (0.26)	:	0.04551370	0.04551327	–4.26798e-07
y (0.31)	:	0.05253068	0.05253019	–4.91941e-07
y (0.36)	:	0.05864152	0.05864097	–5.48305e-07
y (0.41)	:	0.06370597	0.06370537	–5.94580e-07
y (0.46)	:	0.06758639	0.06758576	–6.29504e-07
y (0.51)	:	0.07014810	0.07014745	–6.51867e-07
y (0.56)	:	0.07125974	0.07125908	–6.60520e-07
y (0.61)	:	0.07079354	0.07079289	–6.54376e-07
y (0.66)	:	0.06862570	0.06862507	–6.32419e-07
y (0.71)	:	0.06463666	0.06463606	–5.93707e-07
y (0.76)	:	0.05871141	0.05871087	–5.37380e-07
y (0.81)	:	0.05073980	0.05073933	–4.62660e-07
y (0.86)	:	0.04061676	0.04061639	–3.68859e-07
y (0.91)	:	0.02824264	0.02824238	–2.55380e-07
y (0.96)	:	0.01352337	0.01352325	–1.21725e-07

The error field confines to the range [– 1.77206e-08, – 1.21725e-07]. The approximations are correct to within this domain.

Example 18

BVP : $y'' - 11y' - 12y + 12x + 11 = 0$

$P = 11$, Q = 12.0, R = – (12x + 11)

PS : $y(x) = x + e^{-x}$

IC : $y(0)$: 1, $y(1) = 1.36787944$, $0 \le x \le 1$

W : 0.01

The Computer Solution of the BVP of Order 2

x-value		*Approx value*	*Exact Value*	*Error*
y (0.01)	:	1.00004992	1.00004983	–8.92152e-08
y (0.06)	:	1.00176491	1.00176453	–3.73531e-07
y (0.11)	:	1.00583441	1.00583414	–2.76297e-07
y (0.16)	:	1.01214333	1.01214379	4.57007e-07
y (0.21)	:	1.02058195	1.02058425	2.29475e-06
y (0.26)	:	1.03104549	1.03105159	6.09491e-06
y (0.31)	:	1.04343353	1.04344696	1.34254e-05
y (0.36)	:	1.05764918	1.05767633	2.71485e-05
y (0.41)	:	1.07359776	1.07365025	5.24856e-05
y (0.46)	:	1.09118469	1.09128365	9.89590e-05
y (0.51)	:	1.11031165	1.11049558	0.00018
y (0.56)	:	1.13087000	1.13120906	0.00034
y (0.61)	:	1.15272879	1.15335087	0.00062
y (0.66)	:	1.17571314	1.17685113	0.00114
y (0.71)	:	1.19956490	1.20164420	0.00208
y (0.76)	:	1.22387129	1.22766643	0.00380
y (0.81)	:	1.24793462	1.25485807	0.00692
y (0.86)	:	1.27053526	1.28316208	0.01263

x-value	Approx value	Exact Value	Error
y (0.91) :	1.28949936	1.31252422	0.02302
y (0.96) :	1.30091098	1.34289289	0.04198

The error field confines to the range [–8.92152e-08, 0.04198]. The approximations are correct to within this domain.

9.3. Nonlinear Equations

Earlier in section 7.4 the subject matter on the nonlinear diferential equations was studied and the suitable solutions were found. These are the equations that describe the events of interaction. Such equations have been encountered casually in the real world. The nonlinear differential equations of order 2 have been occurred in higher branches of modern physics, for example, in quantum mechanics, electrodynamics etc.

The solution to a nonlinear boundary-value problem cannot be expressed as a linear combination of the solutions as in the case of initial-value problems of order 2. We need, in this case, the solutions to a series of initial-value problems and on that ground the requirement of an iterative procedure for the solution is inevitable. The approximation to the boundary value problem of second order has been carried out by applying the C++ program named BVP2NLFD using the method of **Finite Difference**. The results for approximation of a BVP would be appropriate if we follow the points mentioned below :

a) The values of P, $\dot{Q}$ and R will be created in the Function DEFINITION Block placed at the end of the program.

b) The boundary conditions of the problem, in this case the values for $x0$, $x1$, yB & yF are to be put in the DEFINITION Block of BC of the program when called for.

Example 1

BVP : $y'' - 2y^3 + 6y + 2x^3 = 0$

$P = 0,\ Q = 2y^2 - 6,\ R = 2y^3 - 6y - 2x^3$

PS : $y(x) = x + \dfrac{1}{x}$

IC : $y(1) : 2,\ y(2) : 2.5,\ 1 \le x \le 2$

W : 0.01

The Computer Solution of the BVP of Order 2

x-value		*Approx value*	*Exact Value*	*Error*
y (1.01)	:	1.99598864	2.00009901	0.00411
y (1.06)	:	1.97896829	2.00339623	0.02443
y (1.11)	:	1.96707974	2.01090090	0.04382
y (1.16)	:	1.96037808	2.02206897	0.06169
y (1.21)	:	1.95886960	2.03644628	0.07758
y (1.26)	:	1.96251603	2.05365079	0.09113
y (1.31)	:	1.97123860	2.07335878	0.10212
y (1.36)	:	1.98492191	2.09529412	0.11037
y (1.41)	:	2.00341743	2.11921986	0.11580
y (1.46)	:	2.02654675	2.14493151	0.11838
y (1.51)	:	2.05410427	2.17225166	0.11815
y (1.56)	:	2.08585948	2.20102564	0.11517
y (1.61)	:	2.12155860	2.23111801	0.10956
y (1.66)	:	2.16092567	2.26240964	0.10148
y (1.71)	:	2.20366248	2.29479532	0.09113
y (1.76)	:	2.24944999	2.32818182	0.07873
y (1.81)	:	2.29794337	2.36248619	0.06454
y (1.86)	:	2.34877338	2.39763441	0.04886
y (1.91)	:	2.40154117	2.43356021	0.03202
y (1.96)	:	2.45581406	2.47020408	0.01439

The error field confines to the range [0.00411, 0.01439]. The approximations are correct to within this domain.

Example 2

BVP : $y'' - y^3 + yy' = 0$

$P = -y,\ Q = y^2 - y',\ R = y^3 - yy'$

PS : $y(x) = (x + 1)^{-1}$

IC : $y(1) : \frac{1}{2}, y(2) : \frac{1}{3}, 1 \le x \le 2$

W : 0.01

The Computer Solution of the BVP of Order 2

x-value		*Approx value*	*Exact Value*	*Error*
y (1.01)	:	0.49748934	0.49751244	2.30982e-05
y (1.06)	:	0.48530153	0.48543689	0.00014
y (1.11)	:	0.47369461	0.47393365	0.00024
y (1.16)	:	0.46263215	0.46296296	0.00033
y (1.21)	:	0.45208019	0.45248869	0.00041
y (1.26)	:	0.44200705	0.44247788	0.00047
y (1.31)	:	0.43238318	0.43290043	0.00052
y (1.36)	:	0.42318099	0.42372881	0.00055
y (1.41)	:	0.41437476	0.41493776	0.00056
y (1.46)	:	0.40594045	0.40650407	0.00056
y (1.51)	:	0.39785565	0.39840637	0.00055
y (1.56)	:	0.39009939	0.39062500	0.00053
y (1.61)	:	0.38265213	0.38314176	0.00049
y (1.66)	:	0.37549560	0.37593985	0.00044
y (1.71)	:	0.36861272	0.36900369	0.00039
y (1.76)	:	0.36198757	0.36231884	0.00033
y (1.81)	:	0.35560527	0.035587189	0.00027
y (1.86)	:	0.34945191	0.34965035	0.00020
y (1.91)	:	0.34351452	0.34364261	0.00013
y (1.96)	:	0.33778099	0.33783784	5.68451e-05

The error field confines to the range [2.30982e-05, 5.68451e-05]. The approximations are correct to within this domain.

Example 3

BVP : $y'' - 6y^2 = 0$

$P = 0$, $Q = 6y$, $R = 6y^2$

PS : $y(x) = \dfrac{1}{(x+1)^2}$

IC : $y(0) : 1,\ y(0.5) : \dfrac{4}{9},\ 0 \le x \le 0.5$

W : 0.005

The Computer Solution of the BVP of Order 2

x-value	*Approx value*	*Exact Value*	*Error*
y (0.005) :	0.98978787	0.99007450	0.00029
y (0.055) :	0.89541685	0.89845242	0.00304
y (0.105) :	0.81368303	0.81898405	0.00530
y (0.155) :	0.74275278	0.74961114	0.00686
y (0.205) :	0.68106359	0.68869338	0.00763
y (0.255) :	0.62727885	0.63491056	0.00763
y (0.305) :	0.58025026	0.58719044	0.00694
y (0.355) :	0.53898659	0.54465489	0.00567
y (0.405) :	0.50262772	0.50657920	0.00395
y (0.455) :	0.47042304	0.47236098	0.00194

The error field confines to the range [0.00029, 0.00194]. The approximations are correct to within this domain.

Example 4

BVP : $2y'' = (1 + x + y)^3$

$$P = 0,\ Q = \frac{y^2 + 3y(1 + x) + 3(1 + x)^2}{2},\ R = \frac{(1 + x + y)^3}{2}$$

PS : $y(x) = \dfrac{2}{2 - x} - x - 1$

IC : $y(0) : 0,\ y(1) : 0,\ 0 \le x \le 1$

W : 0.01

The Computer Solution of the BVP of Order 2

x-value	*Approx value*	*Exact Value*	*Error*
y (0.01) :	–0.00486542	–0.00497487	–0.00011
y (0.06) :	–0.02841523	–0.02907216	–0.00066

x-value		*Approx value*	*Exact Value*	*Error*
y (0.11)	:	–0.05059544	–0.05179894	–0.00120
y (0.16)	:	–0.07129918	–0.07304348	–0.00174
y (0.21)	:	–0.09041068	–0.09268156	–0.00227
y (0.26)	:	–0.10780301	–0.11057471	–0.00277
y (0.31)	:	–0.12333531	–0.12656805	–0.00323
y (0.36)	:	–0.13684953	–0.14048780	–0.00364
y (0.41)	:	–0.14816657	–0.15213836	–0.00397
y (0.46)	:	–0.15708176	–0.16129870	–0.00422
y (0.51)	:	–0.16335944	–0.16771812	–0.00436
y (0.56)	:	–0.16672665	–0.17111111	–0.00438
y (0.61)	:	–0.16686560	–0.17115108	–0.00429
y (0.66)	:	–0.16340484	–0.16746269	–0.00406
y (0.71)	:	–0.15590862	–0.15961240	–0.00370
y (0.76)	:	–0.14386443	–0.14709677	–0.00323
y (0.81)	:	–0.12666789	–0.12932773	–0.00266
y (0.86)	:	–0.10360489	–0.10561404	–0.00201
y (0.91)	:	–0.07382989	–0.07513761	–0.00131
y (0.96)	:	–0.03634005	–0.03692308	–0.00058

The error field confines to the range [–0.00011, –0.00058]. The approximations are correct to within this domain.

Example 5

BVP : $y'' - 2y' + y'^2 - e^y = -2 - e^x(\text{Cos } x + \text{Sin } x)$

$P = 2 - y1,\ Q = 0.0,$

$R = 2y1 - y1^2 - 2 + e^y - e^x(\text{Cos } x + \text{Sin } x)$

PS : $y(x) = Ln[e^x(\text{Cos } x + \text{Sin } x)]$

IC : $y(0) : 0,\ y\left(\dfrac{\pi}{2}\right) : \dfrac{\pi}{2},\ 0 \le x \le \dfrac{\pi}{2}$

W : 0.01570796

The Computer Solution of the BVP of Order 2

x-value		Approx value	Exact Value	Error
y (0.01570796)	:	0.02931292	0.03117173	0.00186
y (0.17278759)	:	0.31959357	0.31865125	–0.00094
y (0.32986722)	:	0.60084781	0.56888631	–0.03196
y (0.48694685)	:	0.86652117	0.78830654	–0.07821
y (0.64402648)	:	1.10873878	0.98057363	–0.12817
y (0.80110611)	:	1.31848876	1.14755633	–0.17093
y (0.95818574)	:	1.48600655	1.28975668	–0.19625
y (1.11526537)	:	1.60142913	1.40641649	–0.19501
y (1.27234500)	:	1.65580144	1.49535523	–0.16045
y (1.42942463)	:	1.64253191	1.55246044	–0.09007

The error field confines to the range [0.00186, – 0.09007]. The approximations are correct to within this domain.

Example 6

BVP : $x^5y'' - x^2y'^2 + 9y^2 = 4x^4$

$$P = x^{-3}y1,\ Q = -9x^{-5}y,\ R = \frac{(x^2y1^2 - 9y^2 + 4x^4)}{x^5}$$

PS : $y(x) = x^3\ Lnx$

IC : $y(1) : 0,\ y(2) : Ln\ 256,\ 1 \le x \le 2$

W : 0.01

The Computer Solution of the BVP of Order 2

x-value		Approx value	Exact Value	Error
y (1.01)	:	0.01076815	0.01025184	–0.00052
y (1.06)	:	0.08021324	0.06939920	–0.01081
y (1.11)	:	0.17789729	0.14272599	–0.03517
y (1.16)	:	0.30586958	0.23166819	–0.07420
y (1.21)	:	0.46495361	0.33769559	–0.12726
y (1.26)	:	0.65485967	0.46231034	–0.19255

x-value		*Approx value*	*Exact Value*	*Error*
y (1.31)	:	0.87436396	0.60704558	–0.26732
y (1.36)	:	1.12151547	0.77346423	–0.34805
y (1.41)	:	1.39384277	0.96315787	–0.43068
y (1.46)	:	1.68854290	1.17774566	–0.51080
y (1.51)	:	2.00264298	1.41887333	–0.58377
y (1.56)	:	2.33313103	1.68821237	–0.64492
y (1.61)	:	2.67705683	1.98745905	–0.68960
y (1.66)	:	3.03160544	2.31833373	–0.71327
y (1.71)	:	3.39414745	2.68258005	–0.71157
y (1.76)	:	3.76227006	3.08196426	–0.68031
y (1.81)	:	4.13379320	3.51827452	–0.61552
y (1.86)	:	4.50677415	3.99332034	–0.51345
y (1.91)	:	4.87950373	4.50893191	–0.37057
y (1.96)	:	5.25049672	5.06695964	–0.18354

The error field confines to the range [– 0.00052, – 0.18354].

Example 7

BVP : $\frac{D^2y}{dx^2} - y' - 2(y - Lnx)^3 = -\frac{1}{x}$

$P = 1, Q = 6(Lnx)^2, R = y1 + 2(y - Lnx)^3 - \frac{1}{x}$

PS : $y(x) = Lnx + \frac{1}{x}$

IC : $y(1) : 1, y(2) : Ln\,2 + \frac{1}{2}, 1 \le x \le 2$

W : 0.01

The Computer Solution of the BVP of Order 2

x-value		*Approx value*	*Exact Value*	*Error*
y (1.01)	:	0.99484917	1.00004934	0.00520
y (1.06)	:	0.96970533	1.00166513	0.03196
y (1.11)	:	0.94529974	1.00526092	0.05996

x-value		*Approx value*	*Exact Value*	*Error*
y (1.16)	:	0.92127718	1.01048897	0.08921
y (1.21)	:	0.89730294	1.01706664	0.11976
y (1.26)	:	0.87305133	1.02476251	0.15171
y (1.31)	:	0.84819561	1.03338592	0.18519
y (1.36)	:	0.82239866	1.04277882	0.22038
y (1.41)	:	0.79530407	1.05280956	0.25751
y (1.46)	:	0.76652739	1.06336794	0.29684
y (1.51)	:	0.73564702	1.07436131	0.33871
y (1.56)	:	0.70219465	1.08571146	0.38352
y (1.61)	:	0.66564477	1.09735219	0.43171
y (1.66)	:	0.62540301	1.10922724	0.48382
y (1.71)	:	0.58079293	1.12128869	0.54050
y (1.76)	:	0.53104079	1.13349563	0.60245
y (1.81)	:	0.47525794	1.14581303	0.67056
y (1.86)	:	0.41242020	1.15821090	0.74579
y (1.91)	:	0.34134359	1.17066345	0.82932
y (1.96)	:	0.26065570	1.18314855	0.92249

The error field confines to the range [0.00520, 0.92249]. The approximations are correct to within this domain.

Example 8

BVP : $x^2 \dfrac{d^2y}{dx^2} - x^2yy' - 2\left(1 + \dfrac{4}{x}\right) = 0$.

$$P = y,\ Q = y1,\ R = yy1 + \frac{2\left(1 + \frac{4}{x}\right)}{x^2}$$

PS : $y(x) = 1 + \dfrac{2}{x}$

IC : $y(1) : 3,\ y(2) : 2,\ 1 \le x \le 2$

W : 0.01

The Computer Solution of the BVP of Order 2

x-value	*Approx value*	*Exact Value*	*Error*
y (1.01) :	2.98027495	2.98019802	–7.69307e-05
y (1.06) :	2.88725798	2.88679245	–0.00047
y (1.11) :	2.80260709	2.80180180	–0.00081
y (1.16) :	2.72518698	2.72413793	–0.00105
y (1.21) :	2.65406862	2.65289256	–0.00118
y (1.26) :	2.58848550	2.58730159	–0.00118
y (1.31) :	2.52780028	2.52671756	–0.00108
y (1.36) :	2.47147902	2.47058824	–0.00089
y (1.41) :	2.41907120	2.41843972	–0.00063
y (1.46) :	2.37019378	2.36986301	–0.00033
y (1.51) :	2.32451862	2.32450331	–1.53135e-05
y (1.56) :	2.28176233	2.28205128	0.00029
y (1.61) :	2.24167791	2.24223602	0.00056
y (1.66) :	2.20404801	2.20481928	0.00077
y (1.71) :	2.16867927	2.16959064	0.00091
y (1.76) :	2.13539760	2.13636364	0.00097
y (1.81) :	2.10404425	2.10497238	0.00093
y (1.86) :	2.07447236	2.07526882	0.00080
y (1.91) :	2.04654419	2.04712042	0.00058
y (1.96) :	2.02012860	2.02040816	0.00028

The error field confines to the range [– 7.69307e-05, 0.00028]. The approximations are correct to within this domain.

Example 9

BVP : $\dfrac{D^2y}{dx^2} + y'^2 + y = Ln\ x$

$P = -y1,\ Q = -1,\ R = Ln\ x - y1^2 - y$

PS : $y(x) = Ln\ x$

IC : $y(1) : 0, y(2) : Ln\ 2, 1 \le x \le 2$

W : 0.01

The Computer Solution of the BVP of Order 2

x-value		*Approx value*	*Exact Value*	*Error*
y (1.01)	:	0.00957149	0.00995033	0.00038
y (1.06)	:	0.05644747	0.05826891	0.00182
y (1.11)	:	0.10173105	0.10436002	0.00263
y (1.16)	:	0.14547846	0.14842001	0.00294
y (1.21)	:	0.18774282	0.19062036	0.00288
y (1.26)	:	0.22857451	0.23111172	0.00254
y (1.31)	:	0.26802151	0.27002714	0.00201
y (1.36)	:	0.30612970	0.30748470	0.00136
y (1.41)	:	0.34294309	0.34358970	0.00065
y (1.46)	:	0.37850406	0.37843644	–6.7621e-05
y (1.51)	:	0.41285352	0.41210965	–0.00074
y (1.56)	:	0.44603110	0.44468582	–0.00135
y (1.61)	:	0.47807523	0.47623418	–0.00184
y (1.66)	:	0.50902331	0.50681760	–0.00221
y (1.71)	:	0.53891179	0.53649337	–0.00242
y (1.76)	:	0.56777625	0.56531381	–0.00246
y (1.81)	:	0.59565146	0.59332685	–0.00232
y (1.86)	:	0.62257146	0.62057649	–0.00199
y (1.91)	:	0.64856961	0.64710324	–0.00147
y (1.96)	:	0.67367860	o.67294447	–0.00073

The error field ccnfines to the range [0.00038, –0.00073]. The approximations are correct to within this domain.

Example 10

BVP : $8 \dfrac{D^2y}{dx^2} + y \dfrac{dy}{dx} = 32 + 2x^3$

$$P = -\frac{y}{8}, Q = -\frac{y1}{8}, R = \frac{32 + 2x^3 - yy1}{8}$$

PS : $y(x) = x^2 + \dfrac{16}{x}$

IC : $y(1) : 17, y(3) : 14.33333333, 1 \le x \le 3$

W : 0.02

The Computer Solution of the BVP of Order 2

x-value		*Approx value*	*Exact Value*	*Error*
y (1.02)	:	16.72082667	16.72667451	0.00585
y (1.22)	:	14.57111726	14.60315410	0.03204
y (1.42)	:	13.29048715	13.28400563	–0.00648
y (1.62)	:	12.57999089	12.50094321	–0.07905
y (1.82)	:	12.25378237	12.10360879	–0.15017
y (2.02)	:	12.19748301	12.00119208	–0.19629
y (2.22)	:	12.34239952	12.13560721	–0.20679
y (2.42)	:	12.64948524	12.46797025	–0.18151
y (2.62)	:	13.09932687	12.97127023	–0.12806
y (2.82)	:	13.68588061	13.62615887	–0.05972

The error field confines to the range [0.00585, – 0.05972]. The approximations are correct to within this domain.

Example 11

BVP : $\dfrac{D^2y}{dx^2} + \dfrac{y1^2}{2} + 1 = 0$

$$P = -\frac{y1}{2},\ Q = 0,\ R = -\frac{y1^2}{2} - 1$$

PS : $y(x) = 2Ln\left[\dfrac{\text{Cos}\,(2x-1)\left(\dfrac{\sqrt{2}}{4}\right)}{\text{Cos}\left(\dfrac{\sqrt{2}}{4}\right)}\right]$

IC : $y(0) : 0, y(1) : 0, 0 \le x \le 1$

W : 0.01

The Computer Solution of the BVP of Order 2

x-value		*Approx value*	*Exact Value*	*Error*
y (0.01)	:	0.00495	0.00516259	0.00021
y (0.06)	:	0.02820	0.02929116	0.00109
y (0.11)	:	0.04895	0.05066046	0.00171
y (0.16)	:	0.06720	0.06932886	0.00213
y (0.21)	:	0.08295	0.08534636	0.00240
y (0.26)	:	0.09620	0.09875509	0.00256
y (0.31)	:	0.10695	0.10958984	0.00264
y (0.36)	:	0.11520	0.11787836	0.00268
y (0.41)	:	0.12095	0.12364167	0.00269
y (0.46)	:	0.12420	0.12689430	0.00269
y (0.51)	:	0.12495	0.12764440	0.00269
y (0.56)	:	0.12320	0.12589368	0.00269
y (0.61)	:	0.11895	0.12163829	0.00269
y (0.66)	:	0.11220	0.11486700	0.00267
y (0.71)	:	0.10295	0.10556289	0.00261
y (0.76)	:	0.09120	0.09370226	0.00250
y (0.81)	:	0.07695	0.07925460	0.00230
y (0.86)	:	0.06020	0.06218223	0.00198
y (0.91)	:	0.04095	0.04243992	0.00149
y (0.96)	:	0.01920	0.01997441	0.00077

The error field confines to the range [0.00021, 0.00077]. The approximations are correct to within this domain.

Example 12

BVP : $\dfrac{D^2y}{dx^2} - 2y^3 = 0$

$P = 0, Q = 0, R = 2y^3$

PS : $y(x) = \dfrac{1}{x}$

IC : $y(1) : 1, y(2) : 0.5, 1 \le x \le 2$

W : 0.01

The Computer Solution of the BVP of Order 2

x-value		*Approx value*	*Exact Value*	*Error*
y (1.01)	:	0.98897460	0.99009901	0.00112
y (1.06)	:	0.93674419	0.94339623	0.00665
y (1.11)	:	0.88907860	0.90090090	0.01182
y (1.16)	:	0.84563396	0.86206897	0.01644
y (1.21)	:	0.80608415	0.82644628	0.02036
y (1.26)	:	0.77012027	0.79365079	0.02353
y (1.31)	:	0.73745020	0.76335878	0.02591
y (1.36)	:	0.70779816	0.73529412	0.02750
y (1.41)	:	0.68090419	0.70921986	0.02832
y (1.46)	:	0.65652372	0.68493151	0.02841
y (1.51)	:	0.63442706	0.66225166	0.02782
y (1.56)	:	0.61439898	0.64102564	0.02663
y (1.61)	:	0.59623823	0.62111801	0.02488
y (1.66)	:	0.57975703	0.60240964	0.02265
y (1.71)	:	0.56478065	0.58479532	0.02001
y (1.76)	:	0.55114692	0.56818182	0.01703
y (1.81)	:	0.53870576	0.55248619	0.01378
y (1.86)	:	0.52731872	0.53763441	0.01032
y (1.91)	:	0.51685850	0.52356021	0.00670
y (1.96)	:	0.50720848	0.51020408	0.00300

The error field confines to the range [0.00112, 0.00300]. The approximations are correct to within this domain.

Chapter 10

C++ Programs For Numerical Solutions

Running the Turbo C++ Programs

The C++ programs are so designed that they can run properly under any c++ compiler from BORLAND International. The commands or instructions used in the program are specific to BORLAND C++ (Turbo version 3.0) for the operating system MS-DOS (version 6.0). The program you want to run is to be typed at first and saved on the hard disk. If you type at the command prompt provided that you have the C++ compiler

C : \ > **tree tc**

You get a picture on the screen as follows :

```
C : TC
 |
 |________Bin
 |
 |________Include
 |
 |________Lib
 |
 |________Bgi
 |
 |________Classlib
 |
 |________EXAMPLES
 |            |
 |            |_______Tcalc
 |
 |________Doc
```

The subdirectory EXAMPLES displayed in bold type is used for saving the program. For storing the program on the hard disk we should follow the steps mentioned below :.

1) Boot the system

2) At the command prompt C : \ > type the command tc to invoke Turbo C++. Finally, the screen will display the following menu selection and waits for further instructions

- File Edit Search Run compile Debug Project options Windows Help

3) Press Alt + F to view the file menu. Select the submenu New

4) Type the required program now that is described in this chapter next.

5) Press Alt + F again to save the program. select the submenu save as ... . Type C :\ tc\ **examples\ intgsimp. cpp**, for example, if you want to store the program INTGSIMP on hard disk.

6) Press Alt + R to run the program. But before running the program you have to create or change the data in the program. About the change or creation of the data I have discussed in each program. Please follow the recommended rules for guidance to perform the specified function.

10.1. *Program : INTGSIMP. CPP for chapter 3*

/*###

PROGRAM FOR SOLVING A DEFINITE INTEGRAL

##

Programname : INTGSIMP.CPP

The program is designed by Arun Ghosh on 23/12/96

The program is constructed to solve a DEFINITE INTEGRAL by means of the extended SIMPSON's rule and is written in C++ (Turbo). The program is executed on any MS-DOS computer.

$L1$ = lower limit, $U1$ = upper limit, K = superscript for m, total number of equal divisions ($2^{**}K = m$) and $w = \frac{U1\text{-}L1}{m}$ = width of each division. We suppose the interval [$L1$, $U1$] to be divided into m equal parts each of length w.

The estimation of the definite integral has been performed by setting the lower and upper limits, $L1$ & $U1$ and the integrand FX in the program.

```
++++++++++++++++++++++++++++++++++++++++++++++++++++++
                 IMPORTANT  TO  NOTE  !!!
++++++++++++++++++++++++++++++++++++++++++++++++++++++++++++
1) Change the DEFINITION Block of IC      (followed by the symbol ∇)
2) Change the FUNCTION Block Fx           (followed by the symbol ∇)
*/
//############################################## HEADER Files
#include <iostream.h>
#include <conio.h>
#include <math.h>
#include <stdlib.h>
#include <dos.h>
//############################################## Define the Symbols
#define Pgname "INTGSIMP"
#define Ititle "ESTIMATION OF THE DEFINITE INTEGRAL"
#define Iline "=================================================="
#define pi 3.14159265
#define eps 2.71828182
//∇∇∇∇∇∇∇∇∇∇∇∇∇∇∇∇∇∇∇∇∇∇∇∇∇∇∇∇∇∇∇∇∇ DEFINITION Block of IC
#define L1 1.0
#define U1 1.3
#define K 4
#define ES 0.3214853
//############################################## MAIN Function
main()
{
int i, j, m;
char ans, tch;
```

```
double Esol, Fx, Fint, Ierr, w;
double Ftemp [4096];
double F0 = 0.0, x = 0.0;
double sumE = 0.0, sumO = 0.0, sumF = 0.0;
//############################################## Clear the SCREEN
clrscr();
gotoxy(60, 1);
cout <<"Program :" <<Pgname;
Setall :
gotoxy(3, 8);
cout<<"\a Have you set up the Function Fx (y/n)?";
ans = getche();
switch (ans)
{ case 'y':
      sleep(1); break;
case 'n':
      cout <<'\a'; sleep(1); return 0;
default :
      gotoxy(6, 10);
      cout <<"\aINVALID CHOICE ... Try again"; sleep(1);
      gotoxy(6, 10);
      cout << "
      goto Setall;
}
PutFunc:
Esol = ES;
m = pow(2, K);
w = (U1-L1)/m;
```

```
for(i = 1; i<= m + 1; i++)
{
    x = L1 + (i-1)*w;
//▽▽▽▽▽▽▽▽▽▽▽▽▽▽▽▽▽▽▽▽▽▽▽▽▽▽▽▽▽▽▽▽▽ FUNCTION Block Fx
    Fx = sqrt(x);
//############################################### Calculation Department
    Ftemp[i-1] = Fx;
    if(i==1)
    F0 = Ftemp[i-1];
}
sumF = F0 + Ftemp[m];
sumO = Ftemp[1];
for(j = 2; j<= m-1; j = j + 2)
{
    sumE = sumE + Ftemp[j];
    sumO = sumO + Ftemp[j + 1];
}
Fint = (sumF + 4*sumO + 2*sumE)*w/3.0;
Ierr = Esol-Fint;
//################################################### Print out the Heading
clrscr();
gotoxy(60, 1);
cout<<"Program:" <<Pgname;
gotoxy(5, 1);
cout<<Ititle;
gotoxy(5, 2);
cout<<Iline;
```

```
//############################################### Print out the RESULTS
cout.precision(8);
gotoxy(5, 5);
cout<<"Lower Limit: "<<L1;
gotoxy(25, 5);
cout<<", Upper Limit:"<<U1;
gotoxy(5, 6);
cout<<"Width:"<<w;
gotoxy(25, 6);
cout<<", Division:"<<m;
gotoxy(5, 7);
cout<<"==========================================================";
cout.precision(8);
gotoxy(5, 9);
cout<<"Estimated Value of the Integral: "<<Fint;
gotoxy(5, 11);
cout <<"Exact Value of the Integral:"<<Esol;
cout.precision(5);
gotoxy(5, 13);
cout<<"Error for approximation:"<<Ierr;
gotoxy(5, 14);
cout<<"==========================================================";
//############################################### WAY to EXIT
Again:
gotoxy(12, 16);
cout<<"\aType (e) to exit:";
cin>>tch;
if(tch=='e')
{
```

```
    goto Exit;
}
if (tch ! = 'e')
{
        gotoxy(12, 17);
        cout<<"\aINVALID CHOICE...";sleep(1);
        gotoxy(12, 17);
        cout<<"
        goto Again;
}
Exit:
    return 0;
}
```

10.2. *Programs: INTGAREA.CPP and INTGDOBL.CPP for chapter 4*

/*##

PROGRAM FOR SOLVING AREA OF PLANE CURVES

##

Programname: INTGAREA.CPP

The program is designed by Arun Ghosh on 23/01/97

The program that is written in C++ (Turbo), is provided to solve the AREA of PLANE CURVES involved in Definite Integral by means of the SIMPSON's Formula and is processed by the operating system MS-DOS.

Lb = lower limit, Ub = upper limit, K = superscript for m, total number of equal divisions (2**K = m) and w = $\frac{\text{(Ub-Lb)}}{\text{m}}$ = width of each division. We suppose the interval [Lb, Ub] to be divided into m equal parts each of length w.

The estimation of the Definite Integral has been performed by setting the lower and upper limits, Lb & Ub, and the integrand Fx in the program.

```
++++++++++++++++++++++++++++++++++++++++++++++++++++++++
                IMPORTANT TO NOTE !!!
++++++++++++++++++++++++++++++++++++++++++++++++++++++++
1) Change the DEFINITION Block of IC      (followed by the symbol ∇)
2) Change the FUNCTION Block Fx           (followed by the symbol ∇)
*/
//################################################ HEADER Files
#include <iostream.h>
#include <conio.h>
#include <math.h>
#include <stdlib.h>
#include <dos.h>
//################################################ Define the Symbols
#define Pgname "INTGAREA"
#define Atitle "ESTIMATION OF AREA OF PLANE CURVE"
#define Aline "══════════════════════════════════════════"
#define pi 3.14159265
#define eps 2.71828182
//∇∇∇∇∇∇∇∇∇∇∇∇∇∇∇∇∇∇∇∇∇∇∇∇∇∇∇∇ DEFINITION Block of IC
#define Lb 1.0
#define Ub 1.3
#define K 4
#define ES 0.3214853
//################################################ MAIN finction
main()
{
int i, j, m;
char ans, rep;
double Esol, Fx, Farea, Aerr, w;
```

```
double Ftemp[4096];
double F0 = 0.0, sumE = 0.0, sumO = 0.0, sumF = 0.0, x = 0.0;
//############################################# Clear the SCREEN
clrscr();
gotoxy(60, 1); cout<<"Program:"<<Pgname;
SetFunc:
gotoxy(3, 8);
cout<<"\aHave you set up the Function Fx (y/n) ?";
ans = getche();
switch(ans)
{ case 'y':
      sleep(1); break;
case 'n':
      cout<<'\a';sleep(1); return 0;
default:
      gotoxy(3, 10);
      cout<<"\aINVALID CHOICE...Try again"; sleep(1);
      gotoxy(3, 10);
      cout<<"
      goto SetFunc;
}
InpArea:
Esol = ES;
m = pow(2, K); w = (Ub-Lb)/m ;
for(i = 1; i<= m + 1; i ++)
{ x = Lb + (i-1)*w;
//∇∇∇∇∇∇∇∇∇∇∇∇∇∇∇∇∇∇∇∇∇∇∇∇∇∇∇∇∇∇∇ FUNCTION Block Fx
   Fx = sqrt(x);
```

```
//########################################## Function Calculation
    Ftemp[i-1] = Fx;
    if(i==1)
    F0 = Ftemp[i-1];
}
sumF = F0 + Ftemp[m];
sumO = Ftemp[1];
for(j = 2; j<= m-1; j = j + 2)
{
    sumE = sumE + Ftemp[j];
    SumO = sumO + Ftemp[j + 1];
}
```

$$\text{Farea} = \frac{(\text{sumF} + 4*\text{sumO} + 2*\text{sumE})*w}{3.0};$$

```
Aerr = Esol-Farea;
//################################################ Print out the Heading
clrscr();
gotoxy(60, 1);
cout<<"Program:"<<Pgname;
gotoxy(5, 1);
cout<<Atitle;
gotoxy(5, 2);
cout<<Aline;
//############################################ Print out the RESULTS
cout.precision(8);
gotoxy(5, 5);
cout<<"Lower Limit:"<<Lb;
gotoxy(25, 5);
cout<<", Upper Limit:"<<Ub;
```

```
gotoxy(5,6);
cout <<"Width : "<< w;
gotoxy(25,6);
cout <<", Division    : " <<m;
gotoxy(5,7);
cout<<"==================================================================";
cout.precision(8);
gotoxy(5,9);
cout <<"Estimated value of the Integral : " <<Farea ;
gotoxy(5,11);
cout <<"E x a c t value of the integral : "<<Esol;
cout.precision(5);
gotoxy(5,13);
cout <<"E r r o r for approximation : " <<Aerr;
gotoxy(5,14);
cout <<"==================================================================";
//############################################### WAY to go OUT
Tryagain:
    gotoxy(12,16);
    cout << "\a Type (e) to exit : " ;
    cin >> rep;
    if (rep == 'e')
    {
        goto Exit;
    }
    if (rep != 'e')
    {
        gotoxy(12,18);
        cout <<"\aINVALID CHOICE ......  "; sleep(1);
```

```
        gotoxy(12,18);
        cout <<"                    "; goto Tryagain;
    }
Exit:
    return 0;
    }
/*##################################################################
```

PROGRAM FOR SOLVING THE DOUBLE INTEGRAL

##

Programname : INTGDOBL.CPP

The program is designed by Arun Ghosh on 07/04/97

The program has been constructed to solve a DOUBLE INTEGRAL by means of SIMPSON's Formula and has been written in programming language C++ (turbo). This program is executed on the operating system MS-DOS.

L1x & L1y = lower limits of x & y, U1x & U1y = upper limits of x & y, K = superscript for m, total number of equal divisions (2**K = m), w= width of each division.

We suppose the interval (L1x, U1x) to be divided into m equal parts each of length w.

The estimation of the Definite Integral (DI) has been performed by setting the lower and upper limits, L1x/L1y/U1x/U1y, and the integrand Fx in the program.

##

IMPORTANT TO MENTION !!!

##

1) Change the DEFINITION Block of IC (followed by the symbol ∇)

```
    2) Change the FUNCTION Block Fx          (followed by the
symbol ∇ )
*/
//########################################### HEADER Files
#include <iostream.h>
#include <conio.h>
#include <math.h>
#include <stdlib.h>
#include <dos.h>
//############################################# Define the symbols
#define pgname "INTGDOBL"
#define Dbltitle "ESTIMATION OF THE DOUBLE INTEGRAL"
#define Dblline "---------------------------------------------"
#define pi 3.14159265
#define eps 2.7182818
// ∇∇∇∇∇∇∇∇∇∇∇∇∇∇∇∇∇∇∇∇∇∇∇∇∇∇∇∇∇∇∇ DEFINITION Block of IC
    #define L1x - 1
    #define U1x 1
    #define L1y 0
    #define Uly 3
// ------------------
    #define K 5
    #define ES 2
//############################################# MAIN function
main ( )
{
    int i,j,m,n;
    char ans,tch;
    double Wx, Wy;
```

```
    double Es1n,Fx,Appint,Dint,Derr;
    double Ftemp[4096];
    double F0=0.0,x=0.0,y=0.0;
    double smO=0.0,smE=0.0,smO=0.0,smF=0.0;
    double sumE=0.0,sumO=0.0,sumF=0.0;
//############################################ Clear the SCREEN
    clrscr();
    gotoxy(60,1); cout <<"Program :" <<Pgname;
//############################################ FUNCTION setting
FuncSet:
    gotoxy(10,8);
    cout <<"\aHave you set up the FUNCTION Fx";
    gotoxy(10,9);
    cout <<"and the INITIAL Conditions ( y/n ) ? ";
    ans=getche();
    switch(ans)
{ case 'y':
        gotoxy (10,5); cout <<"Wait please, it takes 2x60 seconds ... ";
break;
    case 'n':
        cout <<'\a'; sleep(1); return 0;
    default :
        gotoxy(10,12);
        cout <<"\aINVALID OPTION ......";sleep(1);
        gotoxy(10,12);
        cout<<"                    ";
        goto FuncSet;
}
```

```
PutInp :
    Es1n=ES;
    m=pow(2,K):
    Wx=U1x-L1x;
    Wx=Wx/m;
    Wy=U1y-L1y;
    Wy=Wy/m;
    for(i=1; i<=m; i++)
    {
      y= L1y+(i-1)*Wy;
      for(j=1;j<=m+1;j++)
      {
        x=L1x+(j-1)*Wx;
//∇∇∇∇∇∇∇∇∇∇∇∇∇∇∇∇∇∇∇∇∇∇∇∇∇∇∇∇∇∇  FUNCTION Block Fx
      Fx = x*x;
//########################################  Calculation of Function
      Ftemp[j-1]=Fx
      if (j==1)
      F0=Ftemp[j-1];
      }
      sumF= F0 + Ftemp[m];
      sumE=0.0; sumO=0.0;
      sumO= Ftemp[1];
      for (n=2; n<=m-1; n=n+2)
      {
        sumE= sumE + Ftemp[n];
        sumO= sumO + Ftemp[n+1];
      }
```

```
        Appint= (sumF + 4*sumO + 2*sumE)* Wx/3.0;
    if (i==1)
        sm0=sm0+Appint;
    if (i==m)
    {
        smF=smF +Appint;
        goto Dblitg;
    }
    if (i % 2 == 0)
        smE=smE+Appint;
    if (i % 2!= 0)
        smO=smO+Appint;
    }
Dblitg:
    Dint=(sm0 +4*smO +2*smE + smF) *Wy/3.0;
    Derr=Es1n-Dint;
//############################################# Print the RESULTS
    clrscr();
    gotoxy(5, 1);
    cout<<'\a'<<Dbltitle;
    gotoxy(60, 1);
    cout<<"Program:"<<Pgname;
    gotoxy(5, 2);
    cout<<Dblline;
    cout.precision(6);
    gotoxy(5, 4);
    cout<<"Limits:"<<L1x<<","<<U1x<<", "<<L1y<<","<<U1y;
    gotoxy(5, 5);
    cout<<"Increments(Wx & Wy):"<<Wx<<" & "<<Wy;
```

```
gotoxy(44, 5);
cout<<", K:"<<K<<", m:"<<m;
gotoxy(5, 6);
cout<<"==============================================";
cout.precision(8);
gotoxy(5, 7);
cout<<"Estimated Value of the Integral:"<<Dint;
gotoxy(5, 9);
cout<<"Exact Value of the Integral:"<<Esln;
cout.precision(5);
gotoxy(5, 11);
cout<<"Error for approximation:"<<Derr;
gotoxy(5, 12);
cout<<"==============================================";
//############################################## EXIT OPERATION
TRYagain:
      gotoxy(9,14);
      cout<< "Type (e) to exit :";
      cin>>tch;
      if (tch=="e')
      {
        goto Exit;
      }
      if (tch !='e')
      {
        gotoxy(9,16);
        cout <<"\aOPTION is invalid ...;" sleep(1);
        gotoxy(9,16);
        cout <<"
        goto TRYagain;
```

```
        }
Exit:
        return 0:
}
```

10.3 *Program : IVPD1SES.CPP for chapter 5*

```
/*##################################################################
```

PROGRAM TO SOLVE THE DIFFERENTIAL EQUATIONS OF FIRST ORDER : VARIABLES SEPARABLE / EXACT / SEPARATION BY SUBSTITUTION

```
####################################################################
```

Programname : IVPD1SES

The program is designed by Arun Ghosh on 01/01/97.

The program is constructed to approximate an INITIAL VALUE PROBLEM applying the Runge-Kutta formulas. One can approximate a problem dealing with one of the three types of Differential Equations: Variables separated,Exact and separation by substitution. The program is written in C++ (Turbo) and is executed on the system MS-DOS.

x0= initial value of x,y0= initial value of y, w= width of each step, m= number of divisions.

++

IMPORTANT TO NOTE !!!

++

The estimation of the Differential Equation has been performed by setting

1) The initial conditions in DEFINITION BLOCK of IC (followed by the symbol ∇)

2) The function of y for particular solution in MEMBER FUNCTION set ACT (followed by the symbol ∇)

3) The terms assosiated with the Differentials, dx & dy in MEMBER FUNCTION setDE (followed by the symbol ∇)

*/

```
//################################################## The Header Files
#include <iostream.h>
#include <fstream.h>
#include <iomanip.h>
#include <conio.h>
#include <math.h>
#include <stdlib.h>
#include <dos.h>
//############################################ define m / w /pi / eps
#define Pgname "IVPD1SES"
#define Xval "x-value"
#define Appval "Approx. value"
#define Extval "Exact value"
#define Aerr "Error"
#define m 10
#define w 0.01
#define pi 3.14159265
#define eps 2.71828182
//∇∇∇∇∇∇∇∇∇∇∇∇∇∇∇∇∇∇∇∇∇∇∇∇∇∇∇ DEFINITION BLOCK of IC
    #define x0 pi/6
    #define y0 -0.5
//##################################### Define CLASS
Class SevEqn
{   int k;
    double Fxy,SEVdx,SEVdy,RGxy,PSy,Dx,Dy;
    double ACT[11],RK[11],Vx[11],Severr[11];
    double  x,y,X1,Y1,Ftemp,F0,F1,F2,F3,F4;
public:
    void setx0y0()
```

```
   {
      x=x0; y=y0;
   }
//∇∇∇∇∇∇∇∇∇∇∇∇∇∇∇∇∇∇∇∇∇∇∇∇∇∇∇∇ MEMBER FUNCTION set ACT
   void setACT()
   {
      PSy = sin(x)-1;
   }
//∇∇∇∇∇∇∇∇∇∇∇∇∇∇∇∇∇∇∇∇∇∇∇∇∇∇ MEMBER FUNCTION set DE
   void setDE()
   {
      SEVdx = 1+y;
      SEVdy = tan(x);
   }
//################################### Temporary setting
   void setTemp()
   {
      RGxy=SEVdx/SEVdy;
      Fxy=RGxy*w;
   }
//#################################### Calculation Block
   void setVAL0()
   { k=0; }
   void setVAL00()
   { Dx=x;Dy=y; }
   void setVAL1()
   { X1 =x; Y1 =y; }
   void setVAL2()
   { Ftemp=Fxy;
```

```
    F1=X1+w/2.0;
    F2=Y1+Fxy/2.0;
    x=F1;
    y=F2;
}
void setVAL3()
{   Ftemp=Ftemp+2.0*Fxy ;
    F3=Y1+Fxy/2.0;
    x=F1;
    y=F3;
}
void setVAL4()
{ Ftemp=Ftemp+2.0*Fxy;
    F0=X1+w;
    F4=Y1+Fxy;
    x=F0;
    y=F4;
}
void setVAL5()
{ Ftemp=Ftemp+Fxy;
    y=Y1+Ftemp/6.0;
    x=X1+w;
}
void setVAL6()
{
    k=k+1;
    ACT[k]=PSy;
    RK[k]=y;
    Vx[k]=x;
```

```
    }
    void Sevtitle1()
    {
        cout<<"\t[ y("<<setprecision(8) <<Dx <<" ) = " <<Dy<<", Width :";
        cout <<" "<< w <<"]"<<endl;
    }
    void Sevtitle2()
    {   gotoxy(12,k+6);
        cout<<Xval; gotoxy(29,k+6); cout<< Appval;
        gotoxy(47,k+6);
        cout <<Extval<<"   "<<Aerr;
        gotoxy(12,k+7);
        cout <<"_________;"gotoxy(29,k+7);cout<<"_______________";
        gotoxy(47,k+7);
        cout<<"____________ _______________ " <<endl;
        }
void Sevdata()
{
    k=k+1;
    Severr[k]=ACT[k]-RK[k];
    gotoxy(9,k+7);
    cout <<"y(" <<setprecision(8) <<Vx[k];
    gotoxy(23,k+7);
    cout <<" ) : "<<setprecision(8) << RK[k];
    gotoxy(47,k+7);
    cout<< setprecision(8) <<ACT[k];
    gotoxy(62,k+7);
    cout <<setprecision(5) << Severr[k] <<endl;
    }
};
```

```
// ################################## CENTRE PLACE of the program

main()

{

    SevEqn deqn;

    int i, j,k;

    char tch,ans;

    double F0,F1,F2,F3,F4,RGxy,ACTy;

    double x,y,X1,Y1;

    double ACT[11],RK[11],Vx[11];

    double Severr[11];

deqn.setVAL0();

//######################################## Data modification block

    clrscr();

    gotoxy(60,1);

    cout <<"Program : " <<Pgname;

Allset :

    gotoxy(5,8);

    cout << "\aHave you setup the IC/PS/DE (y/n)? ";

    ans=getche();
    switch(ans)

    { case 'y':

        sleep(1); break;

    case 'n':
        cout << '\a'; sleep(1); return 0;

 default :

        gotoxy(8,10);

        cout <<"\aINVALID CHOICE ...... Try again"; sleep(1);

        gotoxy(8,10);
```

```
    cout <<"
    goto Allset;
}
  deqn.setx0y0();
  deqn. setVAL00();
//################################################## The function F1
  for(i=1;i<=m; i++)
  { deqn.setVAL1();
    deqn.setDE();
    deqn.setTemp();
//################################################## The function F2
    deqn.setVAL2()
    deqn.setDE();
    deqn.setTemp();
//################################################## The function F3
    deqn.setVAL3();
    deqn.setDE();
    deqn.setTemp();
//################################################## The function F4
    deqn.setVAL4();
    deqn.setDE();
    deqn.setTemp();
//############################################## PS-calculation Block
    deqn.setVAL5();
    deqn.setACT();
    deqn.setVAL6();
  }
 clrscr();
```

```
//######################################## PRINT OUT THE RESULTS
    deqn.setVAL0()
    gotoxy(59,1);
    cout<<"Program:"<<Pgname;
    cout<<"\n\tThe computer solution of the IVP of order 1\n";
    cout<<"\t===================================================\n";
    deqn.Sevtitle1();
    deqn.Sevtitle2();
    for(j=1;j<=m;j++)
    {
        deqn.Sevdata();
    }
//############################################################ Way to EXIT
Tryagain :
    gotoxy (9,18);
    cout<<"                                                    ";
    gotoxy(9,19);
    cout<<"Type (e) to exit: ";
    cin>>tch;
    if (tch !='e')
    {
        gotoxy(15,20);
        cout <<"\a Wrong choice ... ";sleep(1);
        gotoxy(15,20);
        cout<<"                ";
        goto Tryagain;
    }
Exit:
    return 0;
}
```

10.4. *Program: IVPD1LIN.CPP for chapter 6*

```
/*###########################################################################

PROGRAM FOR THE SOLUTION OF DIFFERENTIAL
EQUATIONS OF FIRST ORDER: LINEAR HOMOGENEOUS
AND NONHOMOGENEOUS, BERNOULLI AND RICCATI.

###########################################################################

Programname: IVPD1LIN.CPP

The Program is designed by Arun Ghosh on 01/01/97.

The program is constructed to approximate an INITIAL VALUE PROBLEM
applying the Runge-Kutta formulas. The problem deals with differential
equation of the form: linear homogeneous and nonhomogeneous, Bernoulli
and Riccati.

The program built in C++(Turbo) has been executed on the system MS-
DOS.

x0= initial value of x, y0= initial value of y, w= width of each step, m=
number of divisions.

+++++++++++++++++++++++++++++++++++++++++++++++++++++++++++++

IMPORTANT POINTS TO NOTE !!!

+++++++++++++++++++++++++++++++++++++++++++++++++++++++++++++

The estimation of the Differential Equation has been performed by setting

1) The Initial conditions in DEFINITION BLOCK of IC ( followed by the
symbol ∇)

2) The Function of y for particular solution in MEMBER FUNCTION set
ACT (followed by the symbol ∇)

3) The Terms associated with the Differentials, dx & dy in MEMBER
FUNCTION setDE.( followed by the symbol ∇ )

*/

//################################################## The Header Files

#include <iostream.h>

#include <fstream.h>

#include <iomanip.h>
```

```
#include <conio.h>
#include <math.h>
#include <stdlib.h>
#include <dos.h>
//################################################## Define m and w
#define Pgname "IVPD1LIN"
#define Xval "x-value"
#define Appval "Approx.value"
#define Extval  "Exact value"
#define Errval "Error"
#define m 10
#define w 0.01
#define pi 3.14159265
#define eps 2.71828182
//∇∇∇∇∇∇∇∇∇∇∇∇∇∇∇∇∇∇∇∇∇∇∇∇∇∇∇∇ DEFINITION BLOCK of IC
    #define x0 1
    #define y0 0.0
//################################################## Define CLASS
class LinEqn
{   int k;
    double Fxy,EXTdx,EXTdy,RGxy,PSy,Dx,Dy;
    double ACT[11],RK[11],Vx[11],Linerr[11];
    double  x,y,X1,Y1,Ftemp,F0,F1,F2,F3,F4;
Public:
    void setx0y0()
    { x=x0; y=y0; }
//∇∇∇∇∇∇∇∇∇∇∇∇∇∇∇∇∇∇∇∇∇∇∇∇∇∇ MEMBER FUNCTION set ACT
    void setACT()
    {
```

```
 PSy = x* (x-1) ;
 }
//∇∇∇∇∇∇∇∇∇∇∇∇∇∇∇∇∇∇∇∇∇∇∇∇∇∇∇∇ MEMBER FUNCTION set DE
 void setDE()
 {
 EXTdx = x+2*y
 EXTdy = x ;
 }
//############################################### Temporary setting
 void setLin()
 {
 RGxy=EXTdx/EXTdy;
 Fxy=RGxy*w;
 }
//############################################### Proper Setting
 void setVAL0()
 { k=0; }
 void setVAL00()
 { Dx=x; Dy=y; }
 void setVAL1()
 { X1=x; Y1=y; }
 void setVAL2()
 {
     Ftemp=Fxy;
     F1=X1+w/2.0;
     F2=Y1+Fxy/2.0;
     x=F1;y=F2;
 }
```

```
void setVAL3()
{
    Ftemp=Ftemp+2.0*Fxy;
    F3=Y1+Fxy/2.0;
    x=F1;y=F3;
}
void setVAL4()
{
    Ftemp=Ftemp+2.0*Fxy;
    F0=X1+w;
    F4=Y1+Fxy;
    x=F0;y=F4;
}
void setVAL5()
{
    Ftemp=Ftemp+Fxy;
    y=Y1+Ftemp/6.0;
    x=X1+w;
}
void setVAL6()
{
    k=k+1;
    ACT[k]=PSy;
    RK[k]=y;
    Vx[k]=x;
}
void Exttitle1()
{
    cout <<"\t[ y("<<setprecision(8)<<Dx <<" ) = "<< Dy <<", Width
```

```
        cout <<" " << w << " ]" << endl;
    }
    void Exttitle2()
    {
        gotoxy(12,k+6);
        cout << Xval;
        gotoxy(29,k+6);
        cout<< Appval;
        gotoxy(47,k+6);
        cout << Extval <<" " << Errval;
        gotoxy(12,k+7);
        cout <<"_____________ "; gotoxy(29,k+7); cout <<"___________ ";
        gotoxy(47,k+7);
        cout <<"________________ ____________________" <<endl;
    }
void Lindata()
{
    k=k+1;
    Linerr[k]=ACT[k]-RK[k];
    gotoxy(9,k+7);
    cout <<"y( " <<setprecision(8) << Vx[k]
    gotoxy(23,k+7);
    cout <<" ) : " <<setprecision(8) << RK[k];
    gotoxy(47,k+7);
    cout << setprecision(8) <<ACT[k];
    gotoxy(62,k+7);
    cout << setprecision(3) << Linerr[k] <<end1;
    }
```

```
//######################################################## MAIN Function
main()
{
    LinEqn deqn;
    int i, j, k;
    char tch,ans;
    double F0,F1,F2,F3,F4,RGxy,ACTy;
    double x,y,X1,Y1;
    double ACT[11],RK[11],Vx[11],Exterr[11];
    deqn.setVAL0()
    c1rscr();
    gotoxy(60,1);
    cout <<"Program:" <<Pgname;
preset:
    gotoxy(5,8);
    cout << "\aHave you set up the IC/PS/DE (y/n)?";
    ans=getche();
    switch (ans)
    {
        case 'y' :
            sleep(1); break;
        case 'n' :
            cout <<'/a'; sleep(1); return 0;
        default :
            gotoxy(8,10);
            cout<<"\aINVALID CHOICE ...... Try again ";sleep(1);
            gotoxy(8,10);
            cout<<"
            goto Preset;
```

```
    }
    deqn.setx0y0();
    deqn.setVAL00();
//####################################################### the function F1
    for(i=1;i<=m; i++)
    {
    deqn.setVAL1();
    deqn.setDE();
    deqn.setLin();
//####################################################### the function F2
    deqn.setVAL2();
    deqn.setDE();
    deqn.setLin();
//####################################################### The function F3
    deqn.setVAL3 ();
    deqn.setDE();
    deqn.setLin();
//####################################################### The function F4
    deqn.setVAL4();
    deqn.setDE();
    deqn.setLin();
//################################################## TheFunction for PS
    deqn.setVAL5();
    deqn.setACT();
    deqn.setVAL6();
 }
clrscr();
```

```
//######################################## PRINT OUT THE RESULTS
  deqn.setVAL0();
  cout<<"\n\tThe computer solution of the IVP of order 1
  (Program:"<<Pgname<<")\n";
  cout<<"\t=================================================\n";
  deqn.Exttitle1();
  deqn.Exttitle2();
  for(j=1; j<=m;j++)
  {
  deqn.Lindata();
  }
//################################################## TRY TO EXIT
Tryagain:
  gotoxy (9,18);
  cout <<"_______________________________________________";
  gotoxy(9,19);
  cout <<"Type (e) to exit : ";
  cin>> tch;
  if (tch != 'e')
  {
     gotoxy(9,20);
     cout<<"\a TRY again ...... "; sleep(1);
     gotoxy(9,20);
     cout<<"           ";
     goto Tryagain;
  }
Exit:
   return 0;
}
```

10.5 *Program : IVPD2LIN.CPP for chapter 7*

```
/*#################################################################
PROGRAM FOR INITIAL VALUE PROBLEM OF ORDER 2:
LINEAR AND NONLINEAR DIFFERENTIAL EQUATIONS
##################################################################

Programname : IVPD2LIN.CPP

Program is designed by Arun Ghosh on 19/01/97

The Program is constructed to approximate an Initial Value problem by
means of the RUNGE-KUTTA formulas. The problem deals with differential
eqation of order2. The program is written in programming language C++.

x0= initial value of x,y0= initial value of y, Dy0= initial value of dy/dx, w=
width of each equal step,m=number of equal divisions.

++++++++++++++++++++++++++++++++++++++++++++++++++++++++++++++++++

                    Important points to note !!!

++++++++++++++++++++++++++++++++++++++++++++++++++++++++++++++++++

The estimation of the Differential Equation has been performed by setting

1)    The Initial Conditions in DEFINITION BLOCK of IC
                                        (followed by the symbol ∇)
2)    The Functions: PSy and PSy1 for Particular Solutions in MEMBER
FUNCTION setACT                         (followed by the symbol ∇)
3)    The expression on right side involving differentials in MEMBER
FUNCTION setDE                          (followed by the symbol ∇)
*/

// ################################################## The Header Files
#include <iostream.h>

#include <fstream.h>

#include <iomanip.h>

#include <conio.h>

#include <math.h>
```

```
#include <stdlib.h>
#include <dos.h>
// ################################################ Define m and w
#define Pgname "IVPD2LIN"
#Define Xval "x-value"
#define Yapp "y-Approx."
#define Yext "y-Exact"
#define Errl "Error"
#define Ylapp "y'-Approx."
#define Ylext "y'-Exact"
#define Err2 "Error"
#define m 10
#define w 0.01
#define pi 3.1415927
#define eps 2.7182818
// ∇∇∇∇∇∇∇∇∇∇∇∇∇∇∇∇∇∇∇∇∇∇∇∇∇∇∇ DEFINITION BLOCK of IC
#define x0 0.0
#define y0 1.0
#define Dy0-1.0
// ################################################ Define CLASS
class LnhIv2
{
    int k;
    double x, y, y1, X1, X2, Y1, Yfd, Dx, Dy, Dy1;
    double Ftemp, F0, F1, F2, F20, F21, F30, F31, F4, F40, F41;
    double Fxy, PSy, PSy1, LNHxy, YErr [11], Y1Err [11];
    double RK [11], RK1 [11], Vx[11], ACTy[11], ACTy1 [11];
public:
```

```
    void setx0y0()
    {x = x0;y = y0;y1 = Dy0;}
//∇∇∇∇∇∇∇∇∇∇∇∇∇∇∇∇∇∇∇∇∇∇∇∇∇∇∇ MEMBER FUNCTION setACT
    void setACT()
    {
    PSy = 1 - x - pow(x, 3)/6 + 2*pow(x,4)/24;
    PSy1 = - 1 - x*x/2 + pow(x,3)/3;
    }
//  ∇∇∇∇∇∇∇∇∇∇∇∇∇∇∇∇∇∇∇∇∇∇∇∇∇∇∇ MEMBER FUNCTION setDE
void setDE()
{
    LNHxy = - x*y;
}
// ############################################ Temporary Calculation
void tempDE()
{
    Fxy = LNHxy*w;
}
void setVAL0()
{k = 0;}
void setVAL00()
{Dx = x; Dy = y, Dy1 = y1;}
void setVAL1()
{X1 = x; X2 = y; Y1 = y1;}
void set VAL2()
{
    F2 = X1 + w/2.;
```

F20 = X2 + Y1*$\frac{w}{2}$.;

F21 = Y1 + $\frac{Fxy}{2}$.;.

F0 = Fxy; F1 = Fxy;

x = F2;y = F20; y1 = F21;

}

void set VAL3()

{

F30 = F20 + F0* $\frac{w}{4}$.;

F31 = Y1 + $\frac{Fxy}{2}$.;

Ftemp = Fxy;

F0 = F0 + Fxy;

F1 = F1 + 2.*Fxy;

x = F2; y = F30; y1 = F31;

}

void setVAL4()

{

F4 = X1 + w;

F40 = X2 + w* $\left(Y1 + \frac{Ftemp}{2}.\right)$;

F41 = Y1 + Fxy;

F0 = F0 + Fxy;

F1 + F1 + 2.*Fxy;

x = F4; y = F40; y1 = F41;

}

void setVAL5()

{

F1 = F1 + Fxy;

```
    Yfd = Y1 + F1/6.0;
    y = X2 + w* (Y1 + F0/6.0);
    x = X1 + w;
}
viod setVAL6()
{
    k = k + 1;
    ACTy[k] = PSy;
    ACTy1[k] = PSy1;
    Vx[k] = x;
    RK[k] = y;
    RK1[k] = Yfd;
}
void Lnhtitle()
{
    cout <<"\t[IC : y("<< Dx <<") = " << Dy <<", y'("<< Dx <<")
=   "<< Dy1 <<", Width : "<<w <<"] "<< endl;
}
void Lnhtitle1()
{
    gotoxy(3,k + 6);
    cout <<Xval;
    gotoxy(11,k + 6);
    cout <<Yapp;
    gotoxy(22,k + 6);
    cout <<Yext;
    gotoxy(36,k + 6);
```

```
    cout <<Err1;
    gotoxy(46,k + 6);
    cout <<Y1app;
    gotoxy(58,k + 6);
    cout <<Ylext;
    gotoxy(72,k + 6);
    cout <<Err2;
    gotoxy(3,k + 7);
    cout <<; --------------";
    gotoxy(11,k + 7);
    cout <<"--------------"; .
    gotoxy(22,k + 7);
    cout <<"--------------";
    gotoxy(34,k + 7);
    cout <<" --------------";
    gotoxy(46,k + 7);
    cout <<" --------------";
    gotoxy(58,k + 7);
    cout << "--------------";
    gotoxy(70,k + 7);
    cout <<"--------------" <<endl;
}
void showdata()
}
     k = k + 1;
     YErr[k] = ACTy[k] – RK[k];
     Y1Err[k] = ACTy1[k] – RK1[k];
     gotoxy(3,k + 7); cout <<setprecision(5) <<Vx[k];
     gotoxy(11,k + 7); cout <<setprecision(8) <<RK[k];
```

```
        gotoxy(22,k + 7); cout <<ACTy[k];
        gotoxy(34,k + 7); cout <<setprecision(3) <<YErr[k];
        gotoxy(46,k + 7); cout <<setprecision(8) <<RK1[k];
        gotoxy(58,k + 7); cout <<ACTy1[k];
        gotoxy(70,k + 7); cout <<setprecision(3) <<Y1Err[k] <<endl;
        }
};
main()
{
    LnhIv2 deqn;
    int i,j,k;
    char tch, ans;
    double ACTy[11], ACTy1[11], RK[11], RK1[11], Vx[11];
    double YErr[11], Y1Err[11];
    deqn.setVAL0();
    clrscr();
    gotoxy(61,1);
    cout <<"Program : "<<Pgname;
Setall:
    gotoxy(5,8);
    cout <<"\a Have you setup the IC/PS/DE (y/n)?";
    ans = getche();
    switch (ans)
    {
    case 'y':
        sleep(1); break;
    case 'n':
        cout <<'\a'; sleep(1); return 0;
    default :
```

```
        gotoxy(8,10);
        cout <<"\aINVALID CHOICE ...... Try again"; sleep(2);
        gotoxy(8,10);
        cout <<"
        goto Setall;
}
deqn.setx0y0();
deqn.setVAL00();
// ################################################### The function F1
for(i = 1; i< = m; i++)
{   deqn.setVAL1();
    deqn.setDE();
    deqn.tempDE();
// ################################################### The function F2
    deqn.setVAL2();
    deqn.setDE();
    deqn.tempDE();
// ################################################### The function F3
    deqn.setVAL3();
    deqn.setDE();
    deqn.tempDE();
// ################################################### The function F4
    deqn.setVAL4();
    deqn.setDE();
    deqn.tempDE();
// ############################################## The function for PS
    deqn.setVAL5();
    deqn.setACT();
    deqn.setVAL6();
```

```
}
clrscr();
deqn.setVAL0();
gotoxy(62,1);
cout <<"Program:" <<Pgname;
cout <<"\n\tThe Computer Solution of the IVP of Order 2\n";
cout <<"\t ==========================================================\n";
deqn.Lnhtitle();
deqn.Lnhtitle1();
for(j = 1; j< = m; j++)
{
    deqn.showdata();
}
// ########################## WAY TO EXIT ######################
Tryagain;
    gotoxy(3,18);
    cout <<"------------------------------------------------------------";
    cout <<"--------------------";
    gotoxy(9,19);
    cout <<"Type (e) to exit :";
    cin >> tch;
    if (tch! = 'e')
{   gotoxy(9,21);
    cout <<"\aINVALID CHOICE … "; sleep(1);
    gotoxy(9,21);
    cout <<"
    goto Tryagain;
}
Exit:
```

```
    return 0;
}
```

10.6 *Program : IVPD1SYS.CPP for chapter 8*

```
/* ####################################################################

        PROGRAM FOR SOLVING THE SYSTEM OF
        DIFFERENTIAL EQUATIONS OF FIRST ORDER

######################################################################

Programmame : IVPD1SYS.CPP

The program is designed by Arun Ghosh on 01/05/97

The purpose of the construction of the program is to solve the system of two
differential equations by means of the extended RUNGE-KUTTA Formulae.
The Program is written in programming language C++.

Here t is the independent variable, x and y are dependent variables, w is the
width of each step or increment, that has a constant value throughout this
chapter. m is the number of increments.

The process of estimation of the system of differential equations starts by
setting the initial conditions that I mention next.

+++++++++++++++++++++++++++++++++++++++++++++++++++++++

            IMPORTANT POINTS TO NOTE !!!

+++++++++++++++++++++++++++++++++++++++++++++++++++++++

1) The MEMBER FUNCTION setDE should be furnished with the
Differential Equations to be solved          (followed by the symbol ∇)

2) The initial values of t, x and y are to be inserted when the MEMBER
FUNCTION IC is called for.

*/

// ################################################# HEADER files

#include <iostream.h>

#include <fstream.h>

#include <iomanip.h>

#include <conio.h>
```

```
#include <math.h>
#include <stdlib.h>
#include <dos.h>
#define m 10
#define w 0.01
#define Pgname "IVPD1SYS"
// ################################################## Define CLASS
class DiffSys
{   int k;
    double x, y, t, Dx, Dy, Dt;
    double SysDx, SysDy, SysFx,SysFy;
    double X1,Y1,T1,Temp1, Temp2;
    double F0,F1,F2,F3,F4,F5,F6,F7;
    double SysX[11],SysY[11],Vt[11];
public:
// ∇∇∇∇∇∇∇∇∇∇∇∇∇∇∇∇∇∇∇∇∇∇∇∇∇∇∇∇ MEMBER FUNCTION setDE
void setDE()
{
    SysDx = x*x / y;
    SysDy = -x;
}
// ########################################## MEMBER Function IC
void getdata(void)
{
    gotoxy(5,4);
    cout <<"x(";cin >> t;
    gotoxy(18,4);
    cout <<") = ";cin >>x;
```

```
    gotoxy(5,5);
    cout <<"y("<<t;
    gotoxy(18,5);
    cout <<") = "; cin >> y;
}
// ############################################# Temporary Function setting
void tempDE()
{
    SysFx = SysDx*w;
    SysFy = SysDy*w;
}
// ############################################### Setting of the Variables
void setVAL0()
{   k = 0;}
void setVAL00()
{   Dx = x; Dy = y; Dt = t;}
void setVAL1()
{   X1 = x; Y1 = y; T1 = t;}
void setVAL2()
{
    Temp1 = SysFx;
    Temp2 = SysFy;
```

$$F1 = T1 + \frac{w}{2.0};$$

$$F2 = X1 + \frac{SysFx}{2.0};$$

$$F3 = Y1 + \frac{SysFy}{2.0};$$

```
    t = F1; x = F2; y = F3;
}
```

```
void setVAL3()
{
    Templ = Temp1 + 2.0*SysFx;
    Temp2 = Temp2 + 2.0*SysFy;
```

$$F4 = X1 + \frac{SysFx}{2.0};$$

$$F5 = Y1 + \frac{SysFy}{2.0};$$

```
    t = F1; x = F4; y = F5;
}
void setVAL4()
{
    Templ = Templ + 2.0*SysFx;
    Temp2 = Temp2 + 2.0*SysFy;
    F0 = T1 + w;
    F6 = X1 + SysFx;
    F7 = Y1 + SysFy;
    t = F0; x = F6; y = F7;
}
void setVAL5()
{
    Templ = Temp1 + SysFx;
    Temp2 = Temp2 + SysFy;
```

$$x = X1 + \frac{Temp1}{6.0};$$

$$y = Y1 + \frac{Temp2}{6.0};$$

```
    t = T1 + w;
}
void setVAL6()
{
```

```
    k = k + 1;
    SysX[k] = x;
    SysY[k] = y;
    Vt[k] = t;
}
void showtitle()
{
    cout <<"\t[IC : x("<<Dt <<") = "<<Dx <<", y("<<Dt <<")
    = "<<Dy <<", Width : "<<w <<"]" <<endl;
}
void showdata()
{
    k = k + 1;
    gotoxy(9, k + 5);
    cout <<"x("<<setprecision(5) <<Vt[k];
    totoxy(18, k + 5);
    cout <<") : "<<setprecision(8) <<SysX[k];
    gotoxy (40,k + 5);
    cout <<"y("<<Vt[k];
    gotoxy(49, k + 5);
    cout <<") : "<<SysY[k] <<endl;
}
    };
// ################################################## MAIN Function
main()
{
    DiffSys deqn;
    int i,j;
    char tch,ans;
```

```
    double x,y,t,X1,Y1,T1;
    double  F0,F1,F2,F3,F4,F5,F6,F7,SysFx,SysFy;
    double SysX[11],SysY[11],Vt[11];

    deqn.setVAL0();
// ################################################## Function Setting
    clrscr();
    gotoxy(60,1);
    cout <<"Program :" <<Pgname;
Allset:
    gotoxy(3,8);
    cout <<"\aHave you set up the DIFFERENTIAL EQUATIONS (y/n) ?";
    ans = getche();
    switch(ans)
    {case 'y':
        sleep(1);break;
    case 'n':
        cout <<'\a'; sleep(1); return 0;
default :
        gotoxy(3,10);
        cout <<"\aINVALID CHOICE ... Try again"; sleep(1);
        gotoxy (3,10);
        cout <<"
        goto Allset;
}
PutIC:
// ################################################## IC Setting
    clrscr();
    cout <<"Initial Conditions (IC): Press the ENTER-key after\n";
```

```
    cout <<" =============================== insertion of each Value\n";
    deqn.getdata();
    cout <<" ———————————————\n";
Chgsec:
    gotoxy(3,7);
    cout <<"\aAny change in IC (y/n);";
    ans = getche();
    switch(ans)
{   case 'y':
        sleep(1); goto PutIC;
    case 'n':
        sleep(1); break;
default :
        gotoxy(2,9);
        cout <<"\aTry again …"; sleep(1);
        gotoxy(2,9);
        cout <<"  ";
        goto Chgsec;
}
deqn.setVAL00();
// ############################################ Calculate the Function F1
for(i = 1; i<=m; i++)
{
   deqn.setVAL1();
   deqn.setDE();
   deqn.tempDE();
// ############################################## The Function F2
   deqn.setVAL2();
   deqn.setDE();
```

```
    deqn.tempDE();
// ################################################ The Function F3
    deqn.setVAL3();
    deqn.setDE();
    deqn.tempDE();
// ################################################ The Function F4
    deqn.setVAL4();
    deqn.setDE();
    deqn.tempDE();
// ################################################ The Function F5
    deqn.setVAL5();
    deqn.setVAL6();
}
// ############################################ PRINT OUT the Results
clrscr();
deqn.setVAL0();
cout <<"\n\tThe Computer Solution of the SYSTEM of DE :\n";
cout <<"\t================================================\n";
deqn.showtitle();
for(j = 1; j< = m; j++)
{
    deqn.showdata();
}
cout <<"\n\t------------------------------------------------";
// ########################################## To END the Program
Tryagain:
    gotoxy(9,19);
    cout <<"Type (e) to exit :";
    cin>> tch;
```

```
  if (tch ! = 'e')
{
  gotoxy(9,20);
  cout <<"\aWrong Choice…"; sleep(1);
  gotoxy(9,20);
  cout <<"               ";
  goto Tryagain;
}
Exit:
  return 0;
}
```

10.7 *Programs : BVPD2LIN.CPP and BVP2NLFD.CPP for chapter 9*

```
/* ############################################################
```

PROGRAM FOR SOLVING LINEAR BOUNDARY VALUE PROBLEM OF SECOND ORDER

```
##############################################################
```

Programname : BVPD2LIN

The Program is designed by Arun Ghosh on 10/01/97

The program is constructed to solve a linear boundary-value problem by means of FINITE-DIFFERENCE method.

The initial boundary conditions of the Differential Equation are xB/xF/yB/yF. w is width of each subdivision and m is the number of equal subdivisions. The coefficients or factors of y'/y/x are P, Q and R. The Differential Equation is solved by means of the program C++ (Turbo).

The estimation of the BVP has been performed by setting the boundary conditions, xB/xF/yB/yF and the factors: P, Q & R in the program.

```
++++++++++++++++++++++++++++++++++++++++++++++++++++++++++
```

IMPORTANT POINTS TO NOTE !!!

```
++++++++++++++++++++++++++++++++++++++++++++++++++++++++++
```

1) The initial boundary conditions of the mathematical problem, xB/xF/yB/yF which are the starting values of x and y, are to be put in the DEFINITION Block of BC of the program. (followed by the symbol ∇)

```
2) The MEMBER FUNCTION setDE is furnished with the values of P, Q
and R as mentioned in the example                (followed by the symbol ∇)
*/
// ############################################ HEADER Files
#include<iostream.h>
#include<fstream.h>
#include<iomanip.h>
#include<conio.h>
#include<math.h>
#include<stdlib.h>
#include<dos.h>
//############################################ Define the Symbols
#define Pgname "BVPD2LIN"
#define pi 3.1415927
#define eps2.7182818
#define m 99
//∇∇∇∇∇∇∇∇∇∇∇∇∇∇∇∇∇∇∇∇∇∇∇∇∇∇∇∇∇∇∇ DEFINITION Block of BC
#define xB 0
#define xF 1
#define yB 1
#define yF 2
//########################################## Define CLASS
class BvpDeqn
{ int k, l;
   double A[100], B[100], C[100], D[100];
   double G[100], L[100], U[100], V[100], Z[100];
   double P, Q, R, x, y1, xV1, xV1. xV2, yV1, yV2, xInc, xInc1;
   double w, wDbl,wHlf,wSqr;
public:
```

```
    void setx0y0()
 {
     xV1 = xB; xV2 = xF;
     yV1 = yB; yV2 = yF;
 }
//∇∇∇∇∇∇∇∇∇∇∇∇∇∇∇∇∇∇∇∇∇∇∇∇∇∇∇∇∇ MEMBER FUNCTION setDE
 void setDE()
 {
     P = 2*x-1;
     Q = 2;
     R = 1-4*x;
 }
//############################################## Temporary setting
 void setTmp()
 {
     R = P*y1 + Q*y + R;
 }
void setL0()
{l = 0;}
void setL12()
{l = 11;}
void setK1()
{k = 1;}
void setK2()
{k = 2;}
void setK90()
{k = 90;}
void setW()
{
```

$w = \frac{(xV2\text{-}xV1)}{(m + 1)}$;

wSqr = pow(w, 2);

wDb1 = w*2; wH1f = $\frac{w}{2}$;

}

void setG()

{

G[k] = yB + k*w* $\frac{(yF\text{-}yB)}{(xV2\text{-}xV1)}$;

k = k + 1;

}

void set XY1()

{

x = xV1 + w;

y = G[1];

y1 = $\frac{(G[2] - yB)}{wDb1}$;

}

void setVAL1()

{

A[1] = 2. + wSqr*Q;

B[1] = – 1. + wH1f*P;

D[1] = – (2.*G[1] – G[2] – yB + wSqr*R);

L[1] = A[1];

U[1] = $\frac{B[1]}{A[1]}$;

Z[1] = $\frac{D[1]}{L[1]}$;

}

void setXY2()

{

```
    x = xV1 + k*w;

    y = G[k];

          (G[k + 1] - G[k - 1])
    y1 = ---------------------;
                 wDb1
}

void setVAL2()

{

    A[k] = 2. + wSqr*Q;

    B[k] = - 1. + wH1f*P;

    C[k] = - 1. - wH1f*P;

    D[k] = - (2.*G[k] - G[k + 1] - G[k - 1] + wSqr*R);

    k = k + 1;

}

void setXY3()

{

    x = xV2 - w;

    y = G[m];

          (yF - G[m - 1])
    y1 = ---------------;
              wDb1
}

void setVAL3()

}

    A[m] = 2. + w.Sqr*Q;

    C[m] = - 1. - wH1f*P;

    D[m] = - (2.*G[m] - G[m - 1] - yF + wSqr*R);

}

void setVAL4()

{

    L[k] = A[k] - C[k]*U[k - 1];
```

```
    U[k] = B[k] / L[k] ;

    k = k + 1;

}

void setVAL5()

{   L[m] = A[m]-C[m]*U[m-1];}

void setVAL6()

{ k = k + 1;

    Z[k] = (D[k]-C[k]*Z[k-1]) / L[k] ;

}

void setVAL7()

{V[m] = Z[m];

    G[m] = G[m] + V[m];

}

void set VAL8()

{

    k = k-1;

    V[k] = Z[k]-U[k]*V[k + 1];

    G[k] = G[k] + V[k];

}

void setVAL9()

{

    xInc = xV1 + k*w;

    xInc1 = xInc + w;

}

void showtitle()

{

    cout<<"\n\ty("<<xB<<"): "<<yB<<",\ty("<<xF<<"):"
        <<yF<<",\tWidth : "<<w<<"\n";
```

```
}
void showdata()
{  l = l + 1;
   G[100] = yF;
   gotoxy(9, l + 4); cout <<"y("<<setprecision(8)<<xInc;
   gotoxy(22, l + 4); cout <<"): "<<G[k];
   gotoxy(42,l + 4); cout <<"y("<<xInc1;
   gotoxy(55, l + 4);
   cout<<"): "<<G[k + 1] <<endl;
   k = k + 2;
   }
};
//####################################### The MAIN GATE of the Program
main()
{
BvpDeqn bvp;
int i, j, k, l:
char tch, ans;
clrscr();
gotoxy(60, 1);
cout<<"Program:"<<Pgname;
Allset:
gotoxy(5, 8);
cout<<"\aHave you set up P/Q/R (y/n)?";
ans = getche();
switch(ans)
{case 'y':
   break;
case 'n':
```

```
        cout<<'\a';
        sleep(1); return 0;
default:
        gotoxy(5, 10);
        cout<<"\aINVALID CHOICE...Try again"; sleep(1);
        gotoxy(5, 10);
        cout<<"
        goto Allset;
}
bvp.setx0y0();
bvp.setW();
bvp.setK1();
for(i = 1; i<= m; i++)
{
    bvp.setG();
}
bvp.setXY1();
//######################################## First Call of the BV-function
bvp.setDE();
bvp.setTmp();
bvp.setVAL1();
bvp.setK2();
for(i = 2; i<= m-1; i++)
{
bvp.setXY2();
//################################ Second Call of the BV-function
bvp.setDE();
bvp.setTmp();
bvp.setVAL2();
```

```
}
bvp.setXY3();
//######################################## Third Call of the BV-function
bvp.setDE();
bvp.setTmp();
bvp.setVAL3();
bvp.setK2();
for(i = 2, i<= m-1; i++)
{
    bvp.setVAL4();
}
bvp.setVAL5();
bvp.setK1();
for(j = 2; j<= m; j++)
{
bvp.setVAL6();
}
bvp.setVAL7();
for(i = m-1; i>= 1; i--)
{
bvp.setVAL8();
}
//######################################## PRINT OUT THE RESULTS
clrscr();
gotoxy(9, 1);
cout<<"The Estimated Values of the BVP";
gotox(58, 1);
cout<<"(Program:"<<Pgname<<")";
gotoxy(9, 2);
```

```
cout<<"==============================================================";
bvp.showtitle();
bvp.setL0();
bvp.setK1();
for(j = 1, j<= 10; j++)
{   bvp.setVAL9();
    bvp.showdata();
}
cout<<"\t--------------------------------------------------------------";
bvp.setL12();
bvp.setK90();
for(j = 1; j <=5; j++)
{
    bvp.setVAL9();
    bvp.showdata();
}
again:
    gotoxy (9,22);
    cout <<"Type (e) to exit :";
    cin >> tch;
    if (tch! = 'e')
  {
    gotoxy(40,22);
    cout <<"\aWrong INPUT…";sleep(1);
    gotoxy(40,22);
    cout <<"                ";
    goto again;
  }
```

```
Exit:
    return 0;
}
/* ##############################################################
```

PROGRAM FOR SOLVING THE NONLINEAR BOUNDARY VALUE PROBLEM OF SECOND ORDER

##

Programname : BVP2NLFD.CPP

The Program is designed by Arun Ghosh on 23/01/97

The program is constructed to solve a NONLINEAR Boundary-Value Problem of 2nd-order Differential Equation by means of the FINITE-DIFFERENCE method. The Differential Equation is treated by the program C++ (Turbo).

The initial conditions are x0 / x1 / yB / yF. w is the width of each equal subdivision and m is the number of divisions of the interval.

The estimation of the BVP has been performed by setting the bounds: x0 / x1 / yB / yF and the functions: P / Q / R in the program.

The following POINTS are to be noted:

1) The variables P/Q/R in Function DEFINITION Block placed at the end of the Program are to be created before start (followed by the symbol ∇)

2) The Boundary Conditions x0/x1/yB/yF are to be put in the DEFINITION Block *of BC* when called for

*/

```
// ################################################ HEADER files
#include<iostream.h>
#include<conio.h>
#include<math.h>
#include<stdlib.h>
#include<dos.h>

#define Pgname "BVP2NLFD"
```

```
#define pi 3.1415927
#define eps 2.7182818
#define m 99
//########################################### Function initialisation
double P,Q,R;
double Bvp11(double x, double y double y1);
double Bvp12(double x, double y, double y1);
double Bvp13(double x, double y, double y1);
// ################################################## MAIN Function
main()
{
    int  i,j,k,1;
    char ans,tch;
    double FnY1,FnY,FnXY,w,wDb1,wHlf,wSqr;
    double x,y,x0,x1,xInc,xInc1,y1,yB,yF;
    double A[100],B[100],C[100],D[100];
    double G[100],L[100],U[100].V[100],Z[100];
    P = 0.0; Q = 0.0; R = 0.0;
// ######################################### Chance of Function setting
    clrscr();
    gotoxy(58,1);
    cout <<"Program: "<<Pgname;
RptFunc:
    gotoxy(10,5);
    cout <<"\aHave you set up P/Q/R(y/n)?";
    ans = getche();
    switch(ans)
{   case 'y':
        break;
    case 'n':
        cout <<'\a'; sleep(1);
```

```
        return 0;
default:
        gotoxy(10,7);
        cout <<"\aWrong selection...";sleep(1);
        gotoxy(10,7);
        cout <<"                              ";
        goto RptFunc;
}
clrscr();
gotoxy(58,1);
cout <<"Program: "<<Pgname;
gotoxy(10,5);
cout <<"Input the BOUNDARY CONDITIONS of x and y.";
gotoxy(10,6);
cout <<"First the x-values and then the y-values,";
gotoxy(10,7);
cout <<"each separated by a BLANK.";
gotoxy(10,8);
cout <<"------------------------------------------------------------------";
gotoxy (10,9);
cout <<"x0 x1 yB yF :";
SelectBC:
    gotoxy (32,9);
    cin >> x0 >> x1 >> yB >> yF;
    gotoxy(10,10);
    cout <<"------------------------------------------------------------------";
Select1:
    gotoxy (10,11);
    cout <<"\aAny change of BC (y/n);";
```

```
    ans = getche();
    switch(ans)
{   case 'n':
        break;
    case 'y':
        cout <<'\a';
        gotoxy(32,9); cout <<"
        gotoxy(10,10); cout <<"
        gotoxy(10,11);cout <<"
        goto SelectBC;

default:
        gotoxy(10,13);
        cout <<"\aWrong selection…"; sleep(1);
        gotoxy(10,13);
        cout <<"                    ";
        goto Select1;
}
// ############################################ Width block
```

$$w = \frac{(x1 - x0)}{(m + 1)};$$

```
wDb1 = 2.0*w;
```

$$wHlf = \frac{w}{2.0};$$

```
wSqr = pow(w,2);
// ######################################## Development of G-functions
for (i = 1; i<= m + 1; i++)
{
```

$$G[i] = yB + i*w*\left(\frac{(yF-yB)}{(x1 - x0)}\right);$$

```
}
```

x = x0 + w;

y = G[1];

$y1 = \frac{(G[2] - G[1])}{wDb1};$

// ## *First Call of the function*

FnY1 = Bvp11(x,y,y1);

FnY = Bvp12(x,y,y1);

FnXY = Bvp13(x,y,y1);

A[1] = 2. + wSqr*FnY;

B[1] = – 1. + wH1f*FnY1;

D[1] = – (2.*G[1] – G[2] – yB + wSqr*FnXY);

L[1] = A[1];

$U[1] = \frac{B[1]}{A[1]};$

$Z[1] = \frac{D[1]}{L[1]};$

for(i = 2; i< = m – 1; i++)

{ x = x0 + i*w;

y = G[i];

$y1 = \frac{(G[i + 1] - G[i - 1])}{wDb1};$

// ####################################### *Second Call of the function*

FnY1 = Bvp11(x,y,y1);

FnY = Bvp12(x,y,y1);

FnXY = Bvp13(x,y,y1);

A[i] = 2. + wSqr*FnY;

B[i] = – 1. + wH1f*FnY1;

C[i] = – 1. – wH1f*FnY1;

D[i] = – (2.*G[i] – G[i + 1] – G[i – 1] + wSqr*FnXY);

}

x = x1 – w;

```
y = G[m];

y1 = (G[m + 1] - G[m - 1]) / wDb1;

// ######################################## Third Call of the function

    FnY1 = Bvp11(x,y,y1);

    FnY = Bvp12(x,y,y1);

    FnXY = Bvp13(x,y,y1);

    A[m] = 2. + wSqr*FnY;

    C[m] = - 1. - wH1f*FnY1;

    D[m] = - (2.*G[m] - G[m - 1] - yF + wSqr*FnXY);

// ########################################## Tridiagonal Calculations

for(k = 2; k< = m - 1; k++)

{

    L[k] = A[k] - C[k]*U[k - 1];

    U[k] = B[k] / L[k];

}

L[m] = A[m] - C[m]*U[m - 1];

for(i = 2; i<=m ; i++)

{

    Z[i] = (D[i] - C[i]*Z[i - 1]) / L[i];

}

V[m] = Z[m];

G[m] = G[m] + V[m];

// ############################################ Final Countdown

    for(i = m - 1; i> = 1; i-)

{   V[i] = Z[i] - U[i]*V[i + 1];

    G[i] = G[i] + V[i];

}

// ######################################## PRINT OUT the Results

clrscr();
```

```
gotoxy(5,1); cout <<"The Estimated Values of the BVP";
gotoxy(39,1); cout <<"Program: "<<Pgname<<")";
gotoxy(5,2);
cout <<"==========================================================";
gotoxy(5,3);
cout.precision(5);
cout <<"[y("<<x0<<") = "<<yB<<", y("<<x1<<") = "<<yF;
cout <<", width = "<<w<<"]";
1 = 0; k = 5;
// ########################################### Print out the Results
for(j = 1; j< = m + 1; j = j + 10)
{   1 = 1 + 1;
    xInc = x0 + k*w;
    xInc1 = xInc + 5*w;
    gotoxy(5, 1 + 4); cout <<"y(";cout.precision(5); cout<< xInc;
    gotoxy(14, 1 + 4); cout<<"):"; cout.precision(8); cout<<G[k];
    gotoxy(36, 1 + 4); cout<<"y("; cout.precision(5); cout<<xInc1;
    gotoxy(46, 1 + 4); cout <<"):"; cout.precision(8); cout<<G[k + 5];
    k = k + 10;
}
gotoxy(5, 15);
cout<<"......................................";
Repeat:
gotoxy(9, 17);
cout<<"Type (e) to exit:";
cin>>tch;
if(tch ! = 'e')
{   gotoxy(9, 18);
    cout<<"\aWrong Choice..."; sleep(1);
    gotoxy(9, 18);
```

```
    cout<<"      ";
    goto Repeat;
}
Exit:
return 0;
}
//∇∇∇∇∇∇∇∇∇∇∇∇∇∇∇∇∇∇∇∇∇∇∇∇∇∇∇ Function DEFINITION Block
double Bvp11 (double x, double y, double y1)
{
//-------------------------------------------- Coefficient of dy/dx
P = - y;
//=====================================================
return double (P);
}
double Bvp12(double x, double y, double y1)
{
//-------------------------------------- Coefficient of y
Q = y*y-y1;
//=====================================================
return double (Q);
}
double Bvp13(double x, double y, double y1)
{
//----------------------------------- Total Right-side Function
R = pow(y, 3)-y*y1;
//=====================================================
return double (R);
}
```

Chapter 11

Differential Equations to be Worked out

Chapter 3 *(Program : INTGSIMP.CPP)*

Find the approximations of the Definite Integrals:

1. DI: $\int_{0}^{1} e^{-x^2} dx$, ES: 0.7468241, K: 5

2. DI: $\int_{0}^{1} \frac{1-x}{1+x} dx$, ES: $2Ln2 - 1$, K: 6

3. DI: $\int_{-10}^{-6} \frac{1}{x+2} dx$, ES: $Ln2$, K: 5

4. DI: $\int_{1.0}^{1.6487212} x \, Lnx \, dx$, ES: $\frac{1}{4}$, K: 3

5. DI: $\int_{0}^{1} \frac{x}{\sqrt{1+x^2}} dx$, ES: $\sqrt{2} - 1$, K: 5

6. DI: $\int_{1}^{e} Ln\, x \, dx$, ES: $x(Ln\, x - 1)$, K: 6

7. DI: $\int_{0}^{1} \frac{1}{\sqrt{x^4 + 1}} dx$, ES: 0.9270374, K: 5

8. DI: $\int_0^1 \frac{e^{-x}}{x + 1} dx$, ES: 0.4634221, K: 5

9. DI: $\int_{-2}^{3} e^{-x/2} dx$, ES: $2(e - e^{-3/2})$, K: 5

10. DI: $\int_0^{1.0} Ln(x^2 + 1) dx$, ES: 0.2639435, K: 5

11. DI: $\int_3^5 \frac{1}{\sqrt{x^2 + 16}} dx$, ES: $Ln\ 0.5$, K: 4

12. DI: $\int_{-1}^{2} \frac{1}{x^2 - 9} dx$, ES: $\frac{Ln\ 0.1}{6}$, K: 6

13. DI: $\int_1^3 Ln\ (x + \sqrt{x^2 - 1}) dx$, ES: 2.458019, K: 5

14. DI: $\int_0^{\pi/4} Ln\ (1 + \text{Tan}\ \theta) d\theta$, ES: $\frac{\pi}{8} Ln 2$, K: 5

15. DI: $\int_0^1 \frac{1}{(x^2 + 1)^2} dx$, ES: $\frac{\pi + 2}{8}$, K: 5

16. DI: $\int_0^1 \frac{1}{(1 + x)\sqrt{1 + 2x - x^2}} dx$, ES: $\frac{\pi}{5.656854}$, K: 6

17. DI: $\int_0^1 x^6 \sqrt{1 + x^2}\, dx$, ES: $\frac{5\pi}{256}$, K: 10

18. DI: $\int_{-1}^{0} \frac{1}{4x^2 - 9} dx$, ES: $-\frac{Ln 5}{12}$, K: 6

19. DI: $\int_0^1 \frac{1}{e^{3x}} dx$, ES: 0.3167377, K: 6

20. DI: $\int_0^1 xe^{-x^2}dx$, ES:. 0.3160603, K: 6

21. DI: $\int_2^4 \frac{x^3 - 2}{x^2(x-1)}dx$, ES: 2.7876821, K: 6

22. DI: $\int_1^3 \frac{2 - x^2}{x^3 + 3x^2 + 2x}dx$, ES: $\frac{Ln9}{10}$, K: 6

23. DI: $\int_2^3 \frac{3 - \theta}{\theta^3 + 4\theta^2 + 3\theta}d\theta$, ES: $\frac{Ln81}{80}$, K: 6

24. DI: $\int_0^1 \frac{3x^2 + 7x}{(x+1)(x+2)(x+3)}dx$, ES: $ln\left(\frac{4}{3}\right)$, K: 6

25. DI: $\int_0^4 \frac{9x^2}{(2x+1)(x+2)^2}dx$, ES: $5Ln3 - 4$, K: 8

26. DI: $\int_1^4 \frac{5x^2 + 4}{x(x^2+4)}dx$, ES: $3Ln4$, K: 6

27. DI: $\int_{\pi/4}^{\pi/2} \frac{\text{Sin } x}{x}dx$, ES: $x - \frac{x^3}{3*3!} + \frac{x^5}{5*5!} - \frac{x^7}{7*7!} + \ldots$, K = 5

28. DI: $\int_0^{\pi/3} \frac{1}{1 - \text{Sin } x}dx$, ES: 2.7320480, K: 6

29. DI: $\int_{-1}^1 x^2 \text{Cos } x\, dx$, ES: 0.4782672, K: 6

30. DI: $\int_0^{\pi/2} \frac{1}{3 + \text{Cos } 2x}dx$, ES: 0.5553602, K: 6

31. DI: $\int_0^{\pi/3} x^2 \text{ Sin } 3x\, dx$, ES: 0.2173927, K: 6

32. DI: $\int_0^{\pi/2} \text{Sin}^6\theta\, \text{Cos}^3\theta\, d\theta$, ES: $\frac{2}{63}$, K: 6

33. DI: $\int_0^{1} \text{Sin}^{-1}x\, dx$, ES: $\frac{\pi}{2} - 1$, K: 10

34. DI: $\int_{\pi/4}^{\pi/2} \frac{1}{\text{Sin}^2 x}\, dx$, ES: 1.0, K: 6

35. DI: $\int_0^{\pi/2} \frac{1 - \text{Sin}x}{\text{Cos}x}\, dx$, ES: $Ln2$, K: 5

36. DI: $\int_0^{\pi/2} e^{\sin x}\, dx$, ES: 3.1041172, K: 4

37. DI: $\int_0^{\pi/4} \frac{1}{\text{Cos}^2 x}\, dx$, ES: 1.0, K: 4

38. DI: $\int_0^{\pi} \text{Sin}^5\theta\, \text{Cos}^4\theta\, d\theta$, ES 0.0507938, K: 5

39. DI: $\int_0^{\pi} (1 - \text{Cos}x)^2\, dx$, ES: $\frac{3\pi}{2}$, K: 3

40. DI: $\int_0^{\pi/2} \text{Sin}^2\theta\, \text{Cos}^3\theta\, d\theta$, ES: $\frac{2}{15}$, K: 6

41. DI: $\int_0^{\pi/4} \frac{1}{\text{Cos}^4 x}\, dx$, ES: $\frac{4}{3}$, K:6

42. DI: $\int_0^{\pi/2} \frac{(\text{Cos } x - \text{Sin } x)}{(1 + \text{Sin } x\, \text{Cos} x)}\, dx$, ES: 0, K:6

43. DI: $\int_0^{\pi} \frac{1}{(2\text{Sin}x + \text{Cos}x + 3)}\, dx$, ES: $\frac{\pi}{4}$, K:8

44. DI: $\int_0^{\pi/2} \frac{\text{Sinx}}{(\text{Sinx} + \text{Cosx})} dx$, ES: $\frac{\pi}{4}$, K: 8

45. DI: $\int_0^{2\pi} \text{Sin}^4\left(\frac{\theta}{2}\right) \text{Cos}^5\left(\frac{\theta}{2}\right) d\theta$, ES: 0, K: 5

46. DI: $\int_0^{\pi/2} \text{Cos}^6\text{x}\, dx$, ES: $\frac{5\pi}{32}$, K: 5

47. DI: $\int_0^{\pi} \text{x Sin}^2\text{x}\, dx$, ES: $\frac{\pi^2}{4}$, K: 5

48. DI: $\int_0^{\pi} \text{x Sinx Cos}^2\text{x}\, dx$, ES: $\frac{\pi}{3}$, K: 7

49. DI: $\int_0^{\pi/2} \text{Sin}^3\text{ x Cos}^3\text{ x}\, dx$, ES : 0.08333333, K: 6

50. DI: $\int_0^{\pi/4} \frac{1}{\text{Cos}^4\text{x}} dx$, ES: 1.33333333, K: 6

Chapter 4 *(Program : INTGAREA. CPP)*

1. Find the area of the region enclosed by the curves $y^2 = 4bx + 4b^2$ and $x + y = 2b$ (when $b = 1$).

   ES: $\frac{64}{3}$

2. Find the area of the region enclosed by the curves $xy = 4$ and $x + y = 5$.

   ES: $\frac{15 - 16Ln2}{2}$

3. Compute the area of the region bounded by the surfaces $y = \frac{8}{x^2 + 4}$, $x = 2y$ and $x = 0$.

   ES: $\pi - 1$.

4. Find the area contained between the parabolas $y = \frac{x^2}{3}$ and $y + \frac{2x^2}{3} = 4$.

ES: $\frac{32}{3}$

5. Compute the area between the catenary $y = 2\,\mathrm{Cosh}\,\frac{x}{2}$, the y-axis and the straight line $y = e + \frac{1}{e}$

ES: $\frac{8}{e}$

6. Find the arc length of the semicubical parabola $y^2 = x^3$ from the origin to the point $x = 4$.

ES: 9.07341528

7. Compute the arc length of the curve $y = \mathrm{Sin}^{-1}(e^{-x})$ from $x = 0$ to $x = 1$.

ES: $Ln[e + \sqrt{(e^2 - 1)}\,]$.

8. Find the arc length of the curve $x = \frac{y^2}{4} - \frac{Ln\ y}{2}$ from $y = 1$ to $y = e$.

ES: $\frac{e^2 + 1}{4}$

9. Solve the equations of the parabolas represented by $y^2 = 10x + 25$ and $y^2 + 6x - 9 = 0$ and find the area.

ES: $16\sqrt{\frac{5}{3}}$

10. Find the area enclosed by the ellipse $(x - 2y + 3)^2 + (3x + 4y - 1)^2 = 100$.

ES: 10π

11. Find the area of the domain enclosed by the ellipse $\frac{x^2}{2} + \frac{y^2}{2} = 1$.

ES: 4π.

12. Find the area of the domain bounded by the curve $\left(\frac{x^2}{4} + \frac{y^2}{9}\right)^2 = \frac{x^2 + y^2}{25}$

ES: $\frac{39\pi}{25}$

13. Compute the equations to find the area enclosed by $y = x^3 - 2x$ and $y = 6x - x^3$.

ES: 16.

14. Find the area in the first quadrant bounded by the x-axis and the curves $x^2 + y^2 = 10$ and $y^2 = 9x$.

ES: $6\frac{3}{4}$

15. Calculate the finite area bounded by the pair of curves $x^{2/3} + y^{2/3} = 1$ and $x + y = 1$.

ES: $\frac{16 - 3\pi}{32}$

16. Compute the area contained between the two parabolas $y = x^2$ and $y = \frac{x^2}{2}$ and the straight line $y = 2x$.

ES: 4.0

17. Find the area of the curve $y = \frac{1}{x}$ bounded by the lines $y = x$ and $x = 2$.

ES: 2.25

18. Calculate the area between the part of the circle $x^2 + y^2 = 1$ and the straight line $x + y = 1$.

ES: $\frac{\pi}{2} - 2$.

Double Integral *(Program : INTGDOBL.CPP)*

Find the approximations of the Double integrals:

1. DI : $\int_0^2 dy \int_0^1 xy\, dx$

   ES : 1

   Wx : 0.001953, Wy : 0.003906, K : 9, M : 512

2. DI : $\int_0^{\pi} dy \int_0^{\pi/2} x \,\mathrm{Sin}(x + y)\, dx$

   ES : $\pi - 2$

   Wx : 0.003068, Wy : 0.006136, K : 9, M : 512

3. DI : $\int_1^3 dy \int_2^5 \frac{1}{(x+2y)^2}\, dx$

ES : $\frac{Ln \frac{14}{11}}{2}$

Wx : 0.005859, Wy : 0.003906, K : 9, M : 512

4. DI : $\int_0^1 dy \int_0^1 \frac{1}{(x+1+y)^2}\, dx$

ES : $Ln \frac{4}{3}$

Wx : 0.001953, Wy : 0.001953, K : 9, M : 512

5. DI : $\int_0^2 dy \int_0^1 (x+2)\, dx$

ES : 5.0

Wx : 0.001953, Wy : 0.003906, K : 9, M : 512

6. DI : $\int_0^1 dy \int_0^1 e^y\, dx$

ES : $e-1$

Wx : 0.001953, Wy : 0.001953, K : 9, M : 512

7. DI : $\int_1^5 dy \int_1^5 \frac{1}{\sqrt{x^2+y^2}}\, dx$

ES : 3.95183553

Wx : 0.007813, Wy : 0.007813, K : 9, M : 512

8. DI : $\int_1^2 dy \int_0^1 \frac{2xy}{(1+x^2)(1+y^2)}\, dx$

ES : 0.31756667

Wx : 0.001953, Wy : 0.001953, K : 9, M : 512

9. *DI* : $\int_0^2 dy \int_0^1 (x^2 + y)\, dx$

ES : $\frac{8}{3}$

Wx : 0.001953, *Wy* : 0.003906, *K* : 9, *M* : 512

10. *DI* : $\int_0^1 dy \int_0^2 (x^2 + 2y)\, dx$

ES : 4.66666666

Wx : 0.003906, *Wy* : 0.001953, *K* : 9, *M* : 512

11. *DI* : $\int_1^{1.5} dy \int_{1.4}^2 Ln(x + 2y)\, dx$

ES : 0.4295545

Wx : 0.001172, *Wy* : 0.000977, *K* : 9, *M* : 512

12. *DI* : $\int_0^1 dy \int_0^1 \frac{x^2}{1 + y^2}\, dx$

ES : $\frac{\pi}{12}$

Wx : 0.001953, *Wy* : 0.001953, *K* : 9, *M* : 512

13. *DI* : $\int_0^{\pi/2} dy \int_0^2 x^2 \text{ Cos} y\, dx$

ES : $\frac{8}{3}$

Wx : 0.003906, *Wy* : 0.003068, *K* : 9, *M* : 512

14. *DI* : $\int_1^2 dy \int_2^4 (x^2 + y^2)\, dx$

ES : $\frac{70}{3}$

Wx : 0.003906, *Wy* : 0.001953, *K* : 9, *M* : 512

15. *DI* : $\int_1^2 dy \int_0^3 (x + y)\, dx$

ES : 9.0

Wx : 0.005859, *Wy* : 0.001953, *K* : 9, *M* : 512

Chapter 5 (*Program : IVPD1SES.CPP*)

Determine the approximations of the differential equations:

1. *DE* : $\frac{Dy}{dx} = 2xy$

   PS : $y(x) = e^{x^2}$

   IC : $y(0) = 1.0$, *Width* = 0.01

2. *DE* : $\frac{Dy}{dx} - 2x(1 + y) = 0$

   PS : $y(x) = 3e^{x^2-1} - 1$

   IC : $y(1) = 2$, *Width* = 0.01

3. *DE* : $\frac{dy}{dx} + xy^2 = 0$

   PS : $y(x) = \frac{2}{x^2 + 1}$

   IC : $y(0) = 2$, *Width* = 0.01

4. *DE* : $\frac{dy}{dx} + 2xy = 0$

   PS : $y(x) = e^{-x^2}$

   IC : $y(0) = 1.0$, *Width* = 0.01

5. *DE* : $y' + y = 0$

   PS : $y(x) = e^{1-x}$

   IC : $y(1) = 1.0$, *Width* = 0.01

6. *DE* : $\frac{Dy}{dx} = \frac{xy}{2}$

   PS : $y(x) = e^{x^2/4}$

   IC : $y(0) = 1.0$, *Width* = 0.01

7. *DE* : $Dy = (2y + 5)\,dx$

PS : $y(x) = \dfrac{11e^{2x} - 5}{2}$

IC : $y(0) = 3.0$, *Width* = 0.01

8. *DE* : $\dfrac{Dy}{dx} - x^2y = 0$

PS : $y(x) = e^{x^2/3}$

IC : $y(0) = 1$, *Width* = 0.01

9. *DE* : $(1 + x)\dfrac{dy}{dx} + 3y = 0$

PS : $y(x) = (1 + x)^{-3}$

IC : $y(0) = 1.0$, *Width* = 0.01

10. *DE* : $(x + y)\dfrac{dy}{dx} + (x - y) = 0$

PS : $Ln(x^2 + y^2) + 2\text{Tan}^{-1}\left(\dfrac{y}{x}\right) = 0$

IC : $y(1) = 0$, *Width* = 0.01

11. *DE* : $e^{3x}\,dx - 2dy = 0$

PS : $y(x) = \dfrac{e^{3x} - 1}{6}$

IC : $y(0) = 0$, *Width* = 0.01

12. *DE* : $xy' - y^2 = 1$

PS : $y(x) = \text{Tan}(Ln\, x)$

IC : $y(1) = 0$, *Width* = 0.01

13. *DE* : $x\dfrac{dy}{dx} + y^2 = 1$

PS : $y(x) = \dfrac{x^2 - 1}{x^2 + 1}$

IC : $y(1) = 0$, *Width* = 0.01

14. *DE* : $y'(x - 2y) = 2x + y$

PS : $y(x) = Ln(x^2 + y^2) = \text{Tan}^{-1}\left(\dfrac{y}{x}\right)$

IC : $y(1) = 0$, *Width* = 0.01

15. *DE* : $8yy' - (3x + 2)x = 0$

PS : $y(x) = \dfrac{x\sqrt{x + 1}}{2}$

IC : $y(3) = 3$, *Width* = 0.01

16. *DE* : $\dfrac{dy}{dx} + xy = 0$

PS : $y(x) = e^{-x^2/2}$

IC : $y(0) = 1.0$, *Width* = 0.01

17. *DE* : $x(1 + x^2y^4)dy = y(1 - x^2y^4)dx$

PS : $x^3y^4 + 2y = 3x$

IC : $y(1) = 1$, *Width* = 0.01

18. *DE* : $\dfrac{Dy}{dx} + 2xy^2 = 0$

PS : $y(x) = \dfrac{1}{1 + x^2}$

IC : $y(0) = 1$, *Width* = 0.01

19. *DE* : $\dfrac{Dy}{dx} = y^2$

PS : $y(x) = \dfrac{1}{1 - x}$

IC : $y(0) = 1.0$, *Width* = 0.01

20. *DE* : $\dfrac{Dy}{dx} = y^3$

PS : $y(x) = \dfrac{1}{\sqrt{1 - 2x}}$

IC : $y(0) = 1.0$, *Width* = 0.01

21. *DE* : $\dfrac{Dy}{dx} = e^y$

PS : $y(x) = Ln\left(\dfrac{1}{1 - x}\right)$

IC : $y(0) = 0$, *Width* = 0.01

22. *DE* : $Dy = [\sqrt{xy} + 1]dx$

PS : $y(x) = x + \frac{x^2}{2} + \frac{x^3}{12} + \ldots$

IC : $y(0) = 0,$ $Width = 0.01$

23. *DE* : $(xe^{-y} + e^x)dy = (e^{-y} - ye^x)dx$

PS : $ye^x - xe^{-y} = 0$

IC : $y(0) = 0,$ $Width = 0.01$

24. *DE* : $[x + 2Ln\ y - (Ln\ y)^2]dy = y\ dx$

PS : $x = y + (Ln\ y)^2$

IC : $y(1) = 1,$ $Width = 0.01$

25. *DE* : $x[Ln\ y - Ln\ x]dy = y\ dx$

PS : $y[Ln\ y - Ln\ x - 1] = -0.6137053$

IC : $y(1) = 2,$ $Width = 0.01$

26. *DE* : $[t\sqrt{t^2 + y^2} - y]dt = [t - y\sqrt{t^2 + y^2}]dy$

PS : $\sqrt{(t^2 + y^2)^3} - 3ty = 89$

IC : $y(4) = 3,$ $Width = 0.01$

27. *DE* : $[3(x-1)^2y + 2]dy = -[2(x-1)y^2]dx$

PS : $y^3(x-1)^2 + y^2 = 9$

IC : $y(1) = 3,$ $Width = 0.01$

28. *DE* : $2xy\ dx = (y^2 - x^2)dy$

PS : $3x^2y - y^3 = 1$

IC : $y(0) = -1,$ $Width = 0.01$

29. *DE* : $x(2 - 9xy^2)dx + y(4y^2 - 6x^3)dy = 0$

PS : $x^2 - 3x^3y^2 + y^4 = 1$

IC : $y(0) = 1,$ $Width = 0.01$

30. *DE* : $\frac{y}{x}dx + (y^3 + Ln\ x)dy = 0$

PS : $4y\ Ln\ x + y^4 = 1$

IC : $y(1) = 1.0,$ $Width = 0.01$

31. *DE* : $\left(\frac{3x^2}{y^2} + 1\right)dx = \left(\frac{2x^3}{y^3} + \frac{5}{y^2}\right)dy$

PS : $x + \frac{x^3}{y^2} + \frac{5}{y} = 5$

IC : $y(0) = 1$, *Width* = 0.01

32. *DE* : $3x^2(1 + Ln\ y)dx = \left(2y - \frac{x^3}{y}\right)dy$

PS : $x^3(1 + Ln\ y) - y^2 = 1$

IC : $y(0) = 1$, *Width* = 0.01

33. *DE* : $\text{Cos}x\ \text{Sin}y\ \frac{dy}{dx} = \text{Cos}y\ \text{Sin}x$

PS : $y(x) = \text{Cos}^{-1}\left(\frac{\text{Cos}x}{\sqrt{2}}\right)$

IC : $y(0) = \frac{\pi}{4}$, *Width* = 0.01

34. *DE* : $(x^2 + 1)y' = 1 + y^2$

PS : $y(x) = \frac{1 + x}{1 - x}$

IC : $y(0) = 1$, *Width* = 0.01

35. *DE* : $y(x^2 - 1)\frac{dy}{dx} + x(y^2 + 1) = 0$

PS : $y(x) = \sqrt{\frac{1 + x^2}{1 - x^2}}$

IC : $y(0) = 1$, *Width* = 0.01

36. *DE* : $xy'\ \text{Cos}\ \frac{y}{x} = y\ \text{Cos}\ \frac{y}{x} - x$

PS : $y(x) = x\ \text{Sin}^{-1}\left(Ln\ \frac{1}{x}\right)$

IC : $y(1) = 0$, *Width* = 0.01

Chapter 6 (*Program : IVPD1LIN.CPP*)

Find the approximations of the following differential equations using the initial conditions and compare the results with the particular solutions.

1. *DE* : $\frac{Dy}{dx} + \frac{3xy}{1 + x^2} = 5x$

PS : $y(x) = 1 + x^2$

IC : $y(1) = 2.0$, *Width* = 0.01

2. DE : $(1 + x^2) \dfrac{dy}{dx} = xy + (1 + x^2)^{3/2}$

PS : $y(x) = (1 + x)(1 + x^2)^{1/2}$

IC : $y(0) = 1.0$, $Width = 0.01$

3. DE : $x \dfrac{dy}{dx} = x^2 - y$

PS : $y(x) = \dfrac{x^3 - 1}{3x}$

IC : $y(1) = 0$, $Width = 0.01$

4. DE : $\dfrac{Dy}{dx} = x + y$

PS : $y(x) = 2e^x - x - 1$

IC : $y(0) = 1.0$, $Width = 0.01$

5. DE : $2y + (x^2y + 1)xy' = 0$

PS : $y(x) = \dfrac{2x - \sqrt{3x^2 - 2}}{x}$

IC : $y(1.0) = 1.0$, $Width = 0.01$

6. DE : $y\,dx + x(2xy + 1)dy = 0$

PS : $y^2e^{-1/xy} = 0.3678795$

IC : $y(1.0) = 1.0$, $Width = 0.01$

7. DE : $(x + 2y)dx = x\,dy$

PS : $y(x) = x(x - 1)$

IC : $y(1.0) = 0$, $Width = 0.01$

8. DE : $Dy + (3y - 8)dx = 0$

PS : $y(x) = \dfrac{2(4 - e^{-3x})}{3}$

IC : $y(0) = 2.0$, $Width = 0.01$

9. DE : $y' = 8 - 3y$

PS : $y(x) = \dfrac{4(2 + e^{-3x})}{3}$

IC : $y(0) = 4.0$, $Width = 0.01$

10. *DE* : $x\,dy + (1 - y)y\,dx = 0$

PS : $y(x) = \dfrac{1}{(x + 1)}$

IC : $y(1.0) = 0.5$, *Width* = 0.01

11. *DE* : $x\,dy = \left(y + \sqrt{xy}\right)dx$

PS : $y(x) = \dfrac{x(Ln\ x + 2)^2}{4}$

IC : $y(1.0) = 1.0$, *Width* = 0.01

12. *DE* : $\dfrac{Dy}{2 - y} = \text{Tan}\ x\ dx$

PS : $y(x) = 2 - 3\text{Cos}x$

IC : $y(0) = 1.0$, *Width* = 0.01

13. *DE* : $2xy\,dy = (y^2 - x^2)dx$

PS : $y(x) = \sqrt{2x - x^2}$

IC : $y(1.0) = 1.0$, *Width* = 0.01

14. *DE* : $\dfrac{Dy}{dx} + \dfrac{y}{x} = x$

PS : $y(x) = \dfrac{x^3 - 1}{3x}$

IC : $y(1.0) = 0$, *Width* = 0.01

15. *DE* : $x\,dy = (x - y)\,dx$

PS : $y(x) = \dfrac{x}{2} + \dfrac{1}{x}$

IC : $y(1.0) = 1.5$, *Width* = 0.01

16. *DE* : $\dfrac{Dy}{dx} - y\text{Cos}x + 1 = 0$

PS : $y(x) = 1 - \dfrac{x^3}{6} - \dfrac{x^4}{24} + \dfrac{x^6}{72} + \ldots$

IC : $y(0) = 1.0$, *Width* = 0.01

17. *DE* : $(x + y)\dfrac{dy}{dx} = y$

PS : $y(x) = \dfrac{x}{Ln\left(\dfrac{y}{2}\right)}$

IC : $y(0) = 2.0$, *Width* = 0.01

18. *DE* : $(x + y)\dfrac{dy}{dx} = y$

PS : $y(x) = \dfrac{x}{(\text{Lny} + 1)}$

IC : $y(1.0) = 1.0$, *Width* = 0.01

19. *DE* : $\dfrac{Dy}{y} = (y^2 e^{x^2} - x)\,dx$

PS : $y^2(x) = \dfrac{e^{-x^2}}{(4 - 2x)}$

IC : $y(0) = 0.5$, *Width* = 0.01

20. *DE* : $2x^3 y \dfrac{dy}{dx} + 3x^2 y^2 = -7.0$

PS : $x^3 y^2 + 7x + 8 = 0$

IC : $y(-1.0) = 1.0$, *Width* = 0.01

21. *DE* : $(1 - 2xy)\dfrac{dy}{dx} = \dfrac{y}{x}$

PS : $y(xy - 1) = 2x$

IC : $y(-1.0) = 1.0$, *Width* = 0.01

22. *DE* : $\dfrac{Dx}{dy} - x\text{Cos}y = \text{Sin } 2y$

PS : $x(y) = 3e^{\sin y} - 2(1 + \text{Sin}y)$

IC : $y(1.0) = 0$, *Width* = 0.01

23. *DE* : $Dy = \left(\dfrac{x}{y}\, e^{2x} + y\right)dx$

PS : $y(x) = \sqrt{[(x^2 + 1)}\; e^{2x}$

IC : $y(0) = 1.0$, *Width* = 0.01

24. *DE* : $(x^2 + y^2)\dfrac{dy}{dx} = \dfrac{y^3}{x}$

PS : $y(x) = \dfrac{2x}{(x + 1)}$

IC : $y(1.0) = 1.0$, *Width* = 0.01

25. *DE* : $y'\dfrac{x}{y} + 2xy\, Ln\, x = -1$

PS : $y(x) = \dfrac{1}{x[(Ln\, x)^2 + 1]}$

IC : $y(1.0) = 1.0$, *Width* = 0.01

26. DE : $xy \, Ln\, x \, dy = (y^2 - Ln\, x)dx$

PS : $y^2 = Ln\, x(2 - 0.804021 * Ln\, x)$

IC : $y(2.0) = 1.0$, $Width = 0.01$

27. DE : $x\dfrac{dy}{dx} = y(y\, Ln\, x - 1)$

PS : $y(x) = \dfrac{1}{1 + Ln\, x - 0.5x}$

IC : $y(1.0) = 2.0$, $Width = 0.01$

28. DE : $x\dfrac{dy}{dx} - y(1 - y) = 0$

PS : $y = \dfrac{x}{x + 0.5}$

IC : $y(-1.0) = 2.0$, $Width = 0.01$

29. DE : $y\dfrac{dy}{dt} + (y^2 + t^2 + t) = 0$

PS : $y(t) = -\sqrt{5e^{-2(t+2)} - t^2}$

IC : $y(-2.0) = -1.0$, $Width = 0.01$

30. DE : $t\dfrac{dy}{dt} + 2y = 3t$

PS : $yt^2 = t^3 + 200$

IC : $y(-5.0) = 3.0$, $Width = 0.01$

31. DE : $t\dfrac{dx}{dt} - x - Ln\, t = 0$

PS : $x(t) = 101t - 1 - Ln\, t$

IC : $y(1.0) = 100$, $Width = 0.01$

32. DE : $2xt\dfrac{dx}{dt} = 3t^2 + x^2$

PS : $x(t) = -\sqrt{3t^2 + 2t}$

IC : $y(2.0) = -4.0$, $Width = 0.01$

33. DE : $2yy' + x^2(1 + y^2) = 0$

PS : $y(x) = \sqrt{2e^{-x^3/3} - 1}$

IC : $y(0) = 1.0$, $Width = 0.01$

34. *DE* : $xy^2\,dy = (x^3 + y^3)dx$

PS : $y^3 = 3x^3\,Ln(Cx),\ C = 1.39561242$

IC : $y(1.0) = 1.0,\quad Width = 0.01$

Chapter 7 *(Program : IVPD2LIN.CPP)*

Find the approximations of the following differential equations using the initial conditions and compare the results with the particular solutions.

1. *DE* : $y'' - y = 0$

PS : $y(x) = e^{-x},\qquad y'(x) = -\,e^{-x}$

IC : $y(0) = 1,\quad y'(0) = -\,1$

W : 0.01

2. *DE* : $y'' + 2y' = 0$

PS : $y(x) = 1.0,\qquad y'(x) = 0$

IC : $y(0) = 1,\quad y'(0) = 0$

W : 0.01

3. *DE* : $y'' + xy = 0$

PS : $y = 1 - x - \frac{x^3}{3!} + \frac{2x^4}{4!} + \ldots,\qquad y' = -\,1 - \frac{x^2}{2} + \frac{x^3}{3} + \ldots$

IC : $y(0) = 1,\quad y'(0) = -\,1$

W : 0.01

4. *DE* : $y'' - y^2 = x^2$

PS : $y = 1 + \frac{x^2}{2!} + \frac{x^4}{3!} + \ldots,\qquad y' = x + \frac{2x^3}{3} + \ldots$

IC : $y(0) = 1,\quad y'(0) = 0$

W : 0.01

5. *DE* : $y'' - 2 = 0$

PS : $y(x) = x^2 + 2x + 1,\qquad y'(x) = 2(x + 1)$

IC : $y(0) = 1,\quad y'(0) = 2$

W : 0.01

6. *DE* : $y'' - y'e^y = 0$

PS : $y(x) = -1.0, \quad y'(x) = 0$

IC : $y(0) = -1, \quad y'(0) = 0$

W : 0.01

7. *DE* : $yy'' + y'^2 - yy' = 0$

PS : $y(x) = \sqrt{e^x + 2}, \quad y'(x) = \dfrac{0.5e^x}{\sqrt{e^x + 2}}$

IC : $y(Ln\ 2) = 2, \quad y'(Ln\ 2) = 0.5$

W : 0.01

8. *DE* : $y'' - y' - 2y = 0$

PS : $y(x) = 2e^{-x} + e^{2x}, \quad y'(x) = 2(e^{2x} - e^{-x})$

IC : $y(0) = 3, \quad y'(0) = 0$

W : 0.01

9. *DE* : $(D^2 - 4)y = 0$

PS : $y(x) = \dfrac{5e^{2x}}{8} + \dfrac{3e^{-2x}}{8}, \quad y'(x) = \dfrac{5e^{2x} - 3e^{-2x}}{4}$

IC : $y(0) = 1. \quad y'(0) = 0.5$

W : 0.01

10. *DE* : $D^2y - 4Dy + 4y = 0$

PS : $y(x) = e^{2x}(3 - 2x), \quad y'(x) = 4e^{2x}(1 - x)$

IC : $y(0) = 3, \quad y'(0) = 4$

W : 0.01

11. *DE* : $y'' - 5y' + 6y = 0$

PS : $y(x) = e^{3x-1}, \quad y'(x) = 3e^{3x-1}$

IC : $y(1) = e^2, \quad y'(1) = 3e^2$

W : 0.01

12. *DE* : $y'' + 4y' + 2y = 0$

PS : $y = e^{-0.5857x} - 2e^{-3.4142x}$,

$y' = -0.5857e^{-0.5857x} + 6.8284e^{-3.4142x}$

IC : $y(0) = -1, \quad y'(0) = 6.2427$

W : 0.01

13. *DE* : $y'' + 4y' + 13y = 0$

PS : $y(x) = e^{-2x}(4\text{Cos } 3x + 3\text{Sin } 3x)$,

$y'(x) = e^{-2x}(\text{Cos } 3x - 18\text{Sin } 3x)$

IC : $y(0) = 4, \quad y'(0) = 1$

W : 0.01

14. *DE* : $y'' + 4y' + 4y = 0$

PS : $y = 2e^{-2x}(1 + x), \qquad y' = -2e^{-2x}(1 + 2x)$

IC : $y(0) = 2, \quad y'(0) = -2$

W : 0.01

15. *DE* : $y'' - y^2 - 1 = 0$

PS : $y = \dfrac{x^2}{2} + \dfrac{x^6}{120} + \ldots, \qquad y' = x + \dfrac{x^5}{20} + \ldots$

IC : $y(0) = 0, \quad y'(0) = 0$

W : 0.01

16. *DE* : $y'' + y - 4e^x = 0$

PS : $y(x) = 2\text{Cos } x - 5\text{Sin } x + 2e^x$,

$y'(x) = -2\text{Sin } x - 5\text{Cos } x + 2e^x$

IC : $y(0) = 4, \quad y'(0) = -3$

W : 0.01

17. *DE* : $y'' - 2y' - 2e^x = 0$

PS : $y = e^{2x-1} - 2e^x + e - 1, \qquad y' = 2(e^{2x-1} - e^x)$

IC : $y(1) = -1, \quad y'(1) = 0$

W : 0.01

18. *DE* : $y'' + 2yy' = 0$

PS : $y(x) = \text{Tanh } x, \qquad y'(x) = \text{Sech}^2\, x$

IC : $y(0) = 0, \quad y'(0) = 1$

W : 0.01

19. *DE* : $(1 - x^2)y'' - 2xy' + 6y = 0$

PS : $y(x) = \dfrac{3x^2 - 1}{2}$, $y'(x) = 3x$

IC : $y(0) = -0.5$, $y'(0) = 0$

W : 0.01

20. *DE* : $(1 - x^2)y'' - 2xy' + 20y = 0$

PS : $y = \dfrac{35x^4 - 30x^2 + 3}{8}$, $y'(x) = \dfrac{5x(7x^2 - 3)}{2}$

IC : $y(0) = 0.375$, $y'(0) = 0$

W : 0.01

21. *DE* : $yy'' + y'^2 - y^4 = 0$

PS : $y(x) = \dfrac{1}{\text{Cos } x}$, $y'(x) = \text{Sec } x \text{ Tan } x$

IC : $y(0) = 1$, $y'(0) = 0$

W : 0.01

22. *DE* : $2yy'' - y'^2 = 1$

PS : $y(x) = \dfrac{x^2 + 1}{2}$, $y'(x) = x$

IC : $y(1) = 1$, $y'(1) = 1$

W : 0.01

23. *DE* : $xy'' - y' = 0$

PS : $y(x) = \dfrac{x^2 - 1}{2}$, $y'(x) = x$

IC : $y(1) = 0$, $y'(1) = 1$

W : 0.01

24. *DE* : $y^2y'' - 1 = 0$

PS : $2y^2 - 4x^2 = 1$, $y'(x) = \dfrac{2x}{y}$

IC : $y(0.5) = 1$, $y'(0.5) = 1$

W : 0.01

25. *DE* : $4\dfrac{d^2y}{dx^2}+4\dfrac{dy}{dx}+y=\text{Cos}\,\dfrac{x}{2}$

PS : $y(x)=\dfrac{\text{Sin}\,\dfrac{x}{2}}{2}-\dfrac{xe^{-x/2}}{4}$,

$\dfrac{dy}{dx}=\dfrac{\text{Cos}\,\dfrac{x}{2}}{4}-\dfrac{e^{-x/2}\left(1-\dfrac{x}{2}\right)}{4}$

IC : $y(0)=0,\quad y'(0)=0$

W : 0.01

26. *DE* : $\dfrac{D^2y}{dx^2}-3\dfrac{dy}{dx}+2y=e^{2x}(3x^2+2\text{Cos}\,x)$

PS : $y(x)=e^x+e^{2x}(x^3-3x^2+6x+1+\text{Sin}\,x-\text{Cos}\,x)$,

$\dfrac{dy}{dx}=e^x+e^{2x}(2x^3-3x^2+6x+8+3\text{Sin}\,x-\text{Cos}\,x)$

IC : $y(0)=1,\quad y'(0)=8$

W : 0.01

27. *DE* : $\dfrac{D^2y}{dx^2}-5\dfrac{dy}{dx}+6y=3x^2-4$

PS : $y(x)=\dfrac{9e^{2x}}{4}-\dfrac{10e^{3x}}{9}-\dfrac{5}{36}+\dfrac{5x}{6}+\dfrac{x^2}{2}$,

$\dfrac{dy}{dx}=\dfrac{9e^{2x}}{2}-\dfrac{10e^{3x}}{3}+\dfrac{5}{6}+x$

IC : $y(0)=1,\quad y'(0)=2$

W : 0.01

28. *DE* : $yy''+y^2y'-y'^2=0$

PS : $y=\dfrac{3e^{3x}}{2+e^{3x}}$, $\quad y'=\dfrac{18e^{3x}}{(2+e^{3x})^2}$

IC : $y(0)=1,\quad y'(0)=2$

W : 0.01

29. *DE* : $2yy''-y'^2+y^2=0$

PS : $y(x)=\text{Sin}\,x+1,\qquad y'(x)=\text{Cos}\,x$

IC : $y(0)=1,\quad y'(0)=1$

W : 0.01

30. *DE* : $y'' + y' - 2y = 0$

PS : $y(x) = 2e^{x} + e^{-2x}$, $\quad y'(x) = 2(e^{x} - e^{-2x})$

IC : $y(0) = 3$, $\quad y'(0) = 0$

W : 0.01

31. *DE* : $y'' - 4y' = 0$

PS : $y(x) = \dfrac{e^{-2x} + 3e^{2x}}{4}$ $\quad y'(x) = \dfrac{3e^{2x} - e^{-2x}}{2}$

IC : $y(0) = 1$, $\quad y'(0) = 0$

W : 0.01

32. *DE* : $Q''(t) + 4Q'(t) + 20Q(t) = 16e^{-2t}$

PS : $Q(t) = e^{-2t}(1 + \text{Sin } 4t + \text{Cos } 4t)$,

$Q'(t) = e^{-2t}(2\text{Cos } 4t - 6\text{Sin } 4t - 2)$

IC : $Q(0) = 2$, $\quad Q'(0) = 0$

W : 0.01

33. *DE* : $y''(x) = 3x - 2$

PS : $y'(x) = \dfrac{3x^2 - 4x - 5}{2}$, $\quad y(x) = \dfrac{x^3}{2} - x^2 - \dfrac{5x}{2} + 2$

IC : $y(0) = 2$, $\quad y'(0) = -2.5$

W : 0.01

34. *DE* : $y'' - y = x$

PS : $y(x) = -x + \dfrac{e^{x}}{2} - \dfrac{3e^{-x}}{2}$,

$y'(x) = -1 + \dfrac{e^{x}}{2} + \dfrac{3e^{-x}}{2}$

IC : $y(0) = -1$, $\quad y'(0) = 1$

W : 0.01

35. *DE* : $y'' + 3y' + 2y = 4e^{2x}$

PS : $y = -7e^{x} + 4e^{2x} + 4xe^{2x}$, $\quad y' = -7e^{x} + 12e^{2x} + 8xe^{2x}$

IC : $y(0) = -3$, $\quad y'(0) = 5$

W : 0.01

36. *DE* : $\frac{D^2q}{dt^2} + 8\frac{dq}{dt} + 25q = 150$

PS : $q(t) = 6 - e^{-4t}(6\text{Cos } 3t + 8\text{Sin } 3t), \quad q'(t) = 50e^{-4t}\text{ Sin } 3t$

IC : $q(0) = 0, \quad q'(0) = 0$

W : 0.01

37. *DE* : $\frac{D^2y}{dx^2} - x\frac{dy}{dx} + y^2 = 0$

PS : $y(x) = 1 + 2x - \frac{x^2}{2} - \frac{x^3}{3} - \frac{x^4}{3} + \ldots,$

$y'(x) = 2 - x - x^2 - \frac{4x^3}{3} + \ldots$

IC : $y(0) = 1, \quad y'(0) = 2$

W : 0.01

38. *DE* : $\frac{D^2y}{dx^2} - \left(\frac{dy}{dx}\right)^2 - xy = 0$

PS : $y(x) = 4 - 2x + 2x^2 - 2x^3 + \frac{19x^4}{6} + \ldots,$

$y'(x) = -2 + 4x - 6x^2 + \frac{38x^3}{3} + \ldots$

IC : $y(0) = 4, \quad y'(0) = -2$

W : 0.01

39. *DE* : $\frac{D^2y}{dx^2} + \frac{2x\left(\frac{dy}{dx}\right)^2}{y} = 0$

PS : $y = \left[\frac{8(x+2)}{(3-x)}\right]^{1/5}, \quad y' = \frac{8}{(3-x)^2}\left[\frac{8(x+2)}{3-x}\right]^{-4/5}$

IC : $y(2) = 2, \quad y'(2) = 0.5$

W : 0.01

40. *DE* : $y'' - 5y' + 6y = 2e^x$

PS : $y(x) = e^x, \quad y'(x) = e^x$

IC : $y(0) = 1, \quad y'(0) = 1$

W : 0.01

41. *DE* : $y'' + y = \text{Sin } 2x$

PS : $y(x) = \dfrac{2\text{Sin}x}{3} - \dfrac{\text{Sin } 2x}{3}$, $y'(x) = \dfrac{2(\text{Cos } x - \text{Cos } 2x)}{3}$

IC : $y(0) = 1$, $y'(0) = 0$

W : 0.01

42. *DE* : $y'' + y' - 2y = 0$

PS : $y(x) = e^x$, $y'(x) = e^x$

IC : $y(0) = 1$, $y'(0) = 1$

W : 0.01

43. *DE* : $\dfrac{D^2y}{dx^2} + y = x$

PS : $y(x) = x + \text{Cos } x - 3\text{Sin } x$, $y'(x) = 1 - \text{Sin } x - 3\text{Cos } x$

IC : $y(0) = 1$, $y'(0) = -2$

W : 0.01

44. *DE* : $\dfrac{D^2y}{dx^2} + 4y = 0$

PS : $y(x) = 2\text{Cos } 2x + \text{Sin } 2x$, $y'(x) = 2(\text{Cos } 2x - 2\text{Sin } 2x)$

IC : $y(0) = 2$, $y'(0) = 2$

W : 0.01

45. *DE* : $\dfrac{D^2y}{dx^2} - Dy - 2y = 4x^2$

PS : $y(x) = 2e^{2x} + 2e^{-x} - 2x^2 + 2x - 3$,

$y'(x) = 4e^{2x} - 2e^{-x} - 4x + 2$

IC : $y(0) = 1$, $y'(0) = 4$

W : 0.01

Chapter 8 *(Program : IVPD1SYS.CPP)*

Solve the following system of equations and find the approximations of x and y :

1. *SYS* : $Dx + \dfrac{2x}{t} = 1.0$, $Dy - x - y - \dfrac{2x}{t} + 1 = 0$

PS : $x = -\dfrac{1}{3}t^2 + \dfrac{t}{3}$, $y = 0.36787945*e^t - x$

IC : $x(1) = 0$, $y(1) = 1$

W : 0.01

2. *SYS* : $t\dfrac{dx}{dt} + x = yt\,,\qquad t^2\dfrac{dy}{dt} + 2x = yt$

PS : $x = 3 - t\,,\qquad y = \dfrac{3}{t} - 2$

IC : $x(1) = 2,\qquad y(1) = 1$

W : 0.01

3. *SYS* : $\dfrac{dx}{dt} + 7x - y = 0,\qquad \dfrac{dy}{dt} + 2x + 5y = 0$

PS : $x(t) = e^{-6t}(\text{Cos } t + \text{Sin } t),\qquad y(t) = 2e^{-6t}\text{ Cos } t$

IC : $x(0) = 1,\qquad y(0) = 2$

W : 0.01

4. *SYS* : $\dfrac{dx}{dt} - 2x + y = 0,\qquad \dfrac{dy}{dt} - 2y + x = -5e^t\text{ Sin } t$

PS : $x(t) = e^t\,(2\text{Cos } t - \text{Sin } t - 2),\qquad y(t) = e^t\,(3\text{Cos } t + \text{Sin } t - 2)$

IC : $x(0) = 0,\qquad y(0) = 1$

W : 0.01

5. *SYS* : $\dfrac{dx}{dt} = \dfrac{y-1}{y}\,,\qquad \dfrac{dy}{dt} = \dfrac{1}{x-t}$

PS : $x(t) = t - e^t\,,\qquad y(t) = e^{-t}$

IC : $x(0) = -1,\qquad y(0) = 1$

W : 0.01

6. *SYS* : $t\dfrac{dx}{dt} = -2x,\qquad t\dfrac{dy}{dt} - yt = x(t+2)$

PS : $x(t) = \dfrac{e}{t^2}\,,\qquad y(t) = 2e^t - \dfrac{e}{t^2}$

IC : $x(1) = e\,,\qquad y(1) = e$

W : 0.01

7. *SYS* : $t\dfrac{dx}{dt} + y = 0,\qquad t\dfrac{dy}{dt} + x = 0$

PS : $x(t) = 0.5t + \dfrac{1.5}{t}\,,\qquad y(t) = -0.5t + \dfrac{1.5}{t}$

IC : $x(1) = 2,\qquad y(1) = 1$

W : 0.01

8. *SYS* : $x\dfrac{dx}{dt} - y^2 = 0, \quad y\dfrac{dy}{dt} - x^2 = 0$

PS : $x^2 = 2.5e^{2t} + 1.5e^{-2t}, \quad y^2 = 2.5e^{2t} - 1.5e^{-2t}$

IC : $x(0) = 2, \quad y(0) = 1$

W : 0.01

9. *SYS* : $\dfrac{dx}{dt} + \dfrac{2(x-y)}{t} = 1, \quad \dfrac{dy}{dt} + \dfrac{x+5y}{t} = t$

PS : $x + y = -\dfrac{0.45}{t^3} + \dfrac{t}{4} + \dfrac{t^2}{5}, \quad x + 2y = -\dfrac{0.53}{t^4} + \dfrac{t}{5} + \dfrac{t^2}{3}$

IC : $x(1) = 0, \quad y(1) = 0$

W : 0.01

10. *SYS* : $\dfrac{dx}{dt} - y = \text{Tan}^2\, t - 1, \quad \dfrac{dy}{dt} + x = \text{Tan}\, t$

PS : $x(t) = \text{Cos}\, t - \text{Sin}\, t + \text{Tan}\, t, \quad y(t) = 2 - \text{Sin}t - \text{Cos}\, t$

IC : $x(0) = 1, \quad y(0) = 1$

W : 0.01

11. *SYS* : $\dfrac{dx}{dt} - 2y + x = 0, \quad \dfrac{dy}{dt} - 4y + 3x = \dfrac{e^{3t}}{e^{2t} + 1}$

PS : $x(t) = X + 2Y - Z + 2U, \quad y(t) = X + 3Y - Z + 3U$

$X = e^t\,(Ln\, 2 - 2), \quad Y = e^{2t}\,(1 - \text{Tan}^{-1} 1),$

$Z = e^t\, Ln(e^{2t} + 1), \quad U = e^{2t}\, \text{Tan}^{-1}(e^t)$

IC : $x(0) = 0, \quad y(0) = 1$

W : 0.01

12. *SYS* : $\dfrac{dx}{dt} - 3y - 2x = 5t, \quad \dfrac{dy}{dt} - 2y - 3x = 8e^t$

PS : $x = \dfrac{9e^{-t}}{2} + \dfrac{11e^{5t}}{10} - 3e^t + 2t - \dfrac{13}{5},$

$y = -\dfrac{9e^{-t}}{2} + \dfrac{11e^{5t}}{10} + e^t - 3t + \dfrac{12}{5}$

IC : $x(0) = 0, \quad y(0) = 0$

W : 0.01

13. *SYS* : $\frac{dx}{dt} - y = -5\text{Cos } t, \quad \frac{dy}{dt} - y - 2x = 0$

PS : $x = -\frac{2e^{2t}}{3} + \frac{5e^{-t}}{3} - 2\text{Sin } t - \text{Cos } t,$

$y = -\frac{4e^{2t}}{3} - \frac{5e^{-t}}{3} + \text{Sin } t + 3\text{Cos } t$

IC : $x(0) = 0, \quad y(0) = 0$

W : 0.01

14. *SYS* : $xy\frac{dx}{dt} = t, \quad x^2\frac{dy}{dt} = t$

PS : $x(t) = \left(\frac{3t^2}{2} + 1\right)^{1/3}, \quad y(t) = x$

IC : $x(0) = 1, \quad y(0) = 1$

W : 0.01

15. *SYS* : $\frac{dx}{dt} - x - y = -\text{Cos } t, \quad \frac{dy}{dt} + 2x + y = \text{Sin } t + \text{Cos } t$

PS : $x(t) = \text{Sin } t - \text{Cos } t - t\text{ Cos } t,$

$y(t) = 2\text{Cos } t + t(\text{Sin } t + \text{Cos } t)$

IC : $x\left(\frac{\pi}{2}\right) = 1, \quad y\left(\frac{\pi}{2}\right) = \frac{\pi}{2}$

W : 0.01

16. *SYS* : $\frac{dx}{dt} - 5x + 3y = te^{2t}, \quad \frac{dy}{dt} - 3x + y = e^{3t}$

PS : $x(t) = e^{2t}\left(\frac{t^3}{2} + \frac{t^2}{2} - 3t - 3e^t\right),$

$y(t) = e^{2t}\left(\frac{t^3}{2} - 3t - 2e^t + 1\right)$

IC : $x(0) = -3, \quad y(0) = -1$

W : 0.01

17. *SYS* : $\frac{dx}{dt} + 2x + 4y = 1 + 4t, \quad \frac{dy}{dt} + x - y = \frac{3t^2}{2}$

PS : $x = \frac{4(e^{-3t} - e^{2t})}{5} + t^2 + t, \quad y = \frac{4e^{2t} + e^{-3t}}{5} - \frac{t^2}{2}$

IC : $x(0) = 0, \quad y(0) = 1$

W : 0.01

18. *SYS* : $\frac{dx}{dt} - y = 0, \quad \frac{dy}{dt} - x = e^t + e^{-t}$

PS : $x = 1.5e^t + 0.5e^{-t} + t \text{ Sin } ht,$

$y = 1.5e^t - 0.5e^{-t} + \text{Sin } ht + t \text{ Cos } ht$

IC : $x(0) = 2, \quad y(0) = 1$

W : 0.01

19. *SYS* : $\frac{dx}{dt} - \frac{x}{y} - \frac{t}{y} = 0, \quad \frac{dy}{dt} - \frac{t}{x} + 1 = 0$

PS : $x = \frac{\sqrt{1 + t^2}}{Ln\left(\frac{e}{t + \sqrt{1 + t^2}}\right)}$

$y = \sqrt{1 + t^2}\, Ln \left(\frac{e}{t + \sqrt{1 + t^2}}\right)$

IC : $x(0) = 1, \quad y(0) = 1$

W : 0.01

20. *SYS* : $\frac{dx}{dt} - 9x - 24y = 5\text{Cos } t - \frac{\text{Sin } t}{3},$

$\frac{dy}{dt} + 24x + 51y = -9\text{Cos } t + \frac{\text{Sin } t}{3}$

PS : $x = 2e^{-3t} - e^{-39t} + \frac{\text{Cos } t}{3},$

$y = -e^{-3t} + 2e^{-39t} - \frac{\text{Cos } t}{3}$

IC : $x(0) = \frac{4}{3}, \quad y(0) = \frac{2}{3}$

W : 0.01

Chapter 9 *(Program : BVPD2LIN.CPP)*

Solve the following problems by means of the above program :

1. *BVP* : $\frac{D^2y}{dx^2} - y\text{Cos}^2 x + \text{Sin } xe^{\text{Sin}x} = 0$

$P = 0, \quad Q = \text{Cos}^2 x, \quad R = -\text{Sin } xe^{\text{Sin}x}$

PS : $y(x) = e^{\text{Sin}x}$

IC : $y(0) : 1, \quad y(\pi) : 1, \quad 0 \le x \le \pi$

W : 0.03141593

2. *BVP* : $\frac{D^2y}{dx^2} + 2xy' - y = 2(1 + x^2)\text{Cos } x$

$P = -2x, \quad Q = 1, \quad R = 2(1 + x^2)\text{Cos } x$

PS : $y(x) = x \text{ Sin } x$

IC : $y(0) : 0, \quad y\left(\frac{\pi}{2}\right) : \frac{\pi}{2}, \quad 0 \le x \le \frac{\pi}{2}$

W : 0.01570796

3. *BVP* : $\frac{D^2y}{dx^2} + 9y = \text{Sin } x$

$P = 0, \quad Q = -9, \quad R = \text{Sin } x$

PS : $y(x) = \frac{\text{Sin } x + \text{Sin } 3x}{8} + \text{Cos } 3x$

IC : $y(0) : 1, \quad y\left(\frac{\pi}{2}\right) : 0, \quad 0 \le x \le \frac{\pi}{2}$

W : 0.01570796

4. *BVP* : $y'' - (2x - 1)y' - 2y = 1 - 4x$

$P = 2x - 1, \quad Q = 2, \quad R = 1 - 4x$

PS : $y(x) = e^{x(x-1)}$

IC : $y(0) : 1, \quad y(1) : 2, \quad 0 \le x \le 1$

W : 0.01

5. *BVP* : $y'' + 4y = 2$

$P = 0, \quad Q = -4, \quad R = 2$

PS : $y(x) = \frac{1 - \frac{\text{Cos } 2x}{\text{Cos } 2}}{2}$

IC : $y(-1) : 0, \quad y(1) : 0, \quad -1 \le x \le 1$

W : 0.02

6. *BVP* : $y'' + y + 1 = 0$

$P = 0, \quad Q = -1, \quad R = -1$

PS : $y(x) = \frac{\text{Cos } x}{\text{Cos} 1} - 1$

IC : $y(-1) : 0, \quad y(1) : 0, \quad -1 \le x \le 1$

W : 0.02

7. *BVP* : $y'' + y - 1 = 0$

$P = 0, \quad Q = -1, \quad R = 1$

PS : $y(x) = \dfrac{\text{Sin } x}{\text{Sin} 1} + 1$

IC : $y(0) : 1, \quad y(1) : 2, \quad 0 \le x \le 1$

W : 0.01

8. *BVP* : $y'' + \pi^2 y = 0$

$P = 0, \quad Q = -\pi^2, \quad R = 0$

PS : $y(x) = 2\text{Cos } \pi x$

IC : $y(0) : 2, \quad y(1) : -2, \quad 0 \le x \le 1$

W : 0.01

9. *BVP* : $y'' - 10y' + 25 = 0$

$P = 10, \quad Q = -25, \quad R = 0$

PS : $y(x) = e^{5x}(1 - x)$

IC : $y(0) : 1, \quad y(1) : 0, \quad 0 \le x \le 1$

W : 0.01

10. *BVP* : $y'' + y = 0$

$P = 0, \quad Q = -1, \quad R = 0$

PS : $y(x) = \text{Cos}(x) - \dfrac{\text{Sin } x}{\text{Tan}(1)}$

IC : $y(0) : 1, \quad y(1) : 0, \quad 0 \le x \le 1$

W : 0.01

Chapter 12

A Short Review on FORTRAN V

Microsoft FORTRAN version 5.1 that I want to discuss is an improved version of the already prevailing MS-FORTRAN programming language. The main purpose of this short review on FORTRAN V is to guide the reader to design and understand Computer programs using the FORTRAN language. The name FORTRAN comes from FORmula TRANslation and it is a high-level computer programming language for mathematical and scientific purposes.

The real motivation of this concern is the preparation of a Floppy Disc (1.44MB / 3.5 inch) with FORTRAN and C++ (Turbo) programs for the solution of Differential Equations. The Disc can be available separately by postal system proposed at the end of this textbook.

I want to study the FORTRAN programming language by means of some program segments.

```
C     This program is constructed to solve the Linear Boundary Value
C     Problems using Finite-Difference Methods.
      DIMENSION FnU (10,10) FnV (10,10)
      Integer I, N
      Real Ff1, Ff2,...
C     Data for Boundary Conditions
      DATA Pi / 3.14159265 /
      DATA X0, X1 / 0.0, 1.0 /
```

```
      DATA Y0, Y1 / 1.0, 0.0 /
      Write (*, 100) X0, FnU (1,10), FnV (2,10)
100   FORMAT (F8.5, 3x, 2(F11.7, 2x))
```

The line beginning with 'C' is a line for comment. The two-dimensional arrays FnU and FnV have been declared next with a single DIMENSION statement. For the variable FnU (10,10) 10x10 elements (cells) are allocated to the memory. A DIMENSION statement is non-executable and must be placed before any executable statement in the program. The DATA statement is used to set a value or to initialize a variable. In the program segment the variables X0, X1, Y0 and Y1, have been initialized by a DATA statement that is also nonexecutable.

The write statement tells the computer to print the formatted information on the screen. The output field specifications have been stated in the FORMAT statement. The field specification F 8.5 corresponds to the variable X0 and generates the value of total width 8, namely, XX.XXXXX. 3x means 3spaces or blanks. The variable FnU (1,10) indicates (1,10) th element of the array and the value will be printed on the screen with the field width XXX.XXXXXXX followed by 2 spaces.

```
    N =9
    H =0.1
    Hs =H**2
    X =X0.+ H
    CALL Func  ( X, P, Q, R )
    A ( 1,1 ) = 16.0 --8.0 * H * p
    A ( 1,2 ) = 12.0 * ( Hs * Q -1.0 )
    ... ... ... ...
    ... ... ... ...
    SUBROUTINE  Func ( Dx, P, Q, R )
    Real P, Q, R, Dx
    P = -1.0 / Dx
    Q = 1.0 / Dx ** 2
    R = 3.0
```

```
Return
End
```

SUBROUTINE is a complete and independent program. On that ground it may contain all the characteristics of any program, for example, type declarations, DIMENSION statements, other Functions, the End statement. The communication between a calling program and the subroutine Subprogram is sent out through the parameters placed in parentheses. The Return statement terminates the execution of the function and transfers back to the calling program. The End statement has the same effect as a Return statement. It is important to note that a CALL statement must contain as many actual arguments (parameters) as there are formal arguments in the corresponding SUBROUTINE. A CALL Function calls upon a Subroutine subprogram.

The Assignments A (1, 1), A (1, 2), etc. are then performed with the returned values of P, Q and R.

```
DO 200 I =2, N–1
    Dx = X0 + I * H
    Dy1 = ( W ( I+1 ) – W ( I–1 ))/(2 * H )
    CALL Deqn (Dx, W (I),  Dy1, Fn, FnY, FnY1 )
    A  ( I ) =2 +H ** 2 * FnY
    B ( I ) = –1 +Hlf * FnY1
      .........
      .........
200 Continue
SUBROUTINE  Deqn ( x, y, y1, Fn, FnY, FnY1 )
Real x, y, y1, Fn, FnY, FnY1
FnY1 = –y / 8
FnY = –y1 / 8
Fn = ( 32 + 2 * x ** 3–y * y1 )/8
Return
End
```

Since repeating a process is fundamental in computer programs, it would be very useful to apply the DO statement, a macrolike Command. A DO statement is one of the most powerful structures in FORTRAN language. The first line indicating a Do statement followed by a number that labels the continue statement. The DO - Continue pair instructs the Computer to repeatedly execute the statements between DO and Continue usually called the body of the DO loop. The range of the loop limits to [2, N–1]. The body of the loop contains expressions for calculation, assignments, calling function etc. Here, the Subprogram Deqn with the formal parameters has been called by the CALL statement in the main program.

```
C .................. Main program
Real A1, RKint, Ya, Yb
DATA A1, Ya, Yb, / 0.0, 1.0, – 2.0/
   ... ... ... ...
   ... ... ... ...
RKint = Rung4 ( A1, Ya, Yb )
   ... ... ...
STOP
END
C .................. FUNCTION Subprogram
Function Rung4 ( A, YA, YB )
Integer I, N
Real A, YA, YB, Fxy, Dx, Dy
N =10
H =0.01
   ... ...
   ... ...
CALL Func ( X, Y, Fx )
RKut  = Func ( Dx, Dy, Y1, H, Fxy )
   ... ... ...
```

```
........
Return
End
FUNCTION Func ( x, y, y1, H1, Fxy )
Real Fxy, H1, x, y, y1
Fxy  = H1 * ( x-y + 2.0 * y1 )
Func = Fxy
Return
End
```

In this segment we want to define a FUNCTION subprogram. A FUNCTION subprogram sends back usually only one result whereas the Subroutine sub-program transfers more than one result. A subprogram receives the values (arguments) from the calling station and sends back the result with the Return statement.

The STOP statement terminates the program execution.

Hitherto I have discussed some points on FORTRAN programming that are quite frequently encountered in solving the problems of differential equations and which help us in developing further problems. If you have much more interest on FORTRAN language, I recommend you then to consult the reference book or user's guide from Microsoft FORTRAN or any other textbook on FORTRAN language.

APPENDIX I

Appendix I : Symbols and Abbreviations

Greek alphabets

α	Alpha	ν	Ny
β	Beta	ξ	Xi
γ	Gamma	o	Omikron
δ	Delta	π	Pi
ε	Epsilon	ρ	Rho
ζ	Zeta	σ	Sigma
η	Eta	τ	Tau
θ	Theta	υ	Ypsilon
ι	Iota	ϕ	Phi
κ	Kappa	χ	Chi
λ	Lambda	ψ	Psi
μ	My	ω	Omega

The fundamental constants of Analysis

e (exponential function) having the value 2.71828182.

e is the number whose logarithm is 1, i.e. Ln e = 1. Also called Euler's number.

Ln means natural logarithm (logarithmus naturalis). Natural logarithms are those which have the number e for base.

π (Pi) has the value 3.14159265.

Symbol / Abbreviation	Interpretation
Dy or y'	$\frac{dy}{dx}$
D^2y or y''	$\frac{d^2y}{dx^2}$

$\dot{x}$	$\frac{dx}{dt}$
$\dot{y}$	$\frac{dy}{dt}$
sqrt (x)	square root of x
sin (x)	Sine of x
Asin (x)	$\sin^{-1}x$
pow(x, 3) or x**3	x^3
DE	differential equation
DF	differential function
LL	lower limit
UL	upper limit
ES	Exact Solution
PS	Particular Solution
Sev	Separation of variables
Sub	Substitution method
Ext	Exact
Lih	Linear homogeneous
Lnh	Linear nonhomogeneous
Lin	Linear
Nol	Nonlinear
Ber	Bernoulli
Ric	Riccati
IC	Initial Conditions
BC	Boundary Conditions
W	width

APPENDIX II

Appendix II : Mathematical Relations

Some of the important formulas and relations of mathematics that are often required for the formulation of an equation in the problem, I want to mention here.

Relations from Trigonometry

➘ $\text{Sin}^2\theta + \text{Cos}^2\theta = 1$

$\text{Sec}^2\theta - \text{Tan}^2\theta = 1$

$\text{Cosec}^2\theta - \text{Cot}^2\theta = 1$

➘ $\text{Sin}\,(\alpha + \beta) = \text{Sin}\alpha\,\text{Cos}\beta + \text{Cos}\alpha\,\text{Sin}\beta$

$\text{Sin}\,(\alpha - \beta) = \text{Sin}\alpha\,\text{Cos}\beta - \text{Cos}\alpha\,\text{Sin}\beta$

$\text{Cos}\,(\alpha + \beta) = \text{Cos}\alpha\,\text{Cos}\beta - \text{Sin}\alpha\,\text{Sin}\beta$

$\text{Cos}\,(\alpha - \beta) = \text{Cos}\alpha\,\text{Cos}\beta + \text{Sin}\alpha\,\text{Sin}\beta$

$$\text{Tan}\,(\alpha + \beta) = \frac{(\text{Tan}\alpha + \text{Tan}\beta)}{(1 - \text{Tan}\alpha\,\text{Tan}\beta)}$$

$$\text{Tan}\,(\alpha - \beta) = \frac{(\text{Tan}\alpha - \text{Tan}\beta)}{(1 + \text{Tan}\alpha\,\text{Tan}\beta)}$$

➘ $$\text{Cos}2\alpha = 1 - 2\,\text{Sin}^2\alpha = 2\,\text{Cos}^2\alpha - 1 = \frac{(1 - \text{Tan}^2\alpha)}{(1 + \text{Tan}^2\alpha)}$$

$$\text{Sin}2\alpha = 2\text{Sin}\alpha\,\text{Cos}\alpha = \frac{2\,\text{Tan}\alpha}{(1 + \text{Tan}^2\alpha)}$$

$$\text{Tan}2\alpha = \frac{2\,\text{Tan}\alpha}{(1 - \text{Tan}^2\alpha)}$$

$$\text{Tan}2\alpha = \frac{(1 - \text{Cos}2\alpha)}{(1 + \text{Cos}2\alpha)}$$

➘ $$\text{Sin}\alpha\,\text{Sin}\beta = \frac{[\text{Cos}(\alpha - \beta) - \text{Cos}(\alpha + \beta)]}{2}$$

$$\text{Cos}\alpha\,\text{Cos}\beta = \frac{[\text{Cos}(\alpha + \beta) + \text{Cos}(\alpha - \beta)]}{2}$$

$$\text{Sin}\alpha\ \text{Cos}\beta = \frac{[\text{Sin}(\alpha+\beta) + \text{Sin}(\alpha-\beta)]}{2}$$

$$\text{Cos}\alpha\ \text{Sin}\beta = \frac{[\text{Sin}(\alpha+\beta) - \text{Sin}(\alpha-\beta)]}{2}$$

➘ $$\text{Sin}\alpha = \frac{(e^{i\alpha} - e^{-i\alpha})}{2i},$$

$$\text{Cos}\alpha = \frac{(e^{i\alpha} + e^{-i\alpha})}{2}$$

$$e^{\alpha+i\beta} = e^{\alpha}(\text{Cos}\beta + i\ \text{Sin}\beta)$$

where $i = \sqrt{(-1)},\ i^2 = -1$

➘ $$\text{Sin}^{-1}x + \text{Cos}^{-1}x = \frac{\pi}{2}$$

$$2\text{Sin}^{-1}x = \text{Sin}^{-1}[2x\sqrt{(1-x^2)}] = -2i\ Ln\ [ix + \sqrt{(1-x^2)}]$$

$$2\text{Cos}^{-1}x = \text{Cos}^{-1}(2x^2-1) = -2i\ Ln\ [x + i\sqrt{(1-x^2)}]$$

$$2\text{Tan}^{-1}x = \text{Tan}^{-1}[2x/(1-x^2)] = -i\ Ln\frac{(1+ix)}{(1-ix)}$$

➘ $$\text{Cos}h^2x - \text{Sin}h^2x = 1$$

$$\text{Sec}h^2x + \text{Tan}h^2x = 1$$

$$\text{Coth}^2x - \text{Cosec}h^2x = 1$$

➘ $$\text{Sin}hx = \frac{(e^x - e^{-x})}{2}$$

$$\text{Cos}hx = \frac{(e^x + e^{-x})}{2}$$

➘ $$\text{Sin}h^{-1}x = Ln[x + \sqrt{(x^2+1)}]$$

$$\text{Cos}h^{-1}x = Ln[x + \sqrt{(x^2-1)}]$$

$$\text{Tan}h^{-1}x = \frac{Ln\frac{1+x}{1-x}}{2}$$

➘ $\text{Sin}(ix) = i\ \text{Sin}hx$, $\text{Cos}(ix) = \text{Cos}hx$, $\text{Tan}(ix) = i\ \text{Tan}hx$

Relations from Algebra

➘ Binomial theorem

$$(a+b)^m = \sum_{k=0}^{m} \binom{m}{k} a^{m-k} b^k$$

where m is a positive integer and

$$\binom{m}{k} = \frac{m(m-1)(m-2)\ \ldots\ (m-k+1)}{1.2.3.\ \ldots\ k}$$

Formulae from logarithm

➘ $Ln(ab) = Ln\ a + Ln\ b$

$Ln\ \frac{a}{b} = Ln\ a - Ln\ b$

$Ln\ a^n = n\ Ln\ a$

$Ln\ 1 = 0$

$0! = 1! = 1$ (! is called factorial)

$a^x = e^{x\ Ln\ a}$

Series expansion

➘ $$e^{-x} = 1 - \frac{x}{1!} + \frac{x^2}{2!} - \frac{x^3}{3!} + \ldots = \sum_{l=0}^{\infty} \frac{(-x)^k}{k\ !} \qquad [|x|<\infty]$$

$$Ln\ x = (x-1) - \frac{(x-1)^2}{2} + \frac{(x-1)^3}{3} - \frac{(x-1)^4}{4} + \ldots$$

$$= \sum_{k=1}^{\infty} (-1)^{k+1} \frac{x^k}{k} \qquad [0 \le x \le 2]$$

$$(1+x)^{-n} = 1 - nx + \frac{n(n+1)x^2}{2!} - \frac{n(n+1)(n+2)x^3}{3!} + \ldots$$

$$= 1 + \sum_{k=1}^{\infty} \frac{n(n+1)\ldots(n-k+1)(-x)^k}{k!} \qquad [n>0]$$

$$\text{Sin}\ x = \frac{x}{1!} - \frac{x^3}{3!} + \frac{x^5}{5!} - \frac{x^7}{7!} + \ldots = \sum_{k=0}^{\infty} (-1)^k \frac{x^{2k+1}}{(2k+1)!}$$

$$\text{Cos } x = 1 - \frac{x^2}{2!} + \frac{x^4}{4!} - \frac{x^6}{6!} + \ldots = \sum_{k=0}^{\infty} (-1)^k \frac{x^{2k}}{2k!}$$

$$\text{Tan } x = x + \frac{x^3}{3} + \frac{2x^5}{15} + \frac{17x^7}{315} + \frac{62x^9}{2835} + \ldots \qquad [|x| < \frac{\pi}{2}]$$

$$= \sum_{k=1}^{\infty} 4^k(4^k - 1)\, \frac{|B_{2k}|x^{2k-1}}{(2k)!}$$

where B_{2k} are the Bernoulli Numbers.

$$\text{Sin}^{-1}x = x + \frac{x^3}{6} + \frac{3x^5}{40} + \frac{15x^7}{336} + \ldots \qquad [|x|<1]$$

$$= x + \sum_{k=1}^{\infty} \frac{1.3.5.\ \ldots\ (2k-1)}{2.4.6.\ \ldots\ 2k(2k+1)}\, x^{2k+1}$$

$$\text{Cos}^{-1}x = \frac{\pi}{2} - \text{Sin}^{-1}x$$

$$\text{Tan}^{-1}x = x - \frac{x^3}{3} + \frac{x^5}{5} - \frac{x^7}{7} + \ldots = \sum_{k=0}^{\infty} (-1)^k \frac{x^{2k+1}}{2k+1}$$

$$\text{Sin}hx = x + \frac{x^3}{3!} + \frac{x^5}{5!} + \frac{x^7}{7!} + \ldots = \sum_{k=0}^{\infty} \frac{x^{2k+1}}{(2k+1)!}$$

$$\text{Cos}hx = 1 + \frac{x^2}{2!} + \frac{x^4}{4!} + \frac{x^6}{6!} + \ldots = \sum_{k=0}^{\infty} \frac{x^{2k}}{(2k)!}$$

$$\text{Tan}hx = x - \frac{x^3}{3} + \frac{2x^5}{15} - \frac{17x^7}{315} + \ldots = \sum_{k=1}^{\infty} 4^k(4^k - 1)\, \frac{B_{2k}x^{2k+1}}{(2k)!}$$

$$\text{Sin}h^{-1}x = x - \frac{x^3}{6} + \frac{3x^5}{40} - \frac{15x^7}{336} + \ldots \qquad [|x|<1]$$

$$= Ln\ 2x + \frac{x^{-2}}{4} - \frac{3x^{-4}}{32} + \frac{15x^{-6}}{288} - \ldots \qquad [|x|>1]$$

$$\text{Cos}h^{-1}x = Ln\ 2x - \frac{x^{-2}}{4} - \frac{3x^{-4}}{32} - \frac{15x^{-6}}{288} - \ldots$$

$$\text{Tan}h^{-1}x = x + \frac{x^3}{3} + \frac{x^5}{5} + \frac{x^7}{7} + \ldots = \sum_{k=0}^{\infty} \frac{x^{2k+1}}{2k+1} \qquad [|x|<1]$$

Relations from Differential Calculus (functions with one variable)

↘ $D(C) = \frac{d}{dx}(C) = 0.$ C being a constant.

$$D\frac{f}{g} = \frac{gDf - fDg}{g^2} \qquad \text{(Quotient rule)}$$

$$Dx^m = mx^{m-1} \qquad [m>0]$$

$$De^x = e^x, \qquad D(Ln\ x) = \frac{1}{x}$$

$$Dy = \frac{dy}{du} \cdot \frac{du}{dx} \qquad \text{(Chain rule, } u \text{ is another variable)}$$

↘ $D\text{Sin } x = \text{Cos } x$

$$D\text{Cos } x = -\text{Sin } x$$

$$D\text{Tan } x = \text{Sec}^2 x$$

$$D\text{Sin}^{-1}x = \frac{1}{\sqrt{1 - x^2}}$$

$$D\text{Cos}^{-1}x = \frac{-1}{\sqrt{1 - x^2}}$$

$$D\text{Tan}^{-1}x = \frac{1}{1 + x^2}$$

↘ $D\text{Sin}hx = \text{Cos}hx$

$$D\text{Cos}hx = \text{Sin}hx$$

$$D\text{Tan}hx = \text{Sec}h^2x$$

$$D\text{Sin}h^{-1}x = \frac{1}{\sqrt{1 + x^2}}$$

$$D\text{Cos}h^{-1}x = \frac{1}{\sqrt{x^2 - 1}}$$

$$D\text{Tanh}^{-1}x = \frac{1}{1-x^2}$$

➘ ***Taylor's series***

$$f(x+w) = f(x) + \frac{wDf(x)}{1!} + \frac{w^2D^2f(x)}{2!} + \ldots + \frac{w^{m-1}D^{m-1}f(x)}{(m-1)!} + R_m$$

where R_m (Remainder) denotes

$$\frac{w^mD^mf(x+\lambda w)}{m!} \qquad \text{(Lagrange's form)}$$

and $$\frac{w^m(1-\lambda)^{m-1}D^mf(x+\lambda w)}{(m-1)!} \qquad \text{(Cauchy's form)}$$

λ being a number in the interval $0<\lambda<1$.

Relations from Integral Calculus

➘ $$\int_\alpha^\beta f(x)dx = G(x)\Big|_\alpha^\beta = G(\beta) - G(\alpha)$$

$$\int_\alpha^\beta f(x)dx + \int_\beta^\alpha f(x)dx = 0$$

$$\int_\alpha^\beta f(x)dx = \int_\alpha^\gamma f(x)dx + \int_\gamma^\beta f(x)dx \qquad [\alpha < \gamma < \beta]$$

➘ $$\int_\alpha^\beta \int_\gamma^\delta g(x,y)dx\,dy = \int_\alpha^\beta dy\left[\int_\gamma^\delta g(x,y)dx\right] = \int_\alpha^\beta \left[\int_\gamma^\delta g(x,y)dx\right]dy$$

$$\int_{-\alpha}^\alpha f(x) = \int_0^\alpha [f(x) + f(-x)]dx$$

$$= 2\int_0^\alpha f(x)dx \qquad \text{when } f(x) \text{ is even}$$

$$= 0, \qquad \text{when } f(x) \text{ is odd}$$

$$\int_0^{m\alpha} f(x)dx = m\int_0^\alpha f(x)dx, \qquad \text{when } f(x) = f(\alpha + x).$$

➘ $$D\int g'(x)dx = g'(x)dx$$

$\int C\,dx = Cx$, $\quad C$ being a Constant.

$$\int x^n \, dx = \frac{x^{n+1}}{n+1} \qquad [n \# -1]$$

$$\int x^{-1} \, dx = Ln\ x$$

$$\int e^{mx} dx = \frac{e^{mx}}{m}$$

$$\int \frac{Dg(x)}{g(x)} = Ln\ g(x)$$

$$\int Ln\ x\ dx = x(Ln\ x - 1).$$

↘ ***Integration by Parts***

$\int u\, dv = uv - \int v\, du$, u and v are differentiable functions of x.

↘ $\int \text{Sin}\ x\ dx = -\text{Cos}\ x$

$\int \text{Cos}\ x\ dx = \text{Sin}\ x$

$\int \text{Tan}\ x\ dx = Ln\ \text{Sec}\ x$

$\int \text{Cot}\ x\ dx = Ln\ \text{Sin}\ x$

$\int \text{Sec}^2\ x\ dx = \text{Tan}\ x$

$\int \text{Sec}\ x\ \text{Tan}\ x\ dx = \text{Sec}\ x$

$\int \text{Sec}\ x\ dx = Ln(\text{Sec}\ x + \text{Tan}\ x) = Ln\ \text{Tan}\left(\frac{\pi}{4} + \frac{x}{2}\right)$,

↘ $\int \text{Sinh}x\ dx = \text{Cosh}x$

$\int \text{Cosh}x\ dx = \text{Sinh}x$

$\int \text{Tanh}x\ dx = Ln\ \text{Cosh}x$

$\int \text{Sech}x\ dx = 2\ \text{Tan}^{-1}\ e^x$

↘ $$\int \frac{1}{x^2+\alpha^2}\, dx = -\frac{1}{\alpha}\ \text{Tan}^{-1}\frac{x}{\alpha}, \qquad [\alpha \# 0]$$

$$\int \frac{1}{x^2-\alpha^2}\, dx = \frac{1}{2\alpha}\ Ln\ \frac{x-\alpha}{x+\alpha} \qquad [|x|>\alpha]$$

$$\int \frac{1}{\alpha^2-x^2}\, dx = \frac{1}{2\alpha}\ Ln\ \frac{\alpha+x}{\alpha-x} \qquad [|x|<\alpha]$$

$$\int \frac{1}{\sqrt{x^2+\alpha^2}}\,dx = Ln\left[x+\sqrt{x^2+\alpha^2}\right]$$

$$\int \frac{1}{\sqrt{x^2-\alpha^2}}\,dx = Ln\left[x+\sqrt{x^2-\alpha^2}\right]$$

$$\int \frac{1}{\sqrt{\alpha^2-x^2}}\,dx = \sin^{-1}\frac{x}{\alpha}$$

➘ $$\int \sqrt{(x^2+\alpha^2)}\,dx = \frac{x\sqrt{x^2+\alpha^2}}{2}+\frac{\alpha^2}{2}Ln\left[x+\sqrt{x^2+\alpha^2}\right]$$

$$\int \sqrt{(x^2-\alpha^2)}\,dx = \frac{x\sqrt{x^2-\alpha^2}}{2}-\frac{\alpha^2}{2}Ln\left[x+\sqrt{x^2-\alpha^2}\right]$$

$$\int \sqrt{(\alpha^2-x^2)}\,dx = \frac{x\sqrt{\alpha^2-x^2}}{2}+\frac{\alpha^2}{2}\sin^{-1}\frac{x}{\alpha}$$

➘ $$\int_0^{\pi/2} Ln\,\sin x\,dx = \int_0^{\pi/2} Ln\,\cos x\,dx = \frac{\pi}{2}Ln\,(0.5)$$

$$\int_0^{\pi/2} Ln\,\tan x\,dx = 0$$

➘ $$\int_0^{\pi/2} \sin^n x\,dx = \int_0^{\pi/2} \cos^n x\,dx$$

$$= \frac{n-1}{n}\bullet\frac{n-3}{n-2}\bullet\frac{n-5}{n-4}\cdots\frac{3}{4}\bullet\frac{1}{2}\bullet\frac{\pi}{2}, \text{ when } n \text{ is even}$$

$$= \frac{n-1}{n}\bullet\frac{n-3}{n-2}\bullet\frac{n-5}{n-4}\cdots\frac{4}{5}\bullet\frac{2}{3}\bullet 1, \text{ when } n \text{ is odd}$$

$$\int_0^{\pi/2} \sin^m x\cos^n x\,dx = \int_0^{\pi/2} \cos^m x\sin^n dx$$

$$= \frac{1.3.5.\ldots(m-1).1.3.5.\ldots(n-1)}{2.4.6.\ldots(m+n)}, \text{ when } m \text{ and } n \text{ are even}$$

$$= \frac{2.4.6.\ldots(m-1)}{(n+1)(n+3)\ldots(n+m)}, \text{ when } m \text{ is odd.}$$

Relations from Differential Equations

➘ ***First - order differential equation***

Separation of variables : $g_1(x)f_2(y)dx + g_2(x)f_2(y)dy = 0.$

Method of substitution : $yG(xy)dx + xF(xy)dy = 0.$

Homogeneous equation : $y' = G\left(\frac{y}{x}\right)$

Exact equation : $M(x, y)dx + N(x, y)dy = 0$

where $\frac{\partial M}{\partial y} = \frac{\partial N}{\partial x}$

Linear homogeneous : $y' + P(x)y = 0.$

Linear nonhomogeneous : $y' + P(x)y = Q(x)$

Bernoulli form ; $y' + P(x)y = Q(x)y^n.$

Riccati form : $y' + P_1 y + P_2 y^2 = Q.$

Lagrange form : $y = xf(y') + \phi(y').$

Clairaut equation : $y = p(x) + g(p),\ p = \frac{dy}{dx}$

D'Alembert equation : $y = x\,g(p) + f(p)$

↘ ***Second - order differential equation***

Linear Homogenous : $y'' + \alpha y' + \beta y = 0$, α and β are constants.

Linear nonhomogeneous : $y'' + \alpha y' + \beta y = R(x).$

Euler or Cauchy equation : $x^2 y'' + \alpha x y' + \beta y = R(x).$

Legendre's equation : $(1 - x^2)y'' - 2xy' + n(n + 1)y = 0.$

Bessel's equation : $x^2 y'' + xy' + (\lambda^2 x^2 - n^2)y = 0.$

↘ ***The general form of a linear equation of n-th order :***

$$\frac{d^n y}{dx^n} + P_1 \frac{d^{n-1} y}{dx^{x-1}} + P_2 \frac{d^{n-2} y}{dx^{n-2}} + \ldots + P_{n-1} \frac{dy}{dx} + P_n y = Q,$$

where $P_1, P_2, \ldots, P_{n-1}, P_n$ and Q are constants or functions of x.

APPENDIX III

Appendix III : Graphical Representations

Chapter 8.3 — Example 4

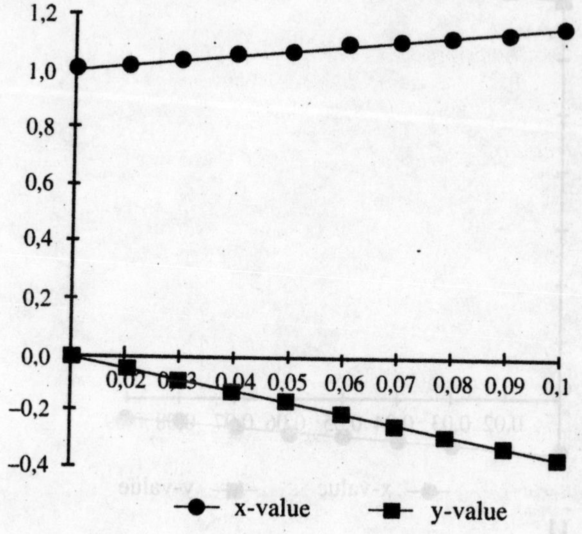

Example 8

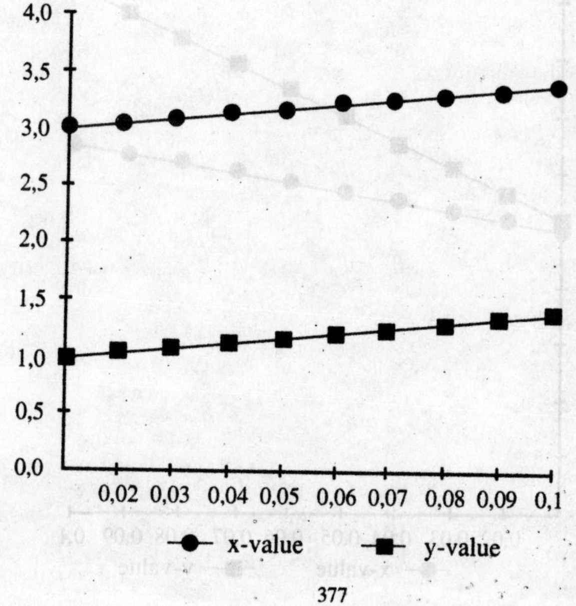

Example 9

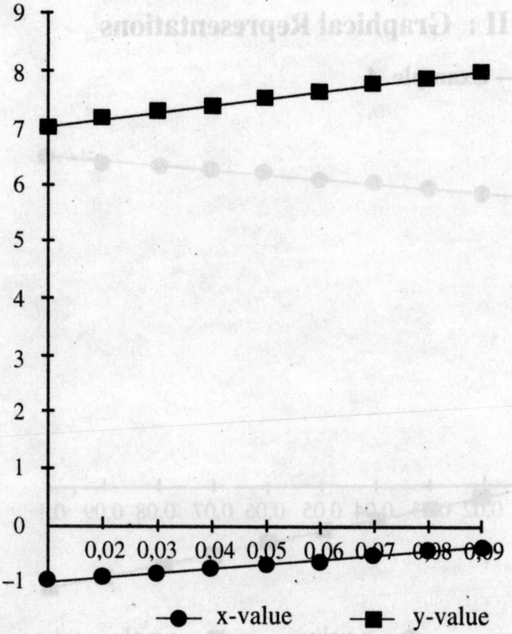

Example 11

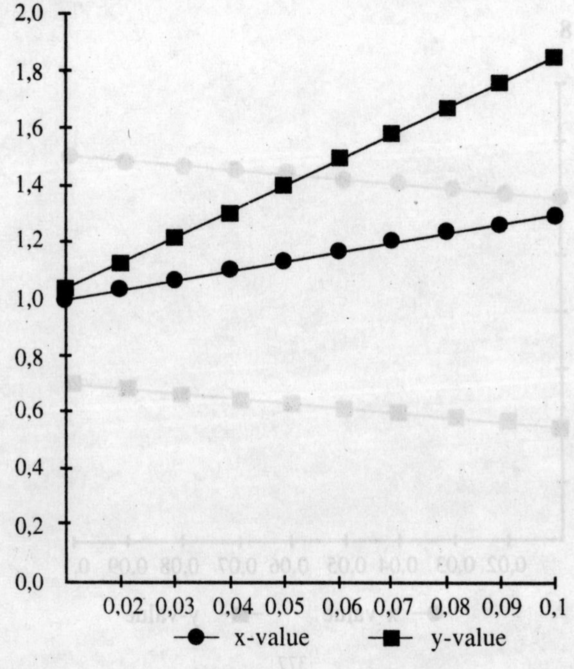

Example 12

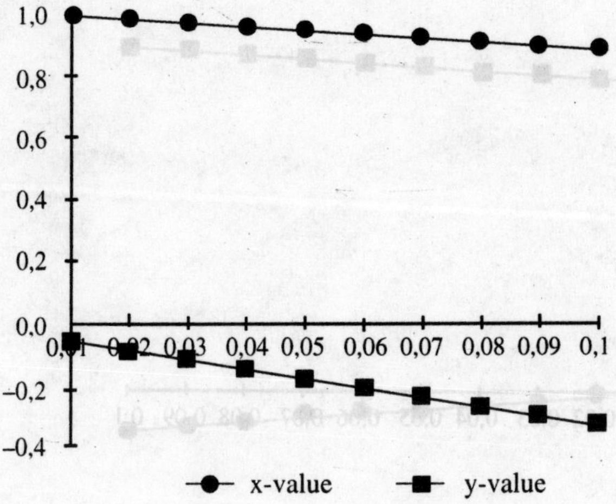

Example 15

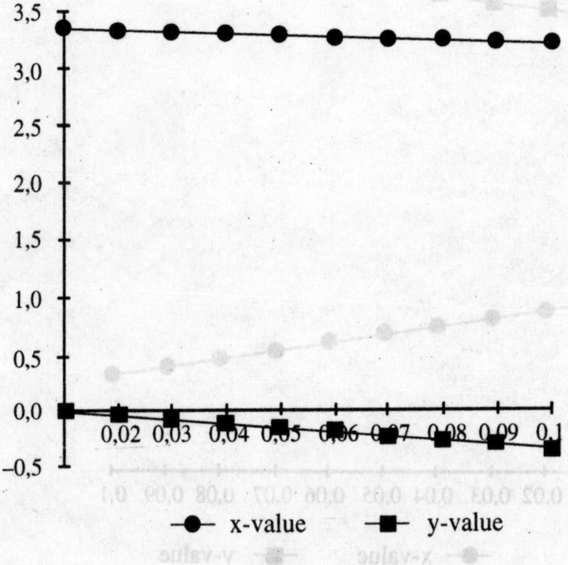

Example 20

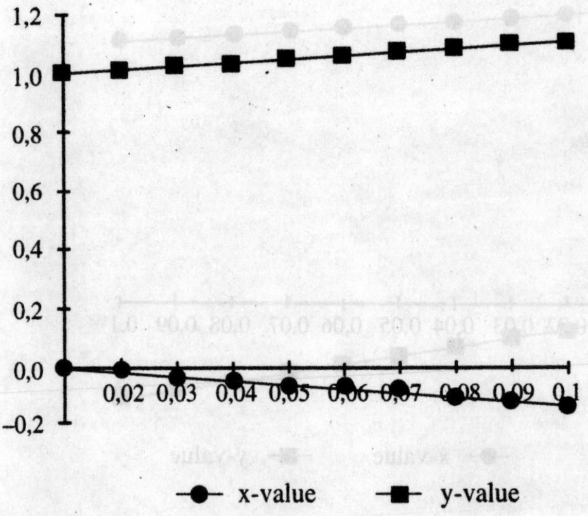

Example 24

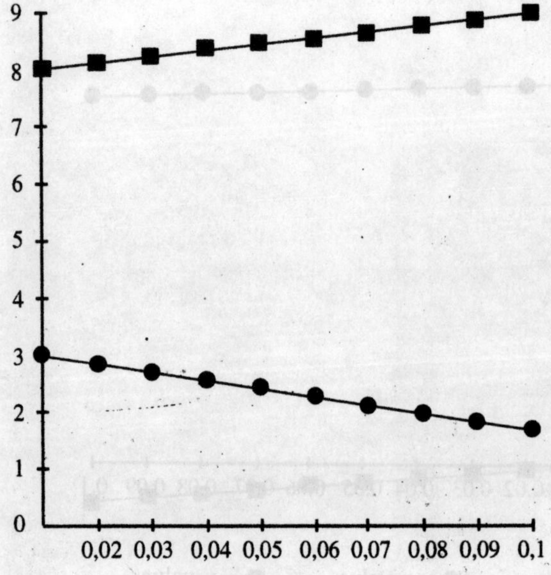

Example 27

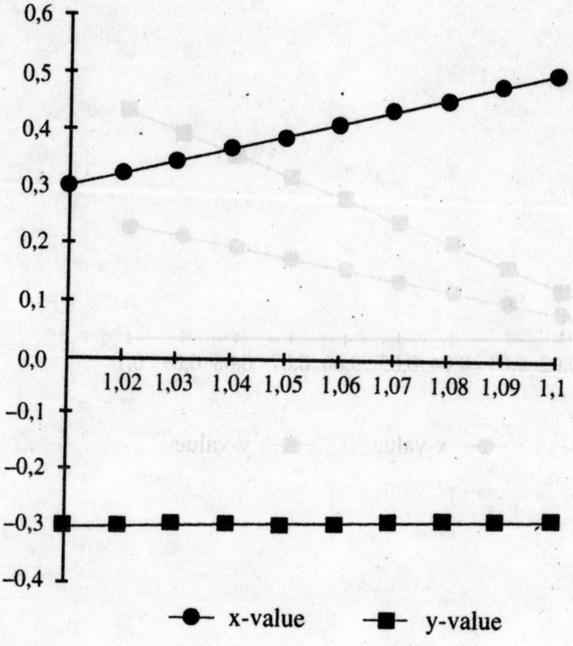

Example 30

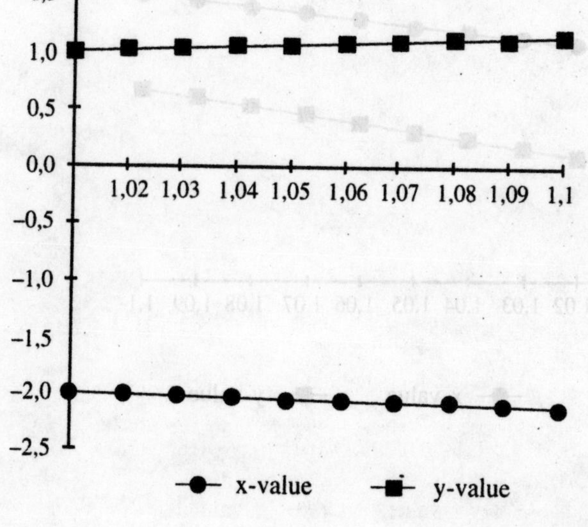

Example 34

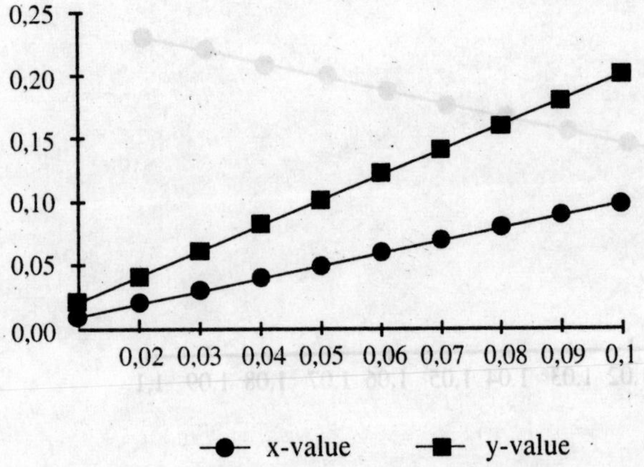

Example 36

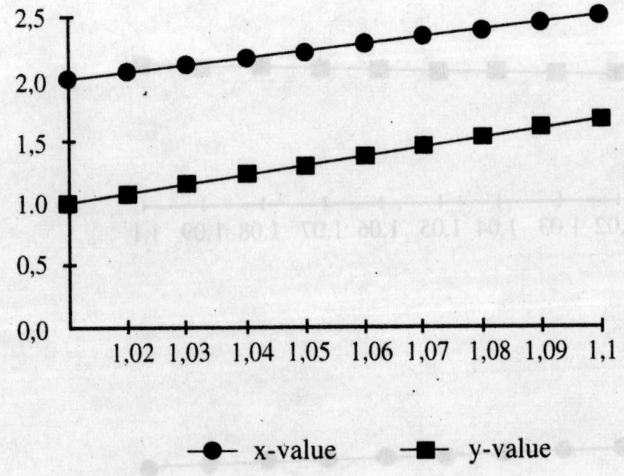

Chapter 9.2 — Example 3

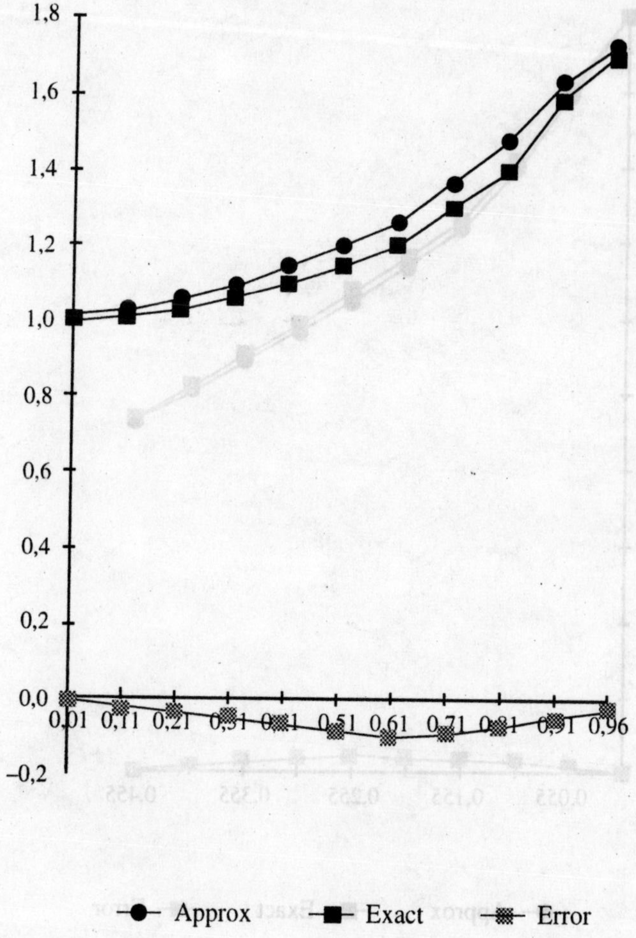

Chapter 9.3 — Example 3

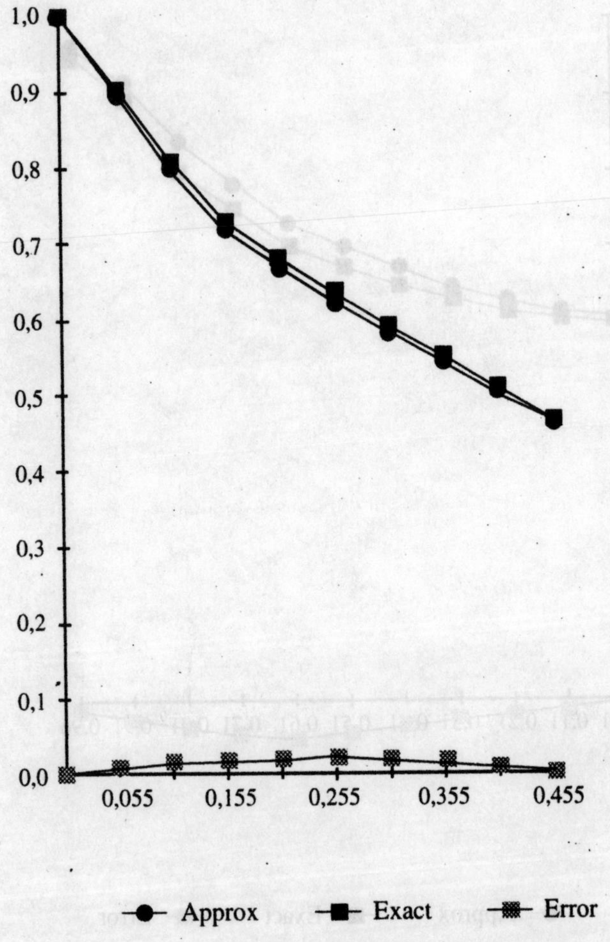

Example 9

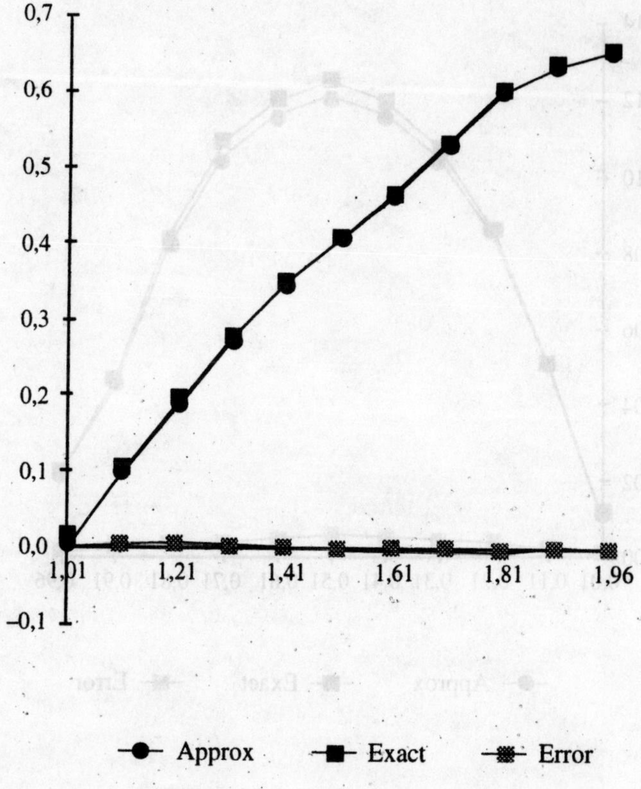
0,7
0,6
0,5
0,4
0,3
0,2
0,1
0,0
−0,1
1,01
1,21
1,41
1,61
1,81
1,96
Approx
Exact
Error

Example 11

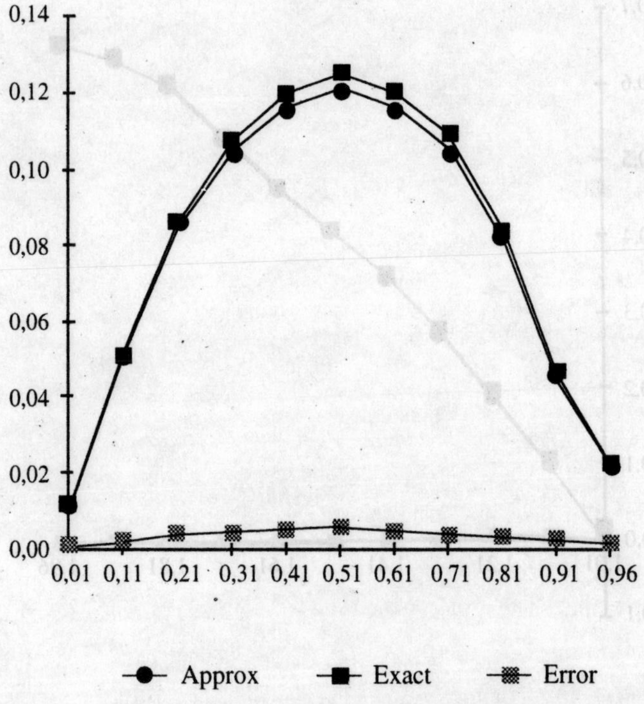
0,14
0,12
0,10
0,08
0,06
0,04
0,02
0,00
0,01
0,11
0,21
0,31
0,41
0,51
0,61
0,71
0,81
0,91
0,96
Approx
Exact
Error

Example 12

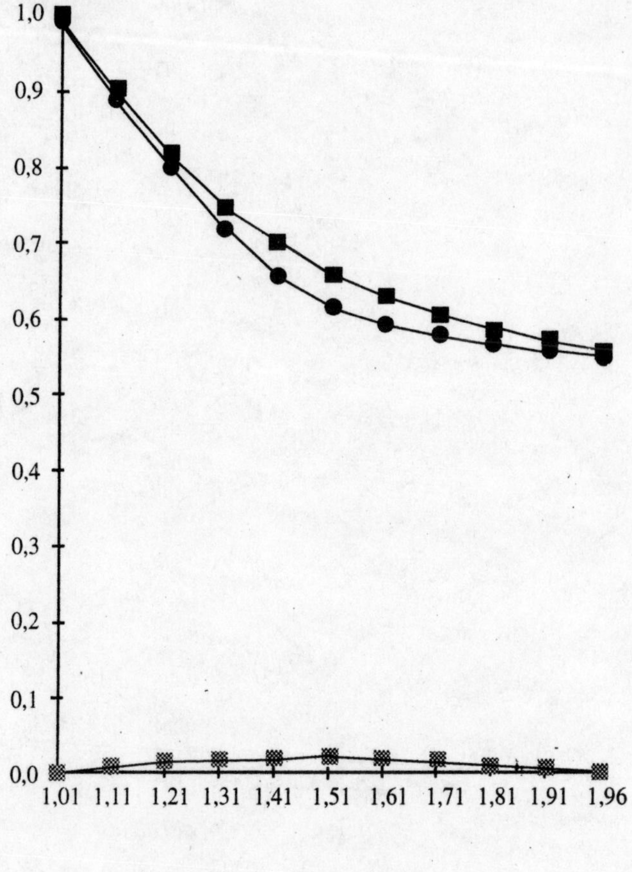
1,0
0,9
0,8
0,7
0,6
0,5
0,4
0,3
0,2
0,1
0,0
1,01 1,11 1,21 1,31 1,41 1,51 1,61 1,71 1,81 1,91 1,96
Approx
Exact
Error

REFERENCES

Agnew, R. P. : Differential Equations, 2nd edition, 1960, p485, McGraw-Hill Book Co., New York.

Brenner, J. L. : Problems in Differential Equations, 2nd edition, 1966, p172, W. H. Freeman and Co., San Francisco.

Conte, S. D. and C. de Boor : Elementary Numerical Analysis—An Algorithmic Approach, 3rd edition, 1980, p432, McGraw-Hill Kogakusha Ltd, Tokyo.

Demidovich, B. : Problems in Mathematical Analysis, 1973, p496, MIR Publishers, Moscow.

Forsyth, A. R. : A Treatise on Differential Equations, 1929, p583, Macmillan and Co. Ltd., London.

Gerald Curtis F. and Patrick O. Wheatley : Applied Numerical Analysis, 1989, p679, Addison Wesley Pub. Co. Reading, Massachusetts.

Ghosh, R. K. and Bagchi, P. K. : An Introduction to Differential Equations, 1971, p200, New Central Book Agency, Calcutta.

Granville, W. A, P.F. Smith and W.R. Longley : Elements of the Differential and Integral Calculus, 1941, p556, Ginn and Co., Boston.

Jain, M. K., Iyengar, S. R. K. and Jain, R. K. : Numerical Methods for Scientific And Engineering Computation, 1995, p454, New Age Int. (P) Ltd., New Delhi.

Kuo, S. S. : Computer Applications of Numerical Methods, 1972, p415, Addison-Wesley Publishing Co., Reading, Massachusetts.

Martin, W. T. and E. Reissner : Elementary Differential Equations, 1964, Addison-Wesley Publishing Co., Reading, Massachusetts.

Mukherjee, K. K. : Numerical Analysis, 1990, p298, New Central Book Agency, Calcutta.

Ortega J. M. and W. G. Poole, Jr. : An Introduction to Numerical Methods for Differential Equations, 1981, p329, Pitman Publishing Inc.

Ralston, A. and Rabinowitz P. : A First Course in Numerical Analysis, 2nd edition, 1978, p556, McGraw-Hill, New York.

Rice John R. : Numerical Methods, Software and Analysis, 1983, McGraw-Hill Book Co, New York.

Ritger, P. D. and Rose N. J. : Differential Equations With Applications, 1968, McGraw-Hill Book Co., New York.

Roberts, S. M. and J. S. Shipman : Two-Point Boundary Value Problems, Shooting Methods, 1972, p269, American Elsevír Pub. Co. Inc.

Shampine, L. F. and Gordon M. K. : Computer Solution of ODES—The Initial Value Problem, 1975, W. H. Freeman and Co.

Scheid, F. : Numerical Analysis, 1988, McGraw-Hill, New York.

Spiegel, M. R. : Mathematical Handbook, 1968, p271, McGraw-Hill Book Co., New York.

Stroud A. H. : Numerical Quadrature and Solutions of Ordinary Differential Equations, 1974, Springer-Verlag.

Index

(The numbers refer to pages)